THE LIVELIEST ART

A PANORAMIC HISTORY OF THE MOVIES

THE LIVELIEST ART

BY ARTHUR KNIGHT • THE MACMILLAN COMPANY
NEW YORK   1957

FIRST PRINTING

PRINTED IN THE UNITED STATES OF AMERICA

LIBRARY OF CONGRESS CATALOG CARD NUMBER: 57-12222

PERMISSION TO QUOTE COPYRIGHT MATERIAL USED IN THIS BOOK
IS GRATEFULLY ACKNOWLEDGED AS FOLLOWS:
AGNES DE MILLE—*Hollywood Saga* BY WILLIAM DE MILLE,
COPYRIGHT 1939 BY E. P. DUTTON & CO., INC.; RKO RADIO
PICTURES—*The Informer,* COPYRIGHT 1935 BY RKO RADIO
PICTURES; THE VIKING PRESS—*Death of a Salesman* BY
ARTHUR MILLER, COPYRIGHT 1949 BY ARTHUR MILLER.

PERMISSION TO REPRODUCE THE ILLUSTRATIONS WAS KINDLY
GRANTED BY CINERAMA, INC.; GEORGE EASTMAN HOUSE;
JOSEPH BURSTYN; METRO-GOLDWYN-MAYER; MUSEUM OF
MODERN ART FILM LIBRARY; EDWARD MORRISON; NATIONAL
FILM ARCHIVES, LONDON; MICHAEL TODD PRODUCTIONS;
UNITED ARTISTS; WARNER BROTHERS.

FOR COLETTE
WHO KNOWS THIS BOOK SO WELL

INTRODUCTION

THIS BOOK BEGAN AS A THREE-HOUR LECTURE DELIVERED ON A SWELTER-
ing July afternoon at the University of Minnesota in Minneapolis.
Its purpose was to trace, not the history of the movies but the high-
points of their artistic growth. To this end, I had assembled a
number of clips from outstanding films—among them *The Great
Train Robbery,* an early Griffith, a reel from *The Last Laugh,* the
Odessa Steps sequence from *Potemkin,* Garbo's entrance in *Anna
Christie,* even Fred Astaire singing and dancing in *Blue Skies.* As a
result, for every point I made there was an immediate, visual reference. (I can now state on evidence that the ancient Chinese proverb
equating one picture to 10,000 words is no exaggeration.) Turning
the lecture into a book was the idea of Rouben Mamoulian, the
distinguished American director who was also speaking at the University that week and had the patience as well as the endurance—
the temperature stood at 103° that afternoon—to sit through the
entire performance. Mamoulian planted the seed; Victor Weybright
of New American Library generously provided the contractual soil.

I doubt very much that any of us knew at the time what was involved in such a project. Mamoulian, I feel sure, envisaged a slim,
three-hour pamphlet. Mr. Weybright expected a small book. I had
been giving a course on the history of the movies at the Institute of
Film Techniques at City College of New York since 1950, and it
seemed to me that the rather sketchy notes I used for those lectures
would admit a certain amount of expansion. Two years later I had a
manuscript that ran close to 200,000 words. Pruning was obviously

necessary—and as a consequence, this explanatory introduction as well. For both in pruning and preparing the manuscript I grew aware of the fact that there would have to be certain important omissions. Since the story I elected to tell is of the development of an art, I had to forgo much of the chatty gossip about personalities or the behind-the-camera maneuverings that so often pass for film history. I have also had to omit mention of many popular and successful films—often personal favorites of my own—if their contributions to the development of the art were negligible. I wanted this to be more than simply a catalog of popular film titles.

Perhaps more serious, a number of well established and highly influential areas of film have had to be wilfully ignored. The animated film, for example, deserves an entire book in its own right; a few paragraphs or even an entire chapter here would be totally inadequate. By arguing that the cartoon field has had an independent growth, a development quite apart from those films made with actors and camera, I was able to justify to myself its absence from these pages. On the other hand, it has always seemed to me that the increasingly important use of film for educational, industrial, sales and training purposes represents a rather deriva-tive form of film making, one whose techniques have been dis-covered first in the fictional or documentary forms and eventually adopted or modified for service in those other fields. Another book may be in order for their *history;* but their *art,* I like to think, has already been recorded in these pages.

Unfortunately, I am forced to admit that aspects of the art itself have also been slighted in the pages that follow. Concentrating primarily on directorial achievements, I have been unable to develop as fully as I should like such problems as music in the movies, the special nature of film acting, the new perspectives for sound or the multiple relationships between a producer and his picture. I can only hope that, as compensation, the main lines of the film's artistic growth emerge more clearly. If not, the fault is all too clearly my own. As I wrote, I became increasingly convinced that only now, when we have had as many years of sound films as there were of silents, has it become possible to achieve any real perspective on the full development of this unique art-industry.

It has been my intention to narrate that development both as simply and as comprehensively as possible. Consequently, I have centered this book on what I consider to be key films, pictures that are important not only in themselves but also that seem to summarize a whole style or movement in film history. Fortunately, through organizations like the Museum of Modern Art Film Library, George Eastman House, the Cinemathèque Française and the British Film Institute, it has been possible for me to see again most of the historic films described in the text. I have tried to visualize these for the reader to the best of my ability. But, since many of these same titles are available in 16mm for either group or home study, it occurred to me that I might add a whole new dimension to the book by listing their sources. They form a kind of living illustration to its pages. I am most grateful, therefore, to Cecile Starr, editor of the *Ideas on Film* column in *The Saturday Review*, for her preparation of the appended *Film Index* and the listing of distributors from which so many of the titles mentioned in the text can be obtained. And while on the subject of acknowledgements, I should like to thank as well Victor Weybright for his patience and encouragement to a book that kept changing its shape before his eyes; to Charlotte Painter and Arabel Porter for their unfailing tact and insight on a most difficult editorial assignment; and to my wife, Colette, who refused to let a sentence into the book that was not perfectly clear to her. She became the representative of all those for whom, ultimately, this book was intended—all those who love the movies and want to know more about them, but unburdened either by technical jargon or the special esperanto of *ciné-club* experts.

CONTENTS

I

AN ART IS BORN

FOR MORE THAN HALF A CENTURY, PEOPLE ALL OVER THE WORLD HAVE been going to the movies, drawn by the mysterious fascination of lifelike images appearing on a screen in a darkened room. They go to relax, to enjoy themselves, just as they read books or listen to music. But while books and music are often discussed as art, movies for the most part remain just movies. There is something so casual about seeing a film. Somehow it is too entertaining, too popular to be identified with the arts. And so it has taken root not because of its occasional masterpieces, but because its way of telling a story, of showing life, stirs both the heart and the imagination of the viewer. It is this abiding affection of audiences everywhere for movies as movies which has provided the stimulus to directors, producers and inventors to push forward from the first crude, flickering images to the technical virtuosity and emotional power of the film today. Through sixty years of trial and error, of box-office hits and box-office failures, the novelty of 1895 has slowly been transformed into the art of the 20th century.

The present moment in film history, with its new 'scopes, new screen sizes and new film widths appearing one after the other, curiously parallels the birth of the motion picture itself. In 1895 a variety of cameras and projectors were introduced almost simultaneously in the United States, in England, France and Germany. They bore such fanciful names as the Kinetoscope, the Vitascope, the Bioscope or Cinématographe, but all produced the same marvelous effects—the black-and-white image of living people who moved and walked in a recognizably real world. In 1929, when talking pictures swept the film industry, again there was a multitude of independent inventions—the Vitaphone, the Movietone, the Cinephone, the Photophone and, in Europe, the Klangfilm. Again, however, they all were working toward an identical goal, this time to reproduce not only the image but the sounds of the world around us.

Throughout the brief history of the motion picture, one finds these mounting waves of technological change that burst over the medium, altering its form and setting new problems for its artists. Indeed, the history of the film is largely an account of directors the world over who, experimenting with the machinery of the inventors, found ways to create entertaining, stimulating pictures for their audiences. Some accepted the medium as they found it, and used it effectively. Some added skill and imagination to make it a more expressive, more affecting art. And some few, the geniuses, perceived within the mechanics of film original ways of handling the camera, fresh methods of combining their shots, new functions for the actor, the settings, the sound track—perceptions that altered the entire course of film creation.

Curiously enough, in this endless pursuit of reality the film makers and the film inventors parallel each other. Sound, color, 3-D, wide screens—indeed, the very invention of the motion picture itself—resulted from the efforts of technicians to enhance the sense of actuality transmitted by the camera. The artists, working with whatever apparatus the inventors had prepared for them at the various stages of the film's development, sought always the reality that lay behind the surface. They discovered first the physical limitations of their medium and then worked out the techniques to go beyond them. Sound was bitterly resented during the first years of its existence precisely because the directors of the silent era had created a rich, subtle and immensely expressive body of techniques that quite overcame the enforced silence. Undoubtedly, some of the resentment directed against the wide screen today comes from the suspicion that the potentialities of the ordinary screen are far from exhausted.

The artist, however, has no control over the inventor, nor over the technological advances that come into his medium. Often the inventors work alone, outside the industry. Their discoveries are incorporated into the film by the businessmen, the "front office" that must, of necessity, worry less about artistic achievements than financial stability. These executives are well aware that the greatest directorial triumphs are meaningless unless someone comes to see them. They know too that there are times when the industry's stock phrase, "There's nothing wrong with the movies that good pictures can't cure," just does not apply. When the box office began to sag during the mid-twenties, the producers turned frantically to sound. When the depression hit the movies, early in the thirties, color was added (and also double features). Now, of course, the threat is from television, and the producers embraced first 3-D, then the wide screens in the theater to eclipse the small screen in the living room.

These, then, are the three points in the triangle of film creation —the inventor, the artist and the businessman. One could scarcely function without the others. But none of them could function without that vast, motley, disorganized throng which, assembled in neat rows in orchestra, mezzanine and balcony, becomes momentarily "the audience." More than in any other art, the artist in film must take his cue from his public, for it is the public that endows the film companies with the hundreds of thousands or even millions of dollars they must spend on each production. He must make pictures that are meaningful and entertaining to vast numbers of people, comprehensible in both theme and technique—popular in the most literal sense of that word. But there is a vast difference between finding a popular response and catering to a least common denominator. It may be going too far to say, with Adolph Zukor, "The public is never wrong"; but the public has been right on so many occasions in the development of the motion picture—recognizing the advances in the art created by D. W. Griffith, discovering star personalities, rejecting the spuriously "arty"—that it is impossible not to recognize the audience's contribution to the dynamics of this development. It was the audience's overwhelming enthusiasm for sound that, in 1929, put a period to the silent film. Today's reception of Cinerama and CinemaScope makes it far too likely that within the next few years we shall all be reconciled to one form or another of the wide screen. And the film makers will begin anew to fill that form with pictures and stories that move us by their power and subtle skill.

THE MACHINE FOR SEEING BETTER

Certainly, it was the enthusiasm of the audiences back in 1895, when Edison in America, Lumière in France and Paul in England first threw a moving picture onto a white sheet, that made their novelty something more than an eight-day wonder. To the inventors, the movies were a scientific toy, just one in a long series of devices exploiting the scientific discoveries of the 19th century. To the public, they were a relevation. It was not merely the fact that movement and the shadow of the real world were captured by these machines—that had been done before—but now everything could be seen as large as life and, curiously, even more real. The first audiences sat entranced by such commonplace views as waves dashing to the shore, fire engines racing through the streets, trains drawing into a station, military parades or even people out walking in the sun. But they moved! And they were real! As far as the inventors were concerned, the movies might have remained at that stage—brief one-minute views of the world around us that exploited the novelty of movement. It was the showmen who transformed the novelty into a form of entertainment; and the directors, cameramen and actors, drawn to the medium from all walks of life and all over the world, who transformed it even further from a simple entertainment into an art.

But if the motion picture has by this time come to be accepted into the sisterhood of the established arts, there is no denying that it was always the child of science. Some of its biographers have insisted on tracing its paternity all the way back to the Greeks' discovery of electricity in amber, back to Leonardo's *camera obscura* and Athanasius Kircher's *magia cystera,* and investigating all the remoter branches of its family tree prior to the 19th century. Once Peter Mark Roget (of *Thesaurus* fame) enunciated his theory of "The Persistence of Vision with Regard to Moving Objects" in 1824, however, the advance toward motion pictures and motion-picture projection was rapid and direct. Almost immediately, scientists throughout Europe began putting his theory to the test. Their devices may have resembled children's toys—whirling discs, twirling coins, booklets of pictures flipped with the thumb —but they quickly established the basic truth of Roget's contention that through some peculiarity of the eye an image is retained for a fraction of a second longer than it actually appears.

On this peculiarity rests the fortune of the entire motion-picture industry. Essentially, the motion picture is simply a series of still pictures printed on a long ribbon of celluloid—generally either 35 or 16 millimeters (written "mm") wide. Each picture, halted momentarily, is projected on a white screen, then removed in a flash and another picture substituted. Whether run at sixteen frames per second, as in silent days, or at twenty-four frames per second as required for sound films, enough phases of an action appear on the screen for the eye to make the connection between one picture and the next, and to create the illusion of continuous motion.

Roget announced his theory in London in 1824; and at the very same time in France, Joseph Nicéphore Niepce was groping toward the fundamentals of photography. In 1822 he had succeeded in producing a crude but permanent photograph. Soon after the famous Louis Daguerre joined him, and the two men continued to experiment until, in 1839, they were able to outline and demonstrate a complete, practical photographic process. Their method was slow and painstaking, necessitating either still life or, if their subject was alive, the metal headclamp and a rigid, motionless pose held for minutes on end. The subsequent introduction, however, first of the wet collodion process and then the gelatin emulsions both speeded up and enormously simplified the taking of pictures— so much so that by 1888 George Eastman was prepared to market his Kodak camera ("You press the button, we do the rest"), bringing photography within the reach of everyone.

Long before there was celluloid for film, however, before photography had developed to the point where it could be used for animation, the parlors of well-to-do Americans and Europeans were adorned with practical demonstrations of Roget's fascinating principle. Perhaps most popular was the Zoëtrope, a slotted revolving drum. As one watched through the slits, hand-drawn clowns or acrobats, horses or dogs seemed to leap through their paces on the strips of paper fitted inside the drum. A simpler device using a similar technique was the Stroboscope, with the figures drawn upon a slotted disc. The image was seen by revolving the disc in front of a mirror and again peeping through the slits. More elaborate was the Praxinoscope of Emile Reynaud. In its center was a ring of little mirrors; a band of images was placed opposite them against the shell of the drum. As the drum revolved, the movement almost flowed from one mirror to the next to create a particularly charming effect. Reynaud was constantly improving his invention. Soon he added a frame and tiny settings, converting the device into a parlor theater. By combining it with the magic lantern, he achieved a form of home projection. By 1889 he was able to enlarge his pictures sufficiently to present them theatrically, and he increased the number of pictures in his bands, mounting them on reels of seven hundred or more separate hand-drawn images. He was to continue with his little Praxinoscope Theater until driven out of business by the rival movies early in the next century.

In all of these devices, of course, the pictures with their tiny phases of movement were drawn by hand. They are, in fact, the precursors of today's animated films, of *Mickey Mouse* and *Mr. Magoo*. No sooner had photography become practicable, however, than it was applied to animation. How much simpler to capture motion with the camera! Although at first each photograph had to be made separately in a sequence of specially posed shots, when such pictures were mounted in their proper order the effect of movement was quite satisfactory. As early as 1861 Coleman Sellers, of Philadelphia, patented a Kinematoscope in which a series of six such photographs were mounted on a paddlewheel and rotated before the individual viewer to create the illusion of movement. Less than ten years later, Henry R. Heyl was projecting similar photographs onto a screen in Philadelphia's Academy of Music for an audience of 1,600 people. He called his machine the Phantasmatrope. And in 1877 Eadweard Muybridge and John D. Isaacs used a battery of twenty-four cameras in sequence to photograph Leland Stanford's race horse in motion. In Paris, Meissonier, the great painter of horses, arranged for a projection of these pictures on yet another device, the Zoöpraxinoscope.

With photography and projection already linked together, the next great problem was to create a camera that would take pictures faster than the ordinary still cameras. Perhaps the first successful step in this direction came in France in 1882 when Dr. E. J. Marey, a physician and physiologist studying the nature of movement, developed a sort of "photographic gun"—a rifle that shot a series of pictures upon a revolving drum set into its chamber. Out of this experiment he evolved during the next decade a series of clumsy but original and practical cameras. Other men, scientists and inventors alike, were challenged by the problem of the camera. In England there was the strange, controversial William Friese-Greene, hero of the recent film *The Magic Box* (1952), who according to some single-handedly solved the problems both of photographing and of projecting motion-picture film. There was the mysterious Frenchman, Louis Leprince, who disappeared from the Dijon-Paris Express in 1890, taking with him the designs for a camera that used strips of perforated celluloid as film.

But the most telling contributions to the development of a motion-picture camera unquestionably came from Thomas Edison and his talented assistant William Kennedy Laurie Dickson. In 1888, after more than a decade of experiment, Edison produced the phonograph, an instrument for recording and playing back sound on wax cylinders. He had already seen the motion photographs of Muybridge, and the idea of combining moving pictures with sound seems to have been in his mind even before the perfected phonograph was offered to the public. In fact, his first efforts in this direction consisted of a strip of small photographs wrapped spirally about just such a cylinder. "Everything should come out of one hole," Edison maintained. When this failed, Edison turned the project over to Dickson—and with it a new film base developed by George Eastman, thin strips of clear, supple, strong celluloid coated with a photographic emulsion. The film began arriving in August of 1889. It was Dickson who solved the mechanical problem of moving it through the camera, devising the sprocket system that is still standard on 35mm film today. Indeed, this ingenious man even managed to link up the pictures with the phonograph, demonstrating the Kinetoscope to his employer on October 6, 1889, with a brief film in which Dickson both appeared and spoke. What was in all probability the first actual presentation of a motion-picture film also marked the debut of the talkies!

Edison's earliest efforts, however, were not directed toward movie projection. He had had considerable success with his penny-in-the-slot phonographs, and it was his opinion that a similar device, offering a brief picture at a penny a look, would ensure a steady profit for his invention. The Kinetoscope was a peep show in which ran a continuous loop of film about 50 feet long. For the moment the sound aspects were ignored as Edison and his crew concentrated on supplying little one-minute subjects for these machines—photographed in the "Black Maria," the world's first film studio, which he built near his West Orange laboratories in 1893. By the fall of 1894, peep-show parlors had sprouted all over the United States and soon appeared in Europe as well. Curiously enough, the inventor seems to have had little confidence in the long-range possibilities of his machine. When in 1891 he took out patents on his battery-driven camera and Kinetoscope, he neglected to pay the additional $150 that would have secured him an international copyright. Within the next few years he was to regret this oversight. In England, Robert W. Paul copied the Edison Kinetoscope and also produced a hand-cranked portable camera. (Edison's first camera had the general shape and weight of a small upright piano.) In France the Lumière brothers, Louis and Auguste, saw the Kinetoscope and promptly invented their own Cinématographe, a machine that not only took pictures but could also print and project them as well. In Berlin, Max and Emil Skladanowski, also inspired by the Edison novelty, produced their Bioskop. These machines were soon to become a serious threat to Edison's market within the United States.

Thus, within fifty years of Roget's presentation of his theory, the theory had not only been recognized but its principle had been incorporated into various forms of entertainment. Animation, photography, projection—each was an indispensable step toward the final emergence of the movies. Significantly, none of these steps was taken in any single country. Roget read his paper before the Royal Society in London. Faraday in England, von Stampfer in Austria, Plateau in Belgium all experimented with the idea, producing the various toys and devices that incorporated its principle. Uchatius, who first projected painted pictures, was a Viennese, Désvignes, inventor of the popular toy Zoëtrope, lived in Paris. Both Sellers and Heyl were Americans. Photography, developed in France, was carried forward by Talbot in England and, immeasurably, by George Eastman in this country. There were no secrets, and everything was pointing in one direction—the projection of moving pictures upon a large screen. It should come as no surprise, then, to discover that the movies were actually invented almost simultaneously in France, England, Germany and the United States. The only wonder is that film historians so often seek to establish priority for the inventors of their own countries, resorting to such dubious phrases as "first accredited showing," "first scientific demonstration" or "first public presentation" to bolster their claims. How much better to recognize the indisputable fact that from the very outset the movies were international, that within a single year films were being projected in New York, London, Berlin, Brussels and Paris.

Once the Europeans had grasped the principles behind Edison's Kinetoscope, they moved directly toward projecting their pictures on a large screen. In the United States too, other inventors—Eugene Lauste, the Lathams, Jean Le Roy, Thomas Armat and F. Charles Jenkins—were also building machines that would project the Edison Kinetoscope reels. Throughout 1895 there were demonstrations of their equipment in New York, Boston, Chicago, Norfolk and Atlanta. Only Edison held back. When, somewhat belatedly, he finally turned to the problems of projection, he borrowed freely (as bitter law suits subsequently revealed) from the discoveries of Le Roy and Latham, and joined forces with Armat whose Vitascope incorporated the essential Maltese Cross movement to hold the film strip momentarily at rest in the aperture of the projector. Even so, not until April 23, 1896, was Edison prepared to present his projecting Kinetoscope to the public. The presentation took place during the vaudeville program at Koster & Bial's Music Hall, 34th Street and Broadway, the present site of the Macy store. A few months later the American Biograph, Edison's keenest rival, made its debut at Hammerstein's Olympia Music Hall. Within the year, movies were being seen in virtually every large city throughout the United States and Europe.

There is an odd and at the same time important observation to be made about the first films from the two continents. In Europe, Lumière, Pathé, Gaumont and the others delighted primarily in movement for its own sake. Anything that moved was grist for their photographic mills—a laborer felling a wall, workers leaving a factory, baby eating breakfast in the garden. As their cameramen wandered ever farther afield, they took views of ordinary street scenes, of native dances and military parades wherever they happened to be. The early European film catalogues are crowded with *actualités* and brief *documentaires,* none of them running over a minute in length, which reflected this intense interest in the world around them. In America, on the other hand, the actualities were apt to be of a more sensational sort—the Empire or Black Diamond Express rounding a bend and pounding down the track toward the camera, prize fights, cockfights, Professor Sandow flexing his muscles or Annie Oakley shooting clay pigeons. Even greater emphasis was placed on bits of staged business— vaudeville and circus turns, glimpses from plays, novelty acts by dancers, jugglers and acrobats. Much of the shooting was actually done in studios such as the "Black Maria," or on the improvised stages that had begun to sprout on rooftops all over New York. In America, at least, the film was firmly linked to a theatrical tradition from the very outset.

THE THEATER SETS THE STAGE

The importance of this theatrical tradition has too often been ignored in tracing the pre-screen history of the film. As Nicholas Vardac has emphasized in his book *Stage to Screen,* the theater of the 19th century, both in this country and in England, did much to create what might be termed a "climate of acceptance" for the movies when they finally did appear. Both in choice of themes and in manner of staging—an emphasis on melodrama, a leaning toward realism—the theater was preparing its audiences for precisely the sort of thing that movies could do better.

The 19th century, in literature, poetry, music and the drama, was an age of unbridled romanticism of spirit combined with a passionate insistence on realism of detail. Perhaps in the theater more than anywhere else this strange and unlikely coupling was most clearly visible. Playwrights might fly to the past, producers might devise elaborate and fanciful pantomimes laid in distant or imaginary lands, but for these to be successful on the stage the scenic designer had to create a palpable, realistic setting. The conventions of an earlier day were simply no longer adequate. The bosky dell painted on a canvas backdrop and framed by flats or cut-outs at the wings, the truncated triangle that served for interiors, gradually gave way to heavier pieces—papier-mâché mountains and trees, elaborately designed box sets for interiors and increased emphasis on such purely mechanical devices as trap doors, elevator lifts and treadmills. The movement toward pictorial realism in the theater, begun in the late 18th century by David Garrick, was projected into the new century by such actor-managers as John Philip Kemble, Charles Macready, Edmund Kean and Edwin Forrest. It reached its apogee in the spectacles and melodramas that crowded the boards during the last half of the 19th century—in the productions of Henry Irving and the Bancrofts in England, and more especially in the work of Steele MacKaye, Augustin Daly and David Belasco in this country. MacKaye, both as dramatist and producer, thought solely in terms of strongly realistic, eye-filling spectacle. One of his plays had as its climax a fight on a drawbridge swung high over the heads of the audience. In another, an entire mining town was swept away by a cyclone. His theater provided a true preview of today's multimillion dollar movie. Belasco produced a gigantic *Passion Play* with a cast including 400 men, women and children, 200 singers and "a flock of real sheep."

This passion for realism, this urge toward size characterized the theater of the late 19th century. *Uncle Tom's Cabin,* the melodramas of Dion Boucicault, adaptations of the novels of Dickens and Victor Hugo were not only extremely popular, but also owed no small part of their popularity to the lavish effects incorporated into their staging. And, to maintain that popularity, the scenery grew heavier and heavier as productions grew more and more elaborate. Treadmills, tanks, trap doors, moving platforms became part of the equipment essential to any well appointed theater.

Although this was all very well for the big cities, where productions were mounted on huge stages fully equipped to handle such spectacular effects, the theater of that period was not confined to a few fortunate centers as it is today. It spread throughout the country; and the road companies of a successful play could spend years traveling from city to city, from town to village. For a really big hit, there might be as many as half a dozen companies working out of New York, Chicago, New Orleans and San Francisco. One night they would appear at a civic center, another evening at a small-town opera house and perhaps the next night in a school auditorium thirty or forty miles away. Naturally, few of these stages had the facilities to fly a heavy show—and even if they did few companies could afford to carry along all the props, scenery and paraphernalia that marked the original big-city production. Not infrequently, a road-company Eliza crossed the ice against a painted river backdrop framed by flies suggesting a palace interior. In short, simplified, makeshift productions had to be worked out for the tours, versions that would fit readily into the limited facilities of most small-town theaters. It meant a reversion to an earlier style of theater, a reversion to scenery that was obviously paint, cutouts instead of solid set pieces, papier-mâché props.

And the inevitable happened. Once audiences had seen a proper production of a Steele MacKaye spectacle, they were no longer satisfied with the road-company facsimiles. Once they had traveled to the big cities and seen *Ben Hur* with three horses to each chariot, they could scarcely be content with the one-horse versions that turned up at their local opera houses. And the ones who didn't get to the big cities, those who remained at home and listened while their friends described the wonders they had seen —they were probably even more dissatisfied. Their imaginations created a richness of detail that no stage could ever hope to match. Thus, throughout the 19th century the theater was unwittingly preparing the public for movies in two important ways: by emphasizing realism and spectacle, and by underlining the inadequacy of most houses to supply them.

At this point the movies made their bow, achieving so readily, so naturally the kind of effects that theater managers could only dream of. Obviously, this did not mean the end of the theater.

Indeed, we find in the early years of the 20th century that the producers in the big cities began to outdo themselves, trying to cram even more spectacle and greater realism onto the stage than ever before. Such plays as *Ben Hur, The Light That Failed, Ramona* and *Judith of Bethulia* were all huge, heavily mounted, prodigally populated pageants, filled with theatrical devices intended to thrill their audiences. Appearing only a few years after the introduction of the film, however, the very illusion of reality that they sought most ingeniously to create on the stage was what the critics attacked most vehemently. Singling out the chariot race from *Ben Hur* as an example, one critic wrote in 1899, "The only way to secure the exact sense of action for this incident in a theater is to represent it by Mr. Edison's invention."

Gradually, the producers began to forsake spectacular spectacles for a somewhat less vast and more detailed realism in their dramas, melodramas and comedies. Belasco reproduced a section of a Childs Restaurant for a scene in his production of *The Governor's Lady.* For the second act of *Brewster's Millions* the entire midships of a yacht was created on the stage, complete with mast, flapping sails and steam whistle; or, for another production, a butcher shop right down to fresh, bleeding carcasses of beef. Even so, audiences that patronized the theater primarily for its visual effects continued to desert to the new medium—and especially in the smaller cities. By the twenties the theater had bowed to the inevitable, turning to expressionism or impressionism to reinforce the mood of the play. In the field of realism, the upstart movies had won hands down.

Even the crudest, most rudimentary early pictures reflect this superiority. *Mary Stuart,* a popular stage drama of the 1880's, reached its climax, naturally enough, as the headsman lowered his ax on Mary's neck. Out of consideration for the actress playing Mary, the curtain was customarily lowered somewhat faster. One of Edison's first Kinetoscope subjects was *The Execution of Mary, Queen of Scots* (1893). This little film, running just under a minute, begins as Mary approaches the chopping block. She kneels, the headsman swings his ax—and the audience is rewarded with the edifying spectacle of Mary's head rolling in the dust! At the crucial moment, of course, the film was stopped in the camera and a dummy substituted for Mary; but the gruesome bit of action continues on the screen without interruption. When the great Joseph Jefferson consented to do scenes from his stage success *Rip Van Winkle* for the Biograph camera in 1896, his theater performance was photographed in a real forest. This difference between stage and screen is perhaps best pointed up in the popular *May Irwin-John C. Rice Kiss* (1896), a scene from the play *The Widow Jones*. Its few moments of magnified osculation resulted in the first scandalized attempt at film censorship. The "kiss" may have been harmless enough in the theater, but seen in full close-up it suddenly became so much more "real."

It was this element of reality that captured for film its first audiences, the novelty of seeing real things in motion. And there is no doubting that they accepted the flat, flickering images as reality. When locomotives thundered down the track, when waves rolled toward the camera, people in the front rows ran screaming for the exits. Soon, however—all too soon—the novelty began to wear thin. The incessant parades, the street scenes, the acrobats, the butterfly dancers and the onrushing trains lost their appeal. The film could make things move, but then what? By the turn of the century, Mr. Edison's invention—along with the Bioscope, the Cinématographe and the Vitascope—had been relegated to the position of "chaser" on the vaudeville bills, the act that would clear out the theater for the next show. They became the last stop in the tour of the wax museums and the penny arcades. Other means had to be found to interest audiences. One showman thought he could solve the problem in a purely mechanical way, installing his projector at the far end of a rocking railway coach and presenting scenic views taken from a moving train. These *Hale's Tours* became a craze, somewhat like miniature golf, and made a fortune for their entrepreneur—but they lasted only a few years. Other movie makers, like J. Stuart Blackton and Albert Smith of the enterprising Vitagraph Corporation, suspected that headline news might bolster interest in the movies. The Boer and the Spanish-American wars afforded Smith a splendid opportunity to test this theory; and an event that he couldn't cover as an eyewitness reporter, like the sinking of the *Maine,* he staged in a bathtub! Still the public's enthusiasm for pictures continued to wane.

DAWN OF THE NARRATIVE FILM: MELIES AND PORTER

What finally saved the movies was the introduction of narrative. In France, Georges Méliès, a professional magician who early became intrigued with the movie camera, was soon combining his magic tricks with pantomimed stories. His *Cinderella* (1900), *Red Riding Hood* (1901) and *Bluebeard* (1901), and above all his celebrated *A Trip to the Moon* (1902), antedated our own *The Great Train Robbery* (1903) in demonstrating the narrative powers of the new medium. In September of 1899 he filmed an extended account of *L'Affaire Dreyfus,* following it with such serious works as *Jeanne d'Arc* (1900), *The Eruption of Mont-Pelé* (1902) and *The Coronation of Edward VII* (1902), all of them created in his fabulous glass-enclosed little studio on the outskirts of Paris. In these and hundreds of others Méliès, always the magician at heart, exploited not only the narrative but also the trick possibilities of the motion-picture camera. He quickly learned how to stop it in the middle of a scene and create miraculous appearances, disappearances and transformations. He mastered the techniques of double exposure and superimposition, producing truly extraordinary effects. A painter as well, he often designed settings that were triumphs of ingenuity, suggesting through forced perspective great vistas despite his tiny stage. He was without question the movies' first creative artist.

But Méliès, like so many of his contemporaries, remained chained to the traditions of the theater. In his hands the camera was made to perform wonderful tricks; but they were tricks ingeniously prepared for it on his specially equipped stage. In *A Trip to the Moon,* for example, to create the effect of the rocket ship en route, Méliès hauled a papier-mâché model of the moon up an elaborately constructed ramp toward the camera. It was as if the camera were the sole spectator at an elaborate pageant or play, occupying the choicest seat in the house but never budging from that seat. Everything happens in his films just about as it would on the stage. The actors come on the scene either from the rear or from the wings. Action is arranged horizontally across the stage. Even his trick of merging one scene into the next Méliès adapted from existing stage techniques, making each scene appear to grow out of the last by cranking the film back a few feet and shooting the start of the new scene over the ending of the old. This device, known as the "dissolve," was quickly accepted by audiences as a movie convention, one that persists to this day.

The films of Georges Méliès—witty, inventive, filled with exuberant activity and fantastic imagination—were widely seen in this country through the first decade of the new century, and played an important part in convincing American producers that pictures could and should be longer than the conventional fifty feet (about one minute on the screen). Unfortunately, such showings were rarely to Méliès's financial advantage. In those days films were not rented but sold outright by the foot. Anyone with a print, of course, could strike off a new negative for a few dollars and sell "dupe" prints at far less than the original producer could afford. This practice, known as "pirating," persisted until authorized film rental exchanges were set up—but by that time Méliès had been driven out of business. He was found, years later, tending a news-stand in the Paris Métro, and died in 1938 in a home for destitute actors.

The sharp business practices of the era, however, were not the sole cause of Méliès's failure. In 1903 a film appeared that was to revolutionize all movie making, breaking decisively with stage forms and stage techniques and pointing toward a genuinely filmic style. *The Great Train Robbery* by Edwin S. Porter, one of America's pioneer director-photographers, revealed for the first time the function and the power of the cut in telling a story on the screen. Closely related to the chases and gun fights of the touring "Wild West" shows at the turn of the century, it tells of a mail train holdup by armed desperadoes, the formation of a posse and the pursuit and annihilation of the gunmen—all in about eight minutes of film. Each scene, taken from a single camera position, is complete in itself and advances the action one step further. Once a scene has been completed, however, Porter makes a flat cut to the next shot without titles, without dissolves or anything but the logic of the story to bridge the gap. Nor does the sequence of his scenes necessarily follow in strict chronological progression, as it had in all films up to that time. We see the robbers enter the station, bind and gag the telegraph operator, then steal aboard the train, all in proper sequence. But after they have held up the train and made their getaway, Porter switches back to the unfortunate operator just as he is discovered by his little daughter at the station. The two lines of action are taking place simultaneously—the robbers escaping, their crime discovered. Porter, boldly juggling with time, here demonstrated the possibilities of parallel editing, the concept that D. W. Griffith was to develop so dramatically a few years later. At another point, the action seems to leapfrog, jumping from the holdup on the train to the formation of the posse and then back to the gang making its escape. Again the scenes are given meaning and coherence by the editing process, the cutting that brings them together and relates them one to the other. In short, the technique that Porter had hit upon in assembling this unpretentious little Western provided the key to the whole art of film editing, the joining together of bits of film shot in different places and at different times to form a single, unified narrative—a principle that Méliès, with his theater background, was never able to grasp.

No less important to the success of *The Great Train Robbery* was its freshness of camera placement. Perhaps one reason for this was its preponderance of outdoor scenes. All of its interiors—the opening scene in the telegraph operator's office, the robbery in the mail car, the "Western" high jinks in the dance hall—were filmed as if they were scenes from a play, with the camera once more the well-placed observer. But as soon as Porter moved his camera away from the studio stage, where all the action could be controlled, he was forced to use set-ups that cut into the scene at an angle, that brought the camera closer to the actors, that required the actors to enter from behind the camera or exit toward it. To keep his horsemen on the screen, he had to swing or "pan" the camera at times. At one point, when the robbers are scrambling down a wooded slope, he tilts the camera downward to follow them. As a final fillip, Porter had a huge close-up of one of the cowboys firing his pistol directly at the camera. "The resulting excitement is great," announced the Edison catalogue of 1904. "This scene can be used to begin or end the picture."

Apparently Porter himself only dimly understood at first the full implications of *The Great Train Robbery*. Soon after, in bringing *Uncle Tom's Cabin* (1903) to the screen, he reverted to the theatrical style of animated tableaux set against painted, two-dimensional settings. It suggests how forcibly the director had been carried along by the logic of his story in *The Great Train Robbery* —and by the fact that he was working out of doors. But the success of this film was too overwhelming to be long ignored. It established the single reel as the standard length for American films (between eight and twelve minutes of film). It set both the fashion and the pattern for Western films. And it inspired other directors to join Porter in exploring the implications of his disjunctive style of editing, his free juggling of time and space. They increased the number of scenes in their little dramas. Their cameras were no longer confined to the studio: scenes taken on location were combined with shots staged against painted sets. And all were assembled and given their final form at the cutting bench, generally by the director himself. As these little stories began to reach the screen, interest in the movies revived throughout the world. In this country, nickelodeons and store shows sprang up in almost every neighborhood. Overnight the movies became the poor man's theater.

TOWARD AN INTERNATIONAL FILM

The demand for these new entertainments was tremendous. To fill it, the movie theaters found it necessary to change their bills every day—and sometimes even twice a day. In their rapidly expanding market, the original pioneer companies soon found themselves competing with dozens of fly-by-night producers with bootleg cameras and evanescent studios. The competition stiffened even further as the leading European producers—Méliès, Pathé, Gaumont from France, England's aggressive Urban Trading Company, the Scandinavian Great Northern, the Italian Itala and Ambrosio—all opened American offices to market their own films. There was no question of showing foreign movies in an "art house" in those days. The titles were simply translated into English (there rarely were subtitles), and they went into the common hopper, turning up on nickelodeon screens cheek by jowl with native productions. Thus, new developments in one country were soon seen and absorbed by the film makers here; while our own pictures, sent abroad in precisely the same way, unquestionably influenced profoundly the European producers. It is not presumptuous to assume that because of this intensive international trade at the dawn of motion-picture techniques an American movie today can be enjoyed in Japan, a Russian film in France and an Italian picture in Scandinavia. Whatever their difference in national temperament, they all spring from a common root of shared discovery and invention. Because the cinematic shorthand of the movies—the way in which a film is put together—remains just about the same all over the world, even a talking picture can provide a purely visual excitement although character relationships and motivations may be obscure.

That this interchange of styles and techniques was neither mystic nor unconscious is readily evidenced by a study of the films of the first decade of this century. Plagiarism of film ideas was rampant. No sooner had a producer released a successful picture, one that proved popular with the audiences, than half a dozen other versions of the same novelty were likely to appear from as many different studios. There can be no doubt that the directors had seen the original version of the films they copied, for not infrequently the special effect or trick that had distinguished the original turned up in the copies as well. Thus, the trick films of Georges Méliès were being imitated by G. A. Smith in England as early as September of 1898, followed by a long series of trick films by Robert Paul beginning in 1899 or early 1900. The popularity of these pictures inevitably produced a school of imitators in this country—led by no less a figure than Edwin S. Porter. In films like *How Jones Lost His Roll* (1905) and *The Dream of a Rarebit Fiend* (1906), he skillfully combined the tricks suggested by the Europeans with home-grown comedy situations. Similarly, the startling financial success of *The Great Train Robbery* caused others to study Porter's own techniques. By 1905 we find them already absorbed, and used proficiently, in such English pictures as Cecil Hepworth's *Rescued by Rover* as well as in most contemporary American films. In effect, it was the audience that dictated which themes, which forms, which techniques the film makers might most profitably follow up.

In France it was the early chase films and trick films that proved most popular. As pictures grew longer—stretching from one minute to ten—these merged into the mad, completely Gallic little farces of men like Ferdinand Zecca, Emile Cohl and Jean Durand. Their construction could not be simpler. Some incident—pumpkins rolling off a wagon, or merely a pretty girl walking down a street—gets a chase under way and then, with incredible inventiveness, complication is piled on complication, camera trick on camera trick, gag on gag until, with a final flourish, everything is righted again and life goes on as unruffled as before. The progress of such films as Zecca's *Slippery Jim* (c1906) or Cohl's *The Pumpkin Race* (1907) is completely straightforward, adding incident to incident without recourse to Porter's more elaborate (and essentially more cinematic) construction. But, shot generally on the streets of Paris, they possessed a superb momentum of their own—and an inspired experimentation with the camera itself. All its resources were explored —fast motion, slow motion, stop motion, reversing the film, superimpositions and ghost effects, comic appearances and disappearances —and always with a lively disregard for the laws of nature and man. It was these comedies that made such an impression on the youthful Mack Sennett and, as he has frankly stated, provided the inspiration for much of his own work as Master of the Revels at Keystone.

By 1910 the international trade in motion pictures had become firmly established, with the Europeans selling in direct competition with the American producers at the going rate of twelve cents per foot (extra if colored—by hand!). Denmark sent a number of somber, starkly lit dramas that impressed, among others, D. W. Griffith. Italy began to contribute its early one-reel spectacle films— rather tacky as spectacles, one finds on re-examination, but drawn from such respectable sources as history or the Bible and filled with crowd scenes and wildly gesticulating actors. A German film industry was still several years away, but Oskar Messter's slightly pornographic comedies were already being imported into the United States. It was, however, the French film that dominated the screens of the world during the first ten years of the new century, a domination secured through Méliès's delightful fantasies, through the comic trick and chase films, through elaborate and dramatic historical reconstructions and, after 1907, the Film d'Art.

THE FIRST FILM D'ART

There have always been those who have sought, whether rightly or wrongly, to combine entertainment with uplift. In France in 1907 a company known as Film d'Art was formed for the express purpose of introducing to lowly cinema audiences the greatest artists of the French national theater in a repertory of great plays. Undoubtedly these people were well meaning. They certainly never stinted in their efforts to obtain the best. They brought before the camera Sarah Bernhardt, Mme. Réjane, Max Dearly and virtually the entire company of the Comédie Française. Ballet was also part of their plan, and dances were filmed with Regina Badet, Trouhanova and La Belle Otero. Stories were drawn from the works of Sardou, Anatole France, Victor Hugo and Edmond Rostand and eventually came to include such standard repertory pieces as *Phèdre*, *The Red Robe*, *Tosca* and even *Werther*. The music to accompany their first film, *The Assassination of the Duc de Guise* (1908), was by no less a composer than Camille Saint-Saëns. Unfortunately, these high ideals never produced a real movie. The actors mouthed their lines even though the films were silent. Their accompanying gestures were those they used on the stage, unmodified for the more intimate camera. The scenery, far richer and more elaborate than that customarily found in any movie studio at the time, was still exposed by the camera for precisely what it was—lath and canvas. Most telling of all, the directors of the Film d'Art, Charles Le Bargy and André Calmettes, had also been imported from the theater. They neither sensed nor cared that their pictures, like those of Méliès, were already out of date. They were bringing culture to the masses—and they expected the masses to be both respectful and grateful for this largesse.

In one respect the sponsors of Film d'Art had an unanticipated success. The masses, suspicious of the whole thing, stayed away in droves; but people who would never have dreamed of going to the nickelodeons to see a cowboy picture, a tear-stained melodrama or a slapstick comedy, somehow felt that movies must be all right if they showed you the classics. For the first time the "right people" began to venture gingerly into the dark, grubby little theaters to see these new, "artistic" films. And, inevitably, the film makers in America, Italy, Germany and England began to follow this new lead. American producers were soon filming Shakespeare in vast quantities—the whole of *Hamlet* in a hectic ten minutes! The Italians intensified their already pronounced predilection for pageant-like pictures based on their historic past. German actors became interested in the disreputable movie business and began to appear in suitably artistic productions. The English turned to both Shakespeare and Dickens for inspiration. Such pictures may have had far less to do with the true art of the film than the primitive *Great Train Robbery;* but they did raise the question of whether melodrama and low comedy were the only materials proper to the motion-picture screen. They conferred a certain begrudging, even misguided, prestige upon the movies. And, perhaps most important of all in the long run, they preserved for us a first-hand document of the theater of half a century ago.

One further effect of these ambitious Film d'Art productions was to help push the motion picture in this country beyond its single-reel length. In 1912 the great Sarah Bernhardt made a film version of her play *Queen Elizabeth* for Film d'Art in four reels. In Italy at the same time *Quo Vadis?* was being readied in eight reels— almost two hours on the screen. In America, on the other hand, film lengths had been arbitrarily frozen at one reel. It was the Motion Picture Patents Company that decided no audience would sit through a movie running longer than about ten minutes, and thus established the single reel as the length for all its films. Composed of the largest producers and distributors in the United States, it sought to control through its pooling of patents every phase of the infant industry. And between 1909 and 1912 its word was law. A Trust in the full Rooseveltian sense, it licensed both cameras and projectors—the cameras solely to its own members, the projectors to those theater men who would agree to purchase only films produced by the member companies. In addition to limiting the length of its movies, the Patents Company also blocked the identification of actors appearing in their films, fearing that they might demand more money if they became well known. Firm believers in the *status quo,* the members of the Trust waged a constant, and frequently bloody, battle with the independents who kept turning up with foreign cameras and fresh ideas.

One of these independents was Adolph Zukor, a young man who, scarcely a decade earlier, had quit the fur business for the penny arcades. He had purchased the American rights to *Queen Elizabeth*, feeling that the time was ripe for longer pictures. Zukor waited long weeks to speak to the Trust officials, to persuade them that Sarah Bernhardt in *Queen Elizabeth* was an attraction most audiences would gladly watch through four full reels. He never got past the gates. Blocked from authorized distribution, Zukor looked outside the normal channels, away from the nickelodeons and store shows. Instead, he convinced one of the leading impresarios of the New York theater, Daniel Frohman, that even on celluloid Sarah Bernhardt deserved a legitimate showcase; and on July 12, 1912, at the Lyceum Theatre, Americans saw their first feature-length film—and paid the unprecedented sum of $1.00 a ticket. No one seemed unduly upset by the fact that the divine Sarah could only be seen, and not heard. The presentation proved an enormous success throughout the country, and led directly to Zukor's formation of "Famous Players in Famous Plays," the ancestor of the present-day Paramount Pictures. As for Sarah Bernhardt, "This is my one chance of immortality," she said when invited, at 65, to film *Camille* and *Elizabeth*.

THE FATHER OF FILM TECHNIQUE: D. W. GRIFFITH

A few years before Bernhardt sought immortality on celluloid, a young stage actor reluctantly consented to appear before the camera—and then only out of direst necessity. "Lawrence" Griffith had spent a decade barnstorming through the United States, more often than not with shows that folded on the road. He had tried his hand at playwriting, at poetry and, when all else failed, had sold subscriptions to magazines, picked hops in the fields, worked on ships and construction jobs. Christened David Wark, the fifth child of an impoverished Confederate colonel, Griffith chose to preserve his real name for the success he felt certain would one day come to him. It was as "Lawrence" that he approached Edwin S. Porter at the Edison Studio in the Bronx with his screen adaptation of the opera *Tosca*. Porter rejected the script, but offered Griffith the leading role in a film he was just about to start, *Rescued from an*

Eagle's Nest (1907). This was an era in which actors from the legitimate stage viewed the movies with the utmost scorn, and felt that to perform in them was degrading. But Griffith, newly married, needed the money badly. He consented to play in it, at $5 a day. A few months later, armed with more scripts, he turned up at the Biograph Studio at 11 East 14th Street, New York City. He not only sold a few, but again was invited to act. Again, presumably, necessity forced his hand; but within a few months Griffith had become a fixture at Biograph and his wife, Linda Arvidson, had also joined the little company. Griffith, however, was still "Lawrence."

What happened within the next few years is probably without parallel in the emergence of any art form. Between 1908 and 1912 Griffith took the raw elements of movie making as they had evolved up to that time and, singlehanded, wrought from them a medium more intimate than theater, more vivid than literature, more affecting than poetry. He created the art of the film, its language, its syntax. It has often been said that Griffith "invented" the close-up, that he "invented" cutting, the camera angle, or even the last-minute rescue. This, of course, is nonsense. What he did was far more important. He refined these elements, already present in motion pictures, mastered them and made them serve his purpose. He discovered ways to use his camera functionally, developed editing from the crude assembly of unrelated shots into a conscious, artistic device. Apparently to Griffith each new film was a challenge, a chance to experiment, to try out new effects. Certainly, Biograph gave him every opportunity. In his first year there he turned out well over a hundred pictures—more than two a week!

One of his first moves was to break the standard distance maintained between audience and actor by changing the camera's position in midscene. There is no need, he argued, to photograph an entire sequence from a single setup when, by simply shifting to a new vantage point, we can always keep the most significant action in screen center. Pursuing the same line of reasoning, he continued to push the camera ever closer to his players to emphasize a gesture or a reaction. "The public will never buy only half an actor," his employers protested. But the public saw, and understood.

Grasping instinctively the fact that the movies are in reality a form quite apart from theater, Griffith went further still. Why go through all the tedious business of having an actor open a door, step into a room, close the door, then walk to the center of the stage before the significant action begins? He started his scenes instead directly upon the action itself, and halted them as soon as the action was completed. Again the audiences understood. He became interested in the composition and lighting of his scenes. He discovered that by placing the camera at an angle to the action he could create a greater dynamism than was possible in the conventional head-on shot, that deep shadows and key high-lights—"Rembrandt lighting," he called it—would intensify the mood and heighten the visual impact of his scenes. He edited his own pictures and found that the length of time a shot remained on the screen could create very real psychological tensions in an audience: the shorter the shot, the greater the excitement. As early as 1909 he introduced this principle to build a climax of suspense in *The Lonely Villa*. A trio of thugs are forcing their way into the house. The father has learned by telephone that his wife and children are in danger, and drives frantically to the rescue. The burglars batter on the doors. The mother stands guard over her little brood. By cutting back and forth from one to the other, making each shot shorter than the last, Griffith heightened the excitement of the situation. It was a device he was to use again and again, a device in which time and space were shuffled freely at the will of the director.

Griffith felt his way gradually, ever more sure of himself, ever widening the gap between film technique and stage methods. He worked his actors to and from the camera, devising groupings and compositions which, while meaningless on the three-dimensional stage, proved highly effective on the two-dimensional screen. As he moved his camera closer to the players, he perceived that the theater's eloquent gestures and overemphatic facial expressions became awkward and artificial. He trained his performers in a quieter, more intimate acting style, and developed a host of young people, preferably without previous stage experience, to work in his films. The Griffith "stock company" at Biograph came to include such future luminaries as Mary Pickford, Lillian and Dorothy Gish, Mae

Marsh, Mabel Normand, Robert Harron, Owen Moore, Blanche Sweet, Mack Sennett, Arthur Johnson, H. B. Walthall and Lionel Barrymore. Actors who could not follow his direction, actors who persisted in the melodramatic style of gaslit melodrama, either left Biograph or worked with other directors there.

Perhaps even more important than Griffith's discovery of how to make film actors act was his realization that in the movies objects could become actors as well. By use of the extreme close-up, a knife, a whisky bottle, a letter, a telephone, a revolver could be made to occupy the entire screen, emphasizing its importance in the developing story. In *The Lonedale Operator* (1911), Blanche Sweet holds a pair of desperadoes at bay with a monkey wrench. We are shown in close-up that it is only a wrench. But the thugs think it is a pistol—and in the long-shots that is what it looks like to us too. It was the close-up that let us in on the secret, when the director was ready to reveal it. Griffith discovered that one basic function of the close-up was to emphasize the inanimate, to make *things* a dynamic part of the world through which the actors move.

But the close-up does more than merely emphasize what is important in a scene: it eliminates everything else. It forces the audience to see what the director wants it to see—and only that. It concentrates attention on the significant detail, whether it be an object, an actor or a portion of an actor. Griffith discovered that the close-up of a hand, an arm, the eyes or lips could often be far more expressive on the screen than the most highly trained actor projecting an emotion in theatrical terms. Unforgettable is the scene of the Little Colonel's homecoming in *The Birth of a Nation* (1915). Only the arms of the mother and sister are seen as they tenderly enfold him and draw him in toward his family. All the tension of the courtroom scene in *Intolerance* (1916) is compressed into the huge close-up of Mae Marsh's hands, the fingers nervously twisting together as the young wife awaits the judge's sentence of life or death for her unfortunate husband. "Visible hieroglyphs," Horace M. Kallen once called such material, "the visible hieroglyphs of the unseen dynamics of human relations." It was Griffith's unique ability to reveal filmically the inmost thoughts and emotions of his characters, to reveal them clearly and intimately to his audiences. Knowing nothing about Griffith, "hieroglyphs" or film technique, people everywhere responded directly to the bitter-sweet sufferings of Little Mary, to the harassed wife of a drunken husband, to courageous Blanche Sweet or terrified Lillian Gish. They found Griffith's pictures more realistic, more convincing, more human than anything shown upon the screen at that time, and they looked forward to each new Biograph release with greater enthusiasm than to the films of any other studio.

It is instructive to compare Griffith's films with the French and Italian spectacles that were imported in great quantities after 1912 by the distributor George Kleine. As early as May, 1911, Griffith had rebelled against the Trust's arbitrary single-reel restriction. When he made *Enoch Arden* in two reels, Biograph, which was one of the leading members of the Trust, insisted on releasing each reel separately. However, in response to audience demand, theater managers were soon showing the two parts together. And by 1912 the two-reeler had become accepted as the standard length for a serious story film. Now, spurred by rumors of the longer films being made abroad, Griffith sought to push further. Working secretly in California, he completed in four reels an opulent version of the biblical story *Judith of Bethulia* (1913). His employers were furious. They shelved the film and declared that henceforth Griffith would supervise production instead of directing. Griffith promptly left the studio, taking with him many of his "stock company" adherents—the Gish sisters, Mae Marsh, Blanche Sweet, Robert Harron, H. B. Walthall and, above all, his trusted and ingenious cameraman, G. W. ("Billy") Bitzer.

Judith of Bethulia was not released by Biograph until late in 1914. Although it appeared a whole year after *Quo Vadis?* had received its Broadway première, and in the midst of a veritable flood of similar European spectacles, the Griffith film reasserted the importance of his discoveries. The Italian and French pictures were longer, had vaster crowds and huger sets, but they were essentially static. They were like watching a tremendous pageant upon a distant stage. One felt no sense of personal involvement. *Judith of Bethulia,* on the other hand, with the most daring close-ups that Griffith had yet attempted, had the power to move audiences, to make them aware of the ancient drama in warm and human terms. Far from the best of his earlier work, it towered over its European contemporaries.

Leaving Biograph, Griffith—now at last David Wark Griffith—

joined the Mutual Company and supervised for them a number of five-reel features, potboilers that, for the most part, reveal all too clearly Griffith's essential lack of interest. For during this period Griffith was gathering together his resources to tackle a subject so great, so ambitious and daring as to astonish the imagination. He had read Thomas Dixon's novel *The Clansman,* a story of the Civil War and the Reconstruction period that followed, a story of the rise of the Ku Klux Klan. Being a Southerner, the son of a Confederate officer, Griffith was drawn instinctively to its theme. But his film sense responded even more strongly to the sweep and melodramatic power of the novel—a little family ruined by the war, then fighting to preserve its integrity amidst carpetbaggers and renegade Negroes. He flung himself into the production, poured into it all his own finances and those of his friends. Working without a scenario, he devised new, unheard-of effects—battle scenes photographed in extreme long-shot and reminiscent of the Brady Civil War photographs, action shots taken in extreme close-up, the climactic ride of the Clans photographed with the camera mounted low on the back of a moving truck. He drew on all the known resources of the camera and invented still more—the iris, the mask, the vignette, split-screen and triple split-screen shots. He worked out every action, every gesture for the principals in his huge cast. He mustered all his knowledge of editing to impart fluency and mounting tension to the scenes that poured from Bitzer's camera. The result was a film of extraordinary eloquence and power, *The Birth of a Nation.*

Released early in 1915, *The Birth of a Nation* took its audiences by storm. Twelve reels long (almost three hours), with a special score performed by a full symphony orchestra, it swept along with a cumulative force that a present-day viewing of the film can only partially suggest. There simply had never been a picture like this before; "like writing history in lightning," Woodrow Wilson described it. The passions it aroused, the tensions it created lasted beyond the theater. They overflowed into the streets, and race riots and mob action followed in the wake of its presentation in many cities. But whether loved or hated, *The Birth of a Nation* established once for all that the film was an art in its own right—and Griffith was its master.

Even today, after more than forty years, the strengths of this remarkable film are still apparent—the characterization through vivid symbol, the epic swelling of its first act from scenes of warm intimacy to the broad panorama of battle, then closing quietly on the Little Colonel's return to his ravaged home; the fevered melodrama of its second half dominated by the sweeping ride of the Clans. Individual scenes reveal still more clearly Griffith's sure instinct for the perfect film image. Incomparable is his portrayal of Sherman's vengeful march to the sea. Beginning with a tight iris shot of weeping women and children huddled together high on a hill, as the iris opens out to fill the screen the camera pans to the right, to an extreme long-shot of Sherman's army far below spreading destruction through the countryside. Individual shots depict the pillage, the burning, the slaughter. The sequence ends with a closing iris glimpse of the tearful women on the hill. The ruthless devastation of war is made poignant by relating it to the innocents who suffer. Again, in a scene that still seems breathtakingly daring, Griffith intercuts shots of the old people at home on their knees in prayer with cold, pitiless glimpses of trenches piled high with corpses frozen in the agony of death. The realism of the scene in the Union hospital, the painstaking authenticity of the reconstruction of Lincoln's assassination, the heart-warming moment of the homecoming, the virtuoso cutting from the wild ride of the Clansmen to the besieged family in a squalid cabin—these are passages of pure film that rank among the greatest in all motion-picture history.

What makes *The Birth of a Nation* difficult to view today is precisely what touched off the controversy that raged about the film in 1915—its use of Negro stereotypes and its sympathetic account of the rise of the Klan. Griffith seems to have been genuinely shocked at the charges of anti-Negro bias leveled against him on all sides when the film appeared, and not without reason. One has only to read *The Clansman,* on which it was based, to become aware of the pains that Griffith had taken to eliminate from his version the rabid hatred that seethes through Thomas Dixon's book. But Griffith was a Southerner, brought up in an embittered, impoverished household. His father had been a colonel in the Confederacy, and Griffith grew up hearing tales of the good old days before the war. He balanced his renegade Negroes and vengeful mulattoes with happy, faithful "darkies," and thought he was being fair. He could never comprehend that to many one stereotype was as repugnant as the other. Set against this, such minor blemishes as Griffith's eternally twittering young girls and a painfully poetic epilogue depicting the arrival of universal brotherhood pale into insignificance. But perhaps the true measure of this film is to be found in the very depth of the passions it aroused. Certainly, not for another ten years was there to be a movie capable of affecting its audiences so profoundly.

It might be a kindness to leave D. W. Griffith at this point, for at 39 he had reached the very pinnacle of his career. With *The Birth of a Nation* he had made all his major contributions to the medium, had transformed the film from a halting, stumbling imitation of theater into a vigorous, eloquent, independent art. There were still years of greatness ahead of him—the daring of *Intolerance* (1916), with its four separate stories from four different eras interlocked by a single unifying theme; the haunting poignancy of *Broken Blossoms* (1919), a small, somber vignette told with great delicacy and refinement; his enormously popular version of *Way Down East* (1920), a gaslight melodrama that Griffith vigorously and resourcefully adapted to the screen; the extraordinary realism of the German-made *Isn't Life Wonderful?* (1924). But along with these films came the potboilers, more and more of them. As an independent, he had to meet the payroll and overhead of his Mamaroneck studio, the expenses of his big productions. When finally the creditors took over, he became just another staff director at Famous Players-Lasky. The end of Griffith's story is not a happy one. It is never pleasant to see greatness humbled or genius left behind. Far better to remember the tireless experimenter, the instinctive artist in an untried art, the man who trained and inspired an entire generation of directors, actors and technicians—the Griffith who declared at the height of his career, "The task I'm trying to achieve is above all to make you see."

THE CREATIVE PRODUCER: THOMAS H. INCE

Soon after Griffith left Biograph for Mutual, he found himself in tandem with two other prominent producer-directors, Mack Sennett and Thomas H. Ince. Each had his own studio, his own autonomy to produce what he liked as he liked; together they contributed the three points to the Triangle Company's offerings—comedies, program features and, from Griffith, the "specials." Of the three, Ince is probably the least known today. At one time, however, his name was as familiar and respected as Griffith's. In France, in fact, the films of "T-H Ince" were generally held to be better than Griffith's, although this can partially be explained by recalling that many—but by no means all—of Ince's pictures were Westerns. The French were attracted by the exotic settings and characters of the Ince films, and especially by "Rio Jim," as they affectionately nicknamed William S. Hart, Ince's top cowboy star. Ince kept his Culver City studio and ranch well stocked with cattle, horses, buffalo and genuine Sioux Indians, and he had a positive genius for finding suitably atmospheric locales for his tales of the American frontier. But no less important is the fact that his pictures were quite devoid of the cloying sentimentality that marred so many of Griffith's films. Working with Hart, Ince created a frontier that was truly primitive, hard and rugged. Here was no romantic compromise, as in the Westerns of Tom Mix, Buck Jones and Hoot Gibson. As for the singing cowboys who populate our Westerns today, Hart would probably have shot them dead on sight. And in the many films that Ince produced without Hart—Westerns and city-based dramas alike—that same unwillingness to compromise is still present. At his best, Ince was a stern realist, a realist with an extraordinary story sense and an ability to remake a picture in the cutting room that has probably never been equaled.

Ince, like Griffith, came to the movies from the theater. Although he had been an actor, he began directing for Biograph in 1910, moving quickly to Carl Laemmle's Imp Company and then to Mutual. By 1914 he was already a major force in the industry, heading his own palatial studio, Inceville, just outside of Hollywood. Gradually Ince found himself devoting far more time to the organization and supervision of his studio than to actual direction, a development that was to prove of considerable importance in the history of film making. It was Ince who introduced the concept of the creative producer to Hollywood—the man who knows so much about pictures that he can plan, organize and supervise the work of others. With himself as the over-all chief, he set up a number of producing units on his lot, each headed by a production manager. This manager, responsible directly to Ince, worked with him and the writer throughout the preparation of a script. When completed, the script was rubber-stamped with the explicit instruction, "Shoot as written." A shooting schedule was then drawn up, indicating what was to be shot where and when. This was equally inviolate. It was a system created for economic production and—at least in Ince's hands—it also resulted in many excellent pictures. His powers of visualization were so strong that, it is said, he could see from the printed page of a script exactly how each completed shot could and should fit with another. In any case, he did much of the final editing of his pictures himself. The system that Ince introduced into his studio between 1915 and 1920 is one that Hollywood, with some modifications, still follows today. The extraordinary thing about Ince's films was the fact that, no matter who directed them, they were all stamped unmistakably with their producer's personality. Few of Hollywood's present producers have quite that degree of creative vigor.

Even though Ince turned out pictures at top speed and invariably had several productions working at once, surprisingly few of his films have survived the years. We have far less opportunity to see again an Ince film than a contemporary Griffith or Sennett. Perhaps his mysterious death in 1924, before there was any considerable literature on the art of the motion picture, has also contributed to the relative obscurity of this gifted pioneer. But while it is difficult today to find a "vintage" Ince—a film produced between 1914 and 1920—those that do turn up are invariably admirable in editing, construction and story. Lean, tight, cut to the bone, the plot advances quickly and tersely, rarely straying from the main line of action for atmospheric, comic or romantic interludes. The characters are solid and three-dimensional, the settings uncluttered and painstakingly realistic. There is a refreshing, unsentimental naturalness about his pictures, whether a hard-hitting, two-reel action story like *The Gangsters and the Girl* (1914), social comment as in *The Italian* (1915) or a small-town comedy romance like *The Clodhopper* (1917). Of the pictures of this period, only the overly ambitious, pseudo-Griffith, semi-pacifist *Civilization* (1916) seems to waver in its point of view or to contain people who are anything less than flesh and blood.

Although Ince continued to make films through the early twenties, they became less and less exciting, more and more routine. It was as if Ince himself had been exhausted by a decade of intense creativity, as if the magnitude of the business operation now drained his energies, leaving little over for his films. Meanwhile, however, both the production techniques that he had devised and the host of directors that he had trained—Frank Borzage, Lambert Hillyer, Rowland V. Lee, Fred Niblo, Victor Schertzinger—were spreading throughout the Hollywood studios. Like Griffith, he had made his contribution.

SENNETT, THE KEYSTONE OF AMERICAN COMEDY

Opposite Ince in the Triangle Company—Griffith, of course, was its apex—stood Mark Sennett, king of the slapstick clowns at Keystone. When Sennett, a huge, gangling, would-be opera singer, arrived at Biograph in January of 1909, he had already steered a hazardous course through circuses, burlesque, vaudeville and walk-ons in the legitimate theater. Like most actors of the period, he was lured into films less by the potentialities of the cinema as an art form than by the $5 daily take-home pay. But Sennett was also possessed by a consuming ambition: he wanted to play a comic policeman. He thought that cops were funny long before he got the opportunity to prove it, frequently arguing this point with D. W. Griffith as the two men rambled together about the streets of New York. Griffith, however, refused to be convinced, and continued casting him in straight roles. Sennett can often be discerned shifting about in the background of the Biograph dramas dressed as a butler, a rube or a tramp "heavy"—but never a comic cop.

From Mary Pickford, Sennett learned that Biograph paid $25 for story ideas, so he promptly became an author. He claims that his first scenario was lifted from something by O. Henry—although not quite far enough to make a sale. In any case, before long he was augmenting his actor's income fairly regularly with acceptable script material, including *The Lonely Villa*. At the same time he was learning to direct—and from Griffith himself. In his autobiography, *King of Comedy,* Sennett pays a warm and heartfelt tribute to his mentor: "He was my day school, my adult education program, my university." Before long, Sennett too had become a director—at a princely $65 a week.

Sennett's years at Biograph were not altogether happy ones. He worked hard, turning out an average of two pictures a week between 1910 and 1912, acting in his own films and occasionally in Griffith's as well. But Sennett had developed some fairly definite ideas about film comedy—and not merely in regard to cops as figures of fun. He remembered the grotesques from circus and burlesque. He was fascinated by the mechanical gags and tricks he saw in the French chase comedies that had been arriving here in great quantities since about 1907, and by the agile comedies of the dapper Frenchman Max Linder (whose style was also at the time being studied by the young Charles Chaplin). Sennett felt that these elements of gag, chase, trick and character could be fused into an American comedy form. Biograph, however, had been prospering under the sober influence of D. W. Griffith. It had gained in prestige and importance. Wallace ("Pop") McCutcheon, the boss of the little studio, enjoyed his new respectability and saw no reason to encourage Sennett's slapstick notions. For Biograph, Sennett turned out a rather routine succession of rube comedies, livened occasionally by the sparkling presence of Mabel Normand.

Sennett's account of the origin of his famous Keystone studio is probably apocryphal—and hardly flattering to his associates in the business, Adam Kessel and Charles Bauman. As he tells the story, Kessel and Bauman were a pair of small-time bookies. Sennett had guessed wrong on too many horse races and owed them a hundred dollars that he didn't have. When finally cornered, Sennett declares he waxed so eloquent about the fortunes to be made in the movies that his creditors not only forgave him his hundred but put up an additional $2,500 to get into the business themselves. The name, he says, was inspired by the insigne of the Pennsylvania Railroad. Just how much of this Runyonesque tale is true, Sennett alone can tell. But in January, 1912—just three years after coming to work as an extra at Biograph—he alighted from a train in Los Angeles and began making pictures at his own studio, the Keystone. And his new bosses, back in New York, were the Messrs. Kessel and Bauman.

At first Sennett was Keystone's director, star, idea man, and

THE TOY
THAT GREW UP

The Praxinoscope, a 19th Century parlor entertainment. Its hand-drawn images, reflected in the mirrors, sprang to life when the drum was revolved.

M-G-M's giant Camera 65 shooting a scene from **Raintree County** (1957). It is one of the many wide-screen variants in use today.

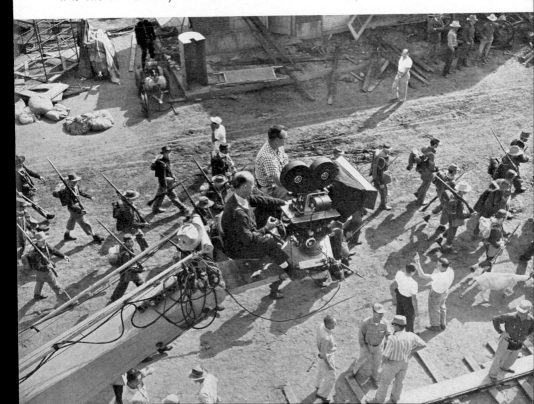

D. W. Griffith (left), the Father of Film Technique, directs a scene from **Intolerance** (1916). Dorothy Gish watches in the background as Miriam Cooper (right) listens to the Master.

Griffith enriched the art of film by heightening its sense of intimacy and reality, as in this shot from **Musketeers of Pig Alley** (1912) . . . While in such films as **The Birth of a Nation** (1915) and, more especially, **Intolerance** (1916), he introduced the sweep and spectacle that continues to delight and astonish audiences to this day.

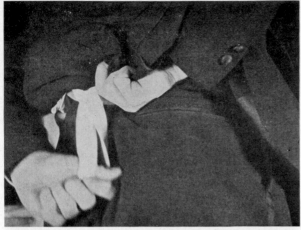

CLOSE-UP

MID-SHOT

LONG-SHOT

As film makers gained mastery over the camera, their basic shots became more precise and expressive. A sequence from Harold Lloyd's **The Freshman** (1925).

sometimes he even helped out on the camera. Stories were improvised on the spot. They might hear of a parade or of a motorcar race, of a lake being drained or a captive balloon released. Sennett and his crew would arrive pell-mell, dreaming up a situation on the way. The key scenes, the scenes involving the incident, would be caught almost on the fly. Then back to the little studio in Edendale to shoot more material that would lead up to it and explain it. The explanation might not be too logical, but Sennett quickly learned to take care of that. "It's got to *move*," he would say, knowing that in a plethora of slam-bang action audiences would find little time to ask embarrassing questions. His favorite axiom for comedy was that a gag should be planted, developed and pointed all within a hundred feet of film (about a minute and a half on the screen).

Now at last he could indulge his fancy for comic policemen, and the Keystone Kops came tumbling into his pictures in their motley, outsized uniforms and collapsible tin lizzies. Now at last he could try out the dizzying camera tricks he had admired in the French chases. Now he could develop his own corps of characters and clowns, of gargoyles and grotesques. Ford Sterling, Mabel Normand, Pathé Lehrman and Fred Mace had made the trip west with him. Soon they were joined by such exuberant types as "Fatty" Arbuckle, Hank Mann, Chester Conklin, "Slim" Summerville, Edgar Kennedy, Charlie Murray, Ben Turpin, Charley Chase, Mack Swain and, of course, Charlie Chaplin. Within the first year of operation, Sennett reports, Keystone had turned out over 140 comedies.

Before long Sennett, like Ince, was forced to withdraw from direct participation in his comedies and become a producer, presiding over the destinies of his studio from a huge bathtub installed in the watchtower office where he held his staff conferences; and no less important, from a creaky rocking chair in the projection room where he viewed every last foot of film his zany crews had photographed. It proved an ideal arrangement. As an actor, Sennett scarcely invites comparison with any of the talented clowns he had gathered around him. His heavy grimaces, his raw-boned, shuffling gait were utterly lacking in precision, finesse or, when you come right down to it, humor. What he did have, born of his years of prentice work at Biograph, was an uncanny instinct for timing and editing his shots. His staff could tell from the squeaks of the rocking chair whether they were pleasing "the Old Man" or not. If not, Sennett could generally tell how to recut a scene to make it play better.

Most of the ideas for the Keystone comedies originated with Sennett himself; nothing was ever purchased from outside. With his writers, he would lay out the basic plot or situation as if planning a straight film. Characters and characterizations were discussed and tailored to fit the personalities on the lot. Only after a proper story line had been hammered out was it forwarded to the "gag room," to the men who would add the humorous scenes and situations. One of Frank Capra's first movie jobs was in the Keystone gag department. Another graduate from this asylum for inspired maniacs was Raymond Griffith, the popular "silk-hatted comedian" of the twenties. Shooting was generally a weird combination of improvisation and script, the natural high spirits and prankishness of the performers often leading to bits of business that even Sennett's accomplished gagsters would have hesitated to devise. Thus Mabel Normand splurched the first custard pie full into the gloriously cockeyed features of Ben Turpin to liven up a faltering scene. Sad-eyed Hank Mann invariably infuriated his Keystone confreres with his scene-stealing acrobatics. But if they pleased Sennett, they stayed. Sennett always thought of himself as the average audience: if he liked a scene, so would the public. He was rarely wrong.

Inevitably, with this incessant flow of ordered insanity, all the comedies were not the masterpieces that the historians, writing with an understandable nostalgia, would suggest. Some of Sennett's satires —*His Bitter Pill* (1916), *A Small Town Idol* (1921), *The Shriek of Araby* (1923)—were perfect gems of parody, generally built around the themes of successful serious dramas. His purely mechanical gags—as in *Dizzy Heights and Daring Hearts* (1916) and *The Clever Dummy* (1917)—were more than merely ingenious: they laughed irreverently at America's increasing worship of the machine. Whole series were built around the leading comics on the lot—Chaplin, Mack Swain ("Ambrose"), "Fatty" Arbuckle, the pixyish Mabel Normand and blustery Ford Sterling. The success of these films rested, of course, upon the antic gifts and graces of their stars. But intermingled with these were great quantities of wholly routine and completely uninspired situation comedies obviously borrowed from vaudeville and burlesque. And a surprising number prove to be rube comedies, all too reminiscent of the pictures Sennett had ground out for Biograph.

By the late twenties, when most of his top clowns and directors had left him for more profitable feature-film jobs, the Sennett pictures had become routine indeed, pale effigies of the speedy knockabout farces that characterized his best production. The props—the cars that fall apart, the crockery that flies into a thousand pieces, the breakaway walls and doors and trees, the pies that sail miraculously on invisible wires—all were still present; but not the great comic gusto that once transformed them into dizzy, devastating parodies of life itself.

Sennett's name today is probably irretrievably wedded to slap-stick and the custard pie. While the connection is perfectly true, its connotations do him an injustice. In his hands slapstick became suddenly, indigenously filmic. He used the camera to exploit the absurd, the impossible, the fantastic. Reason was blurred by the speed of his action and editing. He reduced the real world—or at least something that perilously resembled the real world—to a shambles, and held it up to mockery as a wry joke of a place where little men were married to stern, overpowering women, where lechery abounded, where officialdom was invariably inept, and a swift kick in the pants could settle the most abstruse problems. There was philosophy in the Sennett films, and art as well, although "the Old Man" always expressed polite astonishment whenever anyone found it there. "We played it by ear as we went along," he liked to say.

Perhaps so, but his ear was good and his instincts were sound. Certainly, he discovered and developed a whole generation of top comedians—not only Chaplin and the Keystone Kops but actresses like Gloria Swanson, Phyllis Haver, Bebe Daniels, Marie Prevost, Carole Lombard, Alberta Vaughn, Louise Fazenda and Polly Moran. Marie Dressler, Buster Keaton, Harry Langdon, Harold Lloyd, Wallace Beery, W. C. Fields and Bing Crosby were all on the Sennett lot at one time or another. Perhaps even more important is the training he gave an entire school of directors—men like Frank Capra, Leo McCarey, Mal St. Clair, Roy Del Ruth, Ray Enright, Eddie Cline, George Stevens and George Marshall, many of them still active today. He taught them timing and the need for physical movement on the screen. And he stressed the importance of editing to tighten and sharpen a scene.

Sound and the arrival of the double feature wrote the final chapter to Sennett's story. Perhaps his methods could have prevailed only when the industry was young, enthusiastic and wildly disorganized. His free-wheeling, boldly improvisational techniques were already being toned down during the twenties when Sennett moved to Paramount. In the interest of economy, his films were more carefully planned and budgeted step by step. Sound changed shooting techniques even further, throwing emphasis completely on the written script; and double features virtually eliminated the two-reel comedy from theater bills in favor of the single-reel cartoon or band short. In 1935 Sennett finally withdrew from active production. He, too, had made his contribution.

CHAPLIN AND THE RISE OF THE STAR SYSTEM

Of the many illustrious alumni of the Sennett school, Charlie Chaplin still shines above all the rest. Today, with Chaplin in embittered semi-retirement far from the scenes of his early triumphs and even farther out of contact with the heart and temper of the common man whose image he had created on the screen, it is somewhat difficult to imagine just how popular he once was. Within two years of his first screen appearance, his name had become a household word. There were Chaplin dolls, Chaplin toys, Chaplin contests. People danced "The Chaplin Walk"; children used his name in their counting-out rhymes. There were Chaplin imitators—even in the films—and Chaplin cartoons both in the newspapers and on the screen. "I am here today"—this simple announcement printed over a cutout of Chaplin tipping his hat was all that a theater manager needed to lure the customers into his house. No one bothered to ask either title or story.

Some measure of the whirlwind velocity of Chaplin's career, some estimate of the tremendous popularity of his pictures may be gained from a simple financial statement. He joined Keystone in December, 1913, at a salary of $150 a week—a sizable sum for a young man whose biggest job up to that time had been touring the American vaudeville circuits with an English music-hall act at $50 a week. Just one year later, in January, 1915, Chaplin was signed by Essanay at $1,250 a week. In the following year he joined Mutual at $10,000 a week—plus a bonus of $150,000 simply for putting his name to the contract. And in 1917, at the age of 27, Chaplin signed with First National for a million dollars to deliver eight films in eighteen months—this time with a bonus of $15,000. What makes this sum even more impressive is the fact that all of his pictures had been brief one- or two-reelers. The Chaplin shorts were more prized than any features except those of Mary Pickford. At the time, Mary was earning just under a million dollars a year.

Both Chaplin and Pickford were reaping the benefits of a significant development in the motion-picture industry. Prior to 1910 the identity of the players in movies was completely unknown to the general public. Gradually, as audiences began to recognize their favorites, they would refer to them by the names that were used in the pictures. Thus, the tiny, golden-locked Gladys Smith was known as "Little Mary" long before she acquired the screen name of Mary Pickford; while burly G. M. Anderson, the screen's first cowboy star, was simply "Broncho Billy." Others were known by their studio—"The Biograph Girl," "The Vitagraph Girl," "The Imp Girl." The producers, and particularly those who were members of the Patents Company, sought to maintain this anonymity. They firmly refused to acknowledge the increasingly persistent "who" letters, for if the public learned the names of their players, they reasoned, then the actors might demand more money. It remained for one of the independents, Carl Laemmle, to break this pattern. Florence Lawrence, the popular "Biograph Girl," was lured from that studio by Laemmle's promise not only to pay her more money but to feature her under her own name. Laemmle, always a great believer in advertising, publicized his coup well. A star was born. And with the star, the star system.

Laemmle quickly learned that, while he had to pay more for his actress, he could also charge more rental for her pictures. The devotees, the "fans" of Florence Lawrence could be depended upon to turn up in sufficient numbers at the box office to warrant the increased price. Soon talent raids were taking place throughout the industry. Laemmle swooped down on Biograph again to carry off Mary Pickford and her husband, Owen Moore. Vitagraph, the first of the Patents companies to break the ban, made stars of handsome Maurice Costello and its own "Vitagraph Girl," Florence Turner. Rotund John Bunny was probably the first movie comedian that the public knew by name; Arthur Johnson, the movies' first "matinee idol." By 1911 there was even a dog star—Jean, "the Vitagraph Dog." These early stars came from the ranks of the regular movie players. But after Sarah Bernhardt's success in *Queen Elizabeth,* theater people began to lose some of their traditional antipathy toward the movies and Zukor's idea of "Famous Players in Famous Plays" soon acquired a host of imitators. Between 1912 and 1915 the screen featured such illustrious stage personalities as Nat C. Goodwin, James O'Neill, James Hackett, Minnie Maddern Fiske and Lily Langtry. Naturally, there was never the slightest question about revealing *these* names.

As the studios vied with each other for stars, actors and actresses found their dollar-and-cents value to the studios spiraling upward at a dizzying rate—from $5 to $15 a day before 1910, to from $250 to $2,000 a week in 1914. The true movie stars proved worth their weight even in this much gold, but producers soon learned to their sorrow that a great name in the theater did not automatically assure great popularity on the screen, and that the public often preferred to discover its own stars rather than have them delivered ready-made. Many a top Broadway performer returned to the footlights considerably chastened by his brush with the movies; while many an unknown, yielding to the lure of good money and steady employment in the studios, quickly found himself swept to undreamed-of heights of acclaim and affection. Chaplin was one of the latter.

Few men have ever succeeded in becoming a legend in their own lifetime—especially men who have lived so long and so intensely in the public eye as Charles Spencer Chaplin. Yet Chaplin from the very start met all the requirements for legend-making. His origins are obscure, his parentage, even his name. It is known that he suffered extreme poverty in his youth, including two miserable years in a London orphanage. Coming from a theatrical family, he had learned dancing and miming almost as soon as he learned to walk. He was earning his own living by the time he was seven, dancing in a music-hall act called *The Eight Lancashire Lads;* but this was followed by another period of great hardship when his mother was placed in a mental institution and Chaplin roamed the streets, unwanted and alone. From the time he was ten, however, he began to find fairly regular employment in the theater, first as a child actor (notably in the London company of *Sherlock Holmes*), later in various vaudeville turns. In 1906, with the help of his older brother Sidney, he joined the Karno Comedy Company, an organization that boasted a large and varied repertory of skits, pantomimes, acrobatics, comedy songs and dances. Chaplin was to remain with Karno until the movies tapped him for fame and fortune in 1913.

Mack Sennett has written that when he was in New York in 1912, he and Mabel Normand caught the Karno act "A Night in an English Music Hall." Later, when Keystone's top comedian, Ford Sterling, was bitten by the then prevalent "star fever," Sennett thought it judicious to have a substitute handy. Remembering Chaplin (although not his name), he urged his New York partners to find him and sign him. Adam Kessel handled the arrangements; but although Chaplin signed the contract in May of 1913, he was so filled with doubts and misgivings about his future in films that he refused to leave the Karno troupe until the end of its American tour. When he arrived in Hollywood in December of that year, he was just twenty-four years old.

In Chaplin's first film, a knockabout comedy called *Making a Living* (1914), there is scant suggestion of the beloved tramp to come. Outfitted as a fiercely English dandy, with top hat, monocle, frock coat and long, drooping mustaches, Chaplin played a reporter who took mean advantage of every good turn showed him by others. It was amusing enough at the time, but seen today it seems like the work of a stranger—a deft and hard-working comedian caught up in a series of frantic but meaningless gags. Yet Charlie the tramp was to appear in his very next film. Word had been received on the Keystone lot that there was to be a children's auto race at Venice, the Los Angeles version of Coney Island. Sennett told Chaplin to get himself a funny costume and keep floundering in the way of a cameraman photographing the festivities. The costume proved to be one of those rare combinations of luck and genius. Sharing a dressing room with Arbuckle and Mack Swain, Chaplin borrowed "Fatty's" outsized trousers and, from Swain, a prop mustache. The floppy shoes came from Ford Sterling. The derby, the cane, the too tight coat—all were unerringly chosen in one short afternoon. During the shooting of *The Kid Auto Races at Venice*, Chaplin instinctively fell into the sore-footed shuffle that was also to remain part of the character— the remembered gait of an old peddler he had observed during his days on the London streets.

But if the costume came quickly, and with it the mannerisms that made the little tramp so irresistibly funny—the angular walk, the skidding turn, the inimitable byplay with cane and derby— the full meaning of the character emerged far more slowly. From the outset, Chaplin felt uneasy in the Sennett brand of comedy. The gags flew too swiftly, the pace was too frantic for the kind of pantomime he had mastered in the English music halls. He chafed under the direction of Sennett and Pathé Lehrman. The success of his character, however, was so immediately apparent that within three months Sennett concluded it might be just as well to let the little Englishman have things a bit more his own way. After acting in only a dozen pictures, Chaplin became his own director—a role he never relinquished.

Even so, the demands of the Keystone schedule—almost two films a week—were too great to permit Chaplin to explore and develop the tramp character to any real extent. Here he originated many of the comic bits he was to use again with greater effectiveness in later years, the brash stratagems by which the underdog discomfits his larger or wealthier rival, the visual surprises and transformations by which, in his hands, a doughnut becomes a bracelet or a lamp an object of love. Although the tramp costume remained basic to the character, Chaplin appeared in the Keystone films in a wide variety of garbs, each suggestive of comedy situations—a baker, a waiter, a dentist's assistant, a woman or a squiffy English man-about-town. His flow of comic invention was miraculous. Each of the films is fast and funny. But the gags themselves were often tasteless and vulgar, practical jokes filled with pointless cruelty and brazen dishonesty. Revealing their hasty origins, they were all too frequently laughs for their own sake, unrelated to either character or plot. One of the inducements that Essanay held out to Chaplin to sign with them was the promise of more time for each picture and his own head in production. He accepted gladly.

It was at Essanay that Chaplin began to discover the implications of the little tramp figure he had achieved. Pathos, irony, satire and, above all, a more conscious identification of the character with "the little fellow" everywhere—all of these emerged during his year at Essanay. Here too Chaplin began to build the working team that was to remain with him through the years—cameraman Roland Totheroh, leading lady Edna Purviance, character comics Leo White, John Rand and Billy Armstrong. As his own producer, he paid increasing attention not only to plot incident and story but to the use of the camera itself. Where Sennett's films were swift, choppy and filled with frantic movement, Chaplin evolved a quieter, more intimate style. His camera is more thoughtfully placed, and remains in one position for a longer period of time. Not a technique for flashy, spectacular effects, it is nevertheless wholly functional and, for Chaplin's purposes, admirably economic. Such films of this period as *The Tramp* and *The Bank* reveal a sure instinct for framing, for establishing a dynamic relationship between camera and performer that includes all the essentials and rigorously frames out any extraneous detail. The same economy Chaplin applied to his set dressings. Any property that appears in a scene is there to be used. If the president's office in *The Bank* at first seems a veritable jungle of desks, wastebaskets, telephones, electric fans and scrap paper, within a few moments Chaplin, the bank's handyman, has brought every one of them into play, tangling with them, upsetting them, tripping over them. The electric fan, finally turned on to cool the perspiring Charlie after his arduous clean-up campaign, promptly blows the papers all over the room again. Only when the gag possibilities of the last prop have been exhausted does Chaplin cut to another scene and begin the whole wonderful business all over again.

Not only was Chaplin's cinematic feeling approaching maturity during his year at Essanay, he was also developing the physical capabilities of "the little fellow," as he often called his screen character. "A technique as unfaltering as Réjane," wrote Mrs. Fiske admiringly in 1915. His agility, his precision of gesture, the sudden revelation of character in moments of seemingly unpremeditated byplay (as the delicious bit in which he prudishly slips a lampshade over a nude statuette, then naughtily lifts the skirt for a peek)—all provoked the admiration of professionals and the open adulation of movie audiences everywhere. But these audiences, it should be emphasized, consisted primarily of children and working-class adults. Contrary to the general impression, Chaplin's pictures did not become a cult with the sophisticates until the early twenties. They were too crude, too slapstick—and too popular. Perhaps it was just as well. Chaplin had the common touch, and the enthusiasm of the literati came along too late to sway him from his course.

From *The Tramp* (1915) through *Easy Street* (1917), *Shoulder Arms* (1918), *The Kid* (1921), *The Pilgrim* (1923), *The Gold Rush* (1925), *City Lights* (1931) and *Modern Times* (1936) one observes not a change but a constant deepening and development of the tramp character. Even the costume, assembled by chance and inspiration on a rainy afternoon, began to acquire its own significance— shabby gentility, the wealthy seen from the perspective of the poor, a courageous refusal to admit the stern realities of poverty and contempt. Charlie became the embodiment of the little fellow everywhere, and the marvelous transformation of objects, the sight gags that sparkle through the earlier pictures, Chaplin used increasingly to substantiate the character itself. Thus, in *The Kid* when Charlie removes his fingerless gloves and fastidiously selects a half smoked butt from a sardine-can cigarette case, he makes this thoughtless, habitual gesture seem an act of rare extravagance. In *City Lights* the business with the swallowed whistle that emits little "peeps" at an elegant cocktail party or the paper streamers that become tangled in Chaplin's spaghetti at a nightclub, both wonderfully funny in themselves, also tell us how desperately Charlie wants to conform, to be accepted along with the millionaires and debutantes and the smartly dressed people who surround him. But Chaplin knew that his little fellow could never conform, that he was destined always to stand just outside the circle of the bright lights, waiting, hoping—and always with the inner strength to shrug off disappointment and disaster and go on down the road to his next adventure.

Perhaps there is some special significance in the fact that Chaplin finally abandoned his tramp character in a period of increased conformism. Perhaps he had himself lost faith in "the little fellow" and his abilities to withstand the pressures of society. Or perhaps Chaplin felt that the urgency of his own message to the world required a direct, verbal statement, that the spirit of independence, self-reliance and infinite tenderness always implicit in the tramp character was no longer adequate. As early as *The Great Dictator* (1940) Charlie stepped completely out of character to utter his heartfelt words of hope and courage to all those crushed or cringing under the yoke of the totalitarians. In Chaplin's next film, *Monsieur Verdoux* (1947), the tramp character had disappeared altogether. Probably the most non-conformist picture ever made, *Verdoux* was a mordant satire in which a debonair and presumably humane mass-murderer defends himself by insisting that his crime was merely one of scale: "One murder makes a villain—millions sanctify," he says, pointing a finger at the munitions makers and the military leaders. In *Verdoux* Chaplin brazenly attempted to shock and outrage virtually every organized section of every American community with his pragmatic, unconventional morality. He succeeded all too well. Veteran and religious groups picketed and protested the film so vigorously that theaters were afraid to play it; within the year it was withdrawn from distribution completely.

But this only partially explains its failure in the United States. Chaplin films had been banned and boycotted before—notably his audacious *The Pilgrim* and, after his sensational divorce from Lita Grey, *The Gold Rush*. In the twenties, though, whatever audiences thought about Chaplin the man, they still wanted to see Charlie the comedian. By the time of *Verdoux,* few cared strongly enough either for the man or for the character to protest the suppression of his picture. His most recent film *Limelight* (1952) was brilliant and in many ways Chaplin's most profound work. A summing up of his personal and artistic credo, it was greeted in this country by a mild indifference. The melancholy Calvero was no substitute for the dauntless, infinitely resourceful

Charlie. Chaplin had created one immortal screen figure, and in so doing he had refined the art of projecting character upon the screen far beyond any of his contemporaries. His Charlie still lives— sad, funny, pathetic, heroic. The early comedies, many of them now in public domain, are constantly being revived and re-enjoyed; while Chaplin himself lives in exile in Switzerland, a world away from Charlie and "the little fellow."

MOVIES BECOME BIG BUSINESS

By the end of World War I, profound changes had taken place in the American film industry. Up to 1914 it had shared the world market with England, France, Italy, Denmark, Sweden and Germany. After 1914 those countries directly engaged in the war drastically curtailed their film production: celluloid and high explosives are made from the same ingredients. The Italian, French and English studios suffered a subsequent decline that was to last a generation or more. In Germany, where production was subsidized by the government for morale and propaganda purposes, the motion picture continued to flourish, but the films were created solely for home consumption. Sweden and Denmark, outside the conflict, enjoyed a brief flowering of their industries, particularly in the sober, saga-like dramas of Victor Seastrom (Sjöstrom) and Mauritz Stiller in Sweden and the early works of Denmark's Carl Dreyer. But it was to the United States that most of the world looked for its movies during those troubled years, to the comedies of Charlie Chaplin and Douglas Fairbanks, to the colorful Westerns of William S. Hart and Tom Mix, to the romances and adventures, the dramas and melodramas that poured from the American studios. And a new word appeared in the world's vocabulary—Hollywood!

During the early years of Hollywood's development as a production center American movies changed their complexion, acquiring for the first time the plush and polish, the glamour that has everywhere become synonymous with the name. But Hollywood itself was merely a sleepy little suburb of Los Angeles until the movie people found it and put it on the map. As early as 1910 some of the Eastern companies began junketing to California during the winter months to take advantage of its superb climate and inexhaustible sunshine. Hollywood proved an ideal center for their location work—close to mountains and the sea, desert and farm land. As the Patents war increased in intensity in New York, many of the independents came to settle permanently in Hollywood. Since of necessity they were working with bootleg cameras, it was often convenient to have the Mexican border also close by. By 1915, although the larger companies continued to maintain studios in New York or Chicago, the tide had already turned in favor of California. Taxes in the East drove out more of the companies; the United States' entry into the war, with the drastic rationing of coal and electricity during the hard winter of 1917–1918, proved to be the final blow. Fort Lee, the studio center just across the Hudson from New York, was reduced to a ghost town. California's sunlight—and California's generous inducements in the form of labor laws and lower taxes—soon made Hollywood the capital of American film production. And with the United States clearly dominating world production after 1918, Hollywood became—as it has remained—the world's movie capital as well.

It was a change that permeated every aspect of the industry— production, distribution, exhibition, story content, even the audiences themselves. After 1912 the restrictive Motion Picture Patents Company was virtually eclipsed by the vigorous independents; and the company itself was dissolved as a trust by the Supreme Court in 1917. Meanwhile, its members limped along, clinging to the old ways and the old lengths until finally the competition they had sought to smother drove them from the scene. Almost all of today's major studios trace back to those independents who between 1910 and 1914 cheerfully flouted all the rules of the Patents Company. They lured away their more talented directors and most popular performers. They thrived on the star system. They increased the length of their pictures from two to three and, after 1914, to five reels (with occasional "specials" of seven reels or more). They discovered the value of publicity in popularizing their films and their stars. They established their own exchanges for the more efficient marketing of their product. And, after 1915, they began a race for theater ownership that was to reach fantastic proportions by the twenties.

Up to 1912 the familiar nickelodeon and store show, often furnished with hard chairs or benches rented from a nearby catering or funeral establishment, had been adequate for the working-class audiences who came to the movies for an hour's relaxation. From 1912 on, however, tiny neighborhood houses began to pop up all over the country—"The Idle Hour," "The Gem," "The Bijou Dream," "The Bluebird." Not infrequently they proved to be jerry-built firetraps, but they were far more inviting and far more comfortable than anything hitherto available. And admission prices advanced from a nickel to a dime, or even fifteen cents. Longer films, particularly the "specials" imported from Europe, were generally shown in legitimate theaters rented for the occasion, and at greatly advanced prices. Still the public came.

As more and more features began to appear from Hollywood, it occurred to at least one enterprising showman, Mitchell Mark, that a considerable public could be lured into a theater that was not only clean and comfortable but even elegant. When in April of 1914 he opened his Strand Theatre on Broadway, he inaugurated a whole new era in theater construction—and a new style as well. With gilt and marble and deep pile rugs, crystal chandeliers hanging from the ceiling and original art works on the walls, with luxurious lounges and comfortable chairs, a thirty-piece symphony orchestra to accompany the feature and a mighty Wurlitzer to play for the shorts, the Strand established new standards of luxury for motion-picture audiences—and at only twenty-five cents a ticket! It was an immediate success. The Rialto, formerly Hammerstein's Music Hall, and the Rivoli followed in short order, similarly appointed, similarly equipped. At the Rialto, manager S. L. Rothafel ("Roxy") introduced stage shows to precede the feature film, often bringing in stars of the Metropolitan Opera and the concert stage to emphasize the high plane of his presentations. Most of the other legitimate houses located on Broadway—the Astor, the old Criterion, the New York Theater—also converted permanently to the showing of first-run films. Out in the neighborhoods, only slightly less elaborate theaters were going up. And what was happening in New York was soon being duplicated in every big city across the country. The movies were at last becoming respectable. They were moving into homes of their own. And frequently these were better appointed, better staffed and more comfortable than anything the legitimate theater had to offer.

For their part, the film producers soon learned the value of these first-run houses as a suitably impressive showcase for their wares. Film costs had advanced tremendously in just a few years, from $500 to $1,000 for a two-reel subject in 1912 to between $12,000 and $20,000 for a five-reel feature in 1915. The longer "specials" or films with an expensive star cost still more to make. From the new, large houses the producers could not only obtain a higher rental for their pictures, but the advertising and publicity surrounding these presentations created a stronger demand for them in the subsequent runs. The owners of neighborhood houses would pay more for them, hold them longer and play them at the most favorable time of the week because they knew that their patrons had been pre-sold by the downtown ads, publicity and, with growing frequency, by the newspaper reviews. In fact, producers who were unable to book their pictures into the main-street palaces soon found that they had great difficulty in earning back their investments.

To ensure first-run outlets for their films, the larger companies began to buy into strategic locations, particularly into the downtown theaters of the larger cities. As the competition grew keener, some—notably Fox and Paramount—began to build their own theaters. In consequence, many of the independent theater owners, both frightened by this new competition and outraged by the gouging rentals that the studios had begun to demand, determined to finance their own productions. Organized under the banner of First National in 1917, they won Mary Pickford away from Zukor at Paramount and gave Chaplin his million-dollar contract. Although the original plan called for each star to produce his own pictures, First National soon found it expedient to establish its own studio as well. By 1920 the ties between the producers and the theaters had grown so strong that theater-owner Marcus Loew, in order to maintain a flow of films to his vast chain of movie houses, found it necessary to purchase his own studio, Metro, the forerunner of the formidable Metro-Goldwyn-Mayer company.

Another feature of the Hollywood companies' operations that infuriated the theater owners was the practice of block booking.

As the studios grew in power—and especially in star power—they discovered that they could sell an entire year's output in advance of actual production by tying their pictures together in groups or blocks. The theater owner who hoped to play a Mary Pickford picture, a Fairbanks or Wallace Reid or Charles Ray would have to contract for the dozen or more pictures sold in the block with the few he really wanted. For the studios this made perfect sense. Knowing what their sales would be, they could proceed to budget for their entire year's production. But in consequence the theater men found themselves saddled with many undesirable and sometimes even unplayable titles, all tied in with a possible box-office attraction or two in the form of a star feature still unmade. Despite the anguished cries of the exhibitors, however, the studios with their stars, their own exchanges and their own growing chains of key theaters felt no need to conciliate. Quite the opposite. Notoriously obstreperous theater owners were either bought out or forced out of business if they refused to fall into line. The numerous small, independent studios that owned neither exchanges nor theaters by 1920 found themselves with their backs to the wall. Some few were absorbed into the larger companies; the others quietly expired.

It is difficult to determine at this point whether these fundamental changes in the structure of the industry reflected a change in the composition of the movie audiences or vice versa. Unquestionably, up to 1912 the movies were primarily a working-class entertainment. Representative titles of that year would include *One Is Business, the Other Crime, Man's Lust for Gold, Root of Evil, Loan Shark, A Corner in Wheat,* themes reflecting working-class indignation at favoritism in the courts, usury and big business in general. But as small, comfortable houses—the "Bijou Dreams"—began to appear in neighborhoods all over the country, these audiences became tinctured with the middle classes; while the appeal of such large houses as the Strand and the Rialto was definitely directed toward the middle class. By 1915 the film companies themselves had become oriented toward the audience, drawing their themes now from such popular novels as *David Harum* or *Graustark,* from literary or dramatic classics like *Vanity Fair* and *Peer Gynt,* even from operas. Mary Pickford played Cio-Cio-San in *Madame Butterfly*. Both Geraldine Farrar and Theda Bara starred in productions of *Carmen,* while Chaplin burlesqued both the opera and these two films in still a third version of *Carmen* that same year. In 1912 few recognized actors would dream of appearing in the movies; in 1915 the movies virtually swept the New York theater of its first-string talents, bringing before the cameras such stars as De Wolf Hopper, Fritzi Scheff, Mrs. Leslie Carter, Sir Herbert Beerbohm Tree, Billie Burke, Weber and Fields, Frank Keenan, Blanche Ring and Willard Mack. As early as 1913 the first fan magazine had made its appearance as a house organ of the Vitagraph Company. Within the next few years three independent fan magazines were busily selling Americans on the glamour and romance of the movies.

Laughter, love and make-believe—that was what the world wanted while war raged in Europe, and that was what the new Hollywood concentrated on. Romance, adventure, comedy, glamour —the studios took these basic elements and, in the years between 1915 and 1920, transformed them into a multi-million-dollar industry.

II

THE GROWTH OF AN ART

IN ALL THE ARTS, ONE DISCOVERS IN VARIOUS COUNTRIES AND AT DIF-
ferent times that happy combination of social, cultural and economic forces which provides creative artists with just the right
stimulus to produce their best work. In painting, one thinks of the
Italian Renaissance, the Flemish realists, the English portraitists,
the French impressionists. In music, there are the composers of
the Italian baroque, the Austrian symphonists, the German roman-
ticists and, again, the French impressionists at the dawn of this
century. The same process can also be discerned in the motion
picture, with the sole difference that the creative history of this
art has been crammed into little more than fifty years. Yet even
within that narrow space of time one can glimpse eras in which
the films of one country or another clearly dominated world production and made their most important contributions to the artistic
growth of the medium. Thus, the French chase and trick films
between 1900 and 1907, the Film d'Art of 1907 to 1912, the Italian
spectacles between 1910 and 1914 and the Swedish film of 1918
to 1923 can all be regarded as definite "schools," each with its own
characteristics and each influencing the work of film makers in
other nations. Since World War II we have seen the same process
at work in the emergence of the documentary-style British feature
film, in the vigorous, neorealistic Italian school and, most recently,
in the exquisite mixture of ancient art and modern themes in the
films from Japan. During the twenties, two schools dominated the

artistic development of the film and its techniques. The first was in Germany; the second, in the Soviet Union.

GERMANY'S GOLDEN ERA

Germany's "Golden Era" lasted only a brief six or seven years, roughly from 1919 through 1925. Yet what an era it was! In other lands other directors had already developed the techniques of film. It remained for the Germans to take this vocabulary and extend it, deepening and enriching the entire medium, turning to themes, emotions and relationships never before essayed on the screen. And to treat these new subjects, the German artists evolved additional techniques that are still impressive for their boldness and originality. They discovered the importance of costume and décor and lighting, the nuances of acting for the camera and, perhaps most important of all, they treated the camera itself as a creative rather than simply a recording instrument.

The sources of this extraordinary development of the film in Germany are twofold. During the First World War, although Germany was cut off from contact with all the Allied powers, she was still seeing films from Sweden and Denmark. These pictures, many of them set in the past, were essentially character studies of great power and penetration, handsomely mounted and making dramatic use of natural backgrounds. Their themes were somber, their tone sober, dignified and compassionate. After 1912 the opportunities for film making in Germany encouraged a whole colony of Danish artists to begin working in Berlin—Asta Nielsen and her husband, the designer-director Urban Gad; the directors Carl Dreyer, Stellan Rye and Svend Gade. They formed one nucleus of the German film. Meanwhile, leaders in the German theater—directors like Max Reinhardt and Leopold Jessner, actors like Emil Jannings, Conrad Veidt, Fritz Kortner and Werner Krauss—began to take a genuine interest in the new medium and had none of the prejudice that theater people in France and America had shown toward it. From the very outset they regarded the motion picture as a serious art with its own problems and potentialities. Encouraged by generous subsidies from the government, which in 1917 grouped together most of the leading German studios into

the all-embracing Universum-Film-Aktiengesellschaft (better known
as Ufa), they began the incredible series of pictures that was soon
to establish the German film as the most exciting in the world.

There would seem to be three main types of German productions during this period, all more or less concurrent. First, and
probably most popular, were the great costume spectacles—films
like *Passion* (1919), *Anne Boleyn* (1920) and *Danton* (1921). At
the outset these dealt with less than savory incidents from the
history of Germany's recent enemies; but they did so with great
flair, with a tremendous feeling for the sweep of history in the
mob scenes and an absorbing intimacy and irreverence in their
treatment of the great ones of the past. Indeed, Ernst Lubitsch,
who made his reputation directing many of these films, was dubbed
by one writer, "The great humanizer of history." When eventually
these pictures began to reach England, France and the United
States—often thinly veiled as Danish or Scandinavian productions—
they were promptly hailed as triumphs of picture making, and
their more tendentious aspects overlooked.

The German government had originally subsidized film production for morale and propaganda purposes, to stimulate national
pride and patriotism. It continued to do so because pictures soon
proved a valuable export commodity. Now the tales, the lore and
myths of old German times were revived. Fritz Lang's *Destiny*
(1921) achieved a truly medieval folk-tale quality with its story
of a young girl who bargains with Death for the life of her lover.
The medieval element turns up again and again in the films of
this period—in Paul Wegener's *Golem* (1920), in von Gerlach's
Vanina (1922), in Paul Leni's *Waxworks* (1924) and in Pabst's
The Treasure (1924). The *Nibelungenlied,* that symbol of the
heroic life of ancient Germany, was conjured up in two films by
Fritz Lang, *Siegfried* and *Kriemhild's Revenge* (1924). Massive,
architectural and static, they were based more closely on the
original legend than upon the Wagner operas, despite their rather
operatic flavor.

Possibly such themes afforded an escape from the uncertainties
of the Weimar Republic and the miseries of postwar Germany.
Possibly they were a calculated appeal to the wounded pride and

shattered morale of a defeated people. Certainly, the hardships that the Germans themselves were suffering at the time never turned up on the screen in these elaborately mounted visions of an earlier greatness. Working in the huge new Ufa studios at Neubabelsberg—the largest and best equipped studios in the world—the directors had the facilities to fling up whole towns, whole forests, whole mountains. As Siegfried Kracauer has pointed out in his superb study of the German film, *From Caligari to Hitler,* they rarely ventured outside the studio, preferring to create their settings from the ground up, to control every aspect of their productions. As a result, one is at all times intensely aware of the artistry in each of these pictures, of the skill and planning and technical mastery that went into their making.

THE SHADOW OF CALIGARI

Accompanying, and frequently shading into these historical romances is a group of films without parallel in the work of any other nation, films of macabre and fantastic imagination that were far more than mere horror stories. Paul Wegener's early *Student of Prague* (1913), at once their forerunner and prototype, provides the clue to their strange fascination. Concerned with the problem of identity, it told a Hoffmannesque story of a student whose mirror image is claimed by the devil—and eventually his soul as well. The devil and the supernatural creatures of evil became the motivating forces in these films, exerting their demonic power over weak, will-less, helpless, tormented men. It was the Faustian legend extended into a world of nightmare terrors.

Perhaps the most famous picture in this group—in fact one of the most famous films of all times—is Robert Wiene's *The Cabinet of Dr. Caligari* (1919). It is a story told by a madman (although his madness is not revealed until the end of the picture). Shortly after a strange doctor has displayed his somnambulist at a fair in a small German town, the community is plagued by a series of weird, inexplicable murders. When the hero's best friend is found dead, the young man begins to suspect Dr. Caligari and the somnambulist Cesare. He reports his suspicions to the authorities, but without avail. Beside the wily doctor's powers, the efforts of the police prove childishly ineffectual. The hero persists, however, and discovers that Caligari had gained his power over Cesare through his mastery of medieval witchcraft and had commanded him to commit the murders. Thus, Caligari is presented as evil incarnate, a man who kills solely for the pleasure of killing. But the final scene reveals that Caligari is actually the head of the mental institution in which the young man is confined.

Two things distinguished *Caligari* as a film: the daring of this story-within-a-story and the startling originality of its décor. To suggest that what we see are the ravings of a madman, Wiene deliberately adopted stylized settings—great angular shadows painted a deep black, streets and walls and sky all starkly white. Even the furnishings are unrealistic. When the young man reports his friend's murder to the town constable, he finds that official perched high on a six-foot stool writing in a tremendous ledger—an eerie symbol of authority. The actors too were made to further this sense of irreality—the stark white of Lil Dagover's face emphasized by her huge dark eyes and framed by raven-black hair, the dead white of Cesare's skeletal face contrasted with the black of his skin-tight leotard, the streaks of gray and white on Caligari's face and hair, making him at once more and less than human. And with Werner Krauss as Caligari and Conrad Veidt as the somnambulist, the stylization of make-up and settings was echoed in the performances as well. Veidt clings to wall and tree like a ghastly, attenuated shadow, gliding through each scene like a dark specter of death; while Krauss, peering nearsightedly through his tiny spectacles, stumping stiffly about on bowlegs, bowing and scraping with mock-genial politeness, creates a figure of such sinister malignance as has rarely been equaled on the screen.

Postwar artists and intellectuals, looking upon the movies for the first time as something more than a mere entertainment for the masses, found in *Caligari* a film they could safely admire. Its unconventional story, its Freudian overtones and, above all, its obviously "artistic" settings (related both to the stage work of the expressionists and to the experiments of the cubist painters) won for it an acclaim that was actually somewhat in excess of its contributions to the growing art. For many, however, it was the introduction, the doorway into film. *Caligari* stands alone, a unique picture. Neither its story pattern nor its style of setting has ever been attempted again, but its influence was inestimable. It foreshadowed the vampires, golems and monsters, the personifications of evil that dominated the German screens in the early twenties—*The Golem* (1920), *Destiny* (1921), *Nosferatu* (1922), Fritz Lang's demoniacal *Dr. Mabuse* (1922), the unholy trio in *Waxworks* (1924), right through to the robot girl of Lang's *Metropolis* (1927). As Dr. Kracauer has shown, the shadow of *Caligari* hung over all German films right down to the advent of Adolf Hitler.

THE STREET FILMS: MURNAU AND THE MOVING CAMERA

Less popular than either the costume dramas or the macabre fantasies, but infinitely more important to the art itself, was the extensive series of films dealing realistically with the life of the common man in those depression-ridden years. Dr. Kracauer has aptly called them the "street films" because city streets play such an important role in them. The titles alone are suggestive: *The Street* (1923), *The Joyless Street* (1925), *Tragedy of the Street* (1927), *Asphalt* (1929). Early in the twenties German art in general, and the German film in particular, became tinged with *die neue Sachlichkeit*—"the new realism with a socialistic flavor." The "street films" lent themselves admirably to these expressions of sympathy for the common man in all his misery. Typical is the plot of one of the first in the group, *The Street*. Eugen Klöpfer plays a middle-aged man bored and fretful in the comfort and security of his own home. Venturing out into the lawless, uncontrollable city, he meets with a series of sordid and terrifying adventures, then returns to his wife, sadder, wiser and grateful for the ordered routine that means peace.

Kracauer, studying these films, found their themes symptomatic of a deep-seated German predisposition toward conformity and authoritarianism. But whatever significance they hold for the sociologist and psychologist, for the film makers their greatest interest will always be the new techniques that came from these ingenious attempts to create both the appearance and the feeling of reality within the studio. Reality has always presented the greatest challenge for the film director. The camera's capacity for distortion, for altering reality, may stimulate the imagination and ingenuity of the artist; but it is this same propensity for distortion that the director must control and use to produce his own version of reality upon the screen. To build a city in a studio—even in a studio as vast and splendidly appointed as Neubabelsberg—is not enough. It has to feel like a city. It needs not only a realism of detail— shop windows, electric signs, automobiles—but also the psychic sensations of rushing crowds or loneliness, of opulent good cheer or claustrophobic squalor. To bring the principles of *die neue Sachlichkeit* to the screen, the German directors had to break through the surface reality to the emotions that lay beneath, to the reactions and sensations of the people caught up in this milieu. And to achieve this penetration, directors like F. W. Murnau, E. A. Dupont and G. W. Pabst used their cameras in ways never before attempted or even dreamed of.

It was Murnau's *The Last Laugh* (1924) that brought on this revolution. Throughout the film his camera was constantly on the prowl, roaming freely through city streets, crowded flats and long hotel corridors. But the camera's movement of itself was not the revolution, any more than the close-up was revolutionary in D. W. Griffith's films. There had been close-ups before Griffith; there were moving cameras before Murnau. What was revolutionary in both instances was the creative, interpretative use each man made of these devices. In Griffith's hands the moving camera suggested sweep and spectacle, the excitement of the chase. There was, however, little of sweep, spectacle or excitement about *The Last Laugh*. Another of the "street films," it tells of an aging doorman at a big hotel, proud of his commanding position, proud of his fine uniform, but past his prime: he can no longer lift down the heavy trunks and suitcases from the top of the Berlin taxicabs. The hotel manager, not without a certain malice, gives him a new job more commensurate with his strength and capabilities—and a new uniform: the white jacket of a washroom attendant. Except for a wittingly improbable finale tacked on by screenwriter Carl Mayer as a parody of the Hollywood happy endings, that is just about all the story there is to *The Last Laugh*. Within this frame- work, however, the film thoroughly explores the relationships be- tween the *déclassé* doorman and his family, his friends and his neighbors. And it explores them, for the most part, through the use of what might best be described as a subjective camera.

Theoretically, the camera is an objective instrument, photographing coldly and impassively everything set before it. In point of fact, however, the camera is invariably placed in some special relationship to the material it is photographing, a position determined either by the director or by the cameraman. The very act of choosing a camera position—close or remote, gazing down on the scene from on high or looking up from below—is the product of the director's perception of his subject, his awareness of the emotional reactions he hopes to create in his audience. The camera's "objectivity" is still further delimited by the lens itself. Only in Cinerama does the camera begin to approach the entire field of human vision; the ordinary 35mm camera takes in only a narrow wedge from that field, a 30° to 45° segment of the scene before it. It is the director who determines just what portion of that scene his camera will reveal, what will be included, what will be framed out. The objectivity of the camera is actually nothing more than the mechanism for conveying the director's artistic decision.

When Murnau and his brilliant script writer Carl Mayer set to work on *The Last Laugh*, it occurred to them that the camera might be used not merely to show the objective world of external details but, like a secret eye, to record the inner emotions and reactions of their central character. They wanted to use their camera "subjectively" to reveal the old man's feelings about his degradation, his fear of the people who laughed behind his back, his gratitude to the little night watchman who alone offered him friendship. Mayer, who also wrote *The Cabinet of Dr. Caligari*, had already begun to approach the problem of an objective-subjective camera in that film. The angular settings, the artificial shadows, the accentuated whites and blacks were Mayer's idea: they reflected the distorted image of the world in the mind of the young man telling the story.

While writing *The Last Laugh*, Mayer consulted with Karl Freund, its photographer, to discover the physical limitations of shooting long passages with a camera that moved about continually. When Freund assured him it could be done, Mayer tore up all he had written and began afresh. In his new conception of the film, the camera moved with the old doorman through the courtyard of the apartment building in which he lived, receiving with him the salutations of his neighbors and friends, feeling with him their derisive laughter after he had lost his lofty position. It groped with him down a dark hotel corridor to steal from a cupboard the splendid uniform that had been his cloak of authority. It even, at one point, got riotously drunk for the old man, whirling dizzily around the room until the audience comes to share his vertigo. Through the ingenuity of Mayer and Murnau—and Karl Freund—the camera did as much to create the identity of the old doorman as the actor who played the role, Emil Jannings. It was the first appearance of the camera as actor.

The Last Laugh was far more than a tour de force. It was an innovation—and one that could have been brought off only with the facilities and technicians of the Neubabelsberg studios. The very opening shot strikes the key for all that is to come, a vast long-shot of the lobby of the Hotel Atlantic taken from a descending elevator. The gates open and the camera rushes across the entire lobby up to the revolving door and the proud old doorman. While behind him is a broad city street filled with cars and busses and pedestrians hurrying to get out of the rain! Frequently the walls of the sets were suspended on coasters from the beams overhead, rolling aside to admit the camera as it passed. Special elevators carried the camera aloft. It was wheeled on dollies through corridors and streets. It was strapped to the cameraman's chest as he spun about in a chair during the drinking scene, or suspended by wires and swung in a basket to and fro to suggest visually the sounds of a street band boozily heard. The story is told, as it were, completely in the first person, subjectively, the way the old doorman saw it and felt it. So fully does the camera convey his emotions that not a single dialogue title is needed throughout the entire length of the film.

For Murnau correctly perceived that the camera could be made to shift its point of view in an instant, that it could be the doorman looking up at the supercilious hotel manager at one moment, the manager looking down at the pitiable old man at the next, and a detached bystander looking impersonally at the two of them a moment later. He found that even while the camera was showing the doorman it could still reflect his mood or suggest his emotional state. There is one astonishing scene as Emil Jannings leaves the hotel after his demotion, the precious uniform clutched to his bosom. He dashes across the street, then pauses breathlessly to look back. As he looks, the walls of the hotel heave and sway as if threatening to fall in upon him. Is this objectivity or subjectivity? Are we seeing what the doorman actually saw? Or is the camera telling us how he felt? Or is it perhaps a little of both?

By these constant shifts of personality, of point of view, the film remains constantly vivid and affecting, the psychology of its characters clearly understood. And although *The Last Laugh* employs the moving camera extensively, it by no means exploits it. The use is always logical, motivated and sensitive to every nuance of the script—the more so because Murnau realized that its effectiveness could best be heightened by moments of utter immobility, by scenes in which the camera remains completely at rest. Mention should also be made of the settings by Robert Herlth and Walter Roehrig, so consistent with the tone of the entire picture. The bold gray planes of the hotel façade pierced by great slashes of light, the working-class apartments drably uniform with their dark, square windows all sustain the subjectivity of the camera: this is the way the doorman sees his world.

The Last Laugh made a tremendous impression in America, not only on film people in Hollywood, which one might have expected, but on the general public as well. The absence of subtitles, although not unique in German films, proved an exciting novelty in this country; while the smoothness of the camera movement and the obvious artistry of Jannings's performance won favorable comment everywhere. American producers consciously began shooting their pictures "in the German manner." But the film that completed the revolution, at least as far as Hollywood was concerned, was Jannings's next picture *Variety* (1925), directed by E. A. Dupont and brilliantly photographed by Karl Freund, the cameraman of *The Last Laugh*. Like the earlier film, its story was simplicity itself. A trapeze artist, played by Jannings, discovers that his wife is deceiving him with his handsome partner. He kills him, then goes to prison. Like the earlier film, it was told with a camera that seemed to be everywhere, entering and externalizing the consciousness of each member of its central triangle, building up the atmosphere of seedy sideshow life and the glamour of Berlin's Wintergarten through an infinitude of sharply observed and closely integrated details. Unlike *The Last Laugh,* however, it is impossible to escape the impression that all of this camera movement—darting up to an ear listening at a door, flying through the air with the acrobats, plummeting down from the heights into the very faces of the terror-stricken audience as an aerialist falls to his death—has been created for the effect alone. The discretion, the utter functionalism of Murnau's work is dissipated in a virtuoso show of camera angles and movements, scenes superbly lit and masterfully joined together, but all adding up to an impressive tour de force based on melodrama rather than on the revelation of true characters in a crucial situation.

Nevertheless, the success of *Variety,* when presented to American audiences early in 1926, hastened the already apparent Germanization of Hollywood's studios. Dupont, Freund, Jannings and the female star of *Variety,* Lya de Putti, were all brought to America; and German themes, German acting styles and, above all, German production techniques were incorporated into the most ordinary studio films—a domination that was to continue until sound once again immobilized the camera and sent many of the German artists back to their native land.

PABST AND THE FREUDIAN INFLUENCE

Perhaps of all the "street films" the most famous is G. W. Pabst's *The Joyless Street* (1925)—if only for the adventitious reason that it featured the young Greta Garbo (along with Asta Nielsen, the ubiquitous Werner Krauss and Einar Hanson). A harshly realistic story of inflation-ridden Vienna, it reflected the economic chaos and ruptured moral values of the day through the interlocking lives of the inhabitants of a single street—an impoverished professor and his daughter, an American Red Cross field worker, an oily procuress and the brutal, profiteering butcher who dominates them all. To convey the psychological truth—and horror—of these characters, Pabst began to explore and develop yet another power of the camera, the expressiveness of viewpoint and angle.

As every still photographer knows, the same scene can be photographed from a virtual infinitude of positions to produce an infinity of visual impressions. But always there is one angle, one position that is most revealing. Only after the photographer has decided upon the emotional tone of his scene, the story that it is to convey and his own reaction to it, can he proceed to locate the exact position for his camera. He is helped, of course, by the basic elements of all pictorial composition—the knowledge that predominating horizontals produce a feeling of repose, while strong verticals suggest action and unrest. And there are psychological elements too in the relation of the camera to its subject—close or far, at a strong angle or a non-committal eye level, above it or shooting from below. By his choice of the camera's position, the director creates for the audience an unconscious predisposition toward the scene, the characters and the action.

Pabst applied his own awareness of this technique to his use of the camera throughout *The Joyless Street*. The butcher, always with a huge white hound by his side, is invariably photographed from below, suggesting his domination over the people of the street. The professor in his bare apartment (much of his furniture has been pawned for food) is generally seen from afar—emphasizing the bleakness of his surroundings—and with the camera slightly above eye level. Scenes in the black-market nightclub are taken sensually close, and often at waist level. If the cutting in *The Joyless Street* seems jumpy and disturbingly obvious, it should be emphasized that few have ever seen the film precisely as Pabst planned it; it has been subject to censorship and the whims of its distributors in every country where it has been shown. Even so, the power and penetration of Pabst's later style are already abundantly apparent in this remarkable film.

Pabst did his next work under the supervision of two disciples of Sigmund Freud, Dr. Hanns Sachs and Dr. Karl Abraham. Essentially, *The Secrets of a Soul* (1926) is a case history translated into vivid screen images. An elderly man (Werner Krauss again), alarmed at his impotency and by disturbing dreams in which he pictures himself killing his young wife with a knife, turns to a psychiatrist for help. A few dreams, a few meetings with the psychiatrist, and the cure is completed. Naïve as this may seem today, it marked the first serious treatment of psychiatry on the screen. More important, it emphasized the camera's proclivities toward the use of symbolism. Griffith always had an affection for symbols, but his were almost literary in their connotations. A close-up of Lillian Gish or Mae Marsh followed by a shot of a bird inevitably suggested a childlike innocence; Barthelmess dreamily holding a flower in *Broken Blossoms* bespoke a wistful longing for beauty. In *Secrets of a Soul* Pabst's use of the symbol went beyond this into the more affecting, more revealing—and essentially more cinematic—world of the dream image, of objects charged with a subconscious emotional power.

The knives and doors, the stairs and ladders which, in double and triple exposure, disturbed the slumber of Werner Krauss in *Secrets of a Soul* were to reappear on another, more realistic plane in such subsequent Pabst films as *The Love of Jeanne Ney* (1927) and *Pandora's Box* (1929). Here they exist simply as objects, part of the atmosphere, part of the settings surrounding the characters until the camera moves in to isolate them and underline their significance. Thus, in the opening scene of *Jeanne Ney* the camera sets off on a wordless exploration of Fritz Rasp's sordid, cluttered room—dirty clothes flung about, overflowing ashtrays, erotic pictures and statuettes. We know the character well before laying eyes on him. A shattered mirror in an elegant frame, a spiked iron fence separating two lovers, a knife in the hand of Jack-the-Ripper—all are ordinary objects, but charged by Pabst with emotional overtones as vivid and evocative as dream symbols. Even action is at times deliberately staged for its symbolic effect, as when Rasp preparing to rape Jeanne Ney slowly pulls open his tie.

Above all a director's director, Pabst developed a technique of shooting and editing that was to influence film makers everywhere, and perhaps most especially in Hollywood. In order to maintain the balance between his characters and the objects that surrounded them, he increased the fragmentation of his scenes. The camera leaps incessantly from place to place, from position to position, always discovering the best vantage point to reveal an actor's gesture, action or expression—or to permit the background to make its own eloquent comment upon the action. In one brief section from *The Love of Jeanne Ney*, a scene running less than three minutes on the screen, there are forty separate shots, the longest about twenty sec-

onds in length. But the actual movement from one camera position
to the next is barely perceptible. Pabst consciously sought to eliminate from his films any feeling of jerkiness between shots while
still allowing his camera the utmost freedom. He soon found that
by focusing the audience's attention upon some physical movement,
he could effectively disguise such breaks. By having an actor begin
a gesture in one shot and carry it through to completion in the
next, he created a visual bridge. The eye, following the flow of the
action, ignored the cut itself. This technique of editing on movement, which Pabst discovered and polished with incredible finesse,
was to become fundamental after the introduction of sound.

Pabst's most important work was done during the years that
marked the decline of the German film. Lest this seem curious, it
should be remembered that his pictures never enjoyed the wide
popularity that greeted the work of Lubitsch, Murnau, Fritz Lang
and E. A. Dupont. While his art was essentially cinematic—in some
ways superior to the technique of any of his contemporaries—his
stories were frequently so melodramatic as to alienate all but the
most discerning critics, or so flagrantly erotic as to invite censorial
emasculation. And yet no director of the silent era is more highly
esteemed as a craftsman than Pabst. He had a passion for realism;
and no one excelled him in concretizing that reality. Whether filming an actual flower market in Paris or a misty London street built
in a studio, he sifted each scene for the details that would be at
once most revealing and most evocative, using his camera like a
probing surgical instrument to lay bare in fragmentary glimpses
those secret meanings that lie beneath the surface. He worked with
a sensuous intellectuality, suggesting the emotional and psychological drives of his characters through vivid, affecting and often grotesque screen images. There is a tremendous compression in his films,
a richness of detail that holds layer on layer of meaning. To see
one is a haunting experience, like peering down a darkened corridor at a bright and shadowed world. Long after the story
is done, the images linger and mingle and grow in the realms of
the subconscious, in the phantasms of our dreams.

If the "Golden Era" of the German film was brief, its twilight
was relatively long. Throughout the late twenties the German pictures excelled in sheer physical beauty, in the size and richness of

their mountings, in the artistry of both performances and direction. Instead of being virtues, however, these very qualities soon turned into defects. Such major Ufa productions as *Faust* (1925), *Tartuffe* (1926) and *Metropolis* (1927) were altogether too self-consciously "artistic" for their own good—handsome, impressive, but dreadfully slow and ponderous, lacking the creative vitality that had characterized most German films only a few years earlier. The reasons for this gradual decline are by no means obscure. By the dawn of the twenties, Hollywood had entered into its own "golden era" of giant studios and virtually unlimited financing. Whatever Hollywood could not produce itself, it bought. And as the German pictures began to create a furor in this country, negotiations were soon under way to import the talents that had made them—stars, directors, producers, cameramen, set designers. The first star to arrive was Pola Negri, whose immense popularity with American audiences paved the way for actors like Emil Jannings, Lya de Putti and Conrad Veidt. Ernst Lubitsch was the first important German director to come to Hollywood. His success inspired the wholesale importation of others—Ludwig Berger, Michael Curtiz, William Dieterle, E. A. Dupont, Paul Leni, F. W. Murnau. Even Pabst had a brief, unhappy fling in the Hollywood studios. Top cinematographers like Karl Freund, Karl Struss, Kurt Courant and Theodor Sparkuhl brought German camera techniques to the American films. And finally, in 1927, Erich Pommer himself, the astute production head of Ufa, the man directly responsible for most of the great successes of the "Golden Era," was lured to Hollywood by Paramount. Thus, throughout the late twenties, the German studios were being persistently drained of their best talents.

At the same time the Germans who remained at home were increasingly tailoring their films for the American market, hoping to repeat the box-office success of *Variety*—and hoping, many of them, to receive their own invitations to cross the Atlantic. Their pictures began to shed those specific qualities that had first won attention for the German film; they became vaguely international in tone, following formulas rather than creating styles. This process was hastened when, in 1925, both Paramount and M-G-M negotiated a pact with Ufa to co-produce on the Continent, using mixed casts and technicians. American stars were sent abroad to appear in these films and guarantee their success on both sides of the water. As a result, the already serious drainage of Germany's best creative talent was accompanied by a steady dilution of those creative energies that remained. Dr. Kracauer has described such films of the late twenties as *Homecoming* (1928), *Asphalt* (1929) and *The Wonderful Lie of Nina Petrovna* (1929) as "a synthesis of Hollywood and Neubabelsberg." The marvelous German craftsmanship persisted, but the magic fire of the early twenties was being slowly extinguished.

NEW BEGINNINGS IN RUSSIA

At the very time that the German industry was slipping into a decline, the Western world began to be aware of a vigorous film movement stirring in the Soviet Union. The Revolution of 1917 had virtually severed Russia from the rest of Europe both economically and culturally; but throughout the early twenties travelers were bringing back reports of daring experiments in the arts. Music had become determinedly atonal, imitating cement mixers and riveting drills. In the theater, classic plays were being staged with acrobats and trapeze artists. Films too were sharing in this upheaval. Not until 1925, however, were any of these circulated in western Europe, and the few that did appear were by no means representative. Non-political subjects, they included *Polikushka* (1922), from a story by Tolstoi; Pushkin's *The Stationmaster* (1925) and a film for children, *The Marriage of the Bear* (1925). Seen mainly by critics and film enthusiasts in the numerous film societies and *ciné-clubs* that had begun to spring up in England and on the Continent, this handful of pictures gave barely a hint of the great cycle of Russian films that was to appear between 1925 and 1930. Beginning almost simultaneously with *Potemkin* (1925) and *Mother* (1925), it included such masterworks as *End of St. Petersburg* (1927), *Ten Days That Shook the World* (1928), *Storm over Asia* (1928), *Arsenal* (1929), *Fragment of an Empire* (1929), *Old and New* (1929) and *Earth* (1930). They were films of extraordinary visual impact, revolutionary both in theme and in style. In them, for the first time, the motion-picture medium was treated not only as an art but as a science as well—a science that developed out of the scarcity of film stock and camera equipment that plagued the Russian film makers for almost a decade after the Revolution. Compared to the Germans the Russians were creating films out of thin air.

At the end of the Revolution, the new Soviet Union found itself with the merest shell of a film industry. Its beginnings had been tentative, its roots shallow. Not until 1907 was there a native Russian studio. Up to that time, the only films made there had been shot by itinerant cameramen sent out by the French firms of Gaumont, Lumière and Pathé. Other small studios followed, some of German, some of French and a few of Russian origin. In all of Russia on the eve of the Revolution, there were only 1,045 theaters with 364,000 seats.

Feature production, which began in 1914, was necessarily on a very limited scale, and reflected the producers' determination to woo the middle classes. The great stage director Vsevolod Meyerhold put three of his plays on film, while the most ambitious picture of the period was an adaptation of Tolstoi's *Father Sergius* (1917), directed by Feodor Protazanov. It remains a highly dramatic and impressive film, distinguished particularly by handsome Ivan Mozhukhin's extraordinary performance as the licentious young officer who, after a multitude of sins, becomes a shaggy, tormented old man roaming the countryside in search of redemption. Much of it was actually shot in the sumptuous clubs and marbled palaces described in the novel. Although the film was immediately suppressed by the czarist government for its revelations of corrupt court life, the ban was soon lifted by the Kerensky régime that followed. Not until after the Revolution, however, did the Russian film makers begin to concentrate on the literature, the culture and the life of their own country. But by that time the personnel of the industry and the composition of the audience had undergone a drastic change.

Once the Revolution broke, whatever industry there was promptly disintegrated. The Europeans withdrew and the White Russians hastily followed after, seizing in their flight any bits of film and camera equipment they could lay their hands on. Thus it was almost an empty gesture when, in August of 1919, the Russians nationalized their motion-picture industry and placed it under the

People's Commissariat of Propaganda and Education. Considering the wrecked studios, the meager equipment and the pitiful supplies of raw stock available at the time, Lenin displayed incredibly shrewd foresight in declaring that "Of all the arts, the cinema is the most important for us."

THE EDITING PRINCIPLE: VERTOV AND KULESHOV

It is scarcely surprising to find that during the years of civil war and counter-revolution following the Bolsheviks' accession to power, the Russian film makers were concerned almost exclusively with what would today be called the documentary film. Virtually all available equipment and raw stock was used to record the progress of the Red armies on the various fighting fronts and the changes being effected by the new government. And as the negatives came in from all corners of the Soviet Union, they were shaped and edited by a youthful poet and film enthusiast, Dziga Vertov. Released first in newsreel form, the material was finally assembled into one thirteen-reel film (almost three hours) as *The Anniversary of the October Revolution* (1918). It was the Soviet's first feature. From this experience Vertov developed a theory of film making which he called "The Kino Eye." In a series of bold manifestoes, he argued that the only proper film form for the new Russia was the factual film and that the only true function of film was to bring the facts of the new society to the people who were helping to build it. In 1922 he launched *Kino-Pravda (Film-Truth)*, a weekly newsreel, but a newsreel specially edited to give not only facts but some background for an understanding of these facts— and, not infrequently, an emotional tone coloring the spectator's acceptance of them. Titles punctuated the reel, lettered poster-fashion, bearing propagandist slogans and exultant statistics. From the very outset the Soviet film makers were aware of the importance of editing in their work.

Vertov was to grow increasingly dogmatic in his manifestoes. He compared the motion picture to a living organism, its eye being the eye of the cameraman, its hands the editor who assembles the images, its brain the author-supervisor, Vertov. But Vertov's manifestoes were soon being countered by others. This was an era of manifestoes. As money became more available, new equipment and additional film stock were purchased from abroad and placed at the disposal of artists who promptly enunciated *their* theories on the nature of the film. With the government actively encouraging experiment in every field, technological, scientific and artistic, it was only natural that the motion picture should share in this intellectual ferment. Everything was tried, from straight story-telling pictures (with propagandist overtones) to classic plays featuring the Moscow Art Theatre. One group, calling itself FEX—The Factory of the Eccentric Actor—even sought to apply slapstick, vaudeville and circus techniques to serious themes, using tumblers and acrobats as actors. In such films as *The Adventures of an October Child* (1924) and *The Cloak* (1926), the founder-directors of FEX, Grigori Kozintsev and Leonid Trauberg, achieved a curious form of expressionism based on exaggeration of gesture by the actor and distortion of angles by the camera, both producing an impressive if artificial heightening of the emotional content of the scenes.

Interesting and even audacious as these experiments were, the most fruitful experimentation was to come from the workshop of Lev Kuleshov, one of the few pre-Revolutionary film makers to remain in Russia after the mass exodus of 1917. Kuleshov, like Vertov, insisted on the importance of editing; but where Vertov became increasingly mechanical—even mathematical—in the development of his editing principles, Kuleshov was concerned with the emotional and psychological potentialities inherent in joining one image to the next. And in order to understand fully the fine art of cutting, he began to study and experiment. With raw film still precious and scarce, Kuleshov and his disciples—including Vsevolod I. Pudovkin—set forth upon an intensive investigation of films that had already been made, outstanding among them being D. W. Griffith's *Intolerance*. According to Pudovkin, in his still valuable handbook *Film Technique,* these films were screened over and over again, the mechanics of their construction dissected, analyzed and discussed. The films were physically torn apart and the shots rearranged, the sequences edited in different ways; and each time the new effects were studied to see whether they improved upon or altered the intent of the original.

Perhaps the most famous of Kuleshov's experiments—also recorded by Pudovkin—was one involving an old film with the actor Mozhukhin. From it Kuleshov obtained a close-up in which Mozhukhin appeared perfectly expressionless. This same shot he inserted at various points into another film—once in juxtaposition to a plate of soup, once next to a child playing contentedly with a teddy bear, and again next to a shot of an old woman lying dead in her coffin. Audiences shown the experimental reel praised Mozhukhin's performance—his look of hunger at the bowl of soup, his delight on seeing the child, his grief over the dead woman. For Kuleshov, however, it was a conclusive demonstration of his theory —based on what Griffith had already achieved instinctively—that it is not merely the image alone, but the juxtaposition of images that creates the emotional tone of a sequence. In his film *By the Law* (1926), based on Jack London's taut study of three people snowbound in a cabin for an entire winter, Kuleshov utilized his mastery of the medium to the full. Within a single setting, with only three actors, he created a film in which the emotional tensions, the frictions, the fraying nerves and incipient madness of the characters are experienced almost too intensely by the audience. From Griffith, Kuleshov had learned the kinetic values of longer and shorter shots, the ability to heighten or release emotion by editing. Through his own researches into the relationship of shot to shot, through his calculated assembly of the most revealing movements of an arm, a leg, a hand, his technique of adding detail on detail, he achieved an intensity of emotional identification, of empathy, such as Griffith never attained.

PUDOVKIN AND THE PERSONAL EPIC

Vsevolod I. Pudovkin, the outstanding director to come from the Kuleshov workshop, built upon his teacher's discoveries. For Pudovkin the cut was still fundamental to film technique, but he gave increased attention to the emotional content of his separate shots, broadening Kuleshov's approach to embrace the entire range of human feeling. Because the film is essentially a visual medium, Pudovkin maintained that it was necessary to discover visual means to convey not only story elements but character traits as well. "Plastic material," he called this, the visible manifestations of personality, of attitude, of an inner emotional state. In his book *Film Technique* he cites a crude but unmistakably clear example from an American film by Henry King, *Tol'able David* (1921). To characterize Ernest Torrence as a cruel, heartless, sadistic brute, King introduced him through a brief sequence of shots in which the man, about to enter a house, spies a kitten sleeping in the sun. His eyes glittering with malice, Torrence seizes a rock and prepares to fling it at the tiny creature. This wanton bit of cruelty might, at least in those pre-sound days, have been dispensed with altogether and a title substituted: "The Tramp—a cruel, heartless, sadistic brute . . . Ernest Torrence." But how much more effective to introduce the character visually, through use of this "plastic material"! Pudovkin's films are filled with such shots. In *Mother* the young hero awaits his impending release from jail. His thoughts are of the world outside; and Pudovkin cuts from his smiling face to shots of a thawing mountain stream, of sparkling waters liberated from their wintry prison.

In *Storm over Asia*, Pudovkin refined and polished this technique to an astonishing degree, achieving a precision of plastic expression that has never been excelled. One sequence of great complexity, for example, is played completely without titles, yet every turn of the action, every nuance of mood and motivation is crystal clear. A British soldier has been instructed to take a captured Mongol out to the sand pits beyond the city and shoot him. Clearly reluctant to carry out this command, the soldier carefully finishes binding on his puttees, slowly taps out his pipe and shoulders his rifle. Outside the barracks the Mongol awaits him, not knowing what to expect. Gruffly, the Englishman shoves him forward. They come to a large, muddy puddle in the middle of the road. The soldier makes a wide detour around it; the Mongol splashes straight on through. When they arrive at the sand pits, the scene of the execution, the soldier tries to delay the distasteful business for a moment. He lights his pipe, then offers a cigarette to the Mongol. Smiling, the Mongol refuses. The soldier motions him forward, towards the edge of the pits. Still smiling, the Mongol obeys. In a sudden frenzy, the Englishman tries to unsling his rifle while the Mongol's back is turned. The Mongol sees him and, only half comprehending, is shot down. On the way back to the barracks, his rifle dragging, one of his puttees untied, the soldier sloshes without knowing, without caring, through the puddle he had so fastidiously avoided only a few moments earlier. Each shot has its own significance, carrying us deeper and deeper into an understanding of the characters and their emotions. "Brick by brick," Pudovkin described his method of building a film—brick by brick, solidly, the way a good mason constructs a wall.

When one thinks of Pudovkin, it is invariably in terms of the marvelous moments of character revelation with which his films abound. He knew how to make one feel with them their joy, their pain, their victories, their defeats. From his collaboration with Pavlov on the purely expositional film *Mechanics of the Brain* (1926) he learned, perhaps better than any other film maker, the nature of reflexes and reactions. Certainly, in his pictures one is always tactilely aware of the world in which his characters move— the mud of a road, the steel and stone of a prison, the rough planks and plaster of a peasant hovel; conscious, too, of the impact of a blow or a bullet, of breathless flight or impassioned resistance. Like Pabst, Pudovkin had a keen awareness of the emotional power of carefully chosen and closely observed details. Both men were primarily concerned with revealing the inner impulses that motivated their characters. Both had absorbed much from science— Pudovkin from Pavlov, Pabst from Freud. Quite independently, they had evolved techniques that were strikingly similar: a carefully composed realism of settings and milieu, an abundance of close-ups both of objects and of people, brief shots seen from constantly shifting points of view, and adroit cutting on movement to make all flow together smoothly. For Pabst, however, the interest was always on the individual, on the instincts and passions behind an act of violence, eroticism or death. Pudovkin, on the other hand, portrayed the individual as a social being, and sought to create in his films the dynamic relationship between a man and his background, the impact of ideas and events upon his character.

Pudovkin's films may properly be described as epic. In each of them—*Mother* (1925), *End of St. Petersburg* (1927), *Storm over Asia* (1928), right through his first sound picture, *Deserter* (1933)— the hero is in fact the personification of the masses, an ideal, perhaps even an idealized figure, caught up in the turbulent stream of living history. In this respect Pudovkin's work stands in sharpest contrast to his brilliant contemporary, Sergei Eisenstein. For Eisenstein, the masses themselves were the hero; and at least in *Potemkin* (1925) and *Ten Days That Shook the World* (1928) Eisenstein was able to create a film form in which character and characterization were subordinate to the sweep and turmoil of broad, revolutionary movements. While frequently in bitter opposition to each other during their lifetimes, the names of Eisenstein and Pudovkin will always be linked in film history; they were at once Russia's greatest film makers and most searching theoreticians. "Pudovkin's films resemble a song," wrote the French film historian Léon Moussinac, "Eisenstein's, a shout."

EISENSTEIN AND THE MASS EPIC

Sergei M. Eisenstein, the son of a wealthy shipbuilder, had been trained in architecture and engineering. Drawn to the arts during the period of upheaval just after the Revolution, he worked in the theaters of Foregger and Meyerhold as a designer, then joined the Proletcult Theatre as director. Always he tried to infuse into the theater his own changing, evolving concepts of what he referred to as "Soviet realism." Indeed, his last play before moving into films, *Gas Masks* (1923), was so very realistic that it was not staged in a theater at all. Instead, it was performed against the background of an actual gasworks, the action shifting from place to place within the building itself. One can imagine the audience bustling about after it. In any case, it was this experience that led Eisenstein to suspect that the motion picture—in which the camera can move from place to place while the audience stays put—might provide a happier solution to his artistic problems. He saw quite clearly that the real settings in *Gas Masks* had made the play itself seem quite false. *Strike* (1924), his first film, seems to have come as the logical result of his experience with this play. "The cart fell to pieces and the driver dropped into the cinema," he once wrote. The drop was not without preparation. Eisenstein observed the Kuleshov workshop in production and discussed editing with Dziga Vertov, then engaged the support of the Proletcult collective to produce his film and appear in it. Although *Strike* has never been seen in this country, the final portion of the scenario, reproduced in his book *The Film Sense,* indicates that the climax, with its scenes of strikers being murdered intercut with shots of cattle being slaughtered in an abattoir, was already pointing toward the editing techniques made famous in *Potemkin.*

In recognition of his accomplishments on *Strike,* the Russian government commissioned Eisenstein to make a film commemorating the abortive revolution of 1905. Pudovkin, similarly commissioned, chose Gorki's *Mother* for his theme, but Eisenstein preferred to work without any prepared narrative. He intended to recreate on film key incidents in the nation-wide uprisings and the brutal czarist repression that followed. He had already done some initial shooting in Leningrad before going south to Odessa to take a few brief scenes depicting the famous mutiny of the sailors aboard the battleship *Potemkin.* When he saw the great flight of stairs leading down from the center of Odessa to the waterfront, however, the steps on which Cossacks had methodically shot down hundreds of citizens sympathizing with the rebel sailors, Eisenstein was convinced that here was the heart of his entire picture, the perfect symbol for the whole 1905 uprising. In this one incident he found reproduced in miniature the alignment of social forces that had boiled over throughout Russia in that year—the sharpening lines of class against class, the increasing hatred of the czarist régime and the emergence of a militant revolutionary leadership. The slaughter on the steps epitomized the savage reprisals that followed the uprisings everywhere, one more instance of the czarist government's shocking contempt for the people of Russia. In addition, for dramatic purposes, there was even the indication of a "happy ending." When the *Potemkin* approached the massed ships of the Imperial Navy, the sailors on the other vessels refused to fire upon their comrades, permitting them to escape unchallenged—a symbol of the solidarity of the Russian people and of the eventual victory over their czarist oppressors. In view of all this, Eisenstein dropped his former plans for the 1905 film and expanded the few scenes originally allotted to the Odessa mutiny into a full six-reel feature, which he titled *Potemkin.*

Seen today, *Potemkin* remains as striking and original as when it first appeared in 1925. In no other film has a historic event been reconstructed as the microcosmic symbol of an entire society, nor made so immediate and affecting without an individual hero or personalized story. Its visual excitement, the power of its images and the brilliance of its editing, have retained all their ability to startle and impress. From its opening sequence of increasingly turbulent waters dashing against a quay to its final shot in which the entire ship, seen from below, glides triumphantly across the screen, Eisenstein conceived his film as a series of images assembled in a completely new, revolutionary manner. For him, everything rested on what could be done with the separate shots on the editing table; every shot was made with a view to its position in the completed film. But the theory underlying their assembly was Eisenstein's own, one that he described as "shock attraction."

Eisenstein formulated his theory of editing from his studies of Japanese hieroglyphic writing. The Japanese word picture for crying, he noted, combined the pictures for "eye" and for "water"; sorrow was represented by the hieroglyphics for "knife" and "heart"; and singing joined together their word pictures for "mouth" and "bird." This juxtaposition, Eisenstein felt, did more than simply add one idea to the other: it "exploded" them into a totally new concept—weeping, sorrow or song. Because motion picture editing is essentially the art of bringing together similarly independent images into new relationships, Eisenstein argued that this same technique applied to cinematic construction. Indeed, he insisted that it was basic to any dynamic film technique because it involved the active participation of the audience in comprehending and completing the artist's intentions.

For all the apparent rigidity of his theoretical formulations, Eisenstein on film was a good deal less dogmatic than Eisenstein on paper. While *Potemkin* abounds in marvelous examples of the "shock attraction" technique, the editing is by no means limited to this one method. In fact, it would probably be impossible to base an entire picture on "shock attractions" alone. Out of the hundreds of shots that make up any feature film, only the briefest cluster can be held together in this fashion, unified by a single idea and making a single statement. Yet when Eisenstein did use the "shock" method, as in the incredible "steps sequence" from *Potemkin,* he filled the screen with images of overwhelming power, a power drawn from the audience's own instinctive association of the content of one shot with what is seen in the next. A Cossack in close-up slashes with his saber in one shot; the next shows us a close-up of a woman with her glasses smashed and her face bloody. A line of Cossacks fires and we see a young mother clutching at her vitals, the blood streaming out over her hands. Her baby carriage starts bounding wildly down the steps, and we watch its progress through the horrified eyes of a student crouching down below, his head slowly turning as he follows the descent. Actually, of course, what we are shown is simply a series of independently photographed shots—one of rifles firing, another of a young woman simulating agony, another of a carriage rolling down a flight of stairs, and another of a young man turning his head. It is the editing that establishes their connection for us, the "shock attraction" that binds them together and makes us share with the student his sense of helpless horror. And each shot was arranged and photographed with a precise knowledge of how it would relate to all the others; just as, at the close of the sequence, shots of three stone lions—one lying, one crouching, one rearing up— have been edited together to create the illusion of a single beast suddenly startled and roaring in rage.

In *Potemkin* one finds equally brilliant examples of other edi- torial techniques—techniques that Eisenstein himself was to develop further in *Ten Days That Shook the World* and in *Old and New*. Tonal cutting, in which continuity is provided by the gradual lightening or darkening of the shots in a sequence; directional cutting, in which the flow of movement from one shot to the next establishes the continuity; and cutting on form—the curve of an arm giving way to the arc of a parasol, followed by the bend of an arch—all of these Eisenstein experimented with in *Potemkin* (and all of them have found particular application since that time in the field of documentary film making).

But perhaps Eisenstein's greatest editorial discovery was the dis- crepancy between screen time and real time. Through editing, he found, he could destroy real time altogether. Why pay as much attention, he asked, to one's most insignificant gesture as is given to the most crucial moments in one's life? Psychologists have long been aware of the relativity of time. An agonized moment can seem like an eternity; a happy hour flies by in an instant. Griffith had already shown how to eliminate the inessentials, to concentrate the significant into a single dramatic close-up. Now Eisenstein proceeded to *expand* time, to accentuate the moments of peak significance.

Early in *Potemkin* a young sailor, beaten by his petty officer, half starved on the miserable rations served to the crew, is washing the dishes in the officers' mess. He comes upon a platter on which is inscribed, "Give Us This Day Our Daily Bread." His indignation suddenly wells over and he sends the dish crashing to the floor. To break a dish—to lift it up and throw it down—is the action of only a moment. But this was a moment of tremendous importance, both to the boy and to the development of the entire film, the first external manifestation of the spirit of revolt that was sweeping through the crew of the battleship. Rather than photograph it in a single shot from a single position, which would merely reproduce the action in its ordinary time value, Eisenstein took the same action from a number of angles, then cut the shots together in a slightly overlapping progression. The result was to emphasize the action by the abrupt hail of shots, and to prolong it through the overlaps.

Eisenstein repeated this technique at each crucial moment in *Potemkin*. In the sequence on the quarter-deck, the Marines' growing determination not to fire on their comrades is suggested in a series of shots of clenching fists, flinching eyes and wavering rifles that delay the moment of action long after the officers have given their command. At the climax of the film, as the victorious crew of the ship tensely wait to discover whether the fleet will fire upon them or not, the tension is prolonged through shots of the men waiting motionless, the engines racing and the cannon slowly mounting to the ready position.

This cinematic expansion of time reaches its fullest, most complex expression in the scenes of the massacre on the Odessa steps. The people of Odessa have assembled on the steps to see—and many of them to cheer—the sailors who have thrown off their hated officers. Suddenly, from behind, comes a fusillade of bullets. The Cossacks have been ordered to put an end to this demonstration, to clear the steps. They march slowly, deliberately downward, firing as they go. The crowd immediately breaks in panic, leaping, running, jumping to the foot of the stairs and safety. Now as one look at the steps would show, any reasonably able-bodied citizen could run down the entire flight in a minute or two—particularly if his life depended on it. But Eisenstein realized that for the people trapped on the steps these would be the most terrifying (and for many, the final) moments of their lives. Obviously the scene should not be simply recorded, newsreel fashion, reproducing the atrocity exactly as it happened in time and in incident. To provide a proper psychological expansion and dramatic weight, Eisenstein broke up the mass into its component parts: the Cossacks moving ruthlessly downward and the crowd fleeing in terror before them provide the main motifs. Against them, he set a group that crawls up the steps cringing, begging for mercy; another that huddles together in prayer; and a woman whose child has been shot, defiantly carrying the bleeding body in her arms back to the very barrels of the Cossack rifles. Others are picked out as individuals: a legless cripple who scrambles down the embankment on his hands, the mother with the baby carriage, the horrified student. Each character, each incident provides not only an interruption but a counter-rhythm to the steady, measured tread of the Cossacks. Each action extends the scene upon the steps just a little bit longer until, ultimately, each of these knots of resistance has been broken. The final moments of the sequence capture the sense of headlong flight, of panic and disaster in a rapidly accelerating series of shots of the baby carriage, the student, a praying woman and—in an incredible shot just four frames long—the frenzied face of a Cossack slashing with his saber, cutting off the retreat at the foot of the stairs.

In this one, brilliant sequence of film making, Eisenstein created virtually an editor's handbook, a truly virtuoso display of all the basic cutting principles—parallel editing, rhythmic, tonal, directional and "shock." When later Eisenstein wrote and lectured on his theories, he used the French word for editing, *montage*, which means literally "mounting," or "putting together." But as first *Potemkin*, then *Ten Days* swept through the Western world taking film makers and critics by storm, the word *montage* came to identify not cutting in general, but specifically the rapid, shock cutting that Eisenstein employed in his films. Its use survives to this day in the specially created "montage sequences" inserted into Hollywood films to suggest, in a blur of double exposures, the rise to fame of an opera singer or, in brief model shots, the destruction of an airplane, a city or a planet. It is scarcely necessary to add that this is a far cry from Eisenstein's original conception of the word.

In *Ten Days That Shook the World,* Eisenstein further developed many of the editing techniques he had introduced in *Potemkin.* Time is again extended in the justly famous sequence of the opening of the bridges during a workers' demonstration in St. Petersburg. To cut off the workers from their quarters, the police have been ordered to raise the drawbridges around the center of the city. On one of the bridges is a dead woman, shot by the police. Her long hair lies sprawled across the crevice formed by the two sections of the bridge. As the center begins to rise, the instant of its opening is prolonged in a marvelous series of shots of the hair falling, falling, falling into the abyss. The bridge continues to rise, and the steepness of its ascent is accentuated by a horse hanging over the ledge. The camera rides up with the rising bridge to the very summit, trained on the carriage being held at the tip of the roadway by the weight of the horse. At the last moment the traces part, and a quick succession of shots catches the carriage rolling down the incline on one side, and on the other, the horse plummeting into the water far below. Here not only has time been extended, but the finality of the act, the completeness of the separation between the two parts of the city has been emphasized visually, symbolically.

It was the symbol, the filmic metaphor, that seems to have attracted Eisenstein most strongly during the making of *Ten Days.* Commissioned in celebration of the tenth anniversary of the 1917 Revolution, the film covered the stirring events between Lenin's secret return from exile and the Bolsheviks' seizure of power. As conceived by Eisenstein, it was to embrace activity on many fronts— in the councils of the Kerensky government, in the hectic sessions of the Bolsheviks, at the front and in the workers' quarters, all culminating in the final, decisive attack upon the Winter Palace. Once again he had a broader theme than could be developed through any conventional narrative devices. And even more than in *Potemkin,* he was faced with the necessity of characterizing in sharp, swift visuals all the many elements involved in the history of an era.

Eisenstein found his solution in an elaborate—perhaps even over-elaborate—series of filmic symbols. Thus, the dictatorship of Kerensky is wryly satirized in a sequence showing Kerensky gravely mounting the stairs of the Winter Palace. At each landing he is bowed to by assorted generals and flunkies and saluted with ever more grandiose titles. His Napoleonic ambitions are implied when he carefully assembles the four quarters of a crystal decanter and meticulously places upon them their crown, or gazes upward at an ornate marble statue that extends a wreath of gold over his head. The ceremony of the Old Guard is suggested by richly paneled doors slowly closing; the bustle of the Bolsheviks by the constant banging open and shut of the battered door to their central head-quarters. The symbol, the part for the whole, is used repeatedly to epitomize events. The Army is with the Bolsheviks—a mass of rifles waves in the air. The Kerensky government has lost control of the situation—bureaucrats click vainly on their telephones. The revolutionary forces have won—a young boy sits upon the Romanov throne gaily kicking his legs. The camera—operated by Edouard Tisse, who was to Eisenstein what Bitzer had been to Griffith—adds further emphasis to these meaningful vignettes. Men and women drag a small cannon into position—the camera is tilted to emphasize the difficulty of the operation. A faded woman, a soldier in Keren-sky's Battalion of Death, gazes longingly at a statue of young love —the camera observes her mistily, through soft focus lenses. A gross, mannish woman in the same Battalion is photographed sharply and from below, emphasizing all her corpulence and brawn.

During his making of *Ten Days,* Eisenstein encountered his first difficulties with the Soviet authorities. While the picture was still in production, Stalin and Trotzky had clashed; Trotzky, one of the leading tacticians of the Revolution, fled the country into exile, and Eisenstein suddenly found himself faced with the necessity of removing from his film one of its main protagonists. The sub-sequent re-editing delayed its release for over a year; but one has only to compare *Ten Days* with Romm's *Lenin in October,* pro-duced in 1937 to mark the twentieth anniversary of the Revolution, to realize how dynamic—and, in spirit, how much more authentic—was Eisenstein's version of the Revolution. In Romm's film as the troops charge through the Winter Palace, someone sings out, "Be careful, those are works of art!" Their leader's first action on break-ing into the inner council of the Provisional Government is to comb his hair. Romm's was a self-consciously neat Revolution. In *Ten Days,* the troops charge like troops, smashing as they go; and their leader, a ratty, intense little man in a floppy black hat, plants a revolver on the table the moment he gains the inner chamber, sweeps aside the clutter of books and papers, and declares that the Bolsheviks have taken over. Only at one point does Eisenstein seem to go out of his way to glorify Lenin, introducing a brief but embarrassingly obvious lap-dissolve penetrating Lenin's disguise on his return to Russia to lead the Revolution. It seems almost an afterthought.

Eisenstein's clashes with his government were to continue throughout the remainder of his career—a career, incidentally, in which there were to be only three more completed films, *Old and New* (1929), *Alexander Nevsky* (1938) and Part I of *Ivan the Terrible* (1944). Perhaps he would have clashed with authority under any system of government, such was his temperament, such was his genius. When in 1930 he came to the United States to work for a time at Paramount, he arrogantly submitted his brilliant adaptation of Theodore Dreiser's mammoth *An American Tragedy* with a note that read in part: "Here it is, the miracle completed— *An American Tragedy* in 14 reels . . . And 'Honi soit qui mal y pense.'" The script was rejected, as were all the other projects he originated at Paramount. Later in Mexico, directing *Que Viva Mexico* on funds raised by Upton Sinclair, Eisenstein's relations with his benefactor became so acrimonious that the film was never completed. After he returned to Russia, his film on the Soviet's peasant policy, *Bezhin Meadow,* was scrapped on charges of being "too formalistic." Bureaucrats prevented the realization of other projects—a comedy, a film on Spain, another on the organization of the Red Army in 1917. Work on the first part of *Ivan the Terrible* was delayed repeatedly while Party ideologists tried to decide whether Ivan was a wicked old czar or a national hero who had helped to unify the country. Meanwhile, Eisenstein lectured, taught and directed plays and operas, often creating for them his own scenic and costume designs. He died in 1948, at the age of 49, still planning the completion of the final section of his *Ivan* film.

POETIC SYMBOLISM: DOVZHENKO

Toward the end of the twenties, one more highly original talent emerged in the Russian film to take a place beside Eisenstein and

Pudovkin, the Ukrainian Alexander Dovzhenko. Dovzhensko, it must be admitted, has never shared the popularity abroad of either of his great contemporaries, largely because the symbolism that suffuses his pictures makes them seem strange and difficult to follow. Indeed, many of the symbols in such early works as *Zvenigora* (1927) and *Arsenal* (1929) are so very special as to be quite unfamiliar outside the Ukraine itself. Even so, few pictures are so rewarding to see again and again. With each new viewing their meaning grows clearer, their surface difficulties providing fascinating clues that lead to the rich and complex core of his films. Dovzhenko seems to stand between Eisenstein and Pudovkin. Like Eisenstein, he created bold new film forms, cutting freely to pursue a broad theme rather than a story line. Like Pudovkin, he personalizes his themes, choosing heroes who typify or personify the masses; but where Pudovkin insisted on the reality, the actuality of his central char- actor, Dovzhenko's heroes remain allegorical figures. The protag- onists in Pudovkin's *End of St. Petersburg* and Dovzhenko's *Arsenal,* for example, are remarkably similar—simple men who attain maturity through their contact with the forces of the Revolu- tion. Pudovkin's hero dies in combat. When the hero of *Arsenal,* however, is captured by the counter-revolutionaries and led before a firing squad, he stands impervious to their bullets. The embodi- ment of Ukrainian resistance, he is Dovzhenko's symbol of final victory.

For Dovzhenko, as for Eisenstein, the symbol proved the most natural form of filmic expression. In all his major works from *Arsenal* to *Frontier,* the subject itself—the arsenal, the collective farm in *Earth*, the Dneprostroi Dam in *Ivan*, the new air city in *Frontier*—seems to stand as one gigantic symbol for a new phase in the advancing Soviet economy. Around this central symbol, to build and re-enforce it, Dovzhenko supplies a wealth of additional details, scenes that are themselves filled with symbolic imagery. As a result, his pictures have the kind of compression, the intensity that one associates more often with great poetry. They unfold slowly, revealing new layers of meaning, new levels of perception. And, as in poetry, the more one brings to them, the more one is able to carry away. Dovzhenko's films are odes to life, to the land

and to a better world expressed in terms at once highly personal and deeply affecting.

Perhaps with Dovzhenko more than with any other director, one remembers separate images rather than sequences or stories. There is a vividness in his shots that is tremendously exciting, even though its meaning may be obscure. In *Arsenal,* for instance, audiences never fail to be startled by the scene in which a framed portrait of a Ukrainian national hero suddenly comes to life and spits upon the ikon lamp burning before it. Although few may recognize the portrait, no one can miss the contempt implicit in the action. Dovzhenko's fascination with horses often produced equally startling images. One remembers the revolutionaries in *Arsenal* carrying a dead comrade home in a sleigh with the horses "singing" as they gallop across the snow; when the soldier himself, a rope biting into his frozen mouth, is dumped at the feet of his mother, the horses cry, "Such is our revolutionary life and death, Mother!" One also recalls the faces of the bourgeoisie poised, straining to hear the sounds of the approaching revolution, or the little stationmaster disappearing into nothingness—the end of an era—when he learns that the Communists have commandeered the trains; or the stillness just before the Revolution uncannily captured in a single long-shot of a legless man slowly pushing himself across a darkened street.

The kind of juxtapositions that other directors generally achieve through cutting, Dovzhenko is very likely to encompass within a single shot, finding the perfect visual image through which to transform or alter a meaning with maximum intensity. The very opening shot of *Arsenal,* for example, shows a quiet, peaceful field. Suddenly an explosion bursts the field asunder, and we are carried directly into the war. In *Earth* there is a long moment of ineffable, almost unearthly beauty as its hero walks along a dusty country road, the golden harvest shimmering in the twilight on either side of him. Unable to contain his delight, he breaks into a gay, twirling peasant dance which is rendered by the camera in slow motion. As the dancing figure nears the top of the screen, this vision of pure contentment is shattered by a shot fired by a half-mad boy who fears the approaching collectivization of the land.

It is this same compression, this uncanny ability to bring together within a single shot the few stark details that most sharply characterize a person or a situation, that makes Dovzhenko's images linger in the mind long after the film has past. In *Arsenal,* the war's depletion of a village is implied in one almost motionless scene: a tired woman stands in the doorway of a peasant hovel while in the center of the floor sits a legless cripple wearing a war medal. The realism of such shots, however, did not deter Dovzhenko from combining them into highly unrealistic, poetic patterns, broadening their implications, deepening their meaning. During the sequence in the peasant village in *Arsenal,* he shows a one-armed man plowing a field with a bony old horse. In a sudden frenzy, the man seizes the reins in his teeth and flogs the beast with a stick. The horse says, "It isn't me that you're angry with, old man"; and Dovzhenko cuts to Czar Nicholas sitting before his open diary as if gazing on the distant scene. "Today I shot a crow," writes the czar. And the old man collapses in the field. Or, in the same film, a Ukrainian soldier returns from the front to find his wife holding a baby. "Whose?" he asks. Whereupon Dovzhenko cuts immediately to identical scenes being enacted in the homes of French and German soldiers. From Dovzhenko these references and associations come less as intellectual effects than as outbursts of passion—or compassion—inspired by the material itself.

Dovzhenko, more than any of his Russian contemporaries, infused his films with a deep vein of 19th century humanism. The villains of his pictures—the old kulak of *Earth,* the simple trapper of *Frontier*—are not essentially evil. He never caricatures them or makes them hateful. In his view, they are villains only in their inability to understand the new ways, the new life in the Soviet Union. The most moving scene in all Dovzhenko's work is the death of the old trapper in *Frontier.* The man has sabotaged the air city; he must die. His friend, a partisan of the new order, leads him up into the mountains where for decades the two had roamed free of governments, of cities, of progress. For one long moment the old man's cry of remembrance echoes from mountain to mountain. Then a shot rings out. Progress has won—but there is no delight in the victory.

Not until Akira Kurasawa's *Rashomon*—not even in the later films of Dovzhenko himself—were we to see again such bold stylization, such intensity of visual image, such freedom in cutting, although Dovzhenko's work has had a profound influence upon many of the documentary film makers both in the United States and in England. After 1934, however, film making in the Soviet Union became increasingly art by ukase, with themes dictated to fit national policy and styles altered for ready assimilation by a mass audience. There are still moments of intensity in *Shors* (1939), the story of a popular Red Army commander; some beautifully lyric passages in *Life in Bloom* (1946), the story of the Russian botanist Michurin. But both exude the uncomfortable feeling of having been made to order. They lack the sustained, exalted power of his earlier works. Unfortunately, at the present writing the only Dovzhenko films still available in this country are the early *Arsenal, Shors* and *Life in Bloom*. Each of them, however, gives occasional evidence of his powerful and original filmic intelligence, while *Arsenal* remains one of the true masterworks of the silent screen.

Around these three towering figures in the Russian film of the late twenties are clustered a number of lesser, though far from insignificant, talents—Friedrich Ermler, Abram Room, Kozintzev and Trauberg, V. I. Gardin, Ilya Trauberg, Fedor Ozep, as well as the women directors Olga Preobrashcnskaya and Esther Shub. Lev Kuleshov continued to train new talents and to direct an occasional film. Dziga Vertov, who first had drawn the attention of Russian film makers to the importance of editing, produced an increasingly mechanical and trick-filled series of experiments in *Man with a Movie Camera* (1928), *Enthusiasm* (1931) and *Three Songs About Lenin* (1934). Victor Turin's *Turksib* (1929), a dramatic, factual account of the construction of the Trans-Siberian railroad, proved an early milestone in the development of the documentary film. And Grigori Alexandrov, Eisenstein's assistant on *Potemkin* and *Ten Days,* made the impressionistic *Romance Sentimentale* (1930), while on holiday in Paris, then returned to become Russia's leading director of comedies.

The arrival of sound brought to a close the "Golden Era" of Russian films, a period of tremendous creative vigor and extraordinary artistic accomplishments. One fact stands out clearly in a re-examination of their greatest works, however. With notably few exceptions—Room's *Bed and Sofa* (1926), Ermler's *Fragment of an*

Empire (1929), Eisenstein's *Old and New* (1929)—they were concerned primarily with the past, with the hardships of life under the czars or with the revolutionary events leading up to 1917. It is astonishing that in a land where films were produced not for profit but for enlightenment, the pictures reflected so little of the contemporary scene. Or was it perhaps a case of the policy makers, the Party ideologists, deciding that the "inglorious" past of Russia under the czars was safer matter than the shortages, the famines and the work quotas of Russia under the commissars? Whatever the cause, the Russian film makers developed a technique for recreating the past that produced some of the most exciting and original pictures of the silent era. They helped increase the feelings of national pride within the Soviet Union, and generated considerable prestige for Russia among those who saw the films abroad. As Lenin had predicted, for the Communists the cinema had indeed become "the most important of the arts."

POSTWAR DECLINE IN ENGLAND AND ITALY

In western Europe, recovering slowly from the effects of World War I, films were dominated almost entirely by imports from America. The history of the British film during the twenties is fairly typical of what was happening in most small countries with a restricted home market for their own motion pictures. Native producers could not afford to compete with Hollywood either in scale or in stars. The general public flocked to the American films, and governments found it necessary to assist the home industry either by legislating restrictions upon the American product or through outright cash bounties. In England, for example, the government in 1927 introduced a "quota law" designed to encourage British production. Singularly ill advised both in plan and in execution, it granted to British studios the right to distribute American-made films provided that they produced a certain number of films themselves. To acquire these profitable rights, most of the British firms stuck to the letter of the law. They made pictures cheaply and quickly—"quota quickies," they came to be called—in which they had no real interest.

Despite the unpropitious times, a number of the figures who

were later to carry forward the standards of British film making had already entered the industry. Michael Balcon began his long career as a producer as early as 1922. Alfred Hitchcock, whose first work in films was as a designer of title cards for Paramount's British studio in 1920, had graduated to directing by 1923. His version of Mrs. Belloc Lowndes's *The Lodger* (1926) was one of the few significant British features of the twenties. Until the arrival of sound, Hitchcock, like Anthony Asquith, Herbert Wilcox and other first-rate directorial talents, had to be content with marking time in the production of "quota quickies." In one last effort to compete with the international success of the German films, a group of British financiers invited E. A. Dupont, the director of Germany's biggest box-office hit, *Variety,* to work in England. But the films that resulted, *Piccadilly* (1929) and *Atlantic* (1929), proved to be simply costly hybrids that won neither critical esteem nor popular favor. The English studios entered the sound era with little prestige and meager financial resources.

Italian production throughout the twenties was, if anything, at lower ebb than the British. Cut off from the rest of the world by fascism, the techniques of Italian film making remained at a virtual standstill as producers returned again and again to such scenes of former triumph as *The Last Days of Pompeii, Cabiria, Theodora* and, inevitably, *Quo Vadis?* It was *Quo Vadis?* that had first won international acclaim for the Italian industry back in 1912, the biggest and longest film of its time. In 1924, in an effort to win back some measure of their former prestige, the Italians planned another, more sumptuous version of Henryk Sienkiewicz's hardy perennial. To gain entry into a broader market, Emil Jannings was imported from Germany to play Nero, along with Georg Jacoby to direct and Kurt Courant to photograph—while Gabriellino d'Annunzio's name was added as co-director. Spectacular the film certainly was, filled with crowds, lions, pagan debaucheries and sensational sadism on the grand scale. Unfortunately, the film was also spectacularly dull, combining the worst features of the deliberately-paced German dramas and the remote, pageant-like Italian spectacles. Its reception throughout the world failed to justify the vast sums that had been poured into its production, with the immediate result that the

Italians' enthusiasm for the motion picture as a source of either prestige or profit was considerably dampened.

With capital hard to come by, production fell off drastically. By the middle of the twenties, barely 6 per cent of Italian screen time went to Italian pictures; American features claimed almost 70 per cent. Then for a time it looked as if Hollywood might come to the aid of the enfeebled industry. Henry King brought a company to Italy headed by Lillian Gish and Ronald Colman to film *The White Sister* (1923) and *Romola* (1924), giving employment to many Italian technicians and even more mob extras. Soon it was announced that M-G-M would film *Ben Hur* in Italy as well, promising to out-spectacle the native product. Many Italians felt certain that the influx from Hollywood would set their industry on its feet again, but they were in for a sad surprise. M-G-M changed its corporate mind midway in production, and the Americans sailed for home to reshoot in Hollywood most of the scenes that had already been made abroad. Although *Ben Hur* (1926) was one of the biggest box-office hits of its day, the double shooting made it one of the most expensive pictures of all time. Because of this, American producers continued to regard production in Italy as an unnecessary extravagance and shunned Italian overtures to make pictures in their country for the next two decades. An effort by Italians to make on their own yet another version of *The Last Days of Pompeii* in 1926 only demonstrated again how out of date their techniques and values had become. Indeed, as far as the Italians themselves were concerned, the most popular pictures of this era were the dozens of films featuring the genial giant Maciste (Ernesto Pagani), a sort of home-grown Tarzan. Significantly, Maciste had made his bow in Giovanni Pastrone's spectacular *Cabiria* (1913), when the Italian industry was at the very pinnacle of its success. The sustained popularity of both the character and the star who played him underscores the Italians' reluctance to leave the past.

As in England, the government itself finally began to take an interest in the all but moribund industry. In 1925 the Mussolini government organized LUCE, an agency for the production of educational and propaganda films, and then a central office to supervise all film production. In Rome a Centro Sperimentale was set up to train and encourage new talent to enter the industry. On the verge of the sound era, the Italians were just beginning to catch up with their fellow film makers in other parts of the world, just beginning to absorb influences from the Americans, from Germany and from the Russian films. Few of their efforts, however, received distribution outside Italy itself. For most of the world, the Italian industry had simply ceased to exist until its sudden, dramatic re-emergence at the end of World War II.

ECLIPSE OF THE SCANDINAVIAN FILM

Similarly, the Scandinavian film, which had flowered so intensely during and immediately after World War I, fell into a gradual decline and eventual obscurity as American movies dominated more and more of the world market, and one after another of its major talents departed to studios in Neubabelsberg and Hollywood. But during its own brief "Golden Era" the Scandinavian film made an important impression on film makers in America, Germany and France. The Danish film, though remembered primarily for the work of Carl Theodor Dreyer, proves on the basis of the limited re-examination possible today to have been not only extremely active but richly creative as well. One finds in the early Danish trick and chase films elements derived from popular French and American efforts; but one also finds, as early as 1910, a style of acting already as intimate and expressive as anything that Griffith was doing at the time, an attention to décor and costume equaled only by the French Film d'Art, a photography that clearly foreshadows the Germans of a decade later and, by 1913, a mastery of cutting that not only rivaled Griffith's but was strikingly similar to the style of the Thomas Ince thrillers. It is difficult to say just how much Griffith and Ince were themselves influenced by these remarkable films from Denmark that so closely paralleled their own work. Certainly, after 1908 Danish pictures were shown here in great numbers and were highly popular. It is hard to imagine that men like Griffith and Ince would not seek out such films for study and emulation.

In the case of the Danish influence on German production, the evidence is far clearer. As already noted, even before the First World War Berlin had attracted an entire colony of Danish film makers, working there either for Paul Davidson's Projection A.G.

Union or the German branch of Nordisk. When, late in 1917, the German High Command moved to form the gigantic Ufa combine, both firms were incorporated into it. At first, Danish stars and technicians moved freely back and forth across the border. As Ufa continued to prosper, however, more and more of the Danish nationals came to settle in Germany, working exclusively for the German studios. One has only to look at a few frames of *Toward the Light* (1918), Asta Nielsen's last film in Denmark, to recognize in its photography—dark backgrounds, with the faces and hands of the actors picked out in harsh white light—a style that a few years later was to be identified as peculiarly Germanic. Nielsen's acting technique, with its sparing use of gesture, its suggestion of inner tensions through the innuendo of a glance, was universally admired; but it was the introverted German film of the twenties that could best utilize and copy it. Gradually the Germans robbed Denmark of its best talents—just as a few years later Hollywood was to empty the German studios.

Film making had begun in Denmark as early as 1896, and Nordisk, the major Danish studio, was established ten years later. Not until 1909, however, was there any production at all in Sweden; and not until 1912 did the two men most responsible for the character and development of the Swedish film, Victor Seastrom and Mauritz Stiller, enter the industry. Rather than proving a handicap, this tardy beginning had the real advantage of eliminating from the very outset the theatrical methods of the French and Italian studios. Swedish directors chose as their examples the works of D. W. Griffith and Thomas Ince—especially, it would seem, Ince's Westerns—setting their dramas against the snowy peaks, the rolling meadows and towering forests of their own country. For their themes, they turned ambitiously to their national legends, history and literature—including practically everything by the prolific Selma Lagerlöf. Her vast, saga-like novels provided the basis for most of the outstanding Swedish productions of the period.

Because of their literary origins, and the overwhelming seriousness of purpose with which these works were filmed, the characters emerged with a depth and dimension unprecedented and unparalleled in films anywhere at the time. By the end of World War I, the Swedish film had achieved both critical respect and international popularity. For many intellectuals, particularly on the Continent, such pictures as Seastrom's *The Outlaw and His Wife* (1917) and *The Phantom Chariot* (1920) or Stiller's *Sir Arne's Treasure* (1919) became the first intimation that the motion picture might be taken seriously as an art. Matching the dignity of the material, the acting was notably restrained and the photography often hauntingly beautiful—not merely picturesque, but penetrating into the rough-hewn settings and natural beauties of background to create an almost tactile impression of the world in which the characters moved.

But, as in Denmark and, later, in Germany, the Swedish film paid the price of success. Its best artists were lured away to work in larger, more prosperous studios elsewhere—the technicians, for the most part, in the German studios, Seastrom and Stiller to Hollywood. Before leaving, Stiller made one final grand-scale feature, at once a summary and a swan song of the Swedish film, *The Story of Gösta Berling* (1924). Based on another of the Selma Lagerlöf novels, the story is set in Sweden just after the Napoleonic Wars. Gösta Berling, a wild, defrocked priest, joins the roistering pensioners at Ekeby, a mansion presided over by a wealthy but strange woman. To the house comes a lovely Italian girl, betrothed to an elderly aristocrat. When Berling and the girl fall in love, the curse that hangs over Ekeby threatens to engulf them, but true love saves the day. Conventional narrative, however, was not Stiller's primary object in *Gösta Berling*. Most of Sweden knew the story already (it had won a Nobel prize for its author); what Stiller wanted was to bring alive its host of characters. The extent to which he succeeded can be estimated in the prints of the film presently circulated in this country by the Museum of Modern Art Film Library, a two-hour version of a picture that originally ran twice as long. Whenever the narrative thread becomes lost—which is frequently—the strength of the characterizations, the emotional tone that surrounds them and the perfectly sustained period flavor of the entire film still compel admiration. As one Swedish critic wrote at the time, "No masterpiece . . . it is, of course, one of the really great movies." It was the last great movie to come from Sweden for many a year. On the strength of it, Stiller was invited to Hollywood. He left early in 1925, taking with him the "Italian girl" of his cast—Greta Garbo.

While Hollywood would seem to be the villain of the piece in this steady deflowering of the European cinema throughout the twenties, the fact is that the American studios were simply profiting from the drastic change in film economics that followed World War I. Prior to that time, pictures could be made on a relatively low budget—low enough for a studio in a small country to show a profit through distribution in the home market alone. But as production costs rose, as films became longer, the machinery of film making more complex and skilled stars, directors and technicians more expensive, the home market proved increasingly inadequate. To show a profit, studios had to be able to sell their productions abroad. Only in the United States were producers able to make back their costs in the home market. With this advantage, the larger American studios boldly budgeted their films so that the profit margin depended on the market abroad. They had stars of international popularity, and the money to wage a ceaseless battle for screen time in theaters everywhere. They could afford to gamble on the foreign market. The Europeans, on the other hand—excluding Germany and Russia —were hard pressed to hold even their domestic markets. If they tried to keep production costs down, they lost their best stars and technicians to Hollywood; if they tried to make films of international appeal, they ran the risk of losing the specific national characteristics that had made their pictures interesting in the first place—and bankrupting themselves into the bargain. It was a disastrous dilemma, as the gradual eclipse of the national cinema in one country after another testifies.

FRENCH RENAISSANCE: DELLUC, CLAIR, FEYDER

Only in France was there an industry with sufficient vigor to survive the twenties without governmental assistance. This was due in part to the tremendous interest that French postwar intellectuals took in the medium, in part to a sharply different mode of production than obtained elsewhere. Instead of half a dozen or so large studios grinding out a year's supply of pictures for their affiliated theaters, most of the studios were small, their facilities rented by production firms often set up specifically to make a single picture. A special enthusiasm sparked each new venture, and most films were made primarily because their directors wanted to make them. True, the French pictures of this period are scarcely comparable numerically to production in Germany, Russia or even England (much less the United States); but an extraordinary number of them turned out to be first-rate works.

One man was responsible for the resuscitation of the French film after World War I. Louis Delluc, an author and editor, had become attracted to the motion picture as an art form during the war years. He was impressed particularly by the work of the Swedes and by the American directors Ince, Griffith and Chaplin, and wrote tirelessly about the need for establishing a French cinema. He pleaded for films that would be truly French and also truly cinematic, arguing at once against the re-establishment of the stagy Film d'Art and the imitation of the productions of other nations. Around him he gathered a small but influential group of film makers—Germaine Dulac, Abel Gance, Marcel L'Herbier and Jean Epstein—who came to share his views. Together they initiated a series of pictures that set the style for the first few years of the period. Impressionistic in technique, intimate in form, rather literary in flavor, they were for the most part highly romanticized studies of French low life. Perhaps such films as Delluc's own *Fièvre* (1921) or L'Herbier's *El Dorado* (1921) were too intellectual, too self-consciously artistic to be acceptable today as first-rate examples of film art. Nevertheless, they revealed a new direction for French film makers in the subtlety of their expression, in their feeling for those muted, inchoate passions too tenuous for speech, and in their accenting of atmosphere and milieu. Typical is the gloomy waterfront den in Delluc's *Fièvre* with its hard-faced barmaid, its swaggering sailor-hero and his half-caste wife who crouches dumbly at his feet gazing longingly at a single flower on the bar. "Photogenic" was Delluc's term for such material.

Such films as these continued to recruit new talents, many of them with backgrounds in the older arts. Jean Renoir, youngest son of the famous painter, made his first picture in 1923. Alberto Cavalcanti turned from architecture to set designing, then finally in 1925 to directing. René Clair had been a novelist before coming to films, Jean Epstein a poet and essayist, Dimitri Kirsanov a musician. Each was attracted to the film as a new art form; and each, as artist, brought to the medium a sense of style, of personality. One sees reflected in their works the temperaments of the men themselves—the volatile, impishly witty Clair, the ponderous but sensitive and poetic Renoir, the sharply observant, caustic Jacques Feyder. And the mode of production in France fostered just this kind of individuality.

Of all the French directors of this era, none was more talented or original, or had a greater instinctive feeling for the medium itself, than René Clair. His very first film, *The Crazy Ray* (*Paris Qui Dort*, 1923), made on a shoestring, reveals his sharp eye for the absurd and his enormous appreciation of the comic possibilities inherent in the motion-picture camera. A group of travelers alight from their plane; atop the Eiffel Tower they discover that all Paris is in the grip of a mysterious paralyzing ray. They alone, being above the ray, have escaped its effects. As they pass through the city, they discover its inhabitants frozen into the most delightfully grotesque positions—a pickpocket caught in the act, two sandwich-men bending over to pick up the same franc, a nursemaid with pram kissing a gendarme. Later, they come upon the source of the ray in the home of a mad inventor and prevail upon him to throw the switch that will start life moving again. He does so but, in a manner very reminiscent of the early French trick films, everything goes out of gear, first too fast, then too slow. For all its crudities, *The Crazy Ray* is still fresh and tremendously funny.

The next few years found Clair feeling his way—the brilliant and hilarious Dadaist comedy *Entr'acte* (1924), more fantasy in *Le Fantôme du Moulin Rouge* (1924) and *Le Voyage Imaginaire* (1925); an adventure film, *La Proie du Vent* (1925). Each contributed to the fine art of comedy that burst forth so joyously in his next picture, *The Italian Straw Hat* (1927). Drawn from a popular 19th century farce comedy by Eugène Labiche, it betrays little of its theater origins. As adapted by Clair, it is completely movie, with the camera mobilized in a fashion clearly derived from the post-Murnau German film, its cutting as swift and precise as the best American productions, and all sparked by a crackling Gallic wit and exquisite sense of the ridiculous. In Labiche's story, a young man on his way to his wedding is so unfortunate as to have his horse eat the hat of a respectable married lady while she is embracing her lover, a fierce, mustachioed officer. Since the lady can not return home without her hat, the officer forces the apologetic bridegroom to search for its twin throughout his nuptial day.

Quite apart from making full use of Labiche's highly serviceable plot, Clair kept his picture moving swiftly forward through a veritable cataract of marvelous sight gags. First, there are the characters themselves, the members of the wedding, each endowed with his own comic quality—the bride's father whose new shoes are too tight, her deaf uncle with a wad of paper lodged in his ear trumpet, a very proper cousin who has misplaced one of his white gloves, an elderly gentleman whose tie keeps slipping down. Then there are the incidents—the mayor's florid speech after the ceremony (punctuated by glimpses of the little man with the slipping tie, so intent on every word that he fails to catch his wife's frantic signals which the mayor comes to interpret as being meant for himself), the frequent and abrupt disappearances of the groom from the midst of the wedding festivities, the delightful bit of theater pantomime through which he outlines his version of his predicament to the suspicious husband. And finally there is Clair's virtuoso use of the camera itself, photographing in dreamlike slow motion the officer's wanton destruction of the young man's apartment, in nightmarish fast motion the bridegroom's enforced participation in the dancing after the wedding banquet when he would rather be out searching for the all-important hat—each shot impeccably placed and perfectly timed. *The Italian Straw Hat,* using a minimum of titles, suggests the full fluency of the silent film by one of the most imaginative directors of comedy the medium has yet produced.

The name of Jacques Feyder was frequently linked with René Clair's during the twenties. Like Clair, Feyder worked primarily in comedy. But whereas Clair specialized in the fantastic and satiric, Feyder was an ironic humanist. In such films as *Crainquebille* (1923), a modern rendering of the Anatole France story; in Zola's *Thérèse Raquin* (1928) and *Les Nouveaux Messieurs* (1928), he delivered sharp, cutting criticisms of French justice, French morals and French politics. Indeed, so devastating were his comments on dishonest politicians and parliamentary chicanery in *Les Nouveaux Messieurs*—including a roguish dream sequence in which the benches of Parliament are occupied by charming ballerinas—that the film was banned outright by the French censors. Although later the ban was removed, Feyder had already left for Hollywood in disgust—the first of the French directors to be invited to this country.

Les Nouveaux Messieurs, with its sophisticated boulevard wit, reveals only one aspect of Feyder's tremendous versatility. Less inventive, less spontaneous than Clair, he also had a greater feeling for people and the stresses of ordinary living. It was this quality that enabled him to direct such a variety of pictures well. "A setting, an atmosphere, and a popular plot with a little melodrama in it"— these Feyder once stated were all he needed to make a film. Certainly, he was a master in the art of creating and sustaining an atmosphere, and doing it unobtrusively. *Crainquebille* was praised in its day for the tricky courtroom scene in which Féraudy, the old pushcart vendor, stands tiny between the policemen in front of the looming bench of justice. But its real merits are seen today to lie in such authentically colorful scenes as the old man's heated argument with the gendarme while all the traffic in Paris piles up around them, such closely and wryly observed sequences as the vendor in his prison cell, and such warm and happy moments as his welcome in the newsboy's little room after his return from jail. These vignettes of daily life hold a pathos that makes this film a human comedy, intimate, quiet and often quite poignant. Even in *Thérèse Raquin* there is a certain poignance about the weak and sensual characters of Zola's story. Thérèse seems pitiable though she is a murderess. Feyder asks merely that we understand her, not hate her. Like Zola, he was interested in the human condition in all its manifestations, and excelled in bringing it to the screen with an air of unforced reality. Skilled in realism, comedy, pathos and melodrama, Feyder remained among the most popular French directors of the decade.

Jean Renoir's early work is even less known in this country than Feyder's. After several unsuccessful and imitative efforts, he emerged suddenly as a major talent with his adaptation of Zola's *Nana* (1926), which he both directed and financed. His wife, Catherine Hessling, played the title role, supported by Werner Krauss and Valeska Gert from the German studios. Both a popular and a critical success, *Nana* has been described by the French historian

Georges Sadoul as "one of the best French films of the later twenties
. . . rich in its combination of the pictorial inheritance of impressionism and the realism of Zola's naturalist tradition, and drawing
its inspiration also in part from the films of von Stroheim and the
German school." In all, an impressive combination. Despite its
great success, however, the profits went to the distributors, not to
Renoir. As a result, aside from his *La Petite Marchande d'Allumettes*
(1927), a gloomy and sentimental version of the Andersen fairy tale,
Renoir had to work for other producers, turning out commercial
films like *Tire au Flanc* (1928) and *Tournoi dans la Cité* (1928), a
medieval melodrama. Nevertheless, his handling of the camera in
these pictures reveals his characteristic sensitivity to mood and atmosphere, a quality of carefully suffused light and soft-focus photography that creates scenes of slow, shimmering beauty. Like his
famous father, Renoir painted with light.

Two other members of Delluc's impressionist group whose work
during the twenties deserves mention here are Jean Epstein and
Abel Gance. Epstein's early efforts, created under the influence of
the avant-garde experiments of the time, include the nervous,
rhythmic, technically masterful *Le Cœur Fidèle* (1923) and a version of *The Fall of the House of Usher* (1928) self-consciously full
of moving cameras, double exposures, symbols, Germanic "effects"
—and moments of haunting imagery. Inspired by the Soviet films
that began to appear in Paris around 1927, Epstein abruptly turned
his back on such art-for-art's-sake experiments. His very next film,
Finis Terrae (1928), was a raw, semi-documentary study of the
kelp gatherers on one of the barren islands off the coast of Brittany.
In it Epstein revealed anew the camera's ability to present remote
patterns of life in human and affecting terms. Though frequently
appallingly clumsy both in cutting and in construction, it built its
story of primitive hardships and rude heroism with dignity and
integrity. Meanwhile, Abel Gance, who had won his title as "the
Griffith of France" with the anti-war film *J'Accuse* (1919), continued
to produce grandiose, ponderous spectacles in *La Roue* (1922) and
Napoléon (1926). It was Gance who, in *Napoléon*, introduced the
huge triple screen, a precursor of today's CinemaScope. Vastly admired, vastly praised in their own land and time, his pictures seem
distressingly empty and sentimental today.

THE ART OF FILM: THE MOVING CAMERA

The moving camera, a technique developed in the German studios of the Twenties, was quickly adopted by Hollywood. In this production shot from Mauritz Stiller's **Hotel Imperial** (1927) the camera is mounted in a scaffold that permits it to rise vertically or roll along with the action.

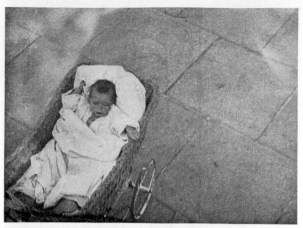

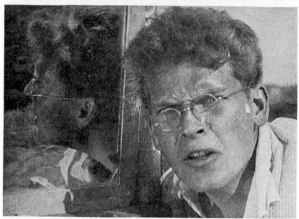

The terror of the Odessa Steps sequence in S. M. Eisenstein's **Potemkin** (1925) was produced through the dynamic assembling of hundreds of separate shots. In these frame enlargements, the power of editing to establish relationships between the rolling carriage, the horror-stricken student and the waiting Cossack with saber poised is clearly illustrated.

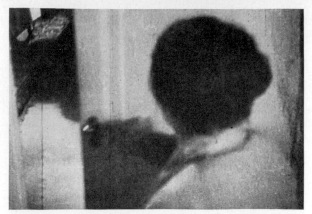

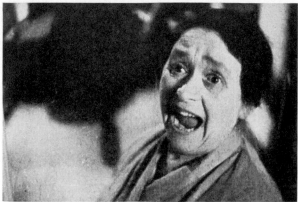

THE ART OF FILM: SOUND MONTAGE

With the addition of sound, the sound track could motivate the cutting. In these frame enlargements from Alfred Hitchcock's **39 Steps** (1935), the landlady discovers a corpse in the hero's room, screams, and her scream merges with the shrill whistle of the train on which the hero is fleeing.

THE SUMMING UP: CARL DREYER

If any single film can be said to characterize and summarize the entire era of production in the twenties, that picture would be Carl Dreyer's *Passion of Joan of Arc* (1928). Though made in France, its cast and crew were extremely international. Its director was a Dane and its star, Falconetti, an Italian. Its gifted cameraman, Rudolph Maté, came from Poland, while its set designer, Hermann Warm, had created the décor for many of the outstanding German films. Inspired by Dreyer, the company worked together with an almost mystic fervor. "It was a film made on the knees," one of Dreyer's assistants has said. Falconetti, who played The Maid, was never able to make another picture, as if drained by the demands made upon her by this extraordinary experience; while Dreyer himself has never again equaled the sustained intensity of his *Joan*. Into it went the distillation of almost a decade of creative film making on the Continent.

The film is centered upon the last day of the trial of Joan and her execution, concentrating within that brief time span a mass of documentation on the trial that had come to light in 1924 and had only just been made generally available. From this material Dreyer drew his portrait of Joan as a simple peasant girl mystically inspired in her heresy. Also from the trial records he established the motives of her tormentors—the compassion of Bishop Cauchon, the sadism of de Courcelles, the prosecutor; and in the case of the British Earl of Warwick, the desire for military revenge. But Dreyer's method for recreating the past was far different from the ordinary historical pageant. To capture a sense of living history, he built his film in a series of huge, revealing close-ups of faces, hands, books, weapons, instruments of torture and symbols of religion. The camera searches constantly for the look, the gesture, the detail that will reveal most tellingly Joan's tragic story, her anguish, her fears and her steadfast convictions. From the very first image—an extended traveling shot across the faces of the priestly jurors—one is startled by the intimacy of these historic figures. Within a moment the spectator has forgotten completely that these are actors; it is less their acting than their eyes, the lines about the mouth, their very gait and carriage that serve as the index to their characters. None of them wore make-up; and Maté's harsh, penetrating photography throws emphasis constantly on the textures of skin and hair, the smooth jowls of a fat priest, the pale eyes of another, the heavy brow of Warwick, the dirt-rimmed fingernails of Joan herself—details that assert the reality of the characters. Similarly, one is always tactilely aware of the cold stone floors, the wooden benches, the rough plaster of the walls, the rude settings of this fierce struggle for the soul of an anguished girl. Even though Dreyer had built a complete town square for the exteriors, the scenic details shown on the screen are the sketchiest—a distant bell tower, the corner of a battlement, a cross against the sky, with the sky always dead white to serve as a neutral background for the earthly drama. The film literally has no long-shots—at least, no long-shots without a huge face in the foreground. By keeping the camera this close to his principals and their surroundings, Dreyer magnified them beyond human dimension, suggesting the monumentality first of his characters and, ultimately, of the trial itself. As the inquisition grows in intensity, tighter and tighter become the shots until, in a final hail of questioning, the camera swoops up to huge mouths that fill the screen, and glimpses of Joan cowering under each new barrage, her hands over her ears, her great eyes flowing with tears.

It is in this sequence that one becomes most disturbingly aware of the limitations of the silent film. The images, for all their power, for all their expressiveness, do not tell all. The subtitles are still necessary; but even when cut to a minimum they are intrusive. They break the rhythm of the visuals, the emotional continuity of the scene. Dreyer seems to have pushed the silent cinema to the very edge of its limitations. It could go no further in baring the soul of its characters; already it was straining toward the added fluency of sound, the added levels of self-revelation possible in speech. Nor was Dreyer himself unaware of this. Sound had already arrived in France as he began work on *Joan of Arc,* and he would have preferred to make it as a talking picture. The financing was not available, however; and what might have been the first masterpiece of the sound era became instead a summing up of all the virtues of silence—the last great work of the French silent film.

THE EUROPEAN AVANT-GARDE

Before returning to the American film, it is important to consider one other aspect of Continental production during the twenties, the work of the avant-garde, the experimentalists. Both individually as artists and collectively as a movement they made a valuable contribution to the development of the art of the film, and especially in France. Officially, however, the movement began in Germany. Two abstract artists, Hans Richter and Viking Eggeling, were wrestling with the problems of developing a visual theme in paint the way a musical theme evolves in the symphony or the sonata. They found a compromise solution in an adaptation of Chinese scroll painting, the gradual unfolding of the scrolls providing movement in time as well as in space. Unfortunately, they discovered, this device provided little control over the pace of the development and afforded no flexibility in surface area. Attracted to the motion-picture medium like so many other young artists of the postwar era, they tried out their ideas in two brief animated films, Richter in his *Rhythmus 21,* Eggeling in *Symphonie Diagonale,* both made in 1921. Richter has remained closely identified with the avant-garde movement ever since. Eggeling, his friend and colleague, died in 1925.

Using masks, cutouts, stop-motion animation and an interesting variety of double exposures, Richter went on to create a whole series of films in which he experimented directly with the camera itself. The tricks, devices, rhythms and effects that he produced were possible only with the motion-picture camera. It became, in effect, the brush of the artist—and he felt it was the proper function of the artist to increase the range and expressiveness of the camera in ways inconceivable in the ordinary, story-telling film. The "absolute film," Richter called his kind of picture, meaning that it had nothing to do with narrative, studio settings or actors. Instead, his films are abstract paintings in motion, a world away from both the intent and the content of the studio film. They explore the changing relationships of shapes moving in space, the effects of varying tonalities of gray, superimpositions of unexpected objects, the distortions made possible by lenses and prisms. Richter was concerned with texture and light, with movement drawn from inanimate things, with rhythms created by cutting.

If any one common purpose motivated all avant-garde efforts of the twenties, it was this desire to break with the increasingly conventional story patterns and forms of the films made for theatrical exhibition, to discover new worlds for the camera to explore. Other artists soon joined Richter in trying their hand at similar abstract, non-objective films. In Germany, Walter Ruttmann worked out a stop-motion technique of improvisation with abstract forms, moving them frame by frame to create fluid, impressionistic designs. It was Ruttmann who created the terrifying dream sequence of the black eagles in Fritz Lang's *Kriemhild's Revenge*. Another prominent artist who contributed films to this movement was Ladislaus Moholy-Nagy, one of the members of the Bauhaus, who made several *Lichtspiele* (light plays) in which forms and textures of specially constructed objects were transformed by shifting lights and shadows. At about the same time, in 1928, Oskar Fischinger began his long series of animated abstractions, using a cartoon technique to create visual accompaniment to standard orchestral works.

By this time the impulse toward filmic experiment had also seized artists in France, with the result that all the main art movements of the twenties—impressionism, cubism, Dadaism, surrealism —were soon to be represented on celluloid. The impressionists had already found their leader in Louis Delluc, who maintained that the story film was itself an art form. His followers looked on movies as a popular entertainment that could be made more artistic by using the camera to capture their own special concepts of mood and atmosphere. In *The Smiling Madame Beudet* (1922), for example, Germaine Dulac chose a fairly conventional little story—an incident involving a romantic middle-aged woman and her stolid, insensitive husband. It was treated almost as an inner monologue on the part of the woman, the camera capturing in shimmering soft-focus photography her mood as she plays Debussy on the piano. In slow motion we see her daydreams of handsome young men stepping out of the pages of a magazine into her arms; in fast motion and with distorting lenses, her vision of her husband angrily banging on the piano, eating his soup or—his favorite prank—threatening to blow out his brains with a revolver. The film conveys, through this mesh of visual fantasy, a full sense of the woman's neurasthenia. By her impressionistic use of the camera, Mme. Dulac proved Delluc's basic contention that a film could be both artistic and entertaining. In Dimitri Kirsanov's poetic, tragic *Ménilmontant* (1925), the subject again was scarcely unique. Two orphaned girls come to Paris where they are both betrayed by the same young man. Kirsanov's nervous, impressionistic camera style, a thing of fleeting glimpses and staccato editing, endowed this drab and sordid story with an intensity that is even today profoundly affecting.

The anarchistic art of Dada, an energetic movement that thumbed its nose at every bourgeois convention during the early twenties, found its first filmic expression in Man Ray's *Le Retour à la Raison* (*The Return to Reason*, 1923). As Man Ray, an American photographer working in Paris at the time, recalls the incident, he made the film overnight for a Dadaist function—a mélange of Dadaist poetry screamed at the top of the lungs, literary works read in pure gibberish and music featuring primarily sirens and bells. His picture was scheduled to close the program. Never having made a film before, he used a technique he had originated in still photography, stretching strips of raw stock upon his work table and sprinkling them with objects lying about the studio—nails, tacks, collar buttons, even the photograph of a nude. As their outlines appeared on the emulsion, he developed the strips and pasted them together as best he could. The effect of this kind of "return to reason," coming at the close of such a session—and heightened by frequent partings of his home-made splices—was to provoke a riot that all but wrecked the hall. It was considered a very successful Dadaist evening.

One true masterpiece of Dada exists, however, in René Clair's incredible *Entr'acte* (1924), with its mock funeral procession patterned after the old French chase films. Commissioned by Rolf Mare as an interlude for his Ballet Suédois, its cast includes the *premier danseur* of the company, Jan Börlin, as well as such prominent representatives of the arts as Erik Satie, Darius Milhaud, Marcel Duchamp, Francis Picabia, Man Ray and Mare himself. Early in the film, amidst the imagery of Paris in miniature and a game of chess played on a rooftop ledge, Börlin is killed by a shot aimed at an amusement park target. The funeral begins with the hearse drawn by a camel, the mourners setting out in majestic slow motion after it. But somehow the hearse breaks loose from its moorings, and soon the entire procession is racing in hot pursuit through the streets of Paris. The leaves blur overhead. Clair cuts in a ride on a roller coaster to heighten the sense of speed, or mounts his camera on the front of a car as it races down a curving mountain road. Suddenly the hearse stops, the coffin falls out, and up pops Börlin smiling and unharmed. Clair punctuated his film with typically Dadaist bits of business. There are repeated shots, photographed from below, of a graceful ballerina whose skirt opens and falls like a lovely flower as she dances—until a final slowly rising shot reveals her to be a heavily bearded gentleman with a pince-nez. A seemingly legless cripple who has been pushing himself along in a cart all during the procession suddenly leaps up and starts running with the rest when the pace grows too fast. Clair's agile filmic imagination responded with characteristic wit to the Dadaists' basic demands for the absurd and the unexpected.

Fernand Léger, one of the first of the cubist painters, turned to film in 1924 with the wholly abstract *Ballet Mécanique*. "To create the rhythm of common objects in space and time, to present them in their plastic beauty, this seemed to me worthwhile," he wrote. "This was the origin of my *Ballet Mécanique*." As its title implies, the film is a dance created out of the movement of levers, gears, pendulums, egg beaters, pots and pans—and incidentally, people whose movements are also mechanized. A girl swinging lazily to and from the camera becomes as automatic as a moving pendulum, an eye opening and closing as mechanical as a piston. Most astonishing of all is a sequence in which a stout washerwoman plods heavily up a steep flight of stairs. Just as she reaches the top, holding out her hand to grasp the rail for the final step, Léger cuts back to the beginning and starts the poor woman again on her weary climb. Twenty-four times he does this, using the same shot over and over and over again at various points in the film until the spectator develops an almost overwhelming desire to hold out his own hand and haul her up the final step himself.

The curious thing is that in this film the machines and other objects set up similar strong physiological reflexes in the audience.

Léger forces the eye to work. Shadows move swiftly across the screen from right to left, from left to right, and the eye follows. A straw hat cuts directly to a ballet slipper, and the eye merges them into a single distending shape. A gleaming pendulum swung directly into the camera lens causes the pupil to dilate and contract, dilate and contract until the rhythm of its movement is felt in every nerve and muscle. Words and numbers are stripped of all their connotations, reduced to meaningless symbols. Circles, triangles and squares, cut rapidly together, create a visual punctuation. Just as Gertrude Stein played with words to find new cadences in the combinations of their sounds, Léger disregarded the function of machinery and the utility of objects to display the abundant vitality of their operation and the intrinsic beauty of their design. Both Richter in *Filmstudie* (1926) and Man Ray in *Emak Bakia* (1927) were to continue this abstract exploration of the object.

An outgrowth of Dadaism, the surrealist movement appeared on the Continent in the mid-twenties. But where Dada was pure anarchy, surrealism had a purpose, a program and a political edge that was sharply Left. One of the most notorious of all surrealist films, *L'Age d'Or,* lashed capitalism and Catholicism so viciously as to provoke a riot when it was first shown in Paris in 1930. The activities of the surrealists spanned the gamut from politics to pathology. Their avowed aim was the destruction of conventional concepts in manners, morals and art, and the exploration of unexpected beauties in the world of the irrational. Through their dynamic manifestoes, through the new vistas they opened up to painters, poets and writers, and through their boundless revolutionary zeal, the surrealists began to attract artists away from all the older movements. By the end of the twenties, surrealism had become the dominant influence in modern art. Inevitably it attracted to it many of the avant-garde film makers. In 1928 alone Man Ray, Germaine Dulac and Jean Epstein added to this latest "ism" such films as *Étoile de Mer, The Seashell and the Clergyman* and *The Fall of the House of Usher*—films based on such pleasant passions as unrequited love, murder, guilt, incest, and general over-all frustration.

Perhaps what most attracted the film makers to surrealism was its heavy dependence on dream imagery. The growing popularity and familiarity of Sigmund Freud's teachings among European intellectuals during the late twenties had created a new and irresistible vocabulary for expressing the subconscious. Sex themes, sex relationships too indelicate to be treated directly on the screen could now be suggested through a kind of visual shorthand that could readily be transcribed by anyone *au courant*. Indeed, watching *The Seashell and the Clergyman* is very much like solving a cryptogram, with Freud holding the key. But such films were more than an intellectual game. They were also a rather disturbing emotional experience, with content more appropriate to the analyst's couch than to the therapy of entertainment. Audiences viewing them often had the uneasy feeling that they were peeping in on someone else's very personal inner turmoil. Because of their nightmare imagery these films could still shock, but the earlier Dadaist exuberance was gone and the atmosphere was now heavy with a referential reverence for everything Freudian.

One of the few surrealist films to avoid this over-intellectual application of Freud was *Un Chien Andalou* (1929) by Luis Buñuel and Salvador Dali. Neither inhibited nor awed by Freud, they plunged into the new subterranean world with curious glee. Like other surrealist film makers, they used dream imagery, but without trying to make it conform to some mechanical, premeditated plan. In preparing their scenario, they pointedly discarded anything which they could either explain or rationalize. Their one aim was to shock and horrify the viewer, and consciously—even self-consciously—they thumbed their noses at all conventional standards of aesthetics, decency and taste. Where others had moved each symbol reverently into place like the pieces of a shadowy jigsaw puzzle, Buñuel and Dali grabbed exuberantly at whatever appealed to them—and the more outrageous, the better.

Its very first sequence sets the tone of the entire film. A young man (Buñuel), stropping his razor, steps out upon a balcony to gaze at the night sky. A young woman is also on the balcony. As a thin sliver of cloud passes across the moon, he takes his razor and in extreme close-up slits the girl's eyeball. Horror falls quickly on horror—a traffic accident, an amputated hand, an attempted rape. As in a dream, there are strange perturbing visions that linger in the mind long after the film has passed: a cocktail shaker that simulates the ringing of a doorbell and, of course, that favorite Dali trade-mark, a swarm of ants crawling out of a hole in a man's hand.

It should not be imagined, however, that *Un Chien Andalou* is composed exclusively of sensational or sickening images. There are glimpses of fragile beauty which are intensified by the horror that surrounds them—moments of wistful tenderness as when the hero, "sixteen years earlier," turns toward the camera remembering what might have been or falls dying in a Corot-like wood. There are many scenes which have the unexpected order and cleanliness, the atmosphere of a Vermeer painting. These seeming inconsistencies were part of the authors' calculated plan to shock the spectator into a new awareness of beauty by laying bare the sensibilities, to create a dream that was, to use the surrealist phrase, "more real than reality."

While the surrealists delved into the imagery of dreams and nightmares, other avant-garde directors found themselves increasingly attracted to the real world that surrounded them. But it was a real world without reality, arbitrarily shaped and organized by the film makers into what they often called "city symphonies," compositions in which documentary shots of ordinary street life provided the raw materials for a semi-abstract *ballet mécanique*. Alberto Cavalcanti's *Rien que les Heures* (1926), an impressionistic study of Paris that sought to capture its characteristic color and rhythms, uses as a recurrent motif shots of a sick old woman creeping ratlike through the back alleys of the city. Contrasts between the lives of the very rich and the very poor were shown but never examined: they were simply part of the texture, part of the kaleidoscope of the city's ever-changing pattern.

At the same time in Germany, Walter Ruttmann produced *Berlin, the Symphony of a Great City* (1927), compressing into five reels a dawn-to-midnight portrait of Berlin. More mechanical, less personal than the Cavalcanti work, its opening passages of a train coming into the city and the shopkeepers raising the iron shutters on their stores beautifully capture the rhythms of a city waking up. In Holland, Joris Ivens made *Rain* (1929), a brief, hauntingly photographed impression of a passing shower in Amsterdam. But the era of the "city symphony" was passing. Stirred by the social realism of the Soviet films, Ivens turned from such pleasant, neutral poetic documentation toward a serious commentary upon society. In his documentary classic *New Earth* (1933), begun in 1929 as a record of the slow painful reclamation of land from the Zuider Zee, he hoped to create an ode to the men whose heroic labor drove back the waters. Its unforeseen ending was tinged with the bitterest irony when in 1933 the Dutch, to protect tumbling wheat prices, dumped their first hard-won harvest back into the sea.

In Germany, Hans Richter had also turned from abstraction to the social scene with an impressionistic study of a horse race, *The Race Symphony* (*Rennsymphonie*, 1928) and *The Stock Exchange* (*Die Börse*, 1929), which described, first through old engravings, then through documentary photography, the history and operation of the exchange. In Ernö Metzner's brief, stark, excitingly photographed *Überfall* (1929), we are back in the world of the German street films of the early twenties; but this time the streets are real, not studio constructed. And the adventures that befall its pitiable hero have none of the comforting reassurance of a happy ending. Another effort to move the camera out of the studio was Billy Wilder and Robert Siodmak's warmly observed *People on Sunday* (*Menschen am Sonntag*, 1929). Photographed in Berlin and its surrounding parks, it is a vivid and frequently poignant little story of four young white-collar workers amusing themselves on their day off. In it appear again many of the details, the rhythmic motifs and experimental techniques of the "city symphonies," but here mobilized for purpose of social comment rather than for purely aesthetic effects.

If the dominating philosophy of the avant-gardists through the twenties had been art-for-art's-sake, the sudden advent of the depression in 1929 soon changed all this. With panic, starvation and ruin all about them, they found it peculiarly inappropriate to be concerned solely with revolving starfish and swinging pendulums, with textures and prisms and the dream world of the subconscious. The penetrating works of Soviet realism had been seen and discussed in the numerous avant-garde *ciné-clubs* that spread throughout the Continent after 1925. For many they were a revelation, a proof that the problems of treating the real world could be as intriguing, as challenging—and as artistically valid—as anything they had done before. After a decade of altering reality, kidding reality, ignoring reality, they suddenly found themselves concerned with reproducing reality, substituting social purpose for aesthetic experiment. For many of the avant-garde film makers—Buñuel, Cavalcanti, Epstein, Ivens, Moholy-Nagy, Rouquier, Ruttmann—the documentary film became the next step. What John Grierson was to call "the dog biscuits of documentary" proved infinitely more attractive to them than a more profitable retreat to the conventions of the studio film they had been railing against for an entire decade.

III

HOLLYWOOD IN THE TWENTIES

BY THE END OF WORLD WAR I, AS WE HAVE SEEN, THE AMERICAN FILM
industry had come to dominate the world market. For movie makers
and movie fans alike, all roads led to Hollywood. Hollywood was
fame and fortune. Hollywood was "the big time." By the turn of
the twenties, Hollywood had become big business as well, the
newest major industry in the United States. Studio stocks began to
be listed on Wall Street in 1919, handled by such respected firms as
J. P. Morgan and Kuhn, Loeb. When United Artists was formed
by Charles Chaplin, Mary Pickford, Douglas Fairbanks and D. W.
Griffith, their combined box-office value had reached the multi-
million-dollar level. The new company could afford to engage as
its legal counsel, at $100,000 a year, William Gibbs McAdoo,
Secretary of the Treasury under Wilson, the man who had floated
the wartime Liberty Loans. In the studios at the dawn of the
twenties, the cost of an average feature with a first-rate star had
reached between $100,000 and $125,000. And this was only the
beginning!

As the companies grew in size and power during the early
twenties, so too did the costs of production. Star salaries continued
to climb, but they soon ceased to represent the sole major item in
a film's budget. Story properties, once an insignificant factor, became increasingly important as the studios acquired the rights to
best-selling novels and hit plays. Expensive settings and costumes,
once used over and over again in picture after picture, were now
designed specifically for each new production. The physical plants

themselves were expanded, the open-air or glass-enclosed stages giving way to huge concrete vaults lit by powerful Klieg lights and arcs; while acres and acres of "back lot" held entire villages, city streets, wharves and railroad stations, awaiting only the designer's touch to transform them into locales appropriate to the current production. Some of the studios even acquired ranches close to Los Angeles, vast areas incorporating many kinds of terrain and kept permanently stocked with horses, cattle, covered wagons and similar properties necessary to the production of Westerns. By the mid-twenties, fully 40 percent of a film's budget went to pay for studio overhead. Naturally, as the lords of such princely domains, the studio heads allocated to themselves correspondingly princely salaries, and men like Adolph Zukor, William Fox, Marcus Loew and Louis B. Mayer emerged as eminent figures on the scene of American high finance.

With hundreds of thousands of dollars—sometimes even millions —riding on each production, inevitably the studios sought to protect their investments as far as possible. A top-ranking star, for example, provided an almost fool-proof insurance of box-office success; and the twenties witnessed a determined effort on the part of the studios to cultivate new stars, new personalities guaranteed to please millions of fans. Whole departments were added to feed tidbits of information to the newspapers and to the increasingly important fan magazines. No stunt was too outlandish, no "angle" too improbable if it might capture a front-page headline or a magazine feature story for the studio's current darlings. Perhaps the most famous publicity man of this era was the irrepressible Harry Reichenbach. It was Reichenbach who, during a temporary lull in Rudolph Valentino's astonishing career, put the Latin lover back on the front page by persuading him to grow a trick beard, kept him there by reporting the protests of women and barbers all over the nation, and capped the climax—months later—with a great public "debearding" performed by representatives of the Master Barbers of America. Such a campaign was typical of the studios' efforts to build or maintain the box-office value of the players they kept under contract. Whole careers were built on what Reichenbach himself referred to as "phantom fame."

And the public responded to this determined star-making. Not only the success but even the approximate box-office "take" could be confidently predicted when films featured such top players as John Barrymore, Rudolph Valentino, Norma or Constance Talmadge, Richard Barthelmess, Milton Sills, Pola Negri or Gloria Swanson. Dozens of other stars, by virtue of some special cuteness or appeal—Clara Bow, Madge Bellamy, Lila Lee, Thomas Meighan, Bebe Daniels, Marion Davies, Jackie Coogan—made any picture they appeared in a reasonably safe investment. The studios, selling their productions on the strength of star names, zealously built up their rosters of reliable box-office performers until, late in the twenties, M-G-M was proud to be identified as "The Home of the Stars." With a contract list that included Greta Garbo, John Gilbert, Norma Shearer, Lon Chaney, Ramon Novarro, Lillian Gish, Marion Davies, Buster Keaton and Joan Crawford, it was by all odds the most profitable, the "safest" studio in the world. The star system, so bitterly opposed by the producers in 1910, proved within ten short years to be the studios' strongest single asset.

Stories, too, provided an important element of control, although inevitably less gilt-edged than star security. Early in the twenties the works of such popular novelists as Blasco Ibáñez, Rafael Sabatini, Joseph Hergesheimer, Booth Tarkington and Elinor Glyn began to appear on the screen with increasing frequency. And the studios watched and charted the public's response to each new offering. When the income at the box office revealed an unexpected interest in some new theme, the studios immediately threw into production whole series of films on the same subject. In short, movies began to run in cycles. The popularity of Cecil B. De Mille's provocative sex comedies just after the war inspired a wave of sophisticated bedroom farces—and incidentally accomplished something of a revolution in screen morality. After the success of Metro's *Prisoner of Zenda* (1922), Graustarkian romances blossomed on every eucalyptus tree. When *The Big Parade* (1925) proved a tremendous hit despite all authoritative insistence that war stories were box-office poison, every studio head immediately ordered a war story.

It was this same desire to give the public what it wanted—or at any rate, what the producers thought the public wanted—that led to the wholesale importation of European talents during the twenties. The public was raving about Pola Negri in *Passion?* Get Negri—and for good measure, her director as well! The Swedes were making great pictures? Get Seastrom! Get Stiller! (For good measure, they got Garbo as well.) *Variety* broke all box-office records for foreign importations? Get Jannings! And Murnau, and Dupont, and Pommer, and Freund, and Leni, and Jacques Feyder, and Lars Hanson, and Einar Hanson, and Lya de Putti. The movement reached avalanche proportions in 1926 and 1927, until the arrival of sound brought it all to a panic-stricken halt early in 1928.

Throughout the twenties Hollywood acquired more and more of the earmarks of a major industry. The roistering, carefree ways that characterized the first two decades of film history became outmoded. A Mack Sennett could no longer arrive in Los Angeles with a camera and a few comedians and consider himself in business. A D. W. Griffith could no longer borrow several thousand dollars from friends and turn out a *Birth of a Nation*. With the acquisition of huge, costly plants in which to make the movies, and vast networks of theaters in which to show them, production had entered a new era—an era of cost accounting, of profit-and-loss statements, of cautious budgeting and cut-throat competition. There was still a virtue in flinging money around. It made good copy. It added to the glamour. It helped to sell tickets. But the money had to be flung with a certain accuracy. It had to get more money. So Hollywood went on paying weekly kings' ransoms to its top stars, paid small fortunes for popular novels and plays, ransacked the European studios for talents guaranteed to please the audiences throughout the United States. Hollywood had become big business—and its first dictum of business was, "The customer is always right."

SIN, SCANDAL AND THE HAYS OFFICE

When the movies first went West, around 1910, Los Angeles boardinghouse keepers were advertising, "Rooms for rent—No dogs or actors allowed." By 1919, mollified by the $20,000,000 the studios were spending annually in salaries and the $12,000,000 for raw materials, this attitude had changed considerably. The natives were now pointing with civic pride to the new Chaplin studio on La Brea Avenue, to Carl Laemmle's Universal City just beyond

Cahuenga Pass, to the way Paramount had expanded from a barn to whole blocks of stages in the very heart of Hollywood. They welcomed the tourists who came to gape at these new wonders of the Western world, and turned their fretful attention to the problem of the thousands of teen-age girls who were pouring into town from all over the country. The vast salaries of the stars, the well-publicized glamour of their lives, led many a small-town belle or beauty-contest winner to head for Hollywood convinced—or at least hoping—that she was the next Mary Pickford or Mabel Normand. Shady "talent schools" added to the influx. Most of these eager young hopefuls were doomed to the cruelest disappointment—or worse. Accounts of vice in Hollywood began to crop up in the newspapers and magazines of America.

Through the early years of the twenties these stories gained substance. The pattern was obvious. Too many people had got too rich too quickly. Unprepared for sudden wealth, unaccustomed to open adulation, many of them began to react like children in a room full of bright new toys—only, their toys included high-powered cars, bootleg whisky, expensive women and drugs. They believed their own publicity. They were kings and queens who could do no wrong. But the very glamour that the publicists had gone to such lengths to concoct proved to be their undoing. The eyes of America were focused upon Hollywood. Newspapers assigned reporters to cover the Hollywood beat, reporters who were not content merely to reprint the studio handouts. They pointed to the rising incidence of prostitution, of studio "call girls," casting couches and orgiastic parties. By 1922 Hollywood had gained the reputation of being not only the most glamorous but also the most corrupt city in the United States.

Part of this can, of course, be explained by the general relaxation of morals following World War I. Hollywood, its publicists argued, was just like any other big city in America, but with the spotlights turned on—and everything magnified by the sudden eminence, the sudden wealth. At the same time, Hollywood in its films was reflecting the change in moral standards. Sophisticated sex had suddenly become big box office, whether in comedies or played straight. Drinking scenes abounded in pictures, despite the recent adoption of Prohibition. Divorce, seduction, the use of drugs were presented in film after film as symbols of fashionable living. America was launched upon an era of high living, and Hollywood was pointing the way. But in towns and hamlets across the nation, the new morality had not taken hold. Many who went to the movies were genuinely shocked by what they saw there—and concluded that what they saw was representative of Hollywood alone.

Their suspicions seemed fully confirmed late in 1922 when, within the space of a few short months, there came in quick succession the sordid "Fatty" Arbuckle rape case, the mysterious and still unsolved murder of director William Desmond Taylor (implicating both Mary Miles Minter and Mabel Normand, two top box-office stars of the time), and the shocking revelation of handsome Wallace Reid's addiction to drugs. Public indignation swelled to alarming proportions. Although their outrage was directed against individuals (Arbuckle and Miss Minter never appeared in films again; Mabel Normand's career was permanently damaged), the protests rapidly assumed the form of a threatened national censorship of all movies. Official and unofficial busybodies suddenly found all sorts of sinister, obscene or salacious material within even the most innocuous pictures, while organizations with their own special axes to grind (such as the temperance societies) lent their voices to the outcry. Everything was condemned, the good with the bad.

Faced with such an overwhelming public protest, the producers ran for cover. Though at one another's throats in the course of normal business, the major studios came together in the face of the common danger to form the Motion Picture Producers and Distributors of America. Organized late in 1922, the M.P.P.D.A. had two immediate tasks: to fight off national censorship and to set up a policy of self-censorship and regulation of their own films that would convince the public of the producers' good faith. Members of the Association pledged themselves to abide by a set of standards mutually drawn up and agreed upon by all. And to enforce this agreement, to supervise its operation, the movie companies appointed as head of the new organization—their "Czar"—Will H. Hays, a Presbyterian elder, Chairman of the Republican National Committee and at the time Postmaster General in the Harding administration.

The choice of Hays proved a wise one. His prominence made him an impressive buffer against outraged citizen groups. Through him the motion-picture producers bought a measure of both political and religious protection. Certainly, they averted national censorship by the federal government. On the other hand, state and municipal censor boards mushroomed on all sides, groups with full local authority to cut offensive sequences out of pictures or even to ban them entirely. Rather than oppose these groups—which in the light of public opinion at that time might have been foolhardy —the Association set about codifying the most frequent censor complaints from all over the country, and advised their member companies just how far they dared go. As the memory of Hollywood's scandals began to fade, however, and the organized voices of protest died to a murmur, the producers became bolder again, often putting on the screen scenes of nudity and debauchery that would be utterly unthinkable today. The M.P.P.D.A.—"The Hays Office," as it came to be known—"advised" its hotly competitive members whenever one of their pictures became too rough, and spent much of its time trying to build good will around the country by assuring civic groups that movies had become cleaner and more moral than ever before.

More moral they certainly were, although in a peculiarly inappropriate sense of the word. The Hays Office promulgated among its producers a theory of "compensating values" to be followed in the production of their pictures. According to this quaintly Victorian theory, if virtue were always rewarded and sin punished, if good eventually triumphed and the evildoer perished miserably, the laws of God, man and the drama would be simultaneously satisfied. The studios were quick to perceive that what this meant, in effect, was that they could present six reels of ticket-selling sinfulness if, in the seventh reel, all the sinners came to a bad end, and that they could go through all the motions of vice if, at the last moment, virtue triumphed. Censors around the country might continue their snipping of occasional scenes, but who could object to movies in which "morality" was so eagerly espoused?

With such a mechanical yardstick as a guide to "jazz age" modes of conduct, there was an inevitable duality, a conflict between thought and deed that made most pictures of the era seem basically dishonest. Thus Clara Bow might invade a bachelor's apartment, dance suggestively in front of him, drink his cocktails and leap provocatively into his bedroom. But when the bachelor made the proper responses, she promptly ran home to mother. Or if a young couple snatched some seemingly illicit hours of love-making, a last-minute "switch" would show that they had been secretly married all the while. Drinking, petting, orgiastic parties—all of these were shown in gleeful detail, but always with a compensating cluck of disapproval to indicate how proper and moral the producers really were.

DE MILLE AND THE NEW MORALITY

The films of Cecil B. De Mille during the middle twenties reveal clearly how superficial, even hypocritical, this new morality essentially was. Apart from D. W. Griffith, De Mille was the best known and most successful director of the era; and no small part of his success lay in his shrewd ability to change with the changing times. He had realized at the very outset of his long career that the public's taste, as revealed at the box office, was the producer's surest guide, and he patterned his films accordingly. His first picture was a Western, *The Squaw Man,* made early in 1914 (and one of the first features produced in Hollywood). It proved an immediate hit, and De Mille quickly made several more movies in the same vein. When in 1915, however, the industry switched to a policy of filming stage plays with famous Broadway stars, De Mille promptly put into production a version of *Carmen* starring the noted diva Geraldine Farrar—and for added insurance, a movie favorite, Wallace Reid. Highly praised at the time for its "theatrical effects," *Carmen* established De Mille as a "name" director. Then, as the war clouds began to gather, he nimbly turned out a series of violently patriotic pictures—*Joan the Woman* (1917), *The Little American* (1917), *The Whispering Chorus* (1918).

Even before the war had ended, De Mille sensed that the demand for such films would soon be over. In casting about for a new popular subject, he released in quick succession a series of pictures in sharply different styles and noted carefully the public's reaction to each of them. The swing, he decided, was toward a more sophisticated approach to sex; and in a long series of modern comedies produced between 1919 and 1923 De Mille catered to the postwar trend toward higher living, heavier drinking and looser morals. Dwelling on both the fashions and the foibles of the fabulously rich, he opened up a whole new world for the films, a world that middle-class audiences, newly won to the movies by the luxurious theaters then springing up, very much wanted to see. *Male and Female* (1919), *For Better, for Worse* (1919), *Don't Change Your Husband* (1919), *Why Change Your Wife?* (1920), *Adam's Rib* (1923)—all promised the last word in elegance, refinement and *haute couture*. And by linking fashion with fashionable undress, De Mille was able to provide something for everyone.

William de Mille, Cecil's brother, who plowed the same field with perhaps less box-office approbation but certainly with greater taste, has amusingly described the elements of a typical De Mille success of this era. In his *Hollywood Saga* he wrote: "He made of the bathroom a delightful resort which undoubtedly had its effect upon bathrooms of the whole nation. The bath became a mystic shrine dedicated to Venus, or sometimes to Apollo, and the art of bathing was shown as a lovely ceremony rather than a merely sanitary duty. Undressing was not just the taking off of clothes; it was a progressive revelation of entrancing beauty; a study in diminishing draperies. The theme was that in no stage of dress or undress, whether in the bathroom, the kitchen, the ballroom or the bedroom, need a woman look unlovely. To this end underclothes became visions of translucent promise, and nightgowns silken poems set to music." De Mille turned out over a dozen pictures in this vein, celebrating the dawn of the jazz age, relishing the sybaritic opulence of the world of fashion and the new freedom from moral restraints. In all of them he condoned the new morality, the flouting of conventions, the hedonistic scramble for wealth and pleasure at any price.

And then, with a conjuror's quickness, he reversed himself. In *The Ten Commandments* (1923) De Mille climbed the mountain with Moses and thundered forth his "Thou shalt not's." The reformers' chorus had reached his ears; the Hays Office had been formed; the women's clubs throughout the land were making known their dissatisfaction with the amount of sex and sin they found in their theaters. The time had come for a change—of sorts. Sex would still sell tickets, but flagrant immorality would not. De Mille solved this dilemma in *The Ten Commandments* by simply masking the kind of sex melodrama that was typical of the era—the very kind that the women's clubs were protesting against most violently—behind a biblical façade. The modern part of the film presents Rod La Rocque as a building contractor who goes to the dogs over sultry Nita Naldi, skimping on the concrete for a cathedral he was building so that he might buy more silks and jewels for his charmer. All of this, of course, De Mille detailed with his customary relish for spicy high life. For the early reels, however, De Mille skipped back to Exodus to demonstrate, parable fashion, the moral lesson, "Thou shalt not kill," "Thou shalt not commit adultery," "Honor thy father and thy mother . . ." For all the impressiveness of such scenes as the Israelites crossing the Red Sea, their wanderings in the desert and Moses receiving the Law on Mount Sinai, none of this had much intrinsic bearing upon the modern story in the film. They were merely the cloak, the smoke screen for the sort of thing that, despite the hue and cry, De Mille felt sure would still make money. And who would dare to protest against a picture that included Moses and the Ten Commandments? Characteristically, even while Moses was receiving the Commandments on the Mount, De Mille made the most of the bacchanalian revels around the Golden Calf below.

Perhaps because De Mille has always trumpeted his moral lessons more sententiously than any other director would dare, his films have also carried more sensational sinning than anyone else's. Better than any other director of the era, he seems to have apprehended a basic duality in his audiences—on the one hand their tremendous eagerness to see what they considered sinful and taboo, and on the other, the fact that they could enjoy sin only if they were able to preserve their own sense of righteous respectability in the process. Certainly, De Mille gave them every opportunity, and his pictures won the crowds. For years *The Ten Commandments* remained among the top-grossing films; while *The King of Kings* (1927), his first all-out essay in the field of sin-cum-morals spectaculars, is still being shown. No one could have remained so completely successful for so long without a shrewd knowledge of his audience—and more than a little willingness to pander to the least common denominator of public taste.

What De Mille did with his special showmanlike flair, most of the other directors of the mid-twenties were also doing, somewhat less flamboyantly, as a matter of studio policy. The Hays Office approach to morality, combined with the mass production of entertainment in the new, huge film factories, resulted in a preponderance of formula pictures—complete with built-in happy endings and an automatic meting out of just desserts to all the "heavies." Their characters were stock and immediately identifiable: the hero was a clear-eyed, clean-profiled young man; the heroine, blond and virginal; the villain was dark, mustached and addicted to cigarettes; the "other woman" was also dark, exotic, given to low-cut gowns and long, long cigarette holders. There was, in addition, generally a middle-aged comic-relief couple. The action was as obvious and predictable as the gaslit melodramas of the late 19th century. Early in the film the hero discovers his girl friend in some terribly compromising position nastily contrived by the villain; there follows a long misunderstanding between the two, the hero's chance discovery of the truth, the punishment of the villain and the big reconciliation scene. Originality lay in dreaming up some especially salacious situation for the misunderstanding and a sufficiently gruesome fate for the "heavies." By comparison, the European films, with no such standardized patterns, with no artificially imposed moral ending, inevitably seemed far more honest and true to life.

HOLLYWOOD IMPORTS "ART"

By the same token, when European directors were brought to Hollywood and asked to adapt their techniques to Hollywood formula stories, the results could not help seeming superficial and forced. The techniques of the Swedish, Danish and German studios had been devised to explore and create the realities of character and background; now they were being used to disguise—or at least, to make more palatable—patently false stories about improbable people. The surprising thing is that so many of the Europeans succeeded as well as they did.

F. W. Murnau, for example, in his first American film, *Sunrise*
(1927), created at least one-half of a masterpiece. Based on Hermann
Sudermann's *A Trip to Tilsit*, it tells of a young peasant seduced
by a vamp from the big city vacationing in his village. They plan
to murder his wife and run away together. But the wife becomes
suspicious and frightened of her husband just as he realizes that he
still loves her and can not kill her. After several clumsy, tentative
efforts at a reconciliation, there is a touching scene of their spiritual
remarriage as the two sit quietly together in a cathedral. The film
might well have ended right there were it not for the fact that the
moral code had still to be fulfilled: the husband had yet to suffer
for his philandering, the vamp had still to be punished for her
vamping. Consequently, the plot takes a sudden, melodramatic turn.
On a trip across the lake, a squall springs up and the newly reconciled couple are separated as the wife is swept out of the boat into
the storm-tossed waters. After a night of agonized search, the re-
morseful husband in a fury turns on his seductress, beats her and
sends her packing even as the wife is discovered safe and alive. This
formula finale quite destroyed the extraordinary depth of character Murnau had created in the first part of his film. These are
no longer people but puppets who have been jerked into a conventional—and singularly unconvincing—moral ending tacked on
to satisfy the demands of the box office and the official custodians
of the public's morals.

The same rigid formula surrounded many of the great European
actors brought to this country during the late silent era. Certainly,
the greatest of these was Emil Jannings, imported on the strength
of the box-office success of his German films *The Last Laugh* and
Variety. In both of them he had played tragic old men broken by
Fate. It was inevitable that Hollywood should cast him again in
the same type of role; what is also clear is that to capitalize on his
European reputation the Paramount script writers deliberately
prepared for him a series of pictures in which tragedy struck in
retribution for the old man's sexual peccadilloes. In *The Way of All
Flesh* (1927), *The Last Command* (1928), *The Patriot* (1928) and
Sins of the Fathers (1929), Jannings was made to feel every sling
and arrow of outrageous fortune that the Paramount script department could devise. He sinned, and he suffered—but his suffering

was so arbitrarily conceived, his retribution so mechanical that not even the great Jannings could conceal the basic falseness of both the stories and their characters. For *The Way of All Flesh* and *The Last Command,* he won the first Academy Award ever given for acting; in neither of them, however, was he able to achieve the sense of truth that had made his old doorman in *The Last Laugh* or his betrayed husband in *Variety* so deeply affecting. Indeed, not until Jannings returned to Germany and made *The Blue Angel* (1930) was he again able to create a role in which tragedy was not confused with maudlin melodramatics, in which disgrace and death came as the inevitable consequence of a shattered life and not the smug punishment of a facile moral code.

Despite their obvious differences in temperament, technique and aesthetic outlook, the Hollywood studios continued to woo the European film makers in great numbers. Nor was their motive purely commercial, although the invitees were invariably the stars and directors of commercially successful pictures. But through the rising tide of film criticism, the idea was getting around that the film was a popular art—one of what Gilbert Seldes had aptly termed in 1924 the "seven lively arts." The films from Europe were being raptly hailed as "artistic." If, the producers reasoned, a European picture could be both artistic and successful at the box office, why not bring its makers to Hollywood to introduce such profitable "art" into American movies? They had no objection to their pictures being "artistic"—not if they showed a good profit as well. The trouble was that, too often, they viewed artistry in terms of camera angles, tricky lighting and specially constructed settings, a technique that was applied to a story rather than to the outgrowth of the story itself. They set their expensive importees to work on formula films, and were naïvely astonished to discover that the pictures they turned out were neither artistic nor, in many cases, commercially successful.

Nor did the native American directors escape these Continental influences. The moving camera, the low-keyed lighting, the slow, deliberate tempo and greater emphasis on pictorial composition all recommended themselves to producers seeking to make their pictures look more impressive and artistic than (too often) they really were. Once the European invasion had begun in earnest, many Americans changed their style overnight. Clarence Brown, who had made his reputation directing Will Rogers' typically American comedies, turned *Flesh and the Devil* (1927) into a full-blown imitation of the Germans, right down to a duel scene staged in picturesquely framed silhouettes. King Vidor's *La Bohème* (1926), Frank Borzage's *Seventh Heaven* (1927), Victor Schertzinger's *Forgotten Faces* (1927), Josef von Sternberg's *Underworld* (1927) and *The Last Command* (1928) all reveal the German influence at its strongest. Whole passages were frequently copied from the German originals; plot incidents were often suspiciously similar; and the increasingly daring camera angles, the extended use of dissolves, the efforts to eliminate or minimize subtitles were similarly German-inspired. Sometimes these effects clashed badly with American themes and formula plots, or with the acting styles of American players. But happily the American directors proved a resilient lot. They not only imitated the new styles; they quickly absorbed them and transformed them from tricks and mannerisms into a strong and highly fluent technique. Indeed, solely in terms of technique, the American films of the late silent era compare favorably with pictures made anywhere in the world.

THE COWBOYS AND THE CLOWNS

There were two major American film forms that had sufficient vitality and integrity to withstand the effects of the foreign invasion throughout the twenties—the slapstick comedy and the Western. Immensely popular all over the world, there was no need to make these more "artistic" by following the latest European fashions. At once too successful and too lowly to warrant such improvements, they were considered "just entertainment." They bore no weighty messages, inspired no cults or schools of aesthetics. But they delighted audiences, both here and abroad, because they were so purely and simply American. Unconsciously, unobtrusively, they epitomized all that was best in America without the slightest trace —or intention—of self-righteous sermonizing. It was there in the ingenuity and eternal optimism of the comics. It shone again in the cowboys' spirit of adventure as they rode the plains in search of the next frontier. To tired Europeans, to cramped city dwellers, to small boys, to people everywhere these films carried the message of the American dream. In them the humble triumphed over their powerful adversaries, the weak outwitted the strong—and always with the implicit promise of riches, freedom and happiness for all. As seen in the Westerns, the world was a simple place for men with the pioneer virtues of honesty, courage, a taste for adventure and a quick trigger finger. The world was a crazy place, said the comics, but with a little faith, a little luck, a little ingenuity—and possibly a couple of prat-falls—it was anybody's oyster.

Perhaps because they were so consistently popular on both sides of the water, perhaps because they had no counterparts abroad— whatever the reason—the Westerns and the comedies were permitted to go their merry ways free of foreign entanglements. It is not surprising, therefore, to discover that these two indigenous forms during the twenties produced not only some of our best directors— men like Frank Capra, John Ford, George Stevens, William Wyler and the many disciples of Thomas H. Ince and Mack Sennett—but also all that is most characteristic of American film style. The speed, the tightness, the brilliant timing of action and editing, the steady progression of story line, the clean, bright photography and, on a somewhat more technical level, the knowing use of camera lenses and filters came primarily from the practice and practitioners of these two schools. A Tom Mix horse opera or a Buster Keaton two-reeler may not have seemed as "artistic" as some of the European imports, but often it had a lot more to do with the genuine art of the film.

Despite their basic simplicity, however, both the Westerns and the comedies changed with the times. Early in the twenties the Westerns veered sharply away from the realistic portrait of frontier life that characterized the William S. Hart pictures. Hart's hero had been the Good Bad Man—a hard-drinking, hard-riding, hard-shooting he-man, often an outlaw, often the enemy of law and order, but always true to the moral code of the old frontier. After the First World War, Hart's descriptions of the West, although essentially truer than anything that has been done since, came to be dismissed as "old-fashioned." Moviegoers—even Westerners— preferred the more romantic version of the West they found in the films of Tom Mix, Buck Jones, Hoot Gibson and Ken Maynard.

Now the hero was a Good *Good* Man, riding the range to protect the weak and bring the outlaws to justice. He never drank, seldom smoked and—unlike Hart with his blazing six-shooters—he used his pistols only when forced to. He was quick on the draw, tall in the saddle, handy with his rope and fists. He lived cleanly and simply, and whatever complications beclouded his life usually came from the machinations of greedy big-city "varmints"—nothing that couldn't be straightened out by the final reel. This was the Old West as city folk, country folk and the cowboys themselves idealized it, and each new Western of the period added its embellishments to this popular myth. Their plots were formula, but their tempo was fast, their technique clean and uncomplicated, and they quickly found their niche in the production scheme of the twenties. Although rarely playing the big theaters in the larger cities, they had a virtually assured audience in the neighborhoods, in rural and Western towns and in theaters abroad. Consequently, every studio then (as now) produced a certain number of Westerns every year. Inexpensive to make, they were one of the few staples in the business.

It was in this spirit that Paramount in 1923 undertook to make *The Covered Wagon* from a *Saturday Evening Post* story of the cross-country trek of the Forty-niners. Impressed with its epic qualities, however, the studio decided to raise the budget and permit director James Cruze to take his cast on location to Snake Valley, Nevada. Here, against the natural splendors of butte and mesa, amidst the same hot sands and torrential rivers that had harassed our ancestors a hundred years ago, Cruze produced a film of tremendous sweep and spirit. Despite the shallow romance that served as its story thread, the essential grandeur of its theme, the vigor and humor of its frontier types and—perhaps above all—the beauties of its backgrounds at a time when pictures were being made increasingly inside a studio, immediately won for *The Covered Wagon* tremendous critical acclaim and, no less important, tremendous support at the box office. By combining the stars and production values that assured big-city box-office appeal with the sure-fire small-town pull of any Western, Paramount had come up with a new kind of winner—the "big Western." For years *The Covered Wagon* remained among the top money-makers in the business.

When the following year Fox produced John Ford's *The Iron Horse* (1924), which romanticized in a similar fashion the construction of the first transcontinental railroad, its resounding success proved that the "big Western" was no mere flash in the pan. It still remains the most consistently lucrative of American film forms, occasionally raising the routine horse opera to the level of a national epic.

In the meantime the slapstick comedy was also undergoing a transformation. Two-reelers persisted right through the twenties under the aegis of such Masters of the Revels as Mack Sennett, Hal Roach and Earle W. Hammons of Educational Pictures (a singularly inappropriate soubriquet). All of them, however, were losing their top comics, their best directors, their cleverest gag men to the feature films. In the face of rising production costs and spiraling star salaries, the shorts field could no longer afford to pay its talent on a scale comparable to the big studios. One by one, the best comedians of the prewar era deserted the two-reelers for feature production. Charlie Chaplin, Harold Lloyd and Buster Keaton led the list, both in popularity and ability, closely followed by such notable clowns as Harry Langdon, Raymond Griffith, Larry Semon, Louise Fazenda and the charming, devil-may-care Mabel Normand. Happily, they carried the slapstick spirit with them.

In their feature-length comedies, each presented a precise and carefully prepared character to the public—generally, some version of the little fellow that everything happens to. But their variations were as different as the performers themselves. Chaplin's tramp had pathos; there was a deeply sentimental vein running through all his films. Keaton was straight-faced, a poignant automaton caught up in a world that was beyond his control or understanding. Lloyd's eager, bespectacled youth understood everything perfectly well but was physically unable to do anything about it—unless Fortune favored him, as she invariably did in the end. Harry Langdon was a baby-faced innocent hopelessly trying to act grown up. Only Raymond Griffith, dapper in spats and silk hat, attempted sophisticated slapstick on the screen, but even he made all the blunders and *faux pas* that harass the average man.

As a group, these feature comedies of the twenties were far more concerned with character and comic incident than with the camera itself. They had little of the effects photography of the early French chases, few of the mechanical gags and tricks of the Sennett Keystones. Their camera work, simple and straightforward, had no room for European angles or fancy lighting; their editing, fast and clean, had no need for European theories. This does not mean, however, that their technique was in any way inferior to that of more portentous productions. To make a sight gag pay off properly required a perfect placement or movement of the camera in relation to its material. To build a laugh to its climax demanded a precision of editing, an acute sense of timing that was nothing short of prodigious.

The camera work throughout Harold Lloyd's *The Freshman* (1925), for example, is superbly functional. The film begins with an iris-shot of Harold in collegiate sweater and cap leading a rousing football cheer, then opens out to reveal that he is leading the cheers in front of his bedroom mirror. In a rash attempt to win friends at college, he offers to stand treat for ice-cream cones; a moving camera keeps pulling farther and farther back as more and more undergraduates join the merry throng en route to the ice-cream parlor. During football practice Harold lands heavily on a tackle dummy—and the camera catches him at just the right angle to imply that he has rather grotesquely broken his leg. In fact, the finest gag in the whole picture depends completely upon a skillful placement of the camera. Harold goes to a ball wearing a new tuxedo that has only been basted. His tailor accompanies him, in case of an emergency. And, inevitably, the emergency arises. Harold, bashfully talking to a girl, twists a bit of thread about his finger— and with each twist the seam of his trouser leg falls open wider. Discovering his error, he beats a hasty retreat to a ringside table where, hidden behind the portieres, the tailor awaits him. Harold sits at the table with his girl, his chin resting on his hands, his legs extending out to the tailor behind him. But the tailor is subject to sinking spells, and chooses just this moment to faint dead away across Harold's legs. The camera moves around front to show Harold sinking lower and lower at the table, still chatting, still smiling and desperately pretending that it is all the most natural thing in the world.

Complementing this unobtrusive but superbly functional use of the camera was an equally incisive editing technique. During the twenties, and primarily owing to the influence of the Chaplin films, the comedy tempo had tamed down considerably from the frantic pace of the Sennett Keystones—although still recognizably swifter than that common in drama or melodrama. A shot remained on the screen just long enough to make its statement—perhaps even less if the gag dictated an accelerating speed. The best comedy directors, aware of the importance of tempo in their films, customarily made more and shorter takes than directors in the other forms, leaping from set-up to set-up in order to provide the editors with a wide variety of angles from which to build a scene. The swift pace of the silent comedies was sustained by the swift changes of point of view, the hail of shots that made up each brief sequence.

Nor were the possibilities of building or prolonging a gag through editing overlooked. The pool game in Buster Keaton's *Sherlock Junior* (1924) affords a brilliant example of this technique. Each shot, each incident plants a laugh that contributes to the cumulative effect of the scene through adroit cutting. The villains, intent on murdering Keaton, invite him to join them at pool—with one of the balls loaded with enough dynamite to blow him to smithereens. To make doubly certain of his sudden demise they also hold in readiness a poisoned glass of wine, while over an inviting chair is poised a mighty halberd triggered to drop the moment he sits down. Cutting from one bit to another—Keaton almost sitting on the chair, almost drinking the wine, almost hitting the loaded ball, the reactions of the villains, the superb innocence of Keaton—the scene builds to a climax that invariably reduces the audience to near hysteria.

In an equally brilliant and even more subtle way, Frank Capra built up one of the comedy scenes in Harry Langdon's *The Strong Man* (1926), prolonging it and capping its climax with a particularly masterful bit of editing. A beautiful but quite large blonde has fainted in Langdon's arms. The little fellow must carry her from the street up to her apartment on the first floor. He tries to carry her but can barely lift her off the sidewalk, much less up an entire flight of stairs. Instead, he places her in his lap and goes up backward step by step. Unfortunately, a workman has placed a ladder at the head of the stairs and Langdon, all unawares, continues to edge his way right on up the ladder. The audience, of course, knows that the moment Langdon and the girl reach the top of the ladder, they both will go over, and the nervous laughter begins to build. Playing on this sense of anticipation, Capra photographs the impending disaster from the front, then from the side, then from the rear. By overlapping each cut just a little, he is able to hold off the moment of climax, the moment when the anticipated will happen and the laughter will cease. It is doubtful if Capra had even heard of Eisenstein in 1926, but he too had mastered the technique of extending time. For comic effect.

Such achievements in editing and photography, however, provide only one aspect, one clue to the great art of the silent comedies. Better than any other form, they also created and sustained a sense of character of such deep persuasiveness that audiences literally could not imagine a smiling Buster Keaton or Harold Lloyd without his glasses. They were characters fashioned out of a thousand richly photogenic details—Chaplin's shuffling walk, Langdon's dead-white face, Keaton's staggering physical dexterity in juxtaposition to his immobile features, the ingenuous smile lurking behind Harold Lloyd's spectacles. These men built their characters for the camera, developing mannerisms and traits that, magnified on the screen, admitted the audience into the secret places of their souls—Langdon's curious, tentative half-gestures of guileless friendship, Lloyd's nervous gulp before tackling the impossible. The scripts, the stories, the plot incidents were all devised to further this one character who reappeared in film after film. Even the world through which they moved was a fantasy of their own creation—the echo of a London slum in the Chaplin films, a world of overwhelming mechanical monsters for Keaton, a cold and insensitive place for Langdon's innocent. In their unique ability to make believable both their private worlds and their public characters lay the genius of the silent slapstick clowns.

To these comedians should be added the name of Douglas Fairbanks. Fairbanks, of course, was not a clown; but he created a true comic character in his earliest films, while his swashbuckling romances of the twenties were invariably enlivened by wonderful sight gags that made splendid use of his incredible athletic prowess.

Brought to Hollywood in 1915 as one of more than sixty Broadway stars scooped up by Triangle in its effort to make the movies "legitimate," he quickly established himself as one of the few real finds in a largely unpopular package. His first pictures were either directed or supervised by D. W. Griffith, who despaired of ever making a film actor out of him. Then Fairbanks had the good fortune to pass, by default, into the hands of John Emerson and Anita Loos. They sensed the brash optimism, the healthy good humor of the man, and set about creating a screen character that incorporated not only his athletic ability but his bracing personality as well. They fashioned for him a series of modern comedies, many of them directed by Emerson, that gave free rein to his natural vitality, but at the same time edged him toward the character once described by Alistair Cooke as "the popular philosopher." During the last half of the teens, Fairbanks became above all the laughing debunker of fads and false standards, the city man who longs restlessly for the West and freedom, the ardent booster of clean living and simple common sense. In most of his comedies he appeared as the "average American male," and the touchstone of his success was the flattering assumption behind all his films that "if I can do it, you can do it too."

Then, on the threshold of the twenties, Fairbanks, like De Mille, underwent a sudden change. But where De Mille had embraced the new, sophisticated pleasures of wine, women and wrong, Fairbanks the optimist, the exponent of clean living and thinking, could take no such course. His alternative was to turn away from the confusions and upheavals of the postwar world, back to a simpler time when the moral values that the Fairbanks screen character had always embodied might have a clearer justification—back to those days when all injustice and oppression stemmed not from the ways of the world but from the malevolence of some master villain, and when a healthy aristocrat with high principles and a lively sword could right all wrongs. In the place of a brisk, clean-shaven, ablebodied young American stood now a mustachioed D'Artagnan, a ringleted Robin Hood, a bronzed Thief of Bagdad. And in place of the everyday, workaday backgrounds of the early Fairbanks films appeared huge, handsome settings and elaborate mechanical and photographic effects. Through these serio-comic extravaganzas, however, Fairbanks continued to romp with his inimitable, balletic grace. His utter ease inspired not envy but admiration, and his screen character rivaled only Chaplin's in world-wide popularity.

SOPHISTICATION AND STYLE: CHAPLIN AND LUBITSCH

The films of Fairbanks, like those of the great slapstick clowns, appealed to people everywhere because their characters were universally recognizable. Fairbanks typified the ideal lover, romantic, nimble and gallant; the others were slightly battered, slightly foolish, often pathetic creatures, but beneath their tattered vests beat the heart of Everyman. What the world recognized and loved was their essential humanity. After World War I, however, another form of film comedy began to appear with increasing frequency. It was the comedy of manners, which specialized in depicting the escapades and excesses of the very rich. Rarely hilarious, not even necessarily funny, it was a wry way of looking at the complications of leisured living. This type of comedy had long been popular in the theater; and when the middle-class audiences began flocking to the movies it soon became a popular film form too. This was the field that Cecil B. De Mille dominated so profitably from 1919 to 1923. He and his imitators turned out countless glittering comedies of high society. Soon other directors were bringing to this form the incisive style and true sophistication that De Mille himself lacked. When in 1923 Charlie Chaplin turned to the comedy of manners in *A Woman of Paris,* and when Lubitsch, soon after, produced *The Marriage Circle,* they introduced a new spice and sparkle that was both more comic and essentially more filmic than anything De Mille had done.

Chaplin seems to have produced *A Woman of Paris* partly to satisfy his own desire to direct a comedy without the tramp character, partly as a gesture to his veteran leading lady, Edna Purviance, whom he rewarded with stardom in the film's title role. (Chaplin himself appears in the picture only for a moment, disguised almost beyond recognition, as a wildly gesticulating porter at a French railway station.) "A drama of fate" was Chaplin's own subtitle for the film—and despite his light, sardonic treatment of its theme, he clearly regarded it as a work with deep social implications. His foreword read, "Humanity is composed not of heroes and villains, but of men and women, and all their passions, good and bad, have been given them by God. They sin only in blindness, and the ignorant condemn their mistakes, but the wise pity them." His story, in outline, might have been the scenario for a tear-jerking tragedy, but his outlook, his approach transformed its bathos into an ironic comedy. Marie St. Clair (Edna Purviance), a girl from a small French village, runs off to Paris after an unfortunate love affair. A year later, Marie has become part of the smart world of Parisian society, the mistress of a suave philanderer, played by Adolphe Menjou (who tootles a saxophone in his more debonair moments). One day, by accident, she meets her former fiancé, now a struggling artist, and commissions him to paint her portrait. Their old love revives, but in the meantime the artist has learned of her new relationship. He persuades her to leave the philanderer but, overhearing a fragment of a conversation, becomes convinced she never will. The young man commits suicide—just as Marie discovers that her fickle lover is planning to marry another. Destitute and disillusioned, she returns to her native village to live with the mother of her dead fiancé.

Chaplin took this maudlin story and by his witty, sophisticated direction turned it into a comedy that set new standards for those American directors who had until then been copying the tasteless excesses of the De Mille extravaganzas. His picture had *style*—the sly implication of an immoral or risqué situation rather than the forthright presentation of one. The nature of the relationship between Menjou and the girl, for example, is adroitly defined when he calls on her at her apartment, then casually goes to her bureau and takes from it one of his handkerchiefs. Again and again Chaplin showed his preference for a tickling innuendo of sex rather than the naked fact. A thinly clad dancer at a Parisian revel twirls out of her costume, but as the last veil falls the camera shows only her twinkling feet. Chaplin filled his picture with wry little incidents that delighted the moviegoers of that day, as when the girl angrily flings a diamond necklace out of the window while Menjou, amused, blows on his saxophone; then, noticing a tramp picking up the jewels in the street below, Marie promptly forgets her pique and dashes out after him to retrieve them. Especially prized was

the ironic note on which the picture ended, a rarity in films of
that time. Chaplin dismissed the entire little tragedy with a cool
cynicism that startled his audiences. The girl, now back in the
country, is riding on a haywagon while Menjou passes by, unknow-
ing, in his high-powered car. "By the way, whatever became of
Marie St. Clair?" his friend asks him. Menjou merely shrugs as
cart and auto continue on their separate ways.

It is impossible to imagine how *A Woman of Paris* would look
today. As a matter of strict policy, Chaplin has refused to permit
this, or any other of the productions that he controls outright, to
be revived or even preserved by any film society or library. All too
often, however, pictures that have played an important role in the
evolution of the techniques of the medium prove strangely disappointing on re-examination. The freshness, the originality, the
sense of innovation that gave them their initial excitement have
disappeared. Their cinematic devices have been copied in film after
film. Their technique, once daring and original, has become part
of the standard repertory of directorial tricks. The same might well
be true of Chaplin's film. In 1923 audiences were tremendously
impressed when a passing train was suggested by the reflection of its
lights on Marie's face. Critics also made much of the fact that the
young artist's suicide was not actually shown but implied in the
close-ups of faces reacting to the sound of the shot. Today, such
effects are commonplace. But it was this kind of inventiveness, this
kind of awareness of the possibilities of the camera for sly, indirect
statement that made *A Woman of Paris* such a revelation in its day.
Several of Chaplin's assistants on the film—Monta Bell, Harry
d'Abbadie d'Arrast and Eddie Sutherland—went on to become directors, working in this same genre and carrying through the same
cinematic suggestiveness that Chaplin had introduced. Many others
were to follow his lead, the most important of them being the erst-
while "humanizer of history" in the German studios, Ernst
Lubitsch.

Lubitsch had been brought to this country in 1923 by Mary
Pickford to direct her in a grand-scale costume drama *Rosita*. It was
a costly flop. Released less than a month before *A Woman of Paris*,
its failure followed by the immediate success of the Chaplin film

seems to have given Lubitsch his cue. He had directed comedies in
Germany before producing the pageant films. Now he turned back
to comedy—and specifically to the comedy of manners, which he
spiced with his own highly Continental brand of humor. His first
film in this style, *The Marriage Circle* (1924), reached the screen
less than four months after the Chaplin film, notably similar to it
both in theme and technique. Contemporary critics made the inevitable comparisons (predominantly in Lubitsch's favor), and
Lubitsch was launched on a new career and a new style in which
he was to remain pre-eminent until his death in 1947.

It should not be imagined, however, that Lubitsch was a mere
imitator of Chaplin. In picture after picture he gave evidence of
his own highly cinematic imagination—*Forbidden Paradise* (1924),
Kiss Me Again (1925), *Lady Windermere's Fan* (1925), *So This Is
Paris* (1926)—until even the general public became aware of the
"Lubitsch touch," that naughty twinkle of sophisticated Continental
wit. He was a master of understatement, compressing in a single
humorous bit of business his own shrewd insights into the ways of
the world. In one of his pictures, for example, Lubitsch wanted to
suggest that a man had grown bored with his wife, that their relationship had become quite matter of fact. The husband's attitude
was made abundantly clear in a brief sequence showing the couple
leaving their apartment for a dinner date. As they enter the elevator,
he is wearing his hat. The car stops a few floors below and a pretty
girl gets on. He takes off his hat. For *Lady Windermere's Fan,*
Lubitsch invented a sequence at a racetrack in which all sorts of
intimate relationships are implied by glances, by quickly averted
eyes, knowing smiles and whispers that neither are explained by
subtitles nor require explanation. Undoubtedly one reason that
Lubitsch became so popular with the smart set during the twenties
—and with other directors as well—was his skillful skirting of the
censor problem. He implied censorable volumes, but offered precious
little that anyone could actually cut out.

Lubitsch also, virtually singlehanded, accomplished a revolution
in American set décors. Prior to *The Marriage Circle,* almost any
decoration would do—either wholly nondescript for a routine film
or, for a more elaborate production, rooms choked with bric-a-brac
and overstuffed chairs set off by loudly ornamental drapes and busy

wallpaper. Lubitsch cleared away the clutter, providing clean playing areas for his action. The advantages were so immediately apparent that they were incorporated into the majority of pictures from that moment on. Few directors, however, have quite his ability to use settings to their fullest advantage. To Lubitsch, a door was always more than simply a way to get into or out of a room: it was a way to end an argument, to suggest pique or coquetry or even the sexual act itself. Corridors, stairways, windows—all had a dramatic function in the Lubitsch films. With his sparkling wit and polished technique, he soon became the leading exponent of the comedy of manners, inspiring and influencing a coterie of directors that came to include such talents as Mal St. Clair, Lewis Milestone, Wesley Ruggles and Frank Tuttle. For them, style was the thing, and the "Lubitsch touch" can be found echoing through such pleasant trifles of the late twenties as *The Grand Duchess and the Waiter* (1926), *Beware of Widows* (1927), *Two Arabian Knights* (1927) and *Gentlemen Prefer Blondes* (1928).

TYPECASTING THE DIRECTOR

During the twenties the studios developed a strong tendency to "type" their directors as thoroughly as they were typing their stars. Lubitsch and his followers were the "smart" directors, invariably assigned to situation comedies. "Gag" comedies went to men like Clarence Badger, H. C. Potter, Erle Kenton, Marshall Neilan and Charles Reisner. Frank Borzage, George Fitzmaurice, Edmund Goulding and Henry King were known for their ability to direct "women's pictures" (a term that, considering the films, women should find particularly offensive); Lambert Hillyer, J. P. McGowan, Al Rogell, Richard Thorpe and William Wyler directed Westerns; action stories were assigned to men like Jack Conway, Victor Fleming, William K. Howard, Rowland V. Lee, W. S. Van Dyke, Raoul Walsh and William Wellman. Tod Browning, who directed most of the Lon Chaney thrillers, found his special niche in tales of horror and the macabre. Rex Ingram, whose *The Four Horsemen of the Apocalypse* (1921) catapulted Rudolph Valentino to fame, became identified with colorful costume romances. Invariably, perhaps even inevitably, the studios saw to it that a director who had scored a hit with one type of film followed it up with more of the same.

As for the general public, there were few directors it either knew or cared about. The studios were selling stars, and their publicity machines were geared to glamorizing their contract players. Nobody saw a director, so why bother about him? The exceptions were men who, either as their own producers or as potent box-office draws, were able to focus some of the attention upon themselves. Perhaps the prototype for all directors, in the public's mind, was the colorful Cecil B. De Mille, who saw to it that his name made the headlines almost as often as the leading stars of the day. He gave the first interview held in an airplane, was the first director to use a megaphone on the set, the first to install a loudspeaker system to address his players. In his broad-brimmed hat, open-throated shirt, riding breeches and leather puttees, De Mille was as familiar a figure in the fan magazines as John Gilbert or Clara Bow. If, however, anyone were asked to name the greatest American director during the early part of the twenties, the answer would still have been D. W. Griffith, even though his name above the title of a picture was no longer a guarantee of box-office success. When Griffith went to work for Paramount in 1925, this order of billing was reversed. Chaplin, of course, was known primarily as an actor, but most people were aware that he also directed his own productions. Ernst Lubitsch, with his perennial cigar, had become fairly well known outside the industry by the late twenties when his ceaseless stream of hit films had elevated him to the slender ranks of the star directors.

Few contemporaries shared either the fame or the independence of these top men. Most directors were simply assigned by their studios to work on a picture, whether its theme was one that interested them or not. The studios had the power to alter their work in any way they saw fit. Few were even accorded the privilege of cutting their picture the way they thought it should be. There was a constant tug-of-war between the "front office" and the directors, who were often bitterly convinced that the studio heads knew nothing about movies and cared less; while the producers, keeping track of the mounting costs on their pictures, resented every change or retake that might send the budget up higher. Perhaps there was some truth in the directors' charge that the producers were secretly craving to be "creative" when they carved up their pictures, but it was equally true that the producers were the men closest to the public and its tastes and therefore most aware of what constituted good box office. At M-G-M during the late twenties, for example, the youthful Irving Thalberg was considered almost infallible in his knowledge of what would please the public. He had full authority to re-edit any film produced on the lot—and has been credited with saving many a picture from disaster. It was the producer's job to make a successful film, and to make it on a budget, whether this meant hurting the director's artistic sensibilities or not. It was also the producer's job to find stories that would assure big box-office receipts, whether they happened to please a director or not.

Fortunately, many of the directors of the twenties were incredibly versatile, able to change their styles to keep abreast of changing public tastes and interests. James Cruze, for example, followed up his big Western, *The Covered Wagon,* with films as diverse as the comic *Ruggles of Red Gap* (1923), the satiric *Beggar on Horseback* (1925) and the sophisticated *Waiter from the Ritz* (1926) before returning to the epic style in *Old Ironsides* (1926). King Vidor, after a number of modest, essentially realistic studies of the contemporary American scene, directed in quick order the epical *Big Parade* (1925), an operatic adaptation of *La Bohème* (1926) and a swashbuckling romance, *Bardelys the Magnificent* (1926). He then turned back to the contemporary scene with *The Crowd* (1928), a heart-warming story of the tragedies and joys of an ordinary man, a clerk in a big office. It was Vidor's masterpiece of the silent era. Herbert Brenon's directorial assignments ranged all the way from sentimental fantasies like *Peter Pan* (1925) and *A Kiss for Cinderella* (1926) to the romantic heroics of *Beau Geste* (1926). A similar versatility is to be found, on occasion, in the works of John Ford, Henry King, Marshall Neilan and many more of the top directors of the twenties.

It was this versatility, above all else, that kept them in the front ranks of the directors. Highly skilled and thoroughly trained through long years of apprenticeship under such masters as Griffith, Ince and Sennett, they had the innate ability to rise to an important theme or a dramatic story. Unfortunately, too few of the films of the period placed such demands upon them. A director was expected to keep the pot boiling with whatever kind of picture was currently in vogue. Consequently, most of them were known as craftsmen rather than as artists, as types rather than as creative personalities.

THE REBEL: VON STROHEIM

And yet the American producers seem to be irresistibly drawn to strong, creative personalities, to artists with a flair for using film to make a highly personal observation on life and the ways of the world. Invariably, the studios put them under contract with considerable fanfare, then proceed to force them into the mold of their own preconceptions of what constitutes good box office. Ironically, what brought them to the producers' attention in the first place was often some independent, off-beat production that was successful precisely because it lacked the conventional themes or values that producers considered "safe." Once under contract, however, a director was expected to conform. For individualists like Erich von Stroheim, Robert Flaherty and Josef von Sternberg, such conformism was difficult if not impossible. The running warfare that always existed between the "front office" and the creative personnel burst forth with added intensity upon such people. For them, there were only three alternatives: complete withdrawal, an uneasy truce or abject surrender.

For von Stroheim, throughout the twenties, it was an uneasy truce. This Austrian-born jack-of-all-trades first won attention during World War I as an actor. In film after film—including Griffith's *Hearts of the World* (1918)—he portrayed a be-monocled, sadistic, lecherous Prussian officer. When he turned to directing with *Blind Husbands* (1919), he again played in it his favorite role, "the man you love to hate"—a professional adventurer, blackmailer and seducer. As an Austrian officer who captivates the bored wife of an American businessman, von Stroheim openly suggested that a married woman whose husband is too busy to be romantic has every right to seek love elsewhere. This attitude, one of the first statements of the new postwar morality to be made in films, shocked many and delighted more. In the ensuing hullabaloo it became one of the box-office hits of the year.

The success of *Blind Husbands* prompted Universal to grant von Stroheim greater leeway on *The Devil's Passkey* (1920) and

Foolish Wives (1921), films that virtually repeated both the theme and the setting of his first picture. All of them were marked by their director's passion for a detailed realism of background and atmosphere. In making *Foolish Wives,* it was reported that he had installed a complete electrical wiring system for each room of a dummy hotel that appeared briefly in the film. In another picture he ordered $10,000 worth of special medals to be struck off for officers in the army of a mythical kingdom, had the royal crest embroidered on his players' underclothes, held up a costly scene for hours until the smoke from a single chimney was rising to his satisfaction. Such details, he argued, may not have added to the physical reality of his pictures, but they did enhance the feeling, the atmosphere that he was trying to create. Given an unlimited budget on *The Merry-Go-Round* (1923), von Stroheim permitted his passion to exceed his discretion and the picture was completed by another, less exacting director. Even so, his reputation was such that the newly formed Metro-Goldwyn studio promptly offered him carte blanche to make for them any picture he wanted. The story that he chose was Frank Norris's *McTeague.* And the film he made from it was *Greed* (1924), one of the great triumphs of American realism.

Written in 1899, at the dawn of the muckrake era of American literature, *McTeague* was a vast, sprawling novel about money and its power to corrupt. Von Stroheim, apparently, had been attracted to it soon after his arrival in America, drawn as much by the harsh realism of Norris's descriptive passages as by the theme itself. Preparing his own adaptation, he proposed to film the book scene by scene, line by line, in the very places so vividly described by the author. Accordingly, he moved his cast out of the studio and up to San Francisco, the locale of the novel. There he commandeered whole blocks of houses, even tearing out the walls to facilitate the photographing of interiors. At one point, a funeral procession had to pass a certain window at a given moment. He tied up city traffic for blocks around until he got the scene just as he wanted it. For the finale, set in Death Valley, he took his principals, Gibson Gowland and Jean Hersholt, into the Valley itself, where they worked for days under the blazing sun. Hersholt has recalled the experience as the most grueling of his long career.

The ironic—and tragic—outcome of all this heroic effort is that von Stroheim's *McTeague* never did reach the public. He had made a film 42 reels long (about ten hours) and suggested to Metro that they release it in two parts. The studio refused. Von Stroheim cut it to twenty reels (or approximately the length of *Gone With the Wind,* released by the same studio just fifteen years later). Again Metro refused, this time taking the film away from him entirely and turning it over to June Mathis, a staff writer, to reduce and re-arrange into a more marketable form. The result was *Greed,* in ten reels. Von Stroheim consistently refused to look at it.

Perhaps the full measure of the greatness of *Greed* is to be found only by comparing what remains with the original novel. So faithful was von Stroheim to the text that his intentions are clear in every scene, even though the structure of the story and the development of its characters were destroyed in the course of re-editing his footage. Such minor characters as the swaggering, cigar-smoking charwoman, or the stooped, evil-looking old junkman, for example, seem much too strongly drawn for the insignificant roles they play in the film, unless one remembers that originally they were the principals in an important subplot, the story of a mysterious treasure to which the charwoman holds the key. Similarly, the strange, sym-bolic inserts of hands caressing golden cups and fingering sparkling jewels which seem so out of keeping with the rest of the picture were actually salvaged from the avaricious dreams of the old junk dealer. Occasionally in the lengthy subtitles used to supplant eliminated action, abrupt references are made to ideas and incidents for which there is no longer any visual preparation. Worst of all, the Mc-Teagues' descent from middle-class respectability to the direst poverty and Trina's disintegration from a gentle, loving wife to a slovenly, penny-pinching shrew takes place so quickly, so baldly as to tax one's credibility. Small wonder that *Greed* remains one of Metro's most expensive flops. It confused and bewildered audiences through what it didn't show—while what it did show is mighty strong meat even for audiences today.

It is strong because von Stroheim, as he said in his foreword to the picture, refused to "truckle," refused to make the kind of picture that ordinarily charmed or amused movie audiences night after night. What he put on the screen was the truth as he saw it— the truth in Norris's characters, the truth of Norris's setting, the truth of Norris's theme. Even in its bowdlerized version, *Greed* remains one of the most uncompromising pictures ever made. Because von Stroheim built his effects primarily within his individual shots rather than through the juxtaposition of shots, the subsequent pruning and condensation could not wholly destroy his intentions. And such sequences as the wedding of Mac and Trina and the grotesque banquet that follows, as well as the scenes in which Mac abandons Trina and subsequently murders her, appear to have been lifted intact from the original versions. As a result, the film still reveals his harsh power and brilliance, his consistency, his integrity, even though the final assembly was the work of another hand. Through shots of disturbing intensity, he created an overwhelming sense of the psychological reality of the slow-witted McTeague, his miserly wife and their false-hearted friend Marcus. And verifying and substantiating these people at every point was a realism of background ordered and organized down to the last minute detail. An old saloon and a butcher shop, the exterior of a church on a Sunday morning, the meeting of Mac and Marcus at the Cliff House with crowds strolling the boardwalk below—all of these made *Greed* appear to be a documentary shot in San Francisco in 1900 instead of 1924. But von Stroheim's technique extends beyond the mere appearance of authenticity. His backgrounds play an active role in his creation of character and incident.

Just what all this means in terms of creating tension and atmosphere in a picture is perhaps better illustrated than described. His was not a technique that can be explained in terms of daring editorial juxtapositions, moving cameras or artistic lighting. It lay instead in the patient invention and addition of thousands of small, skillful, knowingly arranged touches that gradually built up around his scenes and his characters an indefinable aura of reality that made them palpable and alive. The clearest example of the effectiveness of this method is to be found in an almost forgotten von Stroheim film, *Queen Kelly* (1928), which he directed for Gloria Swanson. Shooting had proceeded at his customary leisurely, precise and expensive pace when the advent of sound brought the production to a halt. The producer felt it prudent to stop and salvage what he could. Von Stroheim was removed from the picture and another director brought in to add the few finishing scenes. And one can tell at precisely what moment the new hand took over. The cast is the same, the settings the same, but somehow the pressure has suddenly been taken off. The force, the emphasis, the insistence on minute detail to build character and background alike have suddenly disappeared, and within a moment the picture turns flat and ordinary.

In the four years between *Greed* and *Queen Kelly*, von Stroheim produced only two more films, *The Merry Widow* (1925) and *The Wedding March* (1928). He had become identified as a difficult and expensive director, two unforgivable traits in an industry where mass production and economy had become the watchwords. Not only that, but much of his work—the orgies in *The Merry Widow*, the unsavory sex relationships in *The Wedding March* and *Queen Kelly*—was at once too crude and too sophisticated for the increasingly morals-conscious Hollywood. Von Stroheim suddenly found it impossible to get work. Hopefully he persisted in his efforts throughout the early thirties, writing original scripts and offering to direct them. Only one studio gave him a chance—and even it backed out before the picture was half completed. The film, *Walking Down Broadway* (1932), emerged mutilated beyond recognition. Finally, disheartened, he returned to acting, eventually moving to the Continent. His few American roles since that time—Rommel in *Five Graves to Cairo* (1943), the ex-director Max in *Sunset Boulevard* (1950)—remind us again what a talent we lost. Von Stroheim was a temperamental, tempestuous but authentic artist; Hollywood preferred a more conventional type.

THE POET: ROBERT FLAHERTY

If von Stroheim was driven out of Hollywood, Robert Flaherty voluntarily withdrew. Throughout his career a wholly individualistic film maker, Flaherty had won the attention of Hollywood with the international success of his first film, *Nanook of the North* (1922), a record of Eskimo life based on his own observations as an explorer in northern Canada. At just about the time that von Stroheim was doing *Greed* for Metro, Paramount dispatched Flaherty to the South Seas with instructions to "bring back another *Nanook*." For Flaherty, however, all film making was an exploration. He consistently refused to work from prepared shooting scripts or preconceived stories, preferring to discover his theme, his characters, his settings with his camera. For almost two years he remained in Samoa, talking with the natives, learning their legends and superstitions, observing the daily minutiae of their lives. Only after he had become completely familiar with their ways did he begin to make his picture, shooting it, developing it and editing it himself on the primitive island of Savaii. When finally he presented his completed *Moana* (1926) to the Paramount executives, they were bitterly disappointed. They had envisioned a South Seas equivalent of *Nanook,* complete with typhoons, sharks and more than a touch of dusky romance. Instead, all they got was the loveliest idyll of the silent screen.

What Flaherty had discovered in his slow, patient way, was the astonishing fact that for the Samoans there existed no classic conflict between man and nature. The gods were kind. Food was plentiful, and the raw materials for clothing and shelter grew on every tree. He might have dramatized the influence of traders and missionaries upon a fast-disappearing culture but, as he often said, he had no interest in showing what these people had become under the demoralizing influence of the whites. As far as possible, he recaptured the past, the essence of Samoan life, and placed at the very heart of his film the agonizing ritual of the tattoo which every Samoan youth must undergo to establish his manhood. In the absence of natural hardships, Flaherty found, the Samoans had themselves invented pain to test and protect the fiber of their stock. With this sequence as his key, all the rest of the incidents fitted into place—gathering coconuts, fishing, hunting the wild boar, the women at their cooking and cloth making, the ceremonial feasts and dances. All of these Flaherty observed with a loving eye, over and over again until he had become so completely familiar with them that he could anticipate their movements with his camera, creating the same sense of time-worn smoothness that one associates both with perfect craftsmanship and with ancient ritual. Each frame from *Moana* is almost classically beautiful, with its finely modeled photography (it was the first film to use the new panchromatic stock) and soft, lush lighting. But it is no mere gallery of beautiful stills. Flaherty understood, better than many of his studio contemporaries, the function of edit-

ing and camera placement to keep his film alive, and had an uncanny instinct for the most telling detail and the most revealing
angle for every shot.

Yet Paramount chose to sell this film as "the love story of a
South Seas siren," and the presentation houses brought in bevies of
hula-hula girls as a fitting prologue. Flaherty himself objected to
these tactics, arguing that there were whole sections in every community which, while not habitual moviegoers, could certainly be
brought out in support of a special feature like *Moana*. Furthermore, he proved it by personally selling his picture in six of the
most difficult territories that Paramount's distribution department
could designate. He organized his audiences through the schools,
the Chambers of Commerce, the literary, civic and social clubs in
each community. But, as the Paramount officials firmly pointed out,
it was their job to sell people on the idea of coming to the movies
fifty-two weeks out of the year to see *ordinary* pictures, not once
in a blue moon to see a *Moana*. The "South Seas siren" campaign
went on. (Parenthetically, when Sir Laurence Olivier's *King Henry
V* was brought to this country in 1946, its sales campaign was
handled in precisely the manner that Flaherty had prescribed
twenty years earlier—and it became one of the most successful
foreign films ever to be shown in the United States.)

For a time Flaherty continued in his efforts to convince the
studios that pictures could be made—and sold—his way. At one
point M-G-M sent him back to the South Seas, to Tahiti, to co-direct
with W. S. Van Dyke an adaptation of Frederick O'Brien's *White
Shadows in the South Seas,* a book that he very much admired.
When it turned out that what the studio really had in mind
was a sultry melodrama, Flaherty withdrew. Fox allowed him to
work up a plan for a film on the Pueblo Indians, then lost enthusiasm for the project. In 1929 Flaherty joined forces with F. W.
Murnau, the director of *The Last Laugh* and *Sunrise,* and again set
sail for the South Seas, this time as an independent producer-
director. Although a less likely team could hardly be imagined—
Murnau the studio perfectionist, Flaherty the patient, poetic student
of real people and real settings—the two men remained close
friends even through the throes of picture making. Actually, *Tabu*
(1931), the product of their joint effort, emerged as far more typical

of Murnau's work than of Flaherty's. It had an abundance of
Flaherty's visual magic—laughing girls sliding down a waterfall,
majestic shots of trees, and seas and natives in all their innate
dignity. But there are also cardboard moons and rubber sharks and
a story as patently manufactured as the props. Murnau died soon
after in a tragic motor accident, while Flaherty went on to England
to work with the new documentary movement then forming about
John Grierson. He never returned to the studios, remaining identified with documentary film making until his death in 1951.

THE COMPROMISE: VON STERNBERG

Like Flaherty, Josef von Sternberg also attracted the attention
of the major studios with an independently produced, low-budgeted,
decidedly offbeat production, *Salvation Hunters* (1925). Essentially
a mood piece, it told a simple story of three lost souls, an unemployed, ambitionless family who live on a river scow until a
procurer offers them a room in exchange for the wife's services.
Only when the scabrous villain mistreats their child does the
husband recover his self-respect sufficiently to face up to the man.
The implication is that, having taken this first step, he will lead his
little family on to happiness. The film's dominant mood of hopeless,
spiritual defeat was heavily underlined by long, almost static shots
of the principals drooping in attitudes of picturesque despair. Over-
symbolic details like the great, swinging dredge that scoops up mud
from the bottom of the river into the sunlight, or the billboard
reading "Here your dreams come true" behind the scene of the
fight, were directorial touches that made a profound impression in
their day. Although considerably less impressive when seen today,
Salvation Hunters was hailed as an artistic achievement without
peer, an American film that rivaled anything then being imported
from Europe—an opinion confirmed (and perhaps influenced) by
the ardent championing of the film in Hollywood by two such
influential figures as Charles Chaplin and Douglas Fairbanks.

Both the film's critical reception and its low budget recommended von Sternberg to the major studios. He made one film
(never released) for Chaplin, another for M-G-M, then moved to
Paramount where, to everyone's astonishment, he scored an im-

mediate box-office success with the gangster melodrama *Underworld* (1927). No small part of its popularity was due to Ben Hecht's timely script, virtually written off the headlines of the daily papers. But to this von Sternberg added his own strong pictorial sense, his knowledge of editing, and his ability to draw vivid performances from his casts. George Bancroft, the rugged star of *Underworld*, was a von Sternberg discovery; he never excelled his work as the brutal, blustering gangland chief. Von Sternberg quickly repeated his success with another hard-hitting crime picture, *The Dragnet* (1928), then turned back to the depressed mood and milieu of *Salvation Hunters* in the extraordinary *Docks of New York* (1928). Brilliantly photographed, with deep, glistening blacks and an amazing tonal range of grays and whites, it depicted the dingy bars and rooming houses of the waterfront in a series of strongly composed, superbly atmospheric scenes. Bancroft was starred again, this time as a roistering stoker off a tramp steamer who saves a despondent girl from suicide by promising to marry her, though fully intending to ship out again next day. Von Sternberg's handling of the waterfront types, his skillful use of the sordid settings and, above all, his masterful changes in mood and tempo as the story progresses reveal his artistic growth, his complete grasp of the essentials of his art. Unfortunately, *Docks of New York* did not repeat the resounding commercial success of his previous pictures. Apparently its lack of conventional romance or thrills was too much for audiences expecting another underworld thriller. Von Sternberg was faced with the age-old dilemma of whether to direct artistic failures or less artistic hits.

For a time, von Sternberg continued to waver between the two. *The Last Command* (1928), starring Emil Jannings, reaffirmed his ability to ring the bell at the box office; while *The Case of Lena Smith* (1929) revealed again his masterly ability to create atmosphere and scenes of matchless pictorial beauty—but at the expense of story values and audience interest. As his Paramount contract neared its end, he was happy to accept Emil Jannings's offer to direct him in *The Blue Angel* (1930) in Germany. It proved to be one of the most creative films of the period, filled with movement and a richness of pictorial elements at a time when most movies were stagnant and flat. *The Blue Angel* was an immediate hit in Germany, and almost as successful in its American engagements where, despite the language barrier, it played in the largest theaters. When von Sternberg returned to Hollywood, it was with a new star and a new contract—to direct the films of his German discovery, Marlene Dietrich. He became her mentor, her Svengali. But as Dietrich's star rose, von Sternberg's descended. In a series of handsomely photographed, artfully composed static films, von Sternberg grew increasingly absorbed with the beauty of his images, with Dietrich glimpsed through a clutter of nets and fans and draperies. The style, the sharpness, the originality that had distinguished his earlier, silent efforts degenerated into tricks and mannerisms. He had made the commercial compromise. John Grierson wrote his sad epitaph as early as 1932. "When a director dies," said Grierson, "he becomes a photographer."

In short, throughout the twenties, as the studios became more industrialized, more set in the commercial patterns of producing and marketing their films, they had less room for the highly gifted individual unwilling or unable to accept these patterns. A Chaplin or Fairbanks could afford to ignore them. A De Mille could thrive on them. But they smothered D. W. Griffith and Mack Sennett, drove off von Stroheim and Flaherty, sucked down von Sternberg. Nor were these men alone. Others, less prominent, faced the same alternative of making pictures that were considered commercially safe by the "front office" or not making pictures at all—at least, not in Hollywood. Either way meant an indescribable loss to an industry that is also an art. For the vitality of the film grows out of the daring, the experiments, the originality of the individual artist. Whenever purely commercial considerations are permitted to check that growth, the loss is incalculable—to the art, to the filmgoers, and to the industry itself. It is a shocking waste of the movies' greatest single natural resource, the man of talent.

THE END OF THE SILENT ERA

Despite the fact that Hollywood's films dominated the screens throughout the world, despite the complex mechanisms that had been perfected to make, sell and exhibit them, the industry was ex-

periencing a profound uneasiness during the late twenties. Attendance had fallen off. The radio and the automobile presented new and
powerful competition. The era of Coolidge prosperity had expanded
the income of the average family who could now afford more
elegant entertainments than the movies. At the same time, some of
Hollywood's most reliable, most expensive contract players were
losing their box-office appeal; while the fight for theaters, carried
on during the boom of real-estate values, had saddled many of the
studios with properties costing far more than their actual worth. As
early as 1926 one important company, Warner Brothers, found itself
on the verge of bankruptcy. In desperation they invested their
remaining fortune in a daring novelty—the Vitaphone. In August
of 1926, they introduced a program of Vitaphone talking and singing shorts, and the feature *Don Juan* with a synchronized musical
accompaniment. On October 6, 1927, they presented the first talking
feature on Broadway, Al Jolson in *The Jazz Singer*. Its immediate
success marked the end of an era.

In the United States the silent film died with alarming sudden-
ness, although it lingered considerably longer abroad. Warners
followed *The Jazz Singer*—essentially a silent picure with musical
accompaniment and four talking or singing sequences—with a
cheaply produced "quickie," *The Lights of New York,* the first full-
length, all-talking picture. It was released in July, 1928. In the
meantime, however, every major studio, jealous of the S.R.O. signs
that appeared wherever *The Jazz Singer* was showing, began to
convert to sound as rapidly as possible. Talking sequences were
inserted into pictures that had gone into production as silents. Each
studio rushed into production its own first "all talkie." Within a
single year, every important picture "talked" (although often a
silent counterpart was made for showing in houses not yet wired for
sound). By the middle of 1929, even this protection was no longer
necessary, so swift and final was the transition to sound. At the end
of 1928, of the 20,500 theaters in the United States, only 1,300 had
sound installations. By the end of 1929, there were over 9,000
theaters equipped to handle the new medium. And these included,
inevitably, all the key houses in the big cities around the country,
all the theaters on the major circuits and the important neighborhood houses. Theaters that found the sound systems too expensive,

or had waited too long to put in their order for an installation, soon discovered that it was more economical simply to board up until they too could show the new talkies. Overnight the public seemed to have forgotten that the silent film ever existed.

But if the silent film died swiftly, it did not pass unmourned. Critics and film lovers alike recognized that in a mere three decades the silent film had developed into a subtle, complex and highly expressive art form. They also recognized that the new emphasis on dialogue was robbing the screen of its visual impact. For the sake of a novelty, these critics argued, the discoveries of an entire generation of creative artists were blindly being ignored.

Many of the studio heads were quite willing to agree that talkies were simply a thing of the moment—but at the moment, they pointed out, it was the thing that the public wanted. Indeed, those producers who hesitated to bow to this obviously popular demand, preferring to hold off until the whole thing blew over, were soon out of business entirely. The public's enthusiasm for sound was so strong that attendance leaped from 60,000,000 paid admissions per week in 1927 to 110,000,000 in 1929. When the stock market crashed in the fall of 1929, the impetus provided by the introduction of sound proved strong enough to carry the industry safely through the first years of the depression. By 1930 the silent film was a thing of the past, Charlie Chaplin's *City Lights* (1931) and the Flaherty-Murnau *Tabu* (1931) coming as last, lovely reminders of an art that was no more. By the start of the thirties, in every film-producing nation the studios had converted to sound. It was to take them many a year, however, before they could regain the artistry and power of the best of the silent era.

IV

THE MOVIES LEARN TO TALK

THE SILENT FILM HAD CREATED A WORLD OF PERSUASIVE REALITY despite the absence of voices and the verifying clangor of natural sound. Indeed, much of the art of the silent film lay in the invention of means to circumvent these artificial limitations. Then, suddenly, they were all removed, and the sounds of the real world had become as much a part of the film as its sights. The audience's wholehearted acceptance of the new order, despite all the grave headshakings of industry leaders, despite the shocked protests of the film aestheticians, suggests a certain, dimly sensed inadequacy in the silent film itself. The public positively reveled in the new sensation, the opportunity to hear its favorite stars talking and singing, to hear the crack of a pistol, the roar of a motor or even the ring of a telephone. It was exactly like the first years of the movies all over again. Then, anything that moved was fascinating; now, the most commonplace noises, the most obvious dialogue acquired a marvelous quality simply by virtue of its coming from the screen. From our vantage point today, we can see clearly that the original objections of the aestheticians were based less upon the nature of the sound film than upon the crude excrescences of the first talking pictures. They just never stopped talking!

Actually, in the strictest sense, there probably never was such a thing as a completely "silent" film. From the very outset, from the time when movies were first shown as part of a vaudeville or music-hall presentation, they had some kind of sound accompanying them. Even the nickelodeon theater had its cheap, twangy, upright piano on which "the professor" banged out *Hearts and Flowers* and other tunes more or less appropriate to the emotions emanating from the screen. The large-scale "specials" that began to appear from Europe after 1912 were generally exhibited with a live orchestral accompaniment. Not to be outdone, D. W. Griffith presented *The Birth of a Nation* in its initial engagements with a symphonic score compiled by Joseph Carl Breil and arranged for an orchestra of seventy pieces. The same score was later simplified for smaller orchestras, for trios and for solo piano, to be used with showings of the film in the subsequent runs.

When the big downtown theaters began to spring up after 1914, most of them had large pit orchestras to play at least for the evening shows. Afternoon performances might be accompanied either by a smaller ensemble or by the organ. As de luxe houses extended into the neighborhoods, the standard equipment included a mighty Wurlitzer, that behemoth of mechanical sound with its banks and banks of gleaming keys and special effects. Sometimes it was even augmented by a trio of piano, violin and percussion. Whatever the form, the purpose of such accompaniment was twofold: to provide suitable mood music for the picture, and to blot out for the patrons such distractions as the whir of the projectors, the banging of chairs and (above all) the noises of other patrons. Throughout the twenties the film companies regularly provided cue sheets which suggested standard selections to be played at indicated moments during all their features. Building the musical accompaniments for silent films became something of an art in itself; and when the studios began to "can" their scores on the Vitaphone or Movietone, they turned to such master practitioners of the art as Erno Rapee or Hugo Riesenfeld. In fact, a number of the musical directors in the studios today are men who began as arrangers and conductors of the pit orchestras of the silent era.

During the twenties too, the "effects" became more important as the music was wedded more and more closely to the picture. In the larger theater orchestras, the drummer was virtually a one-man sound effects department, operating with a tremendous variety of drums, whistles, Klaxons, sirens and bells. Some of these men became true virtuosi in synchronizing the sounds of footsteps, knocks, thunderclaps or pistol shots to the visuals on the screen. The range of effects incorporated into the organs was also increased. By the middle of the twenties, directors frequently included sequences in their pictures that depended for their full effect upon some special sound. They knew they could fairly well rely upon the ingenuity of organist, drummer or even pianist to supply it. The battery of drums, thunder sheets and other devices that many theaters installed to provide a realistic accompaniment to such war films as *The Big Parade* and *Wings* were often as elaborate as the effects departments of the first sound studios.

The arrival of sound made possible a far closer integration of music and visuals, a more precise synchronization of the sound effects. But more important, it gave the screen a voice to take the place of the awkward subtitle. Though readily accepted as a convention of the silent film, the subtitle was at best a makeshift arrangement, performing a function that obviously called for sound. At worst, as in Dreyer's *Passion of Joan of Arc,* it could destroy the rhythm of the visuals. Creative directors might try to say as much as possible through their visuals, but even a well made film of the period contained an astonishing number of titles. Run-of-the-mill productions, particularly those adapted from stage plays, would be little more than a succession of big heads in close-up alternating with dialogue subtitles. Many an addict of the silent movie became extraordinarily adept at lip reading, thus providing for himself some of the gratification denied him by the mechanical limitations of the medium. It also provided, from time to time, the odd realization that what the actors were saying was quite at variance with what the titles indicated. Indeed, so adept had the general public become at reading lips by the end of the silent era that when Edmund Lowe and Victor McLaglen, for example, burst out in mute but eloquent profanity in *What Price Glory?,* the studio was flooded with letters of shocked protest.

BREAKING THE SOUND BARRIER

Contrary to popular belief, sound did not burst suddenly upon a completely unprepared public in the winter of 1927. As we have already seen, Edison had conceived of movies accompanied by sound (or, more accurately, sound accompanied by pictures) as early as 1889, synchronizing his phonograph to the Kinetoscope. Quite a number of films were actually made in this fashion in France even before 1900—brief affairs little more than a minute long, but preserving for the world the voice of Bernhardt in *Hamlet,* of Coquelin as Cyrano, the vaudeville turns of Little Tich and Vesta Tilley. Until about 1912 inventors persisted in their efforts to join together sound and visuals, going so far as to run endless belts from the projector motor through the entire length of the theater to a phonograph installed behind the screen. But they soon discovered, as houses continued to grow larger, that the problem was one not merely of synchronization but of amplification as well. The ordinary talking machine simply could not produce the volume of sound required to fill an entire auditorium.

The solution lay in the silenium tube, the so-called "audion amplifier" developed by Lee De Forest shortly before World War I. With it, volume could be controlled, stepped up. Of great importance in long-distance telephone and telegraph experiments, it was basic to the development of the infant radio industry and the talking picture. De Forest sold his amplification patents to Bell Telephone; but soon after the war he began to devote his attention to the problem of sound and films, choosing an entirely new approach. Hitherto, the sound had always been separated from the film strip, a phonograph record to be played along with the picture. De Forest saw that this presented strong disadvantages. The loss of a few frames of film through a break or a splice would throw the whole remaining reel out of synchronization with its accompanying sound, while a broken record could wreck an entire show. In addition, the mechanics of obtaining and maintaining synchronization between the sound and the image became infinitely more complicated when the two were handled on separate machines.

To circumvent this, De Forest developed a method of photographing sound directly on the film itself, recording it in fine striations of grays and blacks along one edge of the strip. Vibrations caught by the microphone broke the current of a photo-electric cell; the resulting fluctuations of light and dark, photographed on motion-picture film, gave back the original sound impulses when passed around another photo-electric cell in the sound head of the projector. As early as 1923 De Forest was presenting his Phonofilm as a novelty in theaters around the country, recording the acts of such top vaudeville personalities as Eddie Cantor, Phil Baker and Weber and Fields. Although his shorts were well received, they caused little stir in the industry.

Even while De Forest was demonstrating his invention, the Bell Telephone Laboratories persisted in their efforts to link movies with sound on disc. By 1926 they had developed a special turntable and 13- to 17-inch records large enough to accommodate the sound for an entire reel of film. It was this process that Warner Brothers acquired and titled the Vitaphone. At the outset, like De Forest, Warners used their process exclusively for novelty shorts, recording the performances of ensembles and stars of the concert and vaudeville stage, among them the New York Philharmonic, Giovanni Martinelli, Mischa Elman and Eddie Foy. On August 6, 1926, when Warners held their Vitaphone première for the general public, they presented a selection of these shorts, preceded by a filmed address by Will H. Hays hailing the new miracle. The feature on the program, John Barrymore in *Don Juan*, was accompanied by a specially recorded symphonic score. Audiences were interested—nothing more. The crude reproduction of a vaudeville act or a concert aria failed to create any wild excitement, and not even Will Hays's eulogy to sound was able to convince them that they were on the brink of a revolution. Indeed, the recorded musical accompaniment for the feature was something of a comedown for audiences accustomed to having large orchestras perform "live" with their pictures. Even so, Warners continued to record the scores for all their more important releases, and particularly those that made heavy demands upon the sound effects department.

Early in 1927, as more and more of the key theaters around the country wired for sound, William Fox secured the rights to the German Tri-Ergon patents, an independently developed sound-on-film system that seems to have antedated De Forest's. At the same time he paid a reputed million dollars to a former associate of De Forest, Theodore W. Case, for the patents and development of yet another sound-on-film apparatus which made its bow under the name of Fox-Case. On it Fox released a series of shorts rivaling the Vitaphone subjects and also began to add scores to his feature films.

(*What Price Glory?* was the first.) In April of 1927 he launched the Fox Movietone News, the first sound newsreel. Its success was instantaneous. The June issue, devoted entirely to Charles A. Lindbergh's triumphal receptions, brought people into the theaters just as, twenty-five years later, the Kefauver investigations were to hold them spellbound at their television receivers. Soon such oddly assorted personalities as Calvin Coolidge, George Bernard Shaw and Benito Mussolini had also faced the Movietone cameras and microphones. There was a special fascination in seeing Coolidge in Indian feathers and hearing him sworn in as a Great White Brother of the Sioux, in listening to Shaw as he paced the gravel path in his garden and spoke jocularly of himself and world affairs. But these were novelties, outside the main stream of picture making. These were the "extra added attractions." What sound still needed was the spark, the flame that would kindle the public's imagination and enthusiasm. And that was Al Jolson's contribution. In *The Jazz Singer* his tremendous vitality and personality were able to break through the primitive recording apparatus to charm audiences in a way that no movie had ever done before. And Jolson did it, not in a Vitaphone short but in a feature-length dramatic film. The panic was on.

THE TYRANNY OF SOUND

In 1929, after little more than a year of talkies, *Variety* wryly reported, "Sound didn't do any more to the industry than turn it upside down, shake the entire bag of tricks from its pocket and advance Warner Brothers from the last place (among the film companies) to first in the league." The films had learned to talk, and talk was uppermost in everyone's mind. Script writers who had trained themselves to think in terms of pictures gave way to playwrights who thought in terms of stage dialogue. Established directors were either replaced by directors from the New York stage or supplemented by special dialogue directors. Many a popular star— especially the European importees—suddenly found himself unemployed; while the Broadway stage was again swept clean to replace those actors whose foreign accents, faulty diction or bad voices the temperamental microphone rejected. To fill the need for dialogue at all costs, plays—good, bad and indifferent—were bought up and rushed before the cameras. It was the era satirized in George S. Kaufman's *Once in a Lifetime,* when the Mr. Glogauers of Hollywood were valiantly but vainly trying to understand the change that had come over their industry, when self-styled geniuses were able to make incredible blunders simply because no one else had any better idea of how the talkies should be made.

And then a new and imposing figure appeared in the studios, the sound expert. It was the sound expert who concealed the microphone in the vase of flowers on the boudoir table, who dictated where actors must stand in order to record properly, who decided where the camera must be placed in order to keep the microphone outside its field. He was the final arbiter on what could and what could not be done, and his word was law. The camera itself, now imprisoned within a sound-proof booth, was robbed of all mobility. And the experts, concerned with nothing beyond the sound quality of the pictures they worked on, continually simplified their problems by insisting that scenes be played in corners, minimizing longshots for the more readily controllable close-up. In no time at all the techniques, the artistry that directors had acquired through years of silent films were cast aside and forgotten in the shadow of the microphone.

As a result, 1929 was for the most part the year of static, photographed stage plays, the year of "all-talking, all-singing" musicals, the year in which raw sound was exploited in every imaginable way. In Mack Sennett's first two-reel talking comedy, *The Family Picnic* (1929), audiences were regaled by the sounds of the picnickers crunching celery or munching potato chips. Warners, not content with having made the first part-talking picture, *The Jazz Singer,* and the first all-talking picture, *The Lights of New York,* soon followed these with the first *all* all-talking picture, *The Terror* (1928). In place of the normal, printed credit titles, it offered Conrad Nagel in mask and opera cape to introduce the picture and its characters. Fox countered with "the first 100% all-talking drama filmed outdoors," *In Old Arizona* (1929). Other studios presented "the first all-Negro all-talking picture," "the first 100% talking, singing college picture," the mathematically absurd "100% talking, 100% singing, 100% dancing" musicals. Warners capped the climax in *On With the Show* (1929). Not only was it "all-talking, all-singing, all-dancing"—it was "100% all-color" as well.

Color, like sound, had long challenged the film makers. Many of the early short films from France were actually colored by hand, frame by frame, producing an utterly charming—if somewhat unpredictable—effect. A practical but overly cumbersome three-color process known as Kinemacolor was introduced in England as early as 1908 (and used to photograph the Coronation in 1910). Other inventions appeared soon after in England, France, Germany and the United States. But color, whether hand painted or mechanically contrived, was merely a novelty, something added to the regular show. And its added realism was in fact at the outset so utterly unrealistic, so obviously false in values and lacking in definition that few producers thought it worth the extra expense and effort. Besides, whenever the suggestion of color was important, they could always print the black-and-white images on tinted stock—blue for night scenes, red for fires, green for fields and forests. The effect could be heightened by "toning" the lighter parts of the shot in a contrasting color—a purple sea with a pink sunset, a green meadow with a sunny yellow sky. Few producers felt any need to go beyond this.

Nevertheless, Herbert Kalmus launched his Technicolor researches in 1918, convinced that color could be reproduced photographically just as readily as shades of gray. By 1923 he was prepared to market a two-color process in which the red-orange-yellow portion of the spectrum was photographed on one negative, the green-blue-purple portion on another. When prints from the two negatives were laminated together, they produced a pleasing though still far from accurate color scale. At first the public was only mildly interested. Enthusiasm began to mount only after producers began to incorporate color sequences into their bigger productions, such as Lon Chaney's frightening appearance as the Mask of the Red Death in *The Phantom of the Opera* (1925). Technicolor scored its first major success in Douglas Fairbanks' *The Black Pirate* (1926), which used the color process throughout. Despite a palette with a strong propensity for blue-green and orange, and flesh tones that altered unpredictably from deep ochre to shrimp-pink, Technicolor definitely enhanced the romantic period flavor of this film and the audiences' enjoyment of it. Soon after, Kalmus perfected his process, eliminating the need for two prints by coating both sides of the celluloid strip with an emulsion. At the very moment that sound arrived, a practicable color process was also ready.

And with the overwhelming success of their sound experiments, the producers were now willing to try almost any novelty. In 1929 several of the major studios added to their pictures not only color but the "grandeur screen" as well, using them for the spectacular musicals that literally streamed out of Hollywood. But the public, attracted by sound, was more irritated than impressed by this additional bounty. The big screens emphasized the graininess of the prints, making them look gray and washed out; while Technicolor, faced by a sudden expansion of business, was totally unprepared to handle the new volume. There were constant laboratory delays, infuriating the producers, and the processing itself left much to be desired. Prints were fuzzy, out of register, painful to the eyes. In addition, the color values were still far from true. Within the year both color and the wide screens had virtually disappeared from the scene, awaiting an era when the public would once more be receptive to the appeal of something altogether "new."

Just as movies had appeared at virtually the same moment in the United States and Europe, so too was sound developed simultaneously in England, Germany, the Soviet Union and America. There had been many versions of the motion-picture camera and projector; now there were numerous sound mechanisms. There was sound on disc (the Vitaphone) and sound on film in half a dozen systems including the Movietone, the RCA Photophone, Cinephone, Phonofilm and, on the Continent, the Tobis Klangfilm. Russia's Dr. Shorin produced a sound-on-film system for the Soviet industry. Except for the Vitaphone, all were compatible with one another. All could be played through the same type of sound head in the theaters, thus permitting the continued world-wide dissemination of pictures. But the struggle for control was a sharp one. For almost three years Warner Brothers asserted not only the priority but the superiority of their Vitaphone system. Meanwhile, William Fox with his German Tri-Ergon patents and a battery of lawyers attempted to dominate sound films all over the world. He failed—ultimately forced out of his own business by his creditors and the combined opposition of the American Telephone Company and its Wall Street representatives. Finally, a patents pool settled matters to everyone's satisfaction (except, of course, Fox, who retired from the scene with a paltry $18,000,000); and after 1931 the sound-on-film system was accepted as standard, with Western Electric and RCA splitting the field between them in the United States, and Tobis supreme on the Continent.

Sound gave the banks and the investment houses their first real hold upon the motion-picture industry. Every studio needed sound, and most of them also needed vast sums of new working capital to make the equipment purchases and studio alterations required to convert to sound. Both the equipment and the financing led ultimately to the same sources, to Western Electric, RCA and their affiliated banking houses. Soon their representatives were sitting on the boards of the motion-picture companies, making policy with— and sometimes in place of—the veteran showmen who had brought their studios from obscurity to world-wide prominence. They appointed the sound experts who dominated the studios through 1929 and 1930. These men knew only about acoustics and microphone characteristics. But because they had the backing of the people who were paying for it all, they often usurped the functions of both producer and director. As a result, a transition that would have been difficult in any case was made more difficult still. Producers whose main stock in trade was their knowledge of entertainment values suddenly found their hands tied. Directors who understood the necessity to keep the picture moving and alive found themselves arbitrarily over-ruled in favor of the microphone.

LIBERATING THE CAMERA: ERNST LUBITSCH

It is to the eternal credit of genuinely creative and courageous men like Ernst Lubitsch, Rouben Mamoulian, Lewis Milestone and King Vidor that they had the ingenuity and vitality to circumvent the experts and lift the new medium out of the rut of dully photographed plays and vaudeville routines into which it had fallen. They had no rules to go on, no precedents to quote. They had the opposition of the sound men to contend with, and the indisputable fact that at the box offices across the nation almost any film was making money as long as it talked. But these men sensed that talk alone was not enough, and that the public would soon tire of the novelty of sound for sound's sake and demand again to see a *movie*. It was their pioneer work that brought forth the techniques to make the movies move again.

Ernst Lubitsch, by 1929 the top director at Paramount, made the important discovery that a talking picture did not have to be *all* talking, nor did the sound track have to reproduce faithfully each sound on the set. In his first talkies, *The Love Parade* (1929) and *Monte Carlo* (1930), he included many passages that were shot without dialogue or any other synchronized sound. For these, he was able to bring the camera out of its sound-proofed box and proceed in the old silent techniques, moving his camera freely, changing its position frequently. Music or effects were put in later. One of the high-points of *The Love Parade* was a running gag with Maurice Chevalier telling a risqué joke to members of the court. Each time he approaches the tag line, his voice sinks to a confidential whisper, a door closes, or the camera leaps outside to view the effect of his story through a window. Audiences of 1929 were delighted to find a new element in the talkies—silence!

Working mainly on the Maurice Chevalier-Jeanette MacDonald musicals, Lubitsch quickly established himself as one of the most inventive directors of the period. With his strong feeling for the relationship between music and visuals, he brought back some of the rhythm that had been present in the silent films. In *Monte Carlo,* for example, Lubitsch cuts together the sounds of a train getting under way. As it picks up speed, the characteristic tempo of the wheels is translated into the music of the theme song, *Beyond the Blue Horizon*. The impressive wedding ceremony in *The Smiling Lieutenant* (1931) was staged without the confining microphone, but each opening door, every step down the great flight of marble stairs, every gesture of the players was timed to the beat of a score that was dubbed in later. He was the first to be concerned with the "natural" introduction of songs into the development of a musical-comedy plot, the first to find a cinematic way to handle verbal humor in the new medium.

But Lubitsch also knew how to use the sound camera to serious purpose. In *Broken Lullaby* (1932), his one dramatic film of this period, he emphasized its anti-war theme in many brilliantly conceived shots. The sights and sounds of an Armistice Day parade are glimpsed between the crutches of a one-legged soldier. Early in the film, while a minister is praying for peace, the camera in ironic counterpoint moves slowly down the center aisle of the cathedral, past row on row of kneeling officers, their spurs gleaming, their swords stiff by their sides. By shooting such sequences silent and adding the sound later, Lubitsch obtained not only greater freedom for his camera but the kind of control of the elements in his scene essential to artistic creation. The "Lubitsch touch," that sparkling combination of wit and irony already famous in the silent film, reached its fullest expression in his early talkies.

Meanwhile, King Vidor in his first talking picture, *Hallelujah!* (1929), explored the possibilities of the sound track to evoke mood and atmosphere. It was an all-Negro picture made, for the most part, in Memphis, Tennessee, and the swamps of Arkansas. The fact that the film was done largely on location, away from rigid studio supervision, gave Vidor an enviable amount of freedom for that time. Much of it he shot silent, later creating an impressionistic sound track for all but the direct dialogue passages. The rhythmic swell of Negro spirituals, a woman's scream or a barking dog heard in the distance, the sounds of the swamp and the river supplied the dominant mood or emotional tone for many of the scenes. The whole final sequence, a frenzied pursuit through the swamps, was shot silent with beautiful, long traveling shots of pursued and pursuer. Only later, back in the studio, did Vidor add the magnified sounds of breaking branches, the screech of birds, agonized breathing and the suck of footsteps stumbling through the mire. Without the present-day equipment for reading sound, without synchronizers or multiple-channel sound mixers Vidor performed a tremendous feat. He showed that the source of a sound is less important than its quality, that sound can create an emotional aura about a scene quite independent of the words and faces of the actors. Lewis Milestone worked in much the same way in making his *All Quiet on the Western Front* (1930), photographing his scenes of troops on the march and in the trenches with a silent camera and adding in later the whine and crash of bombs, the clatter of small-arms fire and the shrieks and moans of the wounded and dying.

This process of adding sound later to scenes shot with silent cameras, known as post-synchronization or dubbing, played an important role in freeing directors from the early notion that everything seen must be heard or that everything heard must be seen. Once post-synchronization had been achieved, such a literal use of sound was clearly no longer necessary. We might see an ordinary street scene, but the dialogue has been post-synchronized to eliminate the irrelevant honks and screeches that would blur the words. Or a director might let us hear the crash of an automobile while showing us only the horrified faces of the onlookers. The experience of post-synchronizing such scenes in the recording studio helped directors to realize that, essentially, the sound track is a composite of many sounds—voices, music and all sorts of noises and effects—and that all of these were completely under his control. Each sound could be independently distorted, muffled, exaggerated or eliminated at will. The director could shoot his scene with a silent camera and dub in the sound for it later.. He could reinforce dialogue passages with music, combine them with noises or bury them under other, post-synchronized sounds. And as the technicians provided more and better equipment to facilitate the handling of sound, these manipulative possibilities within the sound track assumed an ever greater importance. Post-synchronization became the first point of departure in the development of the new art.

The other was an improvement in the camera itself. During the first years of sound, the camera had been forced into a small sound-proofed booth to keep the whirr of its mechanism from reaching the sensitive, cranky microphone. As long as it remained confined, most directors were willing to work in long, static "takes." Often, three cameras simultaneously photographed the same scene from different angles, very much as in television today. This technique vastly simplified the problems of cutting and matching the sound to its proper visual, but it also produced a slow, draggy effect upon the screen. The choice of camera positions was too limited and too arbitrary to produce a truly cinematic effect. During 1930, however, the cameras began to emerge from these boxes, enclosed now in sound-proofed "blimps" which, while still cumbersome, permitted a far greater freedom of movement. It then became the director's problem to force the reluctant sound experts to give that new mobility full rein, to demand from them more flexible microphone set-ups. In shooting his first film, *Applause* (1929), Rouben Mamoulian demanded two microphones on a single set, one to record the voice of Helen Morgan as she sang a lullaby to her daughter, the other to record the child's whispered prayer in bed. The experts argued that this would necessitate the use of two separate channels, a thing unheard of at the time. "Unheard of but not impossible," Mamoulian insisted—and proved his point. Today nine channels is not unusual for a single shot, while on stereophonic epics the number may rise to as many as fifty.

Not only was the number of microphones increased, but their quality improved. They became more "directional," able to hear only in one area so that the director could manipulate other sounds in other portions of his scene. Before long, the stationary microphones were being replaced by mikes suspended on long booms that could be swung to follow the players anywhere. Thus, slowly, the sound experts of Hollywood were defeated by directors with fresh ideas about the nature of the new art—and the prestige and stamina to fight them through.

MASTERING THE SOUND TRACK: RENE CLAIR

Perhaps the first director to appreciate fully the implications of sound was the Frenchman René Clair. Originally opposed to the whole idea, he insisted on the predominant importance of the visual element, declaring that the sound film need not and should not be, to use his own term, "canned theater." This opinion, almost revolutionary among film makers at the time, was brilliantly confirmed in a trio of sparkling comedies that quickly made Clair the most admired and imitated director in the world. In *Sous les Toits de Paris* (1929), *Le Million* (1931) and *A Nous la Liberté* (1931), he worked with a minimum of dialogue, using music, choruses and sound effects to counterpoint and comment upon his visuals. In this principle of asynchronous sound, sound used against rather than with the images, Clair discovered a new freedom and fluidity for the sound medium. Why show a door closing when it is enough merely to hear it slam? Or why listen to a clock's ticking just because it is shown? In *Le Million* there is a brief glimpse of a clock on a mantel shelf, a clock elaborately overdecorated with porcelain cupids blowing trumpets. Clair's sound track at that point carries a blast of trumpets. In *Sous les Toits* a fight takes place at night near a railway embankment. The fight is almost obscured by the shadows, but its force and fury are conveyed in the roar of the passing trains heard on the sound track. In *A Nous la Liberté,* Clair goes so far as to kid the whole notion of synchronous sound by showing his heroine singing away at her window while the hero admires from afar. Suddenly something goes wrong with the voice—it whines and whirrs, then fades away. A moment later, while the young fellow is still looking up at the window, the girl appears in the street, the song begins again and we discover that what we have been listening to all along is a phonograph record from another apartment.

Because Clair's early sound films were both musicals and comedies, he could permit himself an impish audacity denied practitioners of the more serious forms, whose dramatic themes forced them to use more straightforward techniques. Their efforts at realism made it difficult for them to break with the conventional practices that quickly surrounded the microphone soon after it had made its appearance in the studios. Clair, on the other hand, could ignore conventional sound, omitting the characteristic noises of a street, a factory or an opera house altogether unless they served his purpose. It was *his* world, and he did with it as he wished.

And because above all he liked music and the dance, his pictures flash along like ballets. The incessant chases, the scramble after the flying bank notes in *A Nous la Liberté,* the mad party that opens and closes *Le Million*—all are set to gay, infectious tunes. Choruses sing a witty commentary upon the action as it unfolds. Whole sequences are bound together by music alone. In the opening reel of *Sous les Toits de Paris* a street singer is vending the title song of the film. While the camera wanders up and down the street, peering into the apartments and shops, one by one the people of the neighborhood join in the song. In this way Clair quickly introduces the principal characters in his story and gaily sets the mood of the entire film. Throughout his pictures, music functions in dozens of bright and unexpected ways, playing an integral part in the development of his diverting stories.

What Clair had done, what creative directors everywhere were trying to do at the same time, was to discover how to control all the elements that went into the making of a sound film as completely as, in the simpler days of silence, one could control everything that went before the camera. He demonstrated to everyone's satisfaction that much of silent technique was still valid, that it was the image and not the word that kept the screen alive. Sound, and especially asynchronous sound, could add its own grace notes, its deeper perceptions, its enrichment of mood and atmosphere— but not independently of the visual.

Because René Clair had instinctively grasped this principle in his first three films, and turned them out with a flair and finish unmatched anywhere at the time, his pictures had a profound effect upon other directors. He had achieved what they were groping toward. He had brought back into films spontaneity, movement, rhythm. The extent of his influence is immediately revealed by a comparison of the opening reel of his *Sous les Toits* with the first sequences of Geza von Bolvary's *Zwei Herzen im Dreiviertel Takt* (1930) or the "Blue Horizon" number in Lubitsch's *Monte Carlo* (1930). But more important than imitation are the innumerable films of the early thirties that suggest his liberating spirit. In Germany Eric Charrell's *Congress Dances* (1931), in England Victor Saville's *Sunshine Susie* (1932), and in Hollywood films like Frank Tuttle's *This Is the Night* (1932), Gregory La Cava's *Half-Naked Truth* (1932) and Lewis Milestone's *Hallelujah, I'm a Bum* (1933), all reveal not only a new freedom in the use of sound but also—as in the Clair films—a rhythmic structure imparted by the sound track.

Clair's work was especially valuable to those men in the American studios who were themselves seeking to liberate the talking film from the confines of "canned theater." More daring than they dared to be, the fact that such pictures had found considerable popular as well as critical success was helpful in encouraging them to go ahead —quite apart from any technical lessons they might have learned. In this respect the early sound period was very much like the first decade or so of the silent era. The medium itself was still in a highly experimental stage, and directors looked to the box office to tell them how successful they were with the new techniques, and to the works of one another for useful hints that they could incorporate into their own efforts. In this period of search and confusion, Clair's

pictures appeared as beacons to the future. And if Clair had a
tendency to overstress the silent techniques in his early films, they
provided a healthy counter-influence to the over-accenting of the
sound track in the films made by almost everyone else.

EXPLORING THE NEW MEDIUM: ROUBEN MAMOULIAN

Perhaps the leading director of dramatic films in this country
to revolt against "canned theater" movies during the early years
of sound was Rouben Mamoulian—ironically, one of the many
Broadway directors brought to the studios in 1929 specifically to
make "canned theater." Despite his theater background, Mamoulian
sensed at once the differences between the two forms. He felt that
the camera could and should move, appreciated the importance of
the close-up for dramatic emphasis, fought against the prevalent
notion that the source for every sound must be seen. For him, the
camera was far more than a passive observer looking on while actors
recited their lines—and the function of the director was more than
merely helping the actors to say their lines better. He had to help
the audience find what was dramatically significant in a scene,
picking out what was important with his camera, making it seem
fresh and illuminating through the imagination and inventiveness
of his visuals.

In his first two talking pictures, *Applause* (1929) and *City
Streets* (1931), Mamoulian gave repeated evidence of his desire to
move away from stereotyped techniques. A particularly effective
moment in *Applause* began with a close-up of Helen Morgan,
the aging burlesque queen, reminiscing about her youth; as she
speaks, the camera leaves her tired, dissipated face and wanders
across the room to a photograph of her as a lovely young girl. At
another point, a long tracking shot shows only the feet of the
heroine as she leaves the theater, and the feet of the men she encounters as she walks home. The nature of each encounter is
revealed as fully in the footsteps as in the fragments of conversation
accompanying the scene. In *City Streets* a montage of china figurines
is used symbolically over the clash of voices in one of the film's key
dramatic scenes. Dialogue spoken earlier in the picture is heard
again over a huge, tear-stained close-up of Sylvia Sidney as she

recalls the past. Even as in Griffith's day, the producers protested that the public would never understand what was going on, that hearing a sound without seeing its source would only confuse the audience. Mamoulian stuck to his point, however; audiences did understand—and the sound "flash-back" has become a standard technique in talkies ever since.

By the time he made *Dr. Jekyll and Mr. Hyde* (1932), Mamoulian had full control of his new medium. From start to finish, it was a virtuoso work; almost every scene revealed the director's desire to break away from a literal use of the camera and a conventional use of sound. The entire first reel was shot in the first-person technique, the camera assuming the identity of Dr. Jekyll. From that position we see his hands as he plays the organ, the shadow of his head upon the music rack. When Jekyll is ready to go out, the butler hands hat, cloak and cane directly to the camera. After a carriage ride through the streets of London, it enters the doors of a medical school and passes on into the operating theater. Here a complete 360° turn around the hall brings the camera to rest for the first time upon the face of Dr. Jekyll (Fredric March). Quite apart from its indisputable pictorial effectiveness, this use of the subjective camera built a growing suspense, a curiosity about the appearance of the man we know will turn into the monstrous Hyde. The transformations themselves were ingeniously achieved upon the screen (Mamoulian has steadfastly refused to divulge the secret of his technique), accompanied by a vivid, synthetically created sound track built from exaggerated heart beats mingled with the reverberations of gongs played backwards, bells heard through echo chambers and completely artificial sounds created by photographing light frequencies directly onto the sound track. The recordists referred to it as "Mamoulian's stew," but it was probably the screen's first experiment with purely synthetic sound.

Outstanding for its understatement both of sound and visual was Mamoulian's handling of the scene in which Hyde murders "Champagne Ivy" (Miriam Hopkins). Hyde forces the thoroughly frightened girl to sing her pathetic music hall song. Suddenly he bends over her, passing completely out of the frame. For a long moment the shot reveals only the bed-post, a highly ornamental carving of the Goddess of Love. Then the singing stops abruptly, and Hyde's triumphant face rises once more into view. We need be shown no more.

The impact of René Clair's films upon men who, like Mamoulian, were themselves concerned with the creative use of sound is perhaps most clearly revealed in Mamoulian's next picture, *Love Me Tonight* (1932). Although in the tradition of the Jeanette MacDonald-Maurice Chevalier musicals that Ernst Lubitsch had been making so successfully, suddenly the form is freer, lighter, more imaginative than ever before. Greater liberties are taken with reality, and less effort is made to explain or excuse the obviously absurd to the audience. In the midst of a hunt, deer bound across the screen in dreamy waltz time; or characters march about a French château gleefully caroling, "The son of a gun is nothing but a tailor." Through this kind of fantasy, in which trick sound is combined with trick camera to create a world of gay illusion, the literal techniques of the realistic dramas were jolted loose, stirred about. The experience of making such musicals provided directors with new insights into their craft that inevitably carried over into the more serious forms. There was a pronounced tendency toward more vivid imagery, a more imaginative use of sound, even in stories still written mainly in the theatrical tradition.

Mamoulian's own films after *Love Me Tonight* are again indicative. *Song of Songs* (1933) with Marlene Dietrich, *Queen Christina* (1933) with Greta Garbo, *We Live Again* (1934) with Anna Sten had a visual beauty, a sensuous quality that often surmounted the banality of their scripts. Certain scenes—Garbo with the grapes in *Queen Christina* or the long tracking shot to the completely immobile close-up of Garbo that closes the film—linger in the mind as directorial touches that added cinematic life to stories that made their main points through dialogue. Certainly, Mamoulian's concern for the dramatic effect of his imagery made him the logical choice as the director of the first feature-length film shot in the improved, full-color Technicolor, *Becky Sharp* (1935). His handling of the great ball before the battle of Waterloo with its artfully designed shifting patterns of color, its gay pastels mounting to a climax of blood-red cloaks disappearing into the darkness, reveals again his ability to work imaginatively with the raw materials of his art. And when in 1936 he turned once more to musical comedy in the satiric *Gay Desperado,* he showed that he was now able to move as lightly and freely in a realistic world of thieves and radios and high-powered motorcars as in the fantasy world of *Love Me Tonight.* Always the creative director, Mamoulian best exemplifies those talented men of the early thirties who were consciously seeking to transform the talking picture into a genuinely cinematic art.

NEW FORMS, NEW TECHNIQUES

It was perhaps inevitable that, during the first hectic years of sound, the film cycles reappeared with renewed vigor. They seemed to chase each other across the screen, one right after the other—transcriptions of Broadway musicals, prison pictures, gangster pictures, newspaper pictures, back-stage musicals. With the entire industry unsure of itself, any outstanding success was soon followed by the simultaneous release of literally dozens of other films on the same subject from every studio in Hollywood. Curiously enough, this had a salutary effect on the film themselves. The studios did not try merely to imitate what had gone before: they tried to make their films better than their competition. They tried to polish techniques and stories until their own efforts were more attractive, more effective, more "box office." The number of films in each cycle may have driven the moviegoer of the early thirties almost out of his mind by making it seem that every new picture he went to was the one that he had seen the week before. But through these cycles the film forms were themselves able to develop characteristic styles and techniques, an increased mobility and cinematic power.

One of the first and most obvious fields for exploitation by the new sound camera was, of course, the Broadway musical. During 1929 and 1930, a great many of these made the transition to film —*The Vagabond King, The Desert Song, Rio Rita, Sunny, Golden Dawn, Gold Diggers of Broadway, Song of the Flame* . . . The list is endless. Actually, however, very little original thinking went into them. It was enough that they had popular titles, famous stars and familiar tunes. In 1930 Samuel Goldwyn brought to Hollywood a dance director from the New York stage, Busby Berkeley, to handle the musical numbers for *Whoopee,* starring Eddie Cantor. And things began to happen. Berkeley, one of the most original and daring of the directors in this field, saw no reason why the dances should be a mere reproduction of the stage originals. Not with a camera capable of taking scenes from any angle and any position. In *Whoopee* he carried his camera high up into the flies and shot straight down on the dance floor. In subsequent films, he photographed from below, from the sides, from above. He zoomed the camera in from afar to extreme close-ups of his dancing girls or singing stars. He devised trick shots, matte shots and kaleidoscopic lenses to obtain ever more novel effects. For one astonishing moment in "The Shadow Waltz" from *Gold Diggers of 1933,* he tilted the camera at a 90° angle to the floor and photographed the girls mirrored in a lake, pirouetting down either side of the screen. He increased the fragmentation of his dances into a series of all but motionless abstract designs. Meaningless in themselves, they acquired line and continuity when the separate shots were assembled in the editing rooms. Since such dance sequences were generally inserted into well worn backstage stories, purists frequently pointed out that Berkeley's work was ridiculous, that his dances could never conceivably take place on any stage in the world. They were, of course, absolutely right. What they ignored was the fact that the story was merely an excuse for the production numbers, and that Berkeley was producing the purest combination of visual and sound that had yet come from the American studios. His dance sequences were abstract, complete in themselves and, ultimately, self-defeating, an artistic cul-de-sac without links to the more common narrative forms. But, like the avant-garde works of the twenties, they were both stimulating and provocative, suggesting to others new ways of using the freedom that Berkeley had found for himself. Still active today, Berkeley remains unique for his special kind of musical spectacle, although his vogue was to be gradually superseded by the growing popularity of the more intimate style of dance films introduced by Fred Astaire and Ginger Rogers during the mid-thirties.

The popular gangster films of the early thirties—*Little Caesar* (1930), *The Public Enemy* (1931), *Scarface* (1932)—and the almost concurrent cycle of newspaper melodramas also did much to return to the screen some of its former mobility and vitality. Generally written directly for the screen, they eliminated the long, fragrant speeches of the legitimate theater in favor of such pungent phrases as "We're gonna take you for a ride," "He got bumped off," and "You can dish it out but you can't take it." In keeping with the tone of this dialogue, the editing was similarly taut and to the point. In a typical scene from *Little Caesar,* the gang is discussing the fate of one of its members:

"Eddie's turned yellow. He's goin' to rat on us."

"He can't get away with that."

"I just seen Eddie goin' into the church."

"Get Eddie," says Little Caesar. And the scene cuts abruptly to a church exterior, with Eddie coming down the steps. A long black car swings ominously into view; there is a burst of machine-gun fire and Eddie lies sprawling on the steps. Followed by a flat cut to the next scene, Eddie's funeral.

There was a speed, a vigor, a sense of the contemporaneous scene, a realism of character and incident about these films that was in sharp contrast to the talky problem plays that surrounded them. They had action, racy dialogue, the sharply naturalistic performances of people like James Cagney, Edward G. Robinson, Joan Blondell, Lee Tracy, Paul Muni and George Bancroft. They boasted that their incidents were based on fact, that their stories came from the headlines. And they excited audiences in ways that the drawing-room comedies, boudoir romances and static musical comedies did not. They were like a breath of fresh air sweeping through the heavily padded studios of the early sound era, blowing away some of the conventions, some of the stiffness that had crept into the medium with the advent of the microphone.

And directors—even directors who were not working on gangster films—responded to their tonic. In *The Front Page* (1931), one of the first and fastest of the newspaper cycle, Lewis Milestone solved the problem of translating the Hecht-MacArthur play into a film by keeping the camera almost constantly in motion, by cutting frequently and by staging the dialogue at breakneck speed. King Vidor, faced with much the same problem in bringing to the screen Elmer Rice's *Street Scene* (1931), used few moving camera shots but worked out a shooting script in which every single shot was taken from a fresh angle. Josef von Sternberg, in films like *Blonde Venus* (1932) and *Shanghai Express* (1932), used long traveling shots, scenes arrestingly decorated, composed and lit, long lingering lap dissolves and sparse dialogue to sustain the visual interest of his films. By 1932, at least the opening reel of most pictures had strong pictorial values. Typical was William K. Howard's *Transatlantic* (1931), a very ordinary melodrama for the most part, but its first few minutes beautifully captured both the excitement and the mechanics of an ocean liner preparing to leave port. Once the ship got under way, unfortunately, so did the story—and it promptly fell back upon dialogue to make all its points. The film makers, however, were growing increasingly aware of the fact that their medium could not live on words alone.

Nowhere were the dislocations caused by the addition of the sound track more apparent than in the field of film comedy; and yet here too a balance was soon reached that proved of value to film makers in all fields. Prior to the introduction of sound, of course, comedy had been almost entirely a visual medium, with emphasis on character and physical humor. Subtitles—especially those subtitles that introduced the various characters—might carry an occasional wisecrack. ("He had water on the brain. In the winter it froze and everything slipped his mind.") In the sophisticated or folksy comedies of the twenties, there might even be a snappy retort. Will Rogers, for example, punctuated his silent comedies with typical Rogers-isms—but, significantly, Rogers was never as popular on the silent screen as he was after sound came in. In sound, the humor shifted abruptly from visual to verbal, and a whole new crowd of comics—largely imported from the New York stage and from vaudeville—came clamoring through the studios. The Marx Brothers, Ed Wynn, Lou Holtz, Eddie Cantor, W. C. Fields, Jimmy Durante, Frank Morgan, Bobby Clark, Charlie Ruggles and, soon after, Bob Hope were all brought west because they could handle a humorous line or witty repartee. Keaton and Lloyd, Harry Langdon and Raymond Griffith drifted into either the obscurity of studio office jobs or complete retirement. At the same time, such relatively minor comics from the silent days as Laurel and Hardy, Edward Everett Horton and Joe E. Brown were suddenly boosted to stardom. They were stage trained. They could talk.

Typical was the case of Buster Keaton. At the close of the twenties, he was M-G-M's highest paid comedian. Early in the thirties he was cast in a series of comedies with Jimmy Durante. Nominally, Keaton was the star; but whatever success the pictures scored was so clearly due to Durante that Keaton's contract was simply allowed to expire. He had established himself as a silent, frozen-faced comedian. Durante's natural style was volatile, explosive. It was Durante, not Keaton, that the talkies wanted.

Nor were all the stars of the stage completely at home on the talking screen. Ed Wynn's simple-minded funny man, Beatrice Lillie's cool sophistication, Fanny Brice's broad dialect humor and even broader bathos found scant acceptance outside New York. Even Eddie Cantor—successful in theater, radio and now television —was never as warmly received in the movies. Radio stars like Amos 'n' Andy, Jack Benny, Fred Allen and Kate Smith were notably unsuccessful when they tried the screen. The characters that had sparked the imagination of millions when heard in the living room never quite seemed to satisfy those same millions when they came to see them in the movie houses.

On the other hand, the Marx Brothers, W. C. Fields, Will Rogers, Bob Hope, Jimmy Durante and Marie Dressler—each had some special quality of voice and personality that found an immediate response in audiences around the world. Their humor was verbal, but it also had a strong visual quality. It is difficult to think of Will Rogers and Marie Dressler without recalling their shrugs and gesticulations, their special forms of mugging. Jimmy Durante is a veritable fury of activity, magnifying every emotion until it becomes a parody of itself. Bob Hope, with the smooth patina of years of vaudeville trouping, has a cock of the eye, a twist of the lip or a flip of the hand to accompany every line.

INSPIRED MAYHEM: THE MARX BROTHERS AND W. C. FIELDS

It is in the films of the Marx Brothers, however, and of W. C. Fields—and in such rare, offbeat items as *Million Dollar Legs* (1932), *Six of a Kind* (1934) and the Hope-Crosby *Road* series—that one finds the real flowering of comedy in the sound films. Indeed, the Marx Brothers presented a perfect filmic combination—the fast-talking Groucho, the silent, nimble-witted pantomime of Harpo, and Chico, the saturnine fall guy (with statuesque Margaret Dumont generally around to play straight). Even though their very earliest films, *The Coconuts* (1929) and *Animal Crackers* (1930), were nothing more than crudely photographed versions of previous stage hits, the swiftness of the dialogue and Harpo's eloquent by-play all but concealed their technical deficiencies. Such a fantastic colloquy as the one from *Animal Crackers* in which Groucho and Chico discuss the mysterious disappearance of a valuable painting needs nothing beyond a sound track and a well-focused camera:

"We'll search every room in the house," says Groucho.

"What if it ain't in this house?" says Chico.

"Then we'll search the house next door."

"What if there ain't no house next door?"

"Then we'll build one," says Groucho—and the two immediately set about drawing up plans for building the house next door.

All their better pictures had similar sequences. In *Duck Soup* (1932) Groucho as the Prime Minister of Fredonia holds up a document and says to his assembled council, "Why, it's so simple a child of ten could understand it"; then, *sotto voce* to Chico, "Run out and find me a child of ten. I can't make heads or tails of it."

Just as in the gangster films, this dialogue had a racy fascination of its own. It was talk, true; but it was also more than talk. It had, in the most literal sense, a picturesque quality—a quality that was best conveyed by a wholly passive camera. But alternating with and counterbalancing all this dialogue were sequences of frantic activity and pure pantomime—the trick with the mirror in *Duck Soup,* with all three Marxes dressed as Groucho and circling suspiciously about one another; the travesty on opera in *A Night at the Opera* when Harpo inserts "Take Me Out to the Ball Game" into the orchestra's score for *Il Trovatore* and then runs amuck in the scenery; the inspired mayhem of the operating scene from *A Day at the Races,* with Groucho calling for X-rays and Harpo and Chico rushing in with the evening papers.

As a team, the Marx Brothers achieved an almost perfect balance of sight and sound, marred only by the occasional *scènes obligatoires* of Harpo playing the harp and Chico the piano. (In one of their pictures Groucho, as if aware of the letdown in tempo, says directly to the audience, "Look, I have to stay here, but why don't you go out to the lobby for a smoke until this whole thing blows over?") Although directors invariably sought to enliven such sequences with trick shots of Chico at the keyboard, with close-ups of Harpo's unique fingering of his instrument, with zoom shots and striking angles, they were never able to force cinematic life into what remained essentially stagy performances. Apart from such moments, however, the skillful interplay of the Marx Brothers created a kind of humor that was ideally suited to the requirements of the sound camera.

If the Marxes provided perfect foils for one another, W. C. Fields was the perfect sound comedian in himself. The irascible, bumbling braggadocio that was his screen character was also, it would seem, his off-screen character as well. He was an unpredictable eccentric whose confirmed pessimism had been nourished by years of adversity. A lifetime of rigorous training as a juggler in circus and vaudeville had made his every gesture and movement a masterpiece of precise timing. The result was an incomparable blend of half-articulate howls of rage, mumbled bits of private philosophy ("No man who hates small dogs and children can be *all* bad"), and eloquent pantomime. Many of the best sight gags in his earlier pictures were developed from his old stage routines, such as the golfing scene with the bent clubs in *You're Telling Me* (1934), his attempts to sleep on a noisy back porch in *It's a Gift* (1934) and the hilariously crooked poker game in *Mississippi* (1935).

There was always an air of improvisation about a Fields picture, as if his comedy patter and throw-away lines had been caught almost by accident by the camera. One had the feeling that the next time the picture was run, they might not even be there! It gave his films the peculiar fascination of a newsreel, of a one-time happening to a truly unique character. The pictures themselves were invariably abominably constructed, a hodgepodge of plot and gags that shot off in all directions. Indeed, his final film, *Never Give a Sucker an Even Break* (1941), almost defies description, its narrative has so many breaks and changes. But, like all the Fields films, it is full of the most inspired inanities—Fields diving out of an airplane after his whisky bottle and comparing an ordinary cigarette to the new king size as he plummets to earth, his running warfare with the formidable waitress at the local hash house ("I did *not* say this meat was tough. I just said I didn't see the horse that usually stands outside.") And, as in all the Fields films, there were the familiar props —the agile cane, the straw hat that constantly popped out of his hands or flew off his head, the stump of a cigar that half concealed his more scurrilous oaths.

Fields wrote most of his own pictures, using such improbable noms de plume as Otis J. Cribblecoblis or Mahatma Kane Jeeves; probably no one else could have realized quite so well the picaresque qualities inherent in the character, or dreamed up the mass of petty harassments through which Fields fought his way with beady eye and wide-swinging cane. Like the Marx Brothers, like Will Rogers and Bob Hope, Field's humor was verbal; but what gave it character and substance was the bulbous nose, the look of outraged dignity and larcenous innocence that accompanied everything he said or did.

INTEGRATION AND STYLE: ASTAIRE AND HITCHCOCK

The fact is that in the work of the best comedians of the thirties the sound film was coming closer to striking a proper balance between its visual and aural elements. Much of this was instinctive, much was the result of happy accident; but also, out of the accumulating skill and experience of directors and technicians alike, a sure craftsmanship was emerging. And as accident gave way to method, so too did the flamboyant trickery of the early years of sound give way to style. In the series of Fred Astaire and Ginger Rogers musicals that brightened the mid-thirties, for example, a camera technique was evolved that broke sharply with the exuberant, exhibitionistic patterns of the Busby Berkeley dances and permitted the closer integration of musical and story elements. The Astaire films were intimate, the dances coming not as interruptions but as extensions of the story. Astaire and Rogers danced because words alone could not convey their feelings. At first, the problem of getting into the dance was often solved mechanically, with the awkward expedient of the song cue—a bit of dialogue incorporating the title of the number or explaining its presence in the picture ("Listen, dear, they're playing our song!"). Soon, however, the Astaire films were simply letting the music steal in under the dialogue without any attempt at explanation or excuse. The dancers respond to it, and the number is under way. Obviously, Berkeley's swooping cameras and picturesquely posed chorines were out of place under these circumstances. And yet, the Astaire dances were created for the camera every bit as knowingly as Berkeley's. Few of them could be reproduced on a stage, but not because of angles or tricks but because they utilized the camera's innate ability to cover great areas, to fall back as the dancers move forward, to cut nimbly from place to place.

In the exhilarating "Bojangles of Harlem" number from *Swing Time* (1936), there are repeated examples of this new integration of the camera into the choreography of the dance itself. At one point Astaire is working solo to the accompaniment of only guitar and drums, the camera in very close to him. Suddenly he stops and flings out his arms ecstatically, the chorus dances on from either side, and the camera moves up and back to enlarge the scene as the orchestra swells out to full volume. This synchronization of the movement of the dance, the camera and the music creates a moment of rare gratification to both eye and ear. Within this same sequence there is an astonishing shadow play in which three silhouettes of Astaire work first in unison with him, then in tricky counter-rhythms. But though his routines were often tricky, his use of the camera itself was not. After his first few pictures, Astaire began to direct as well as to choreograph his dance sequences, with notable success. He brought his camera increasingly into the play of the dance, judiciously placing it to provide a tight frame for his own solo work, pulling it back to create new dimensions for the ensembles, moving it freely to sustain at all times the line of the dance. It was an unobtrusive, discreet and beautifully functional use of the camera—and one that, for the first time, achieved the balance between camera, image and the sound track that is the true art of the sound film.

What the Astaire films reveal, with their grace and lightness and sureness of touch, is the approaching technical maturity of the

American film makers. From an overemphasis of sound, many had moved to the opposite extreme, to an overemphasis of the visual element. By the middle of the thirties, a happier balance was being achieved. Directors no longer feared sound, nor did they try to conceal long dialogue passages behind a myriad of artifically created scenes. The better writers had long since discovered the difference between stage dialogue and talk on the screen while, at the top level, people like Dudley Nichols, Robert Riskin and Joseph Mankiewicz were writing with a strong awareness of the visual requirements of the medium as well. A whole corps of superbly trained cameramen—many of them, like James Wong Howe, Karl Freund and Arthur Edeson, with experience extending far back into the silent era—were fully prepared to transform their words into striking images. The sound engineers and technicians had, in a brief half-dozen years, supplied the studios with equipment that, for all its complexity, was incredibly flexible and allowed a maximum of control at every point; they stood ready to supply the director with virtually any effect he might request. As is always the case, masterpieces were few and far between. But the period of experimentation was over and the period of integration and consolidation could begin.

One of the first directors to achieve this integration in dramatic films was England's Alfred Hitchcock, whose mystery thrillers began to appear on American screens in 1935. Perhaps because the mystery form has always laid emphasis on visual shocks and surprises, the full extent of his contribution has been somewhat underestimated. Hitchcock did far more than simply bathe his stories in somber lighting and deep shadow to create in his audiences a dread of the unexpected. And also, it should be added, he did more than invent a series of brilliant, equally disquieting surprise effects on the sound track (although some, such as the woman's scream in *The 39 Steps* that merges with the shriek of a locomotive's whistle, have become classics in the field).

One has only to read through the first few pages of John Buchan's *The 39 Steps*, however, and compare the novel with Hitchcock's screen treatment of it to recognize his full stature. From Buchan's description of his hero wandering about London, looking in windows, stopping in bars, taking in a show, Hitchcock selected the one incident—scarcely more than a passing phrase—that lent itself best to dramatic screen treatment. He opens the film at a variety theater—something for the eye, something for the ear—and leads the narrative back there for the dramatic finale. Throughout the film the incidents are suggested by the novel rather than reproducing it scene for scene. Hitchcock, who has always worked on his own screenplays, prefers to invent around an idea, letting it develop in filmic terms rather than in terms of the novel or short story used as source material. His favorite device was the "magguffin," his own term to describe a visual or sound gimmick—a snatch of music, a man with a twitching eye, a ticking time bomb—that runs throughout the picture as a sinister leitmotif. In *The 39 Steps* this "magguffin" is a man with a missing finger. The key figure in the mysterious spy ring, he is wholly Hitchcock's invention: there is no counterpart for him in the original novel.

What contributed to the fascination of such vintage Hitchcocks as *The 39 Steps* (1935), *Secret Agent* (1935), *The Woman Alone* (1936), *The Girl Was Young* (1937), and *The Lady Vanishes* (1938) was his deliberate underplaying of climactic scenes. A woman staggers toward the camera and then, as she collapses, we see the hilt of the dagger in her back. A boy unwittingly carries a time bomb across London; we see him mount a bus and then, in long shot, the bus blows up. We are not shown the kidnaping of the old woman in *The Lady Vanishes*; we only know that suddenly in her place in the railway carriage has appeared a dreadful grim-faced substitute wearing her clothes and claiming to be Miss Froy. In *The Woman Alone*, while Sylvia Sidney is preparing to murder her husband in the shadowy movie house, on the sound track is heard the macabre refrain from Disney's cartoon *Who Killed Cock Robin?* There was a casual urbanity about Hitchcock's most carefully prepared moments, whether visual or aural, that quickly established his supremacy not only as a director of thrillers but as a master of the sound-film medium. His pictures, eagerly awaited during the late thirties, led inevitably to a Hollywood contract. Although Hitchcock frankly admits that he is now doing what he calls "the commercial thing," few directors today can rival him in the grace and polish, the slick surface finish of his star-studded comedy melo-dramas.

THE SCRIPT AND THE STARS

Unquestionably the greatest single difficulty that faced the di-rectors of the mid-thirties was the problem of handling dialogue gracefully. The public had visibly tired of the "100% all-talkies"; the critics railed against them. With sound itself no longer a novelty, audiences grew bored and restless at movies that didn't move, at pictures that told their stories almost entirely in words. Although Lubitsch, Clair, and Mamoulian had got around this by minimiz-ing their dialogue, the majority of films continued to consist solely of long, tedious conversations that came either directly from the theater or—what was just as bad—from stage-trained writers. Fre-quently writers and directors sought to give the screen some sem-blance of mobility by breaking up long dialogue passages into scene fragments. A conversation might begin in a taxi, continue in the living room and wind up in the bedroom. Too often such a device was simply distracting, drawing attention away from the words themselves while adding nothing to the cinematic feeling of the film. Obviously, another approach was needed.

Before any approach could be successful, however, there had to be a drastic revision in the dialogue itself. The script writers, whether recruited from the theater, from radio or the silent movie, had to discover a truly filmic language, a language with a lively fascination of its own. Primarily, it was a dialogue that had to approximate more closely the patterns of ordinary speech than is either necessary—or desirable—on the stage or in literature. The theater demands a richness of verbal imagery to help cloak the immobile and restrictive nature of its settings. Stage dialogue is full of descriptions of off-stage events that must be reported because they can not be shown. It is laced through with psychological in-sights into character and motivation that sound highly artificial in the movies. It is, in a word, "theatrical." Only in the theater can a character say, as in *Death of a Salesman,* "Nobody dast blame this man. You don't understand: Willy was a salesman. And for a sales-man, there is no rock bottom to the life. He don't put a bolt to a nut, he don't tell you the law or give you medicine. He's the man way out there in the blue riding on a smile and a shoestring. And when they start not smiling back—that's an earthquake. And then you get yourself a couple of spots on your hat, and you're finished. Nobody dast blame this man. A salesman is got to dream, boy. It comes with the territory." Such words create their own spell, their own poetry in the theater, but they disintegrate and destroy all sense of character in the more naturalistic film medium.

Nor is the language of literature, particularly as discovered in the novel, any more suitable for direct filming (although there is growing evidence that many of today's writers have been strongly influenced in their conception of dialogue by repeated exposure to the motion picture). Ideally, no screen character can be permitted the paragraphs of introspective speeches that the protagonist of a novel so often indulges in. And certainly the long, discursive passages in which the author explores the ramifications of his theme—always one of the primary attractions of the novel form—defy translation into film in terms of dialogue. When Budd Schulberg reversed the accepted procedure and expanded his screenplay for *On the Waterfront* (1954) into a novel, it was specifically in order to develop themes and ideas that he could not put into the mouths of the illiterate and half-articulate characters he had brought so vividly to life upon the screen.

Screen writers had to invent dialogue that was at once rich and colorful, pungent and amusing, but also stripped of inessentials. They had to learn not only what to say, but also how much could be left unsaid—how much could be left to the camera and the actor and the director to put on the screen through action and gesture or by implication. Here, for example, is a portion of the final scene from Dudley Nichols' splendid script for *The Informer* (1935), a model of terse cinematic writing:

> "*The Vestibule of the Church:* Gypo comes in with the same slow, stiff walk (as in the previous shot), his arms limp at his sides. Dazedly he sees the font and reverently he dips his hand in and tries to cross himself. But that hand weighs a ton and he cannot do it. Stiffly he turns and staggers through the narrow Roman door, and we next see him inside the church,

swaying in the dim, mysterious light. He tries to think where
he is. Then he sees a kneeling figure in a black dress, alone in
the church on the aisle, about halfway up, on the side, and he
staggers on with that stiff, slow walk, finally reaching the kneeling figure. It is Mrs. McPhillip praying for her dead son. Gypo
swallows the blood in his mouth and stands there weaving
before her, and his voice is a thick whisper.

    Gypo: 'Twas I informed on your son, Mrs. McPhillip.
. . . Forgive me . . .

    Mrs. McPhillip: (tears running down her worn, kindly face)
I forgive you Gypo. You didn't know what you were doing."

Here is work for camera, director, actor, set designer *and* the
sound recordist. The scenario provides the mood, the atmosphere,
the dialogue and the main elements of the action in the scene. But
it remained for John Ford, the director, to determine upon the
diffused light from a street lamp as the key illumination behind
Gypo when he stumbles into the church; to follow his leaden movements down the aisle with a camera placed to the rear, emphasizing
at once his bulk and the emptiness of the room; to hold the camera
in close on Mrs. McPhillip during the brief dialogue passage;
and then, a moment later, to move the camera high behind the altar
so that as the dying Gypo cries out, "Frankie! Frankie! Your mother
forgives me!" he seems to be speaking directly to Christ on the altar
cross. The script for a film, in short, is like an orchestral score. It
is the conductor's interpretation of the music that finally brings
it to life for the concert audience. It is the director's visualization
of the script that creates the movie, blending dialogue with action
to produce the most affecting combination of both.

    The Informer demonstrated the advantages of a strong writer-
director team, a collaboration that in Ford and Nichols produced
such memorable films as *The Lost Patrol* (1934), *The Plough and
the Stars* (1936), *Stagecoach* (1939) and *The Long Voyage Home*
(1940). Another outstanding writer-director team of the thirties
was Robert Riskin and Frank Capra. In such enormously popular
comedies as *Lady for a Day* (1933), *It Happened One Night* (1934),
Mr. Deeds Goes to Town (1936), *You Can't Take It With You*
(1938) and *Mr. Smith Goes to Washington* (1939), Capra demon-

strated his confidence in the ability of his colleague to write dialogue that held its own upon the screen by filming long passages without any change in camera position whatsoever. His special skill lay in recreating the speed and humor of silent comedy in the sound medium, feeling out the subtle relationship between dialogue and camera, sensing when cutting or camera movement was required and when words alone could carry the momentum of his scene. If the talk was good, he reasoned, why try to hide it? A favorite technique of his was to start an extended dialogue passage with the camera some distance away from his principals, then slowly, almost imperceptibly, track in to a large two-shot, as if irresistibly drawn by his interest in what the people were saying.

In *It Happened One Night,* with entire sequences played within the confines of a bus or a small tourist cabin, Capra ingeniously contrived to keep his screen alive by scanning the faces of the passengers on the bus, or discovering his stars almost haphazardly among the people and the packages and seats that surrounded them. Only when the dialogue was important, when it bore significantly on the development of the story, did he move in for protracted close-ups. But these close-ups were completely functional: they emphasized the words. Capra sensed when he could count on Riskin's lines to carry a scene without additional visual pyrotechnics, when they could be shot with a static camera or when the full effectiveness of the scene required the extra mobility of the moving camera and staccato editing of silent days. A particularly delightful sequence illustrates his ability to blend the two: Clark Gable and Claudette Colbert are sitting on a fence by the side of the road holding an animated conversation on the best way to thumb a ride from the passing cars; Capra filmed this entire scene in a single shot without moving his camera. But when Gable walks out to the road to demonstrate his hitch-hiking methods (capped by Colbert's conclusive evidence that the knee is mightier than the thumb), Capra builds the scene from short snatches of pantomimed action brilliantly edited together—climaxed with an adroit montage in which a glimpse of Miss Colbert's leg brings a car to a screeching halt.

Capra was also among the first to perceive that the use of dialogue on the screen involved not only the preparation of a taut, vivid, idiomatic prose, but also a more specialized handling of the actors delivering that dialogue. And here was perhaps the final adjustment that directors had to make to sound. In silent days the director could (and often did) build a star's performance out of bits and pieces—a close-up of the actor, a reaction shot, an insert of an object or an image that underscored the emotional content of the scene. With sound, much of this "synthetic" kind of acting was automatically eliminated. Not only did the actors now have to speak their lines, but—as Al Jolson in *The Jazz Singer* so clearly revealed—the sound track itself produced a far greater awareness of their essential personality than the silent camera ever had. Voice, face, mannerisms and temperament were fused together by the sound camera to create that elusive, indefinable quality known as "box-office appeal." These were the elements that the actor brought to his part—along with whatever measure of talent he possessed. More important than acting ability, however, was the photogenic magnetism of the star, around which the director could create a characterization. It was a quality which, when properly used, added its own dynamism to the film. And directors like Capra, Ford, George Cukor and William Wyler who gained the reputation of being "good with actors" were good because they knew how to fit their stars to their roles, and how to utilize their personalities to sustain the momentum of a scene.

THE ART OF THE SOUND FILM

For anyone who can remember the silent film at all distinctly, it is a bit startling to realize that we have had talking pictures for just about as many years as there was silence. The sound film, now barely thirty years old, seems to have been here forever; while the silent film is almost lost in the mists of time—a museum piece, like Etruscan art. Within a year or two of their arrival, the talkies had ousted the silents. Their rapid acceptance soon dissipated the hostility, the bitterness with which critics, aestheticians and many of the film makers themselves first greeted the new medium. The "novelty" of 1928 came to stay, and a whole generation has since grown up without ever having seen a silent movie—except perhaps as distorted by television or burlesqued in *Flicker Flashbacks*.

Today the sound films have had quite as long to reach their maturity as did the silent screen. It would seem that the time has come to assess the art of the sound film as a medium in its own right, a medium that has grown out of the silent days, but one that in growing has developed its own forms, its own techniques.

Considered as a whole, this development has been swifter, but less dramatic, less clear-cut than the evolution of the silent film. There are fewer personalities to whom one can point and say, "He did this," or "He contributed that." The big work of exploration had been done in the silent period. The basic techniques on which the talkies were to build—the many functions of the cut, the interpretive powers of the camera, the evolution of a cinematic style of acting—all of these had been discovered long before the microphone took over. Sound produced no D. W. Griffith to take the raw materials of camera and microphone and forge from them a new medium. Nor is it possible to speak of French symbolism, Russian cutting or German lighting and camera movement in the sound era. Sound produced no such distinctive national styles of film making. Instead, the same technical problems—and very much the same solutions—seem to have presented themselves almost simultaneously in every film-producing nation. First came the period of "canned theater" which vigorously exploited sound for its own sake and filled the screens of every nation with painfully static reproductions of stage plays and musicals. Then came the experimenters, the men who revolted against the rigid camera and theatrical dialogue, directors who sought to return to the screen some of the mobility of silent days, who sought to use the sound track itself for something more than the mere literal reproduction of dialogue. And, since the mid-thirties, there has been the slow, steady search for a balance, an integration of sound and visual—all leading to a new and universal film form that is, ideally, neither "canned theater" nor what Alfred Hitchcock once described as "silent talkies."

Actually, the sound film is a composite of many arts, and the theater was only one of the contributors to the new medium. By the mid-thirties music too was finding its place, not only in the song-and-dance pictures but in the dramas as well. When Max Steiner's score for *A Symphony of Six Million* (1932) won unanticipated enthusiasm for a sentimental story of New York's East

Side, music began to acquire a certain prestige. Soon it was being tossed into films indiscriminately, good or bad, necessary or not: it added "production value" to the picture. By 1935, however, in such films as John Ford's *The Informer,* there was a determined (if still rudimentary) effort to use music to strengthen dramatic values as well. Toward the end of the thirties, serious composers like Aaron Copland, George Antheil and Hanns Eisler were making their way into the American studios, while in the European studios, Arthur Bliss, Arthur Honegger, Dmitri Shostakovich and Sergei Prokofieff were mastering the craft of scoring a film and helping to raise film music to an art.

Obviously, the sound track did not eliminate the need for a creative visual track, although in many ways it altered the nature of that creativity. It required a new perception of the tensions that can be created by dialogue, the spell that can be woven by the actor, the continuity that can be provided by music. Because of his background in radio as well as in theater, Orson Welles brought to his early films a heightened awareness of the full potency of sound. His inventive staging of such classics as *Macbeth, Julius Caesar* and *Doctor Faustus* in the New York theater had set the pulses racing with their incantation-like drumbeats, trumpet flourishes and weird off-stage voices. His radio shows—not only the famous *War of the Worlds,* but his week-in, week-out mystery dramas and suspense pieces—were filled with echo chambers, filters, adroit musical bridges from one scene to the next and, in most cases, featured Welles himself as narrator. Narration—the voice of an all-seeing, all-knowing commentator who sets the scene, threads the story together and, from time to time, offers his special insight into the motivations and thoughts of the characters—was common enough in radio. Films, on the other hand, except for newsreels and documentaries, were still using subtitles for introductions, place names and dates until Welles introduced the narration technique in *Citizen Kane* (1941) and *The Magnificent Ambersons* (1942).

Of these two films, *Kane* has always received the greater attention, partly for its bold presentation of a controversial figure, partly because of its unique four-part story construction. Certainly, the film was experimental in the extreme—wide-angle photography that created the illusion of vast spaces, dramatic lighting that threw deep shadows over great portions of the screen, a camera that was constantly seeking out the important character, the important incident, the important gesture. The score, by Bernard Herrmann, who had composed the music for most of Welles's radio shows, was completely functional, providing dramatic accents, tying scenes together, making transitions—never simply purring in the background. But *Kane* suffered from an excess of experimentation. Angle shots were too often included for their own sake; scenes were played in semi-darkness for purely arbitrary reasons. Its story leaped spasmodically from place to place, from character to character. Its final "explanation" was far too superficial for all the tricks and effects that had gone into the telling of the story. *Kane* was bold and arresting, but also coldly objective and overly intellectual in its handling of the characters. It impressed, but it rarely excited its audience. For his second production Welles was ordered by his studio to be somewhat less experimental. Although *The Magnificent Ambersons* may look like a more conventional film than *Citizen Kane,* actually it is a good deal more inventive—but in subtler, more cinematic ways.

Unfortunately, it is difficult to speak of *The Magnificent Ambersons* as a complete film. The Booth Tarkington novel on which it is based was a shrewd study of the disintegration of a Midwestern "first family" under the impact of the rising industrial aristocracy around 1910, and Welles had filmed it with emphasis both on character and on social background. But bad relations between him and the heads of RKO resulted in the picture's being taken away from his Mercury Productions unit on the RKO lot soon after shooting was completed and while the film was still being edited. The studio reduced his footage to a shorter, "more commercial" picture than he had visualized. Cutting for story, they eliminated scenes calculated to prepare the audience for major changes in the characters, as well as much of the material showing the physical transformation of the town itself. What remains is there because it was essential for purposes of continuity. Still, it is enough to reveal much of Welles's intention and Welles's technique.

The picture opens with an adroit sequence designed to establish the period and to introduce the leading characters of the film. Over Welles's witty narration we see, almost cartoon-fashion, the styles, the customs, the way of life in a small town at the turn of the century. He refers to "that prettiest of all vanished customs—the serenade," and we see a slightly intoxicated Eugene Morgan (Joseph Cotten) with a group of musicians courting Isabel Amberson (Dolores Costello)—and awkwardly falling into his own bass viol. Next, Welles talks about the stovepipe hats then in fashion, and shows another suitor, Wilbur Miniffer, wearing one as he rows Isabel on a quiet lake. And a moment later we learn from the narration that Isabel is going to marry Wilbur even though she really loves Eugene. Thus, within three minutes of film the background, the principals and the central situation have all been brought before the audience, presented with the unique economy made possible by the narration technique. Welles used it at several points in the picture to give insight into character, to comment upon the changing social scene or upon the action itself.

In radio Welles had developed a special montage technique using a crescendo of voices, each saying a sentence or sometimes merely a fragment of a sentence. This he carried over into film, photographing the various speakers in close-up against a blank background. Spliced together in quick succession, the shots gave the impression of a whole town talking—and, equally important, what the whole town was talking about. Welles even altered traditional dialogue techniques to create a more vivid, more realistic feeling in his scenes. It has long been a stage—and now a movie—convention to permit one character to complete a speech before the next begins to reply. Actual conversations, of course, rarely progress in this fashion. One person speaks and then, often before he has finished the sentence, the listener interrupts with his own opinion. In a roomful of people, no one dreams of remaining silent until one speaker has completed his remarks. Numerous conversations take place simultaneously, overlapping one another, even drowning out one another. Welles, after seeking to reproduce this effect in radio, found it even more suitable for films, where the source of the words is always visible. He had toyed with it a bit in *Citizen Kane*, as in the quick succession of breakfast quarrels that signal the growing estrangement between Kane and his wife. In *The Magnificent Ambersons* it became an important element in building the reality of his scenes and his people. The farewells after the last great ball at the Amberson mansion, the tired jumble of voices arguing, questioning, nagging as the Ambersons prepare for bed, the spontaneous gaiety of a family outing in the snow—all of these came alive through Welles's natural use of normal speech patterns. In his drive to get this same kind of naturalism from his performers he sometimes went to extremes. Thus he made Agnes Moorehead repeat and repeat her long climactic scene of near hysteria until what the camera finally captured was no longer an actress acting but a woman truly on the verge of hysterics.

In camera techniques, Welles proved more eclectic than original —but his sources were the best. Von Stroheim seems to have been peering over his shoulder as Welles conceived the long carriage ride through the town's main street, the camera catching in the polished shop windows the reflection of buildings and people on the other side of the street to create an extraordinary sense of the three-dimensional reality of the town itself. The many lingering lap dissolves are reminiscent of von Sternberg. There is even one long, slow iris-out that suggests a familiarity with the work of Griffith. Between Welles's highly original use of sound and imaginative use of the camera, he established an exciting integration of the two—a cinematic style distinguished by its naturalism, its economy and originality. Seen today, *The Magnificent Ambersons* seems, if anything, more impressive than when it first appeared. The gradual absorption of the techniques that it introduced has removed some of its strangeness, and time itself the taint of intellectuality that repelled its audiences in 1942. Its artistry is clearer now, even though—like von Stroheim's *Greed*—the film itself is an emasculated version of what its director had intended.

Welles's subsequent film work has never lived up to its early promise, but much that he experimented with in the early forties— the narrative technique, deep-focus photography, overlapping dialogue, a functional use of music—is today the common practice in the studios. The cameramen, editors, composers, even the producers who worked with Welles absorbed his techniques and ideas and frequently carried them along to their subsequent jobs. Welles as a director is no longer a major force, but his contributions to the medium continue through the men he trained and influenced.

With the appearance of *Citizen Kane* and *The Magnificent Ambersons*, the incessant exploration of the resources of camera and microphone that characterized the best films of the thirties came to a close. The pioneer days of sound were over. In little more than a decade directors everywhere had achieved a technical mastery that made them far less self-conscious in their search for "effects." Soon, in the work of men like Vittorio De Sica and David Lean, John Huston and Elia Kazan, one could discover the growing maturity of the medium. And because their films have won international acclaim, such directors have influenced the work and the thinking of film makers throughout the world. In their personal styles and techniques are to be found the creative potentialities of the art of the sound film.

John Ford, for example, is one of the true veterans of Hollywood, still active, still productive. Not only his sound but even his wide-screen films reveal his long experience, combining the visual continuity of silent editing techniques with a perfect instinct for just how much each shot should tell. He is so certain of his effects that his editors claim he cuts his films himself within the camera, providing them with little more than they actually need to piece the scene together. His takes, generally shorter than most directors', move with incredible precision from point to point, always anticipating the audience's natural curiosity. Typical was the memorable fight scene in *Young Mr. Lincoln* (1939). It takes place at night in a forest, some distance from the festivities of a Fourth of July picnic. At first it is perceived only dimly—heard rather than seen through the trees, the brush and the darkness. Some women rush to the scene, and we see the fright on their faces. The moon appears from behind the clouds, and now we see the fight as the women see it, close, intense and deadly. The moon passes behind a cloud and a shot rings out. When the light returns we are watching from the edge of the scene. A dying man is dancing in agony while a puff of smoke mounts toward the sky, and a boy calls for his mother. Throughout this brief sequence, Ford's cutting and his choice of camera position alike have been dictated by the logic of the material, the flow of its emotion and by his superb instinct for what the audience will want to see from one moment to the next. Never one to cut for shock effect or to create an artificial sense of surprise or excitement, Ford's films demonstrate functional editing at its best—precise, unobtrusive and sure.

England's David Lean, on the other hand, frequently relies on editing techniques for his best moments. His early experiences as cameraman and editor taught him the art of cutting. And in directing such films as *Brief Encounter* (1945), *Great Expectations* (1946), *Breaking the Sound Barrier* (1952) and *Summertime* (1955), he has repeatedly revealed his special awareness of the creative possibilities of the cut. The hilarious moment when Katharine Hepburn tumbles into the canal in *Summertime* was built through some of the neatest cutting since sound arrived. Perhaps the most famous bit of editing in all sound films is Lean's spectacular cut from the boy Pip to the grim Magwitch in the eerie graveyard scene from *Great Expectations.* The convict's sudden appearance invariably frightens audiences just as much as it frightened Pip—precisely the effect that Lean had hoped to achieve. Close examination of the scene shows that the camera was already in motion, moving away from the boy toward the waiting Magwitch when the cut comes, creating a moment of uneasy anticipation and suspense that is more than justified by the shot that follows. It is a sequence that only a director with an awareness of the power of the camera as well as the cut could have realized. And Lean reinforced its power not with a startling crash of "scare music" in the orchestra, but with the creak of trees and the howl of wind in the dark, forbidding graveyard.

Lean's compatriot, Sir Carol Reed, the director of *Odd Man Out* (1947), *The Fallen Idol* (1948), *The Third Man* (1949) and *Trapeze* (1956), came to film from the theater early in the thirties and quickly established his ability to draw outstanding performances from his players. His early pictures were heavily theatrical in style, but a turning point in Reed's directorial career came with the success of *Night Train* (1939), an adventure film made very much in the Hitchcock manner. In it he found a new respect for the camera—the excitement of unexpected angles, of tensions created by artful framing and swift changes of position. Certainly, by the time he made *Odd Man Out,* that taut, tragic story of a hunted and dying man, the camera was completely his instrument. The film opens with an attempted robbery, photographed in stark, documentary style. James Mason, the leader of a band of Irish revolutionaries, is mortally wounded in the getaway and abandoned by his friends. His life ebbing slowly, he turns desperately from one to another for shelter and for help. As the man grows weaker and more feverish, the angles grow wilder and more distorted, the imagery richer and more chaotic—a crowded pub, the rococo studio of a mad artist. In the final shots, with Mason dying in the snow by an iron fence overlooking the Belfast harbor, the photography returns once again to the simplicity of the opening scenes—but darker now, quieter and less intense. Reed seems particularly aware of the camera's ability to suggest a point of view, an inner state of turmoil, torment or confusion. In *The Fallen Idol,* many of the shots are taken from an unusually low angle, photographed as they would be seen by the small boy who is the hero of the story. The sinister, corrupted life of postwar Vienna is suggested in *The Third Man* through hugely distorted angle shots, through great shadows moving over dark rain-glistening streets and interiors over-rich with décor.

Reed invariably enhances his films with a sound track that adds greatly to their expressive power. The changing quality of sound in a city builds both the time progression and the growing confusion and despair of Mason in *Odd Man Out*—sounds of children playing give way to the clamor of the pubs, the street noises, the distant ships in the harbor, and finally the great clock tolling midnight and the death knell of the tragic man. *The Third Man* is perhaps best known for the economy of its nostalgic zither accompaniment, but behind the zither lies the echo of fleeing footsteps across a cobblestoned square, the hollow timbre of voices in a bombed-out building, the labored breathing of pursued and pursuer in the climactic chase through the cavernous sewers beneath the city. Given a good script, Carol Reed is one of the finest film makers working today.

Less facile than Reed in the use of the camera, but at his best more intense and always more searching is the Italian Roberto Rossellini. It was Rossellini who first drew the attention of the world to the postwar Italian film with his memorable *Open City* (1945). In it he marvelously combines a sense of objective reality with a warm, passionate feeling for the people, an effect achieved as much through his use of the camera as by what he places before it. Such scenes as the cold-blooded shooting of a pregnant woman fighting against the arrest of her husband, the torture of the underground leader and the execution of the Catholic priest are made immediate by huge, inescapable close-ups. When a gang of boys blows up a Nazi supply train, on the other hand, the details are left in semi-darkness; not until they clamber up the stairs of their tenement home does Rossellini give us a good look at them—and then not as bold saboteurs but as frightened little children whose parents are anxiously awaiting them. A truckload of Gestapo police is seen from a rooftop where a Resistance leader is hiding; the fright of the ordinary citizen as the men ransack the apartment building is conveyed through the great, looming shots of the Nazis themselves, their uniforms and their gleaming, murderous equipment. Underlying all is the determination to force the camera to the limits of realistic re-creation so that the audience not only sees but feels the terror and the courage of the Romans during the occupation years.

Rossellini's next film, *Paisan* (1946), is without question his greatest, and also one of the greatest of all sound films. Its six-part story, inspired by the suffering, the heartbreak and the innate dignity of the Italian people, covers incidents in the advance of the war up the Italian Peninsula from Sicily to the marshes north of the Po. Each incident, complete in itself, is treated in a slightly different style; but all are united by a common bond of sympathy for the human condition, whether it be manifest in a drunken Negro M.P., a Roman prostitute, or the naïve faith of the priests in a monastery isolated not only from the war but from the world. Despite an unevenness in construction and quality in the separate episodes, Rossellini's mastery of the camera is everywhere apparent. Even the weakest of the stories, the Florence sequence, captures with the impersonal immediacy of a newsreel the feeling of a war with no front lines, no visible troops and sudden death hanging heavy in the air. The Rome interlude is a love story, twisted and defiled by the war. Here Rossellini's photographic style is close, intimate, revealing the exhilaration of an American G.I. and a Roman girl who meet and fall in love on the glorious day of liberation, and the bitter disillusion of their second meeting only six months later. The final and finest episode in *Paisan* depicts the isolation and eventual defeat of a group of partisans cut off and hunted by the Nazis in the treacherous marshlands of northern Italy. Rossellini accentuates the dreariness, the hopelessness of their guerrilla action almost entirely by his use of the camera. Shot after shot reveals the low, distant horizons—empty of help, empty of hope. There is only the constant, veiled menace of the Germans, unseen but vividly implied in such shots as the dead partisan floating grotesquely in the water that opens the sequence, or the glimpse of a baby howling amidst the corpses of its slaughtered family. Rarely have sound and sight been blended so skillfully and economically to assail the emotions, creating out of hopelessness not despair, but a profound admiration for the dauntless courage of the human spirit.

In the films that Rossellini has turned out since *Paisan,* those ideas that interested him particularly are revealed in scenes of extraordinary power and intensity—the suicide of the child in *Germany Year Zero* (1947), the mad girl's torment in the church plaza of *The Miracle* (1948) and the huge close-ups of the insane in *No Greater Love* (*Europa 51,* 1952). In such sequences Rossellini uses the expressive powers of the camera with a mastery that few directors have ever approached. Unfortunately, the creative vigor that sustains these moments soon flickers out and they are followed by long expositional passages that are all too often slipshod and routine. As a result, one looks forward to a new Rossellini film hopefully rather than with high expectation.

Vittorio De Sica, on the other hand, while rarely achieving the heights of Rossellini at his best, directs a film in which artistic control predominates from the first frame to the final fade-out. With the sole exception of *Miracle in Milan* (1951), a fantasy, one searches in vain through his pictures for camera effects, camera tricks or distinctive editing techniques. Instead, what one finds is a kind of compression within the shot, an intensification of an emotion by placing within a single frame visual elements that make their own commentary upon the main action. Thus, early in *The Bicycle Thief* (1949) the wife goes to pawn the family linens so that her husband can buy the bicycle he needs for his new job. As she deposits her bundle at the pawnbroker's window, the camera moves slowly over bin after bin, stack after stack of similar bundles —the family goods of thousands as poor and as desperate as the hero of this film. Later, after his precious bicycle has been stolen and an all-day search for it proves futile, the man and his little boy sit despondent on a curb. Suddenly, between them and the camera flash dozens of cyclists returning from a sports arena. The sight of all these bicycles being used for pleasure passing within inches of a man whose need for one is a matter of life and death creates an irony deeper than words. When the father, furious at the world, turns and spitefully cuffs his little boy, the sudden spiritual gulf between the two becomes visible as the boy scuffs along high on an embankment while the father, already ashamed of his action, walks slowly down the pavement on the other side of the street. No less skillful is the climactic shot from *Umberto D.* (1952) that makes us wait until an entire train has passed before we can discover the fate of Umberto's little dog, his one possession.

After Rossellini and De Sica, only one other Italian director has achieved a similar compression of emotional statement, an ability to reveal a human truth in vivid cinematic terms. The youthful Federico Fellini, a former writer-assistant to Rossellini, proved himself a major talent with only three pictures—*I Vitelloni* (1954), *La Strada* (1954) and *Il Bidone* (1955). In *La Strada* he displayed an individuality of viewpoint, a poetic approach to realism, an eye for the expressive image and a strong feeling for atmosphere; and above all else, an ability to use the camera for revelation, not merely exposition.

In France the outstanding film maker, always excepting René Clair, is that master of cynicism and shock, Henri-Georges Clouzot. With a mere handful of films—*Le Corbeau* (1943), *Manon* (1949), *The Wages of Fear* (1953) and *Les Diaboliques* (1955)—he has established his mastery of a melodramatic kind of realism that is relentless in its pursuit of effects, brilliant in its creation of them. In *The Wages of Fear* the detailed realism of the opening reels, creating a mood of utter hopelessness and degradation, sets the stage for the long, harrowing drive to the burning oil fields with truckloads of nitroglycerin ready to explode at every jolt and jar. The drivers are gambling their very lives against the opportunity to escape from their steaming, sordid environment—the vermin, the filth, the callousness that Clouzot has made explicit with his penetrating camera. Similarly, in *Les Diaboliques* the atmosphere of a third-rate French boarding school provides an extraordinary realism of background for the Grand Guignol horrors of the story. At its climax a panic-stricken woman moves helplessly through darkened corridors closer and closer to her doom. Mysterious gloved hands softly turn a knob, glide relentlessly down a banister; lights flicker on and off, a floor board creaks, the sound of typing is heard from an empty room, water rushes from a distant tap—and the atmosphere grows dense with an expectant terror that is more than justified by the final horror. This is film making of breath-taking virtuosity. To date, virtuosity has been Clouzot's primary concern, mobilizing the camera for melodramatic effects with chilling precision and complete authority. No other film maker today—not even Hitchcock—excels him in this limited but very popular field.

Clouzot has been described as "Hitchcock with a touch of carbolic acid," but this only partially explains the differences between the two men. Certainly, Clouzot lacks Hitchcock's urbane good humor in viewing the eccentricities or even rascalities of the human species. But where Clouzot's primary concern is the effective telling of an exciting story, Hitchcock has in recent years displayed a keener interest in setting himself difficult technical problems to overcome. In *Lifeboat* (1944) he purposely confined his camera to one particularly cramped setting; in *Rope* (1948) he sought to make a film that completely eliminated cutting; while in *Rear Window* (1954) his pursuit of the unconventional led him to photograph most of the action sequences in extreme long-shots. Most of the Hitchcock pictures made in this country reveal his absorption in the creation of special camera effects—the long, slow pan around the empty cottage in *Rebecca* (1940), his first American film; the twisting travelling shot following the supposedly poisoned glass of milk in *Suspicion* (1941); the climactic shot in *Spellbound* (1945), with the camera behind the pistol as it swings away from Gregory Peck, circling 180° to Leo Carroll and then going off point-blank in a sudden burst of Technicolor; the record-breaking kissing scene in *Notorious* (1946), with a peripatetic camera hovering close to Ingrid Bergman in her amorous pursuit of Cary Grant. Characteristically, Hitchcock was the first of the star directors to try his hand at 3-D when the vogue for stereoscopic movies swept the country a few years ago.

And yet, despite his penchant for tricks and effects, Hitchcock continues to be one of the most interesting and accomplished of

IT is INGRID BERGMAN, NOT G. PECK.

America's star directors. Few move their cameras so daringly, frame their action so expertly, or know so well the precise moment to cut from action to reaction. Few have his flair for staging a scene to give it the rare quality of reality caught by chance—a juror blowing his nose in one corner of the screen while another straightens his hair, the red tip of a murderer's cigar glowing ominously in a darkened apartment. He is such a practiced hand that he can afford to throw a trick away, as in his playful insertion of the fireworks during the love scenes from *To Catch a Thief* (1955). What another director might have built into a big effect, Hitchcock tosses off as a little joke. His weakest point seems to be his choice of scripts, yet even his poorest films reveal his flair, his humor and impeccable technique. Whenever Hitchcock's story judgment matches his filmic talents, the results are truly impressive.

Among the top American directors, William Wyler has perhaps the keenest editing sense of all. Although apparently preferring the adapted stage play as the basis for his pictures, he organizes his scenes with a strong, sure instinct for filmic form. In *The Little Foxes* (1941), for example, the horrifying scene in which Regina permits her husband to die upon the stairs is intensified in Wyler's handling by framing within a single shot a huge, immobile close-up of Regina while, deep in the background, the husband is seen desperately trying to make his way up the stairs. No one knows better when to shift the camera's point of view, when to cut, or how to relate the characters in one shot to those in the next. The relationships may be complex, the action involved, but you never have to wonder where you are in a Wyler picture, or from whose viewpoint you are watching the scene. His sense of film geography, his unfailing precision in the placement of his actors as he cuts from one to the other, gives his work a certainty and clarity unmatched by anyone.

Wyler has also developed to perfection a technique that might best be described as cutting within the frame. Realizing that dialogue imposes a slower editing pace than obtained in silent days, he has sought to create the effect of shifting visual patterns by strong regroupings of his characters within the shot, or by sudden changes of background. In the scene of Fredric March's homecoming in *The Best Years of Our Lives* (1946), for example, March enters close to the camera. His wife, Myrna Loy, runs toward him down a long corridor. As she approaches, their daughter, Teresa Wright, moves in from the side and the trio shut out the view of the corridor. Thus, a long-shot has been transformed into a close-up without the need of cutting. Similarly, in *The Heiress* (1949) the constant closing of doors, shutting off room after room as the camera passes through, accomplished very much the same effect. Testing out his dialogue, Wyler felt that repeated cuts would detract both from the importance of the words and the emotional flow of the performances. His solution proved an ideal technique for sound films.

A very similar technique is to be found in the films of George Stevens, another director from the silent era who has emerged as one of the most creative talents in the sound medium. Formerly a cameraman, he shares with Wyler a strong feeling for the dynamics possible within the frame, an ability to shift the dramatic emphasis within a shot without recourse to unnecessary editing. In *Shane* (1953), a "big Western" built around the hackneyed theme of farmers versus cattle ranchers, Stevens managed to infuse a new vitality, a new sense of realism into the time-worn story through the strength and freshness of his visuals. In one incredibly protracted long-shot Alan Ladd and Brandon de Wilde are speaking in the foreground while, from the distant hills, a horse and wagon approach the camera, drawing nearer and nearer until the riders dash into screen center with their important news. By this device Stevens has been able to prepare the audience for their arrival while still concentrating attention on the dialogue between his principals. Stevens habitually spends a long time on his pictures—a year on *Place in the Sun* (1951), two years on *Shane,* even longer on *Giant* (1956). A meticulous craftsman, he has been known to take days lining up a single exterior shot, then months on the final editing and shaping of his film. But out of it come the tremendous compression and richness that typify his best work, the ability to encompass dramatic overtones of atmosphere and characterization within a single shot.

Actually, it would seem that since the arrival of sound, the possibilities of working within the frame have been greatly increased, creating dramatic effects in the shot quite independent of the editing process. To replace the speed and visual action of the pre-dialogue days, directors have been forced to discover new, stimulating forms of composition to hold the spectator's eye even during scenes that are primarily dialogue. Men like Wyler and Stevens have solved the problem by frequently rearranging the composition of their shots during a dialogue passage. John Huston and Elia Kazan, on the other hand, create their effects with an unobtrusive, almost diffident use of the camera. Expert at building the mood of a scene for their actors, they permit the invisible tensions of dialogue and personality to sustain the interest of their audience. In making *On the Waterfront* (1954), for example, Kazan at times permitted his actors to improvise their lines. Before shooting the tense scene between Marlon Brando and Rod Steiger in the black limousine, Kazan worked with them until they thoroughly understood the mood of anger and desperation which he hoped to capture with his camera. Then they went ahead on their own, filling in the scene and bringing it to life by their superb interplaying, Kazan's camera merely providing the frame that focused attention on their performance. John Huston is even more adroit in conveying this sense of spontaneity on the screen. He invents for his actors innumerable bits of naturalistic business that convey the impression of impromptu realism, while by his skillful placement of the camera he accentuates the relationships between his characters. A Huston film, a Huston scene is charged with overtones that echo beyond the frame. Because tension and overtone interest both Huston and Kazan, they are extremely sparing in their use of close-ups, reserving them only for the major accents in their pictures. Most of their scenes high-light two, or at most three characters framed tightly by the camera. They achieve their intensity primarily through their actors—and through their sensitive positioning of the camera in relation to the performers. In their work, the sound film seems to have come full circle, from the early, awkward imitation of theater back to the theater's emphasis on dramatic performance now captured and magnified by the skilled use of filmic techniques.

And so, for almost three decades, directors of imagination and integrity have been refining and elaborating the structure of the sound film. Over the past thirty years they have found fresh ways to balance the performances of their actors against the pictorial excitement of costume and décor. They have discovered how best to enhance dramatic dialogue by combining it with the purely sensory appeals of music and evocative sound. There are no rules for this kind of creation, no one true technique, no single standard of excellence. There are, however, some few directors so gifted that they can work creatively with all the elements of the sound film, and these quickly take their place among the most admired, most sought-after men in the industry. Their work is studied, imitated, absorbed, enriching in time the entire medium.

It is important to recognize that this absorption process is constantly taking place, for it accounts for the steadily improving technical quality of the movies that we see. But it is also necessary to realize that sheer technique does not produce inspired films. There must exist as well a love for the medium, the urge to create, to communicate, and the talent to do so with flair, discipline and imagination. In short, the creative impulses behind all artistic endeavor are more important than technical facility in the production of a great movie. There is at present the possibility that the departmentalization of creativity now dominating studios all over the world will dissipate the single-minded vigor that once produced a *Birth of a Nation* or *Greed,* an *Open City* or *Citizen Kane.* Today, with hordes of specialists and experts each anxious to contribute his own bit of technical perfection to a picture, its identity is constantly in danger of being diluted, watered down to a characterless average. And there lurks the even greater danger that as film making grows more departmentalized—and more expensive—the purely pragmatic interests of box office will take precedence over all other impulses behind film production. Certainly, in motion pictures the *vox populi* can not be safely ignored; but neither can the industry devote itself single-mindedly to the repetition of proven box-office hits. Audiences soon tire of mere technique, while the medium thrives and grows on the efforts and accomplishments—even the box-office failures—of the genuinely creative artist.

V

INTERNATIONAL TRENDS

AMERICAN MOVIES LEARNED TO TALK WITH A SOUND THAT WAS HEARD around the world. To ensure their monopoly of the field, the great American electrical industries bought up the basic patents on existing, competing sound systems both here and abroad, and entered into trade agreements with those firms they could not buy out. With world-wide control assured, they lost no time in marketing their equipment to the European studios and theaters. As a result, sound on film soon became the standard system for talkies all over the world. And because the equipment everywhere was basically the same, the international exchange of films—and filmic ideas— could continue. Despite the language barrier, a French film could be run on German equipment, a Russian film on an American projector. Film makers could still learn from one another, profiting from advances in both the technique and the technology of the new medium. And a curious thing began to happen. The techniques of sound rapidly became standardized throughout the world. The stylistic differences that distinguished a French or Russian film from a Hollywood movie during the silent era virtually disappeared. National differences after sound are to be found less in style than in the emerging themes that, directly or indirectly, revealed each country's reactions to such world-wide crises as the depression, the Second World War and the difficult years of postwar reconstruction.

FRANCE: UNCERTAINTY AND DESPAIR

The arrival of sound in France had a disastrous effect upon its film industry. The new equipment was prohibitively expensive, but the studios had to have it if they were to stay in business. Wily investors seized upon this opportunity to gain control, buying into established companies solely to exploit them. With representatives of the banks, investment houses and equipment manufacturers sitting on their boards, the French studios quickly lost the spirit of independence and individuality that had distinguished their films during the twenties. The pictures that streamed from Gaumont, Pathé and French Paramount during the first years of sound were the cheapest kind of all-talking potboilers. To utilize the new equipment to the full, the same film was shot over and over again in different languages with different casts, but with the same settings and often the same director. Under such conditions, many of the better directors of the silent era simply withdrew from films, or left for studios in America and England. Only René Clair and a handful of others—Jean Benoît-Lévy, Julien Duvivier, Jean Renoir—had the combination of ability and tenacity to bring to the screen any truly distinguished works. And in 1934 even Clair departed, driven out by the cumulative clouds of the depression and political interference.

But all was not lost, for in the meantime two new figures emerged, men whose sharply contrasting viewpoints and techniques provided the main sources of inspiration for all subsequent French production. One was the youthful Jean Vigo, whose strong feeling for imagery, for atmosphere and milieu characterized the best French films during their brief period of optimism between 1935 and 1937, and through the long night of despair and tragedy as France fell under the shadow of World War II. Vigo's strange, almost surrealist approach to the medium found expression in only two pictures, *Zéro de Conduite* (1933) and *L'Atalante* (1934). He had a poet's instinct for the expressive symbol, for the beauty of the unexpected, for the intensity of an emotion captured in a single apt image. *Zéro de Conduite,* a nightmarish recollection of his youth in a boarding school, is filled with grotesques—the dwarfed school supervisor, the angular headmaster spying like a cat on the activities of his young charges, a pillow fight in the dormitories staged in slow motion. Similarly, in *L'Atalante*, a slight story woven around a river-barge owner and his wife, Vigo derives a curiously nostalgic poetry from the drab industrial outskirts of Paris—the tangle of railway tracks and electric wires, its misty waterfront bars and boarding houses. In mood and atmosphere, in sensitivity to the nuances of milieu, his work clearly foreshadows Marcel Carné's sympathetic studies of haunted, tragic lives in the great era of the French sound film that lay just ahead. But Vigo was never to see that era; he died in poverty at the age of 29.

So completely did Vigo create his effects with the camera that one recalls his pictures almost as silent films. At the opposite extreme was the playwright Marcel Pagnol, first attracted to the medium by the successful filming of his satiric comedy *Topaze* (1932). Working for French Paramount, he wrote and supervised the filming of his famed trilogy *Marius* (1932), *Fanny* (1932) and *César* (1933), directing the last himself. Although strenuously attacked by critics of the day for what they termed a reversion to the theatrical style of the Film d'Art, Pagnol's witty and literate dialogue, the veracity of his Marseilles types and the heart-warming performances of his cast—Raimu, Pierre Fresnay, Orane Demazis and Charpin—immediately won for his pictures a wide popularity. Pagnol readily admitted that he used the camera primarily as a means of shifting the scene, but he introduced concepts of characterization and standards of filmic dialogue that soon exerted a strong influence upon the work of other French writers and directors. The best of the French sound films became, in fact, a fusion of Vigo's haunting imagery with Pagnol's pungent, thought-provoking dialogue and fully realized characters. But it took a second crisis in the French film industry to bring this about.

By the end of 1934, all the big studios in France had closed their doors, ruined by the depression and by the corruption and mismanagement of the people who had run the industry since sound. Prudently, Pagnol took the profits from his films and plays and opened his own studio near his beloved Marseilles, where he has continued to work ever since. For the less fortunate film workers, however, there was only panic, unemployment, possibly the end of all film production in France. Their salvation—indeed, the regeneration of the French film—came from the most unexpected source. In place of the few major studios, there suddenly appeared dozens of self-styled producers, promoters hoping to profit from the chaos by raising the capital to make independent productions. And by some miracle, they not only got production going again, but the films were more creative than ever before. Although from all accounts many of these promoters were shady fly-by-night operators, they differed in one important respect from their well-entrenched predecessors. They had no committees, no boards of directors to pass upon the merits of a script, to decide what was commercially safe. They were satisfied if a director came to them with a script he wanted to do, and perhaps the promise of a star name who would appear in it—these were enough to go out and raise money on. Certainly, many an honest man was cheated of his francs in this way, many an artist worked for a salary that he never saw. But under these unlikely auspices the individuality, the creative independence of the director was returned to the French cinema. At that darkest moment in the history of the French film, its artists stood unwittingly on the brink of their own brief "Golden Era."

Events on the entire European scene were helping to pave the way. The new republic in Spain, the Italian invasion of Ethiopia, the unmistakable threat of Hitler's Germany after the Saar plebiscite had the effect of stirring up a profound national consciousness among the French. During 1935, as crisis followed crisis, the traditional divisions of French politics and the French people began to disappear, the liberal and Leftist elements drawing together in that optimistic amalgam known as the "Popular Front." A new confidence pervaded vast sections of the country, the feeling that by working together, by uniting and solving small differences men of good-will could together build a better world. For the next two years, between 1935 and 1937, this optimism dominated the French films—Jacques Feyder's *Carnival in Flanders* (*La Kermesse Héroique*, 1935), Duvivier's *They Were Five* (*La Belle Equipe*, 1936) were almost allegorical in their presentation of the theme that concerted action could overcome any calamity. Other pictures demonstrated a new concern and solicitude for the common man, expressing the need for understanding, for compassion—Renoir's *Toni* (1935) and *La Grande Illusion* (1937), Marc Allegret's *Heart of Paris* (*Gribouille*, 1935).

But quickly the tide began to change. In 1937 the "Popular

Front" saw its hopes dashed in Spain; while the fateful Munich pact clearly foreshadowed the imminence of war, causing a paralysis throughout all of France, a sense of doom that was quickly reflected in her films. Pagnol, in pictures like *Harvest* (*Régain*, 1937) and *The Baker's Wife* (*La Femme du Boulanger*, 1938), counseled a return to the soil, to the simple values of a pastoral existence. But most of the directors, looking at the contemporary scene, saw only despair. Their concern for people remained, but the cheerful image of Jean Gabin joining with his friends to build a new life in *They Were Five* gave way to a Gabin, sullen and alone, awaiting death in his besieged hotel room of *Le Jour Se Lève* (1939). Suffering, suicide, sudden death—these themes became virtually the obsession of French film makers as the thirties drew to a close. Symptomatically, *La Marseillaise* (1938), undertaken by Renoir as the "official film" of the "Popular Front," emerged as perhaps his weakest work. Planned during the period of optimism and realized when disillusion and fear were setting in, it expressed the hope rather than the conviction that France would reunite and, with the strength of a united people, combat the forces of fascism on all sides. Within the year Renoir was in uniform, fighting the Nazi invasion of his country. When the Germans occupied France, he fled to Switzerland, soon to make his way to Hollywood.

Throughout the five years of German occupation, the French studios continued to make films, although many of her best talents —Renoir, Duvivier, Benoît-Lévy, Feyder—had left the country. Those who remained held themselves notably aloof from contemporary themes, finding a kind of spiritual refuge in the past. Where Marcel Carné's *Port of Shadows* (*Quai des Brumes*, 1938) and *Le Jour Se Lève* reflected with grim reality the paralysis that gripped all of France as war drew near, his wartime *Visiteurs du Soir* (1942) and *Les Enfants de Paradis* (1945) were stylized allegories of death and despair set against the romantic backgrounds of bygone days. Scores of films used the old, graceful châteaux, far from the realities of the occupation, as settings for medieval stories tinged with melancholy mysticism and somber fantasy—*Le Baron Fantôme* (1943), *La Fiancée des Ténèbres* (1944), *Sylvie et le Fantôme* (1945). Even Jean Cocteau, returning to the film medium more than a dozen years after his boldly experimental *Blood of a*

Poet (*Sang d'un Poète,* 1930), remained scrupulously in the past with his coldly handsome rendering of the Tristan legend, *L'Eternel Retour* (1943) and his sophisticated adaptation of *Beauty and the Beast* (1946). Lesser talents concerned themselves with pure trivia —a few comedies, a few musicals, many romances.

Of all the films from this period, only Henri-Georges Clouzot's *The Raven* (*Le Corbeau,* 1943) dealt in any way directly and searchingly with the contemporary scene. Devoid of all political reference, it was a melodrama based on the disintegrating effect of a series of poison-pen letters upon a small French town. But because he depicted the community in something less than ideal terms—at a time when national feeling was running particularly high—and because the Germans undertook to distribute the picture outside France under the unflattering title of *A Little French Town,* Clouzot was accused of being pro-German. Once the Nazis had left, his picture was banned and Clouzot himself barred from working for several years. Now that the tides of national feeling have somewhat abated, it can perhaps be said that Clouzot was neither pro-German nor anti-French, but anti-human. Such recent efforts as *The Wages of Fear* (*Salaire de la Peur,* 1953) and *Les Diaboliques* (1955) reveal that fundamentally his mastery lies in exploiting the basest instincts and most sordid elements to produce his brilliantly cinematic effects of shock, surprise and revulsion.

Since the war, the French film industry has been without question the most chaotic and disorganized in Europe. Suffering chronically from lack of funds, aided spasmodically by the constantly shifting governments, many of the producers have sought to stabilize their operations by turning out nothing but Eddie Constantine imitations of American gangster films, Martine Carol sex plays and sordid, sensational melodramas patterned after the worst of the Italian neorealist school. Others have found reassurance in a return to the earlier, literary style of film making based on popular or distinguished novels—*Symphonie Pastorale* (1946), *Devil in the Flesh* (*Le Diable au Corps,* 1947), *L'Idiot* (1947) and the movie versions of Colette's collected works. Nor has the image of the haunted, suffering individual altogether disappeared from the French screen, as may be seen in such films as *The Walls of Malapaga* (1949), *Casque d'Or* (1952) and *The Proud and the Beautiful* (*Les Orgueilleux,* 1954). But these are holdovers from the past. That the present offers no new, clear-cut themes or trends is in itself a reflection of the uncertainties and lack of direction within the country since the war.

What does seem to have survived, despite war and political chaos, is the strong individuality of the best French film makers. One finds it, for example, in the eccentric, highly personal comedies of Jacques Tati—*The Big Day* (*Jour de Fête,* 1949) and *M. Hulot's Holiday* (1953)—done with the kind of pantomime humor once so distinctively Clair's. It is heartening too that such fresh and original talents as René Clément, Robert Bresson, Jacques Becker and Nicole Vedrès have been able to work, even though their output has been limited. Despite the extremely cautious financing behind most French films, they have still on occasion found the backing necessary for such daring and distinctive pictures as *Farrebique* (1946), *Life Begins Tomorrow* (*La Vie Commence Demain,* 1950), *Diary of a Country Priest* (*Journal d'un Curé de Campagne,* 1951) and *Forbidden Games* (*Jeux Interdits,* 1952). And then, of course, there are the remnants of the old guard, the men for whom individuality has always been a banner. Jean Cocteau still pursues his independent way, turning chameleon-like from the rich brocades of *Beauty and the Beast* to the highly theatrical *Les Parents Terribles* (1948) and then the completely cinematic, elusive *Orpheus* (1950). Sacha Guitry, until his death in 1957, continued in the special style he had chosen for himself long before the fall of France—facile, witty, and more loquacious than ever. Above all, there is Réne Clair, once more working in his native land. His *Beauty and the Devil* (1949) and *Beauties of the Night* (1952) reveal a mellower talent, one that is as gay and inventive, as graceful and charming as before, but with a new seriousness and thoughtfulness in his themes. Such works remind us that the true greatness of French film making is still to be found in those directors who regard their medium as primarily a means of personal expression—and in those producers who can still think in terms of a single picture rather than an entire year's "product."

GERMANY: FILMS FOR PROPAGANDA

Even while the German studios were converting to sound in 1929, the danger flags were flying. The National Socialists had already gained a considerable foothold in the Reichstag through the elections of 1928, while the dominant Social Democratic party had sunk into an apathy that was soon to prove disastrous. With the collapse of the stock market in America, the loans on which Germany had been subsisting since 1924 abruptly ceased and, as factory after factory closed its doors, the German people entered upon that period of unemployment and misery that paved the way for Hitler in 1933. The Social Democrats looked on with helpless neutrality while Communists sought to incite the masses to a Russian-style revolution or Nazis brought forward the mystic slogan of "blood and fatherland"—the promise of a better life for all who believed in Hitler and the glorious destiny of the German people. Those who refused to believe had a foretaste of things to come in the bitter street fighting between Communists and Nazis in the years 1930–1933. The Nazis, backed by some of Germany's biggest industrialists, had a program that knowingly exploited many of the deepest fears and dreams of the German people; the other parties wasted their strength by fighting within and between their ranks.

Throughout this period, with its forebodings, its sudden flare-ups of violence, its nightmare terrors of hunger and poverty, the German screen grimly mirrored the sequence of events. *The Blue Angel* (1930), for example, is virtually a tour de force of sustained sadism. Its schoolboys might be Hitlerjugend in their heartless persecution of the professor, the professor himself a symbol of the old authority that had to be destroyed to make way for the new. More explicit reflections of the times were to be found in the many films in which unemployment served as either the background or the springboard for the central situation. The hero, frequently jobless or at best a sidewalk vendor, passes through a series of sordid adventures not unlike those in the "street films" of an earlier era—only this time there is no snug, safe parlor for him to go back to. In innumerable wishful romances and comedies, an impoverished or unemployed youth is transformed into a fabulously successful businessman through the touchstones of a little luck and the right girl. Even the musical comedies reflected the depression. In the popular *Three from the Filling Station* (*Drei von der Tankstelle*, 1930), a trio of bankrupt young men sell their car, buy a gas station, then blithely begin their melodious pursuit of Lillian Harvey. But the depression was not to be whistled away. As an antidote to the growing despair, contemporary dramas solemnly counseled submission and patience, while the incessant mountain films offered their Aryan heroes escape from the world's problems through an arduous climb high above the clouds.

As for quality, the German films of this era seem to have suffered less from the addition of sound than those of other lands. The best directors continued to put the emphasis on imagery rather than on dialogue, and the mobility of the camera was only temporarily impaired. Such men as Pabst, Fritz Lang and Max Ophuls all demonstrated a sustained interest in the emotional and symbolic content of the shot, never permitting their pictures to degenerate to the level of the "100% all-talkie" so prevalent elsewhere. In films like Pabst's *Westfront 1918* (1930) and *Die Dreigroschenoper* (1930), or Lang's *M* (1931), one finds already an impressive integration of sound with the visuals that was decidedly advanced for the time. Even Leontine Sagan's *Mädchen in Uniform* (1931), although adapted from a play, avoided the stigma of "canned theater" through sensitive use of the camera. There is a striking visual contrast between the innocence of Hertha Thiele, dressed always in white and photographed against light backgrounds, and the harsh, black-robed head of the school; while ominous, recurrent shots of the deep stair well in the institution dramatically foreshadow the film's final tragedy. In the early German musicals as well, although scarcely scintillating when seen today, one still notes with considerable pleasure such inventions as the flight of the two butterflies across a hundred years of musical history at the opening of *Zwei Herzen im Dreiviertel Takt* (1930), or the ballet of the chairs in Eric Charrell's *Congress Dances* (1931).

As the depression deepened over Germany and the menace of Nazism became more apparent, a few films were made that seemed to take a positive stand against the growing reaction and rampant nationalism. Victor Trivas's *Hell on Earth* (*Niemandsland,* 1931) was an ingeniously contrived anti-war drama. Five soldiers—a German, a Frenchman, an Englishman, a Negro and a Jew—are trapped together in a bomb crater between the two opposing armies of World War I. In their enforced isolation, they learn to respect one another and their common ambition for peace. But the war brings them death instead, and the film ends with the shadow image of the five marching together in double exposure across the battlefield—a vague assertion of internationalism somewhat negated by the fact that its protagonists are all dead. Slatan Dudow's *Kühle Wampe* (1932) turned directly to the contemporary scene to study the effects of the depression on the German working class, detailing with considerable vigor the ceaseless search for jobs, the evictions, the suicides. Stronger than any film of this era, it presented the Communist viewpoint, but its climax offered no solution to the multiple difficulties of its characters beyond the ambiguous statement that "we must keep on fighting, ever advancing . . ."

Most impressive of all was G. W. Pabst's *Kameradschaft* (1931), the story of a mine disaster on the frontier between France and Germany, with German miners picking their way to the entrapped Frenchmen through an underground tunnel abandoned since the war. In it the theme of the international solidarity of workers is underscored—"Miners are miners," the Germans say in explaining their willingness to risk their lives to save their former enemies. Further, the workers must persuade the mine owners to permit them to form their rescue parties and use the mine's equipment, a permission that is granted with obvious reluctance. All of this Pabst detailed with superb realism, particularly in his scenes of the subterranean terrors of a mine cave-in. But there is also a curious coldness about the film, a remoteness suggesting that Pabst was not above maneuvering scenes to fit Socialist theory. In the finale there are speeches made in favor of international brotherhood by both the French and the German miners, but despite this the underground frontier barrier, torn down by the Germans to reach their French comrades, is gravely replaced by the officials of both nations. There is a special irony in the fact that the German working class, to which *Kameradschaft* was primarily addressed, stayed away from the film in droves.

Such films, with their combination of progressive sentiments and skilled use of the sound camera, were greeted in this country with considerable critical enthusiasm. At a time when the American film was still wrestling with the problem of sound, many of the pictures from Germany demonstrated that talk need not dominate the visual elements when the sound track is handled in a genuinely creative way. It can be seen today, however, that for all their skill with the medium, for all their apparent progressivism, these pictures and their makers had unwittingly been caught up in the storm that was sweeping across Germany. The gestures that seemed noble and brave, the sentiments that sounded boldly radical were in fact so vague, so remote from the realities of the situation—so intellectual at a time when Hitler was capturing the emotions and the imagination of the masses—that they proved pitifully inadequate as tools against the Nazis. Such were the films of dissent, the strongest outcries of protest. But they were not strong enough, nor were there enough of them, to turn the rising tide. The dissenters, taking their hint from the elections early in 1933, escaped whenever possible to other lands. There were concentration camps for the less fortunate.

No sooner had the Hitler régime come to power than it sought to force the German film industry to reflect the Nazi ideology in every way. It is said that one of Propaganda Minister Goebbels's first moves was to call together the heads of the various German studios and run off for them a print of Eisenstein's *Potemkin*. "Gentlemen," he announced when the lights came on, "that's an idea of what I want from you." What he got was a *Hans Westmar* (1934), so blatantly propagandistic that it had to be sent back for extensive revision before Goebbels could permit its release; or films like *Hitlerjunge Quex* (1933) and *SA-Mann Brand* (1934) which delivered their message so unsubtly that not even the most ardent Nazis were completely taken in. Goebbels changed his tack. After the first year or so of the Nazi rule, outright political propaganda became increasingly rare in the entertainment films. True, there were occasional "hate" films—hate the British (*Oom Paul*, 1939), hate the Jews (*Jüd Süss*, 1940)—but for the most part he was content to have the studios turn out old-fashioned, sentimental "waltz dreams," the ever-popular stories of mountain climbers and military comedies, and an occasional stiff, expensively mounted historical film recalling the pomp and splendor of Imperial Germany.

On the other hand, every theater was required to include in its program an officially prepared newsreel and supplementary documentary shorts. It was through these ingeniously, insidiously clever renderings of the "realities" of the Nazi world that Goebbels sought, and held, the German mind and soul. By 1939 his newsreels were often as much as forty minutes long. But the crowning achievement of the Nazi film makers was their documentaries. Repugnant as they are to American eyes, it is impossible not to marvel at the technical brilliance and subtle cunning that produced them. Made under the supervision of Leni Riefenstahl, who had progressed from a mediocre actress in the pre-Hitler era to an able director and brilliant editor, they penetrated all aspects of Nazi life—top echelon party meetings, Göring's new air force, the land army, the Olympic Games. Perhaps best known and most impressive is the massive three-hour spectacle *Triumph of the Will* (1937), ordered by Hitler himself as a film record of the first Party convention at Nuremberg. Every aspect of the historic meeting—the incessant parades, the impassioned oratory, the drilling of troops, their massed sports, even their mass feedings—was captured by cameras that seemed to be everywhere. Some thirty photographers covered the event, and nothing was spared to ensure them strategic positions. For ultimately, both Goebbels and Hitler realized, the enthusiasm of the Party members at Nuremberg was less important than the transmission of that enthusiasm to the millions of ordinary Germans everywhere who would see the film in their theaters. And there is no escaping the conclusion that *Triumph of the Will* had an almost hysterical effect upon its audiences with its endless torchlight parades, its close-ups of speaker after speaker, its rank on rank of Brown Shirts and Black Shirts listening transfixed before bursting out on signal with a roaring *"Sieg Heil!"* To the jaundiced eye, all of this may add up to a spectacle at once bewildering and wearying. Not even the most prejudiced observer, however, can fail to respond to the almost mystic power of the first reel as Hitler flies in his airplane over the waiting city, an ancient God about to walk the earth among mere mortals; or the sequence in the stadium when Hitler and his top Party officials march down a lane of thousands on thousands of Nazi soldiers. One can only imagine the impact of such scenes upon a people who wanted fervently to believe in the Godlike quality of their Führer, who had already elevated Nazism into a religion.

Nor were the Nazis satisfied simply to use the film to feed enthusiasm on the home front. Before long the German fact-film makers had become so adept at presenting their own version of reality that they could permit special editions of their pictures to go abroad. In this fashion, even the Olympic Games provided fodder for the Goebbels propaganda machine: the brilliantly photographed and assembled footage for *Olympia* (1937) was prepared in different "friendly" versions for distribution to each of the participating nations, with generous footage allotted to all their winners—and the Nazi officials ever present as their smiling, sportsmanlike hosts. Later, when Hitler's long-promised "just" war became a frightful reality, cameramen accompanied the Stuka bombers and Panzer divisions as they slashed into Poland. The film record of this brief campaign, *Baptism of Fire* (*Feldzug in Polen*, 1940), was rushed through to celebrate the victory in every German theater; then, as Hitler's armies prepared to move successively against Denmark, Norway, Holland, Belgium, Romania and Yugoslavia, special versions of the same film were shown to the high officials of each of those countries, emphasizing the futility of resistance. *Victory in the West* (*Sieg im Westen*, 1941), a similar report on the fall of France, was shown not only in Germany but in France as well, underscoring the weaknesses of the "decadent" French as opposed to the health and might of the new order. Throughout the war years the German people were frequently reminded by Goebbels that pictures don't lie; and they were constantly being shown newsreels, documentaries and information films in which their final victory was made to seem inevitable. But behind the pictorial realism of these films was a corps of technicians especially trained in distorting and transforming reality into the official version of the "truth." Through editing, commentary and the skillful use of sound the Nazis manipulated the screen as thoroughly and insidiously as they manipulated the minds and souls of their people.

Since the war, with the partition of Germany, the Russian zone has become the scene of the liveliest production activity. Cannily, the Russians took over the finest studios—as well as control of the famed Agfacolor process. They rapidly restored the studios to operation by granting quick amnesties to the best German film makers. Ironically, the very men who just a short while before had been making pro-German films for the Nazis were now making anti-

Nazi films for the Russians. The first pictures to come from this Eastern zone, like *Murderers Among Us* (1946) and *Marriage in the Shadows* (1948), were somber stories probing into Germany's war guilt or condemning Nazi atrocities committed both before and during the war. As might almost be expected, there was a considerable amount of soul-searching realism in the treatment of these dramatic themes. In more recent years, from the limited evidence available, the accent seems to be falling on films that glorify the German Communists and their battles against the Nazis in the years before Hitler. Such pictures as *Mother Courage* (1955), based on a story by Bert Brecht, and Slatan Dudow's *Stronger Than the Night* (1955) are representative of this new line—and as crudely propagandist and unconvincing as the earlier Nazi film versions of these same events.

Denazification proceeded far more slowly in the West German zone, and film production there since the war has been both halting and timid. Despite the presence of Erich Pommer, the great executive producer at Ufa before the Hitler era, the films that have emerged are distinguished primarily by their absence of any point of view whatsoever. Unlike their countrymen in the Eastern zone, the directors are free of the pressure of party lines and propagandist directives. At the same time, they can not help being aware of the surveillance of the Allied powers. As if fearful of offending anyone, the present film makers seem to have deliberately excluded from their pictures subjects that might be controversial or even merely timely. Helmut Käutner's skillfully directed and brilliantly acted film *The Devil's General* (1955), for example, was considered exceptional for West Germany because it actually dared to show the debauchery and disenchantment of top Nazi officials during the last years of the war! Far more of the pictures rely on the old, familiar *genres*. The bitter-sweet musicals, the military romances and the heavy, elaborate historical pageants are all back again, and showing no signs of improvement. Some few films, like Victor Vicas's *Master Over Life and Death* (1955) and Harald Braun's *As Long as You're Near Me* (1955), suggest a growing technical proficiency in the West German studios. For the most part, however, the film makers in the democratic zone seem unwilling or unable to deal in any but the most superficial terms with either the past or the

present-day life of their country. It is as if the tragic history of the
sound film in Germany has bequeathed to them a legacy of fear, the
fear of using the medium significantly in yet another era of crisis
and change.

RUSSIA AND THE SATELLITES

Sound came late in the Soviet Union. Although two systems had
been in the laboratory stages since 1926, the first Russian talking
picture, Nikolai Ekk's *The Road to Life,* did not appear until 1931.
In the meantime critics in Europe and in the United States, recalling
the bold, experimental silent films of the late twenties, looked hopefully to the Russian directors to rescue the new medium from the
stagnation of "canned theater" and stereotyped musicals. Many
were aware that both Pudovkin and Eisenstein had written and
lectured extensively about the possibilities of sound long before
any practical work could begin. Could their teachings inspire a type
of sound film as vigorous and eloquent as their classics of the silent
era? Could they clear a truly cinematic path through the new, un-
charted areas of sound? For a short time it seemed quite possible.
The Road to Life, despite its naïve story of the regeneration of a
group of "wild boys," was encouragingly creative in its use of the
sound track. Subsequent films like Dovzhenko's *Ivan* (1932) and
Frontier (1935), Dziga Vertov's *Three Songs About Lenin* (1934),
and Pudovkin's *Deserter* (1933) freely explored the new medium,
particularly in the use of music, mass chants, choruses and the
orchestration of noise into expressive sound. They created effects
of stunning if somewhat mystifying complexity, seeking always
to intensify the visuals through the sound track, not simply to
verify with sound what the visuals had already shown. Even where
they failed, as in the climax of *Deserter* or the incessant declama-
tions of *Three Songs About Lenin,* they were still provocative.
Many advanced the theory that because the film in Russia was not
motivated by the profit-seeking evaluations of hard-headed businessmen, its directors had greater artistic freedom than directors in
any other country.

But if film making in Russia was not tied to the profit motive, it
was hedged with other restraints that came into sudden prominence

at the dawn of the sound era. One of the aims of the first Five-Year Plan was to increase the amount of projection equipment throughout the country. Within little more than four years, between 1929 and 1932, the number of projectors had trebled to 27,000, drastically altering the status of the film in the Soviet Union. Through this rapid "kinefication" of the country a vast new audience was created for the Russian film; and as this audience increased, so too did the responsibility of the film makers. Unquestionably, such works as *Ten Days That Shook the World, The New Babylon* and *Arsenal* were overly-sophisticated fare for a nation that was still composed in the main of a backward peasantry and illiterate laborers. And because of the film's expanding sphere of influence, Soviet critics began to raise charges of "formalism" against the leading directors, accusing them of carrying on artistic experiment for its own sake without concern for the motion picture as a medium of propaganda and education in a socialist society. In 1932, with the start of the second Five-Year Plan, film makers were pointedly asked, "What kind of propaganda is this that appeals only to intellectuals, that fails to communicate with the broadest masses of the people?" They were urged to turn away from their aesthetic games, their tinkering with technique, and come to grips with what their critics termed "socialist realism." By this they meant the creation of a simple, straightforward, naturalistic kind of realism—and one that corresponded more closely to the Communist Party's aims and objectives at any given moment.

The immediate requirement of the Russian film at this time was for a hero with whom the masses could identify readily—not the "mass hero" of Eisenstein or the symbolic hero of Dovzhenko, but a man of the people who would be easily recognizable as such. Sound suddenly made it possible for the scenarists and directors to create heroes who quite literally spoke the common language. Eschewing experimental forms and simplifying their stories, they concentrated on realism of background, dialogue and character. When toward the end of 1934 two young directors, the brothers Sergei and Grigori Vassiliev, presented their *Chapayev,* it proved to be just what the Soviet propaganda chiefs had in mind. It dealt in clear, often humorous, somewhat romantic terms with a Red guerrilla leader during Russia's civil war, a man of the people who led his peasant partisans to victory and became in turn a well-disciplined Bolshevik. Its popularity within the Soviet Union was enormous; and abroad as well, where its tremendous gusto, its exciting battle scenes and the charm of its hero, as played by Boris Babotchkin, earned for it both critical acclaim and a wide following. *Chapayev* set the pattern for the big Russian films of the late thirties, almost down to the outbreak of war. Such films as *We Are from Kronstadt* (1936), *Baltic Deputy* (1937) and the *Maxim* trilogy (1938-1940) all dealt with the experiences of men who became heroes in the revolutionary events of 1917–1919—and often died for their heroism.

It is interesting to note that in preparing these ideological films the directors of the thirties continued to turn back to the Revolution for their characters and their themes, even as the directors of the silent era had done. Perhaps the present was too drab to be suitably inspiring. Certainly, the few pictures of this era that dealt with contemporary subjects chose the more remote aspects of the Soviet scene—a team of geologists working in the arctic, the creation of an air city at the far end of Siberia, or the difficulties of bringing education to a distant Russian village. The problems of urban life, the proletarian dramas of factory and mill that one might expect to find mirrored with "socialist realism" on the Soviet screen, were scrupulously avoided. It is as if the Soviet film makers suspected what Goebbels had already discovered, that the fiction film resists the outright propagandist treatment of contemporary material. Since the Nazis had no past to utilize for this purpose, Goebbels was forced to reject the fiction forms entirely, resorting to a skillful manipulation of actuality through the documentary film to impress the German people with the justice and invincibility of their cause. The Russians, on the other hand, had a highly serviceable past. By returning to the era of the Revolution, they were able to use the fiction film to dramatize and keep alive the ardor and enthusiasm of those early days when both enemies and issues were sharply defined.

As the sound era progressed, films were cut more and more closely to the needs of political dogma and expediency. Indeed, the history of the Russian film has become increasingly a reflection of the zigs and the zags of the Party line as it changed under one pressure after another. After the 1935 meeting of the Communist

Internationale, for example, the line was drastically altered. As Germany emerged more clearly as a threat to the Soviet Union, Stalin openly abandoned the dream of world-wide revolution to build in Russia the fortress of world Communism. Directors, suddenly encouraged to make films that would strengthen national pride, now looked back not only to the period of the Revolution but on beyond to the Russia of the czars—back to Peter the Great, Alexander Nevsky, Ivan the Terrible, back to the great Russian leaders like Suvorov, Admiral Nakhimov, Minin and Pozharsky, men who had contributed to the unification and aggrandizement of Imperial Russia. One after another they trooped across the screen, but no longer were they wicked oppressors or the warlike representatives of a hated régime. To fan the latent fires of Russian nationalism they had been transformed into folk heroes, the saviors of their country in time of crisis, the men who had made Russia great. For a brief period the Soviet screen glittered with the pomp and glory, the opulence and riches of a world that the Communists themselves had banished.

With the growing tension between Germany and Russia, there could be discerned an increasing hostility in the films of this period. Eisenstein's *Alexander Nevsky* (1938) implied that if the Russians had beaten the Teutonic Knights of the thirteenth century with Prince Alexander as their leader, they could certainly do it again under Stalin. At the same time there were pictures more specifically anti-Nazi. *Professor Mamlock* (1938), *Soldiers of the Marshes* (1938) and *The Oppenheim Family* (1939) presented vivid indictments of Germany's treatment of the Jews and the inhumanity of its concentration camps. The antagonism between the two nations kept mounting, both off screen and on. But when Russia entered into the Nazi-Soviet Pact, all of these anti-German films, including even *Alexander Nevsky,* were arbitrarily banished from distribution. The line had changed again.

The security promised by the mutual non-aggression pact soon proved a delusion. In June of 1941 Hitler's legions rolled across the frontiers of the Soviet Union to open the bloodiest, bitterest campaign of World War II. And immediately the Russian film was fired by a vigor and passion that recalled the finest of their silent classics. The wraps were off. The enemy was clear. And the contemporary scene, with all its blood and tragedy, had at last found the Russian screen. A heightened nationalism inspired film after film recounting Russian heroism in the face of the Nazis. German atrocities provided the theme for many of these—*No Greater Love* (1942), *Girl No. 217* (1944), *Zoya* (1944); resistance on the home front was the subject of many more. Others dealt with the sacrifices and daring of the men and women in the services.

Even more important than the fiction films, however, was the vast series of documentaries, features edited from footage that streamed in from every fighting front, from every guerrilla band operating perilously behind the German lines, from factory and farm, from city and village. These films literally poured upon the screen every aspect of the war in Russia. Many of the best directors and cameramen were assigned to this work, for it was quickly realized that no fiction could ever capture the full sense of the war's horror and destruction, the intensity of battle or the determination of the men and women in the armed forces to throw back the invading armies. During the war, feature production was halved, while the documentaries steadily increased in number. Of those seen in the United States, *A Day of War* (1942), compiled from the reels of a hundred cameramen in all parts of the Soviet Union, created a magnificent cross-section of an entire nation united in its resistance to the enemy. Films describing a single campaign, such as *Moscow Strikes Back* (1942) and *The Siege of Leningrad* (1943), put the actuality of war on the screen with a vividness of detail and an awareness of the human element that has never been equaled anywhere. Unlike the Nazi war documentaries, they did not hesitate to show atrocities in all their horror, nor did they shrink from revealing the toll in human lives that every victory cost them. Neither were they limited by the feelings of implacable hatred for the Nazis that characterized Russian fiction films of this period. There was instead a deep and terrible humanity about these pictures—a compassion that mourned the desolation of land and life and the human spirit everywhere.

Since the war the Russian film has steadily receded from the eloquence and vitality of those days. No sooner had peace been declared than the line on historical pictures was abruptly changed, relegating the czars, their generals and their admirals to their former disrepute. As a result, Pudovkin's *Admiral Nakhimov*

(1946) had to be considerably revised before it could be released, the third part of Eisenstein's *Ivan the Terrible* was never filmed, and a number of other pictures either planned or in production were simply abandoned. The new line placed heavy emphasis on the scientific and cultural advances within the Soviet Union, and film makers obliged with a reverent series of dull biographies on scientists, composers and authors. In response to demands for pictures revealing "the honor and poetry of labor," shallow love stories featuring a girl, a boy and a tractor have become a commonplace of the Soviet screen. More recently, the emphasis has shifted to making the movies quite literally a "theater of the people," a medium for bringing great plays, ballets and operas to the masses living outside the few large cities where such presentations are normally given. Sometimes, as in *The Grand Concert* (1951), these appear as straightforward stage presentations with a slender thread of movie story woven in; and sometimes—as in the ballet film of Prokofieff's *Romeo and Juliet* (1954) or the grand-scale film version of Moussorgsky's *Boris Godounov* (1955)—the work is given a more cinematic adaptation. Needless to say, they still retain to a marked degree the theatrical flavor of the original. At the same time, the documentary techniques developed during the war have degenerated into interminable, full-color presentations of sports events, May Day parades, air shows over Red Square and similar topical displays. Those seen in this country have all shared a crude, perfunctory newsreel quality, naïvely gloating over the sheer abundance of planes, tanks and people that they put on the screen. Today more than ever the film in Russia functions as an ideological tool, a useful weapon in the Soviet's education and propaganda armory. It does a job. It fills a need. But somewhere in the process the idealism and imagination that made the films of the late twenties and early thirties so memorable have vanished without a trace.

Of the film work in other countries behind the Iron Curtain, one is granted only an occasional glimpse—just enough to suggest that it is largely an imitation of the pallid themes and styles currently ordained by the Soviet Union itself. In all of them the industry functions as an agency of the State; and in the years since the war these States have been listening with ever greater attention to the propaganda lines laid down by the Kremlin. Czechoslovakia, which inherited from the German occupation a large and well equipped studio at Barandov, first attracted attention with her trick films—notably *The Emperor's Nightingale* (1949) and the many imaginative puppet shorts by Jiri Trnka. There have also been a number of bitterly anti-Nazi films recalling the years of German domination. Of these, Alfred Radok's *Distant Journey* (1950) is outstanding for the humanity with which its director recreated the Terezin ghetto in Czechoslovakia, a Nazi preconcentration-camp clearinghouse for Jews of all nations. More recently, however, such long and starchy film biographies as *Smetana* (1955) and *Jan Hus* (1955), both carefully researched and handsomely mounted, are strongly reminiscent of the nationalistic biographies coming from Russia since the war.

Poland, too, has been recalling her past through large-scale biographies and stories of the resistance. In Alexander Ford, however, Poland has the advantage of a first-rate director. Each of his films to reach this country—*Border Street* (1949), *Young Chopin* (1952) and *Five Boys from Barska Street* (1954)—has been in a different style, but unified by a remarkable visual sense and an ability to create moving, believable characters despite obviously propagandist themes. Hungary, Romania, Bulgaria—each has its own industry, although none as yet has produced any films either of distinction or even of interest outside her native land. The same may be said of Austria, just emerging from the Russian orbit. Here the everlasting Viennese operettas continue irresistibly to attract the directors, and they are turning them out again as if there had never been a war, two occupying armies or, for that matter, a twentieth century. But there is one exception. G. W. Pabst has returned to his native land, and in *The Last Ten Days* (1955), his dramatic portrait of Hitler's disintegration, reveals that he is still one of the best directors on the European scene. Since 1950 Yugoslavia has been hard at work building up a native industry, dividing its production almost equally among cultural, instructional and entertainment films. As yet, few of these have been seen abroad.

Over all these countries at present hangs the heavy, restrictive pall of the official film maker. Frequently their pictures reveal intelligence and taste. But as long as questions of utility continue to take precedence over problems of artistry and personal expression, one must look elsewhere for the creative growth of the medium.

ENGLAND AND THE DOCUMENTARY TRADITION

The British film, which had muddled through the silent era without distinction or success, reached its lowest ebb during the early years of sound. Production in the late twenties had been maintained primarily by the government's Quota Act of 1927 that granted distribution contracts for the profitable Hollywood films only to those studios that would make English pictures. As a result, the British producer became essentially a distributor, turning out cheap, artless "quota quickies" with his left hand in order to get his right hand on the popular, star-studded entertainments coming from America. In this way the studios survived, although their pictures reflected little credit either on the men or on the country that produced them. When in 1929 the studios were hit simultaneously by sound and the depression, the whole shaky structure collapsed. Sound equipment was too expensive for most of the companies to purchase outright, and the film business was hardly likely to attract investment capital at that moment. Many studios simply went bankrupt. Those that did survive immediately fell into the routine of filming stage plays.

Until the very end of the thirties the British studios remained notoriously devoid of either inspiration or vitality. Disenchanted young men who might have contributed their vigor and talents to the entertainment film abandoned it in favor of the unexplored realms of documentary. While from the harried commercial studios came little more than shabby imitations of Hollywood's poorest offerings. And yet, behind the scenes, techniques and skills, courage and resourcefulness were growing steadily in both the documentary units and the studios. When the war finally brought together these two divergent groups, the result was not a clash but a fusion that marvelously transformed the entire British film.

While the English studios of the thirties continued to jog along in their quota-protected rut (and American television viewers are now well aware of what a rut that was), a few films did break away from the routine of cheap sets, excessive dialogue and hasty camera work. This dramatic departure was inspired by a single success that for a time intoxicated the entire industry and filled many with false hopes. It had always been the dream of the British to break into the rich American market. When Alexander Korda, a Hungarian director who had been only moderately successful in Hollywood and on the Continent, suddenly scored a hit in America with his relatively inexpensive production of *The Private Life of Henry VIII* (1933), the British thought they had their answer. The film starred Charles Laughton, an English actor who had already earned a considerable reputation through appearances in Hollywood films. With Laughton's name as a lever—and a highly salable title—it became the first British film to be booked into big American first-run houses and the major theater chains. Its profits were enormous. Obviously, the way to get British films into American theaters, the producers argued, was to bring over Hollywood stars and feature them in pictures as big and glossy—and possibly slightly less vacuous—than the American spectaculars. After Korda's success, investors were suddenly willing to pour money into such grandiose plans.

Unfortunately, they were doomed to failure. Nobody can out-Hollywood Hollywood. It takes more than money, more than Hollywood stars. The flair, the exuberance, the showmanship that goes into the American super-production was something the British could neither buy nor reproduce. British pacing, British restraint, the clipped British accent made such star-studded films as *Catherine the Great* (1934), *Rembrandt* (1936) and *Things to Come* (1936) strange and unacceptable fare to the vast American public. Outside of the few sophisticated Eastern cities, their popularity was limited. And where *Henry VIII* had been able to show a profit because of its modest budget, the multi-million dollar productions required a mass audience that simply was not available to British films in the American market. Despite the Hollywood stars and directors, despite the European technicians for whom they paid so bountifully, the British studios were unable to produce a type of film that could captivate a wide audience. By 1937 the speculators were reluctantly writing off their losses and once again turning a jaundiced eye upon the movie business.

But out of these costly extravaganzas, as well as from the welter of cheaply produced, indifferent little pictures, there began to appear in the studios for the first time a rising sense of professionalism and a corps of genuinely creative men. What finally liberated their talents was the revised Quota Act of 1938, designed by the government specifically to eliminate the "quota quickie." In order to qualify for quota benefits, the studios now had to spend on their films enough money to ensure a decent level of production.

The Act held out further benefits as an inducement for producers to exceed the £7,500 per reel minimum. While the amount of money spent on a picture is never in itself, of course, any guarantee of quality, the new budgets automatically provided more time for preparation and shooting, more leeway in the number of settings, more opportunity to work on location. At last the craftsmen in the British studios could take some pride in their work, and this new attitude was reflected immediately in their films. Such pictures as *South Riding* (1938), *Bank Holiday* (1938), *Owd Bob* (1938) and *The Stars Look Down* (1939) were all modest efforts by Hollywood standards, but they could stand on their own merits. And they did so in what was, for Britain, a new and important way. For the first time there were English pictures that seemed to be looking with some insight and appreciation at the life and spirit of the country itself. They spoke of the British character, British institutions—even of social problems such as unemployment and nationalization—with unprecedented frankness and awareness. Events on the Continent seemed to have startled the British into a reappraisal of their way of life. And where in France the film makers were already giving way to despair and resignation as the war clouds gathered over Europe, the British suddenly came forward with a sober affirmation of pride and confidence in their traditions and their future. By some rare good fortune, the British screen found its voice just at the moment that the nation needed it most.

In the short time that remained before the war broke out, the studios consolidated their gains. Each month their films seemed surer, more alive, more successful artistically—and, above all, more intensely British. New stars—Wendy Hiller, Deborah Kerr, Michael Redgrave, Ralph Richardson—were emerging with every new picture; while established players like George Arliss, Leslie Howard and

Charles Laughton were returning home from Hollywood to lend their prestige to the reviving industry. New directors like David MacDonald, Michael Powell, Carol Reed and Robert Stevenson came forward to take their places beside such veterans as Anthony Asquith and Alfred Hitchcock. While behind the cameras, at the cutting benches, pounding the typewriters in the studio story departments were many more of the men who were to mold the British film during the years ahead.

In the meantime, the independent documentary movement had also developed into a potent force, one that was to prove of inestimable value not only during the war years but also in shaping the intimate realism of the postwar British feature film. As a movement, documentary may be said to have had its official beginning in 1929 with the formation of the Empire Marketing Board Film Unit by John Grierson, a tough-minded Scot with a background in mass communications and a firm conviction that the motion picture could play a vital educational role in a democracy. Grierson persuaded Sir Stephen Tallents, head of the Marketing Board, to add film to the conventional media of books, pamphlets and posters already being used by that organization in its work of promoting and integrating the nation's food supply. As Grierson conceived it, the function of the E.M.B. Film Unit was to relate these activities in meaningful terms to the people of Britain—"to bring the Empire alive," he termed it. His ability to do so was evident from his very first film, *Drifters* (1929), revealing the drama behind the daily haul of the North Sea herring fishermen, enacted by the men themselves. Coming in the midst of the stilted, stagnant early all-talkies, its views of real people, real seas and storms had the additional impact of novelty. It remains one of the classics of the documentary form.

With the backing of Tallents, Grierson proceeded to gather around himself a group of men to study the techniques appropriate to putting actuality on the screen. In *Drifters* he had broken both with studio staging and with conventional story construction. Now the problem was to discover new ways to make fact exciting and provocative, to get information across without being dull or didactic. The unit spent long months in a critical reappraisal of earlier filmic treatments of reality—the masterworks of Robert Flaherty and von Stroheim, Eisenstein and Pudovkin, the American Westerns with their natural backgrounds, the "city symphonies" of the Continental avant-garde, as well as newsreels and scientific shorts from every nation. And from this study evolved the aesthetic base on which the documentary movement was founded. Grierson once described it as "the creative treatment of actuality," a phrase that indicates the equal stress placed upon artistry and subject matter. Its purpose was to project the facts of life under a democracy; its method, to show man in relation to his institutions.

It was this combination of social purpose and artistic experimentation that gave the British documentary its strength and its direction. As the movement matured, as its relation to government, to industry and to the general public became clearer, documentary was to undergo numerous changes in form and technique. From the early objective recording of fishermen, potters, miners and glass blowers going about their routine tasks, documentaries gradually came to include direct interviews and even dramatic recreations. As themes grew more complicated, it was sometimes necessary to introduce actors and studio settings into the films. Thus, it became increasingly apparent that documentary was less a technique than an approach. Reality was its theme, and the documentary director was properly concerned with the methods of capturing a sense of reality upon the screen. But whatever techniques he chose, his purpose remained the same—to inform and enlighten rather than simply to entertain. Indeed, Grierson himself preferred the stronger word, "propaganda." What he meant by this, of course, was not the calculated, cynical distortion of truth as practiced by the totalitarians, but its function of spreading information. "We can," he wrote, "by propaganda, widen the horizons of the schoolroom and give to every individual, each in his place and work, a living conception of the community which he has the privilege to serve."

In 1933 the Empire Marketing Board Film Unit was moved, virtually intact, to the General Post Office, where it remained until the early years of the war. With characteristic imagination, Grierson seized on the new affiliation as an opportunity to interpret communications in the widest sense of the word to the people of Britain —not just the pickup and delivery of mail but "the gale warning

INTERNATIONAL TRENDS: UNITED STATES

Gangster films like **The Public Enemy** (1931) marked the new realism of
Hollywood's movies as both sound and the depression conspired to intro-
duce a naturalistic style of setting, writing and performance onto the
American screen.

INTERNATIONAL TRENDS: FRANCE

The French sound film flowered in the late Thirties. As war drew near, the studios seemed to specialize in such romanticized studies of disillusion and despair as Marcel Carné's **Port of Shadows** (1938).

INTERNATIONAL TRENDS: ENGLAND

When war came to Britain, the documentary techniques learned through the Thirties were quickly fused with studio productions to create such realistic and effective story films as the Noel Coward-David Lean **In Which We Serve** (1942). Coward clings to the life raft at the lower right.

INTERNATIONAL TRENDS: ITALY

After almost three decades of silence, the Italian film suddenly burst upon the consciousness of the world with **Open City** (1945). It introduced a new director in Roberto Rossellini, a new star in Anna Magnani, and a new style in film-making—neorealism.

behind the Central Telegraph Office, the paradox of nationalism and internationalism behind the cable service, the choral beauty of the night mail, and the drama tucked away in the files of the ship-to-shore radio service." Now began the memorable series of films that, more than any others, have come to represent the highest and most characteristic achievements of British documentary— *Weather Forecast* (1934), *Song of Ceylon* (1934), *Coal Face* (1935), *Night Mail* (1936) and *North Sea* (1938). Within their framework of fact, they experimented with a wide variety of styles. Basil Wright's *Song of Ceylon* remains among the most lyric films of all time, with scenes of ageless native ritual juxtaposed against the jumbled voices of the tea traders, the shippers and the London Stock Exchange. Harry Watt's *Night Mail*, following the nightly run of the mail express from the south of England to Edinburgh, introduced a poetic commentary by W. H. Auden set to the music of Benjamin Britten. Auden's words conveyed not only the magnitude of this routine operation but brought it close to everyone when, over shots of the sleeping, smoky city the narrator's voice says, "Soon they will wake and listen for the postman's knock— for who can bear to feel himself forgot?" In *North Sea* Watt used a story line and actors to dramatize the work of the ship-to-shore radio service in bringing aid to the men of a trawler disabled by storm. It was also at this time that Len Lye began his delightful experiments in the synchronization of abstract animation and popular music, tied to postal messages like "mail early" or "ship via parcel post." In all, the G.P.O. Film Unit produced hundreds of documentaries in dozens of styles before being taken over as the Crown Film Unit to serve the Ministry of Information throughout the war years.

During its formative years, the British documentary movement owed its existence entirely to government support. As the thirties wore on, however, it began to attract an independent following. Although the movie houses paid them scant attention, a regular audience for fact films was growing in the universities, the film societies, in labor organizations and clubs of every kind. And with an established demand for the films, sponsorship by private industry began to appear. In England, it must be remembered, radio broadcasting has always been non-commercial, a function of the government-operated B.B.C. Potential advertisers had to find other ways to reach their public. It was Grierson who persuaded them to invest in institutional advertising, in films that built good-will for the company through documentaries on subjects of broad, general interest rather than in pictures that simply plugged their product. As a result of this farsighted policy, one finds films on nutrition sponsored by the Gas, Light and Coke Company, on slum clearance by the British Commercial Gas Association, on housing by Cadbury's Chocolate, and brilliant instructional films for classroom use paid for by Shell Oil. By 1937, when Grierson withdrew from G.P.O. to form the London Film Centre, more documentaries were being produced for industry than for government; and the Film Centre acted as a clearing house to indicate those subjects on which films were needed, to assist in their planning, and to prevent wasteful duplication of effort. By the time the war broke out, the British documentary movement—headed by men like Paul Rotha, Stuart Legg, Basil Wright, Harry Watt, Alberto Cavalcanti, Arthur Elton and Edgar Anstey—had achieved a world-wide reputation and inspired scores of directors outside England to attempt documentary movements in their own countries.

The quality that made the British documentary so distinctive was the calmness of its presentation. Without resorting to flamboyant techniques or emotion-charged commentaries, it sustained interest and provoked thought. Even where the films took a stand—on the advantages of slum clearance, for example—the argument was generally given through unemphatic but revealing visuals. The facts were organized and presented; the viewer was left free to draw his own conclusions. As Britain prepared for war, the propriety of this approach was questioned for a time. Perhaps the line should become more forthright, more emotional, as in Alexander Korda's studio-made pastiche of documentary combat shots and jingoistic story, *The Lion Has Wings* (1939). Perhaps the documentary people could be used best in the creation of straight poster films, films urging the population to enlist, to buy war bonds, to save fuel and foodstuffs. While the government wavered, the documentary film makers clamored to be permitted to do what they knew best—to put on the screen, with characteristic understatement, the true face of Britain at war. After months of hesitation, the Ministry of Information acceded. The Crown Film Unit was formed, and soon began its extraordinary series of wartime documentaries. Pictures like *London Can Take It* (1940), showing London under the blitz; *Target for Tonight* (1941), an R.A.F. night-bombing mission over Germany; *Desert Victory* (1942), a stirring account of the North African campaign—all of these not only kept up morale on the home front but did much to win sympathy and support for England in the United States during the early years of World War II. As film became increasingly important to the war effort, literally hundreds of young people joined the documentary movement, working on subjects as various as recruiting pictures, training films and movies covering every aspect of the national emergency from *Wartime Factory* (1941) to *More Eggs from Your Hens* (c1943).

Soon after the outbreak of the war, the English studios were mobilized to turn out morale and training films in addition to their entertainment pictures. And here, for the first time, the documentary and fiction film makers of Britain joined forces. Some, like Alberto Cavalcanti and Harry Watt, moved from documentary to fiction; while fiction directors like John Boulting, Thorold Dickinson and Carol Reed became, at least for the time, documentalists. There was a distinct gain on either side. The documentary directors learned to make their pictures more dramatic, more immediate in their appeal to new audiences of tens of millions. The directors of entertainment films mastered the problems of creating a sense of realism on the screen. Dickinson, for example, was assigned to direct a training film for the armed forces that would dramatize the wartime slogan "the enemy is listening." Using an actual incident from official files, he produced in *Next of Kin* (1942) such an exciting spy story that it was shown not only to British and American troops but was also exhibited theatrically in both countries. Another outstanding wartime contribution by studio-trained talents was *The True Glory* (1945). Working with clips from the archives of the American and British Signal Corps, Carol Reed and the American director Garson Kanin supervised the editing and shaping of hundreds of thousands of feet of combat footage. Narrated by General Eisenhower and scores of anonymous soldiers' voices, the film became a vivid, authentic document of the Allied campaign in Europe—and a fervent prayer for the peace.

It was the function of the British wartime documentaries to keep the nation informed on the progress of the war, to strengthen the morale and unity of purpose of the British people during those perilous years. Their appeal was to the intellect and the under-standing—and their effectiveness was beyond question. But another force was needed to touch the emotions of the people, to provide them with a different kind of inspiration; and this became the task of the entertainment film. Like the documentaries, many of them dealt with both the effects of war on the home front and the direct encounters with the enemy on land, at sea and in the air. The pri-mary difference—and in this lay their particular appeal—was their concentration on the personal element.

How well these two film forms balanced each other during the war years may be seen by comparing a documentary with a fiction film on very much the same subject. In the documentary *Target for Tonight,* dealing with a bombing mission over Germany, it is the mission itself that concerns us. We are shown in detail the intricate planning and preparation behind the run, the timing and tech-nical mastery required to carry it through. One cannot watch this film without admiring the efficiency and skill of the operation, and the dedicated spirit with which the men of the R.A.F. faced the perils of what was for them just another routine assignment. But there are no individual heroes, no thrills apart from those intrinsic to such a mission. On the other hand, in Michael Powell's fictional *One of Our Aircraft Is Missing* (1942), also involving a bombing mission over Germany, the audience's sympathies and emotions are immediately engaged. Where the documentary reported on the planes from base to target and home again, in Powell's film the accent falls on the men themselves. Each member of the crew seems to typify some unique and positive aspect of the British character. Their bravery, ingenuity and good cheer in the face of danger became a source of pride and inspiration to the British people. Identifying with them in their struggles and victories, the audience renewed its own strength and in some measure found the courage to carry on.

Other fiction directors followed much this same pattern, producing pictures like *In Which We Serve* (1942), *Nine Men* (1943), *Millions Like Us* (1943) and *We Dive at Dawn* (1944). In each the hero is seen as a member of a team whose sheer survival is often dependent upon concerted, coordinated group action. By 1943 all the studios were releasing this type of film, but it was the Ealing Studio in particular that specialized in them. To heighten their realism Michael Balcon, the head of Ealing, added to his staff a number of leading documentary directors, cameramen and editors—a fact that was to give his studio a distinct edge in the postwar phase of British film making. For the vitality generated by this fusion of documentary and the fiction film was to continue to shape and influence pictures coming out of the studios long after the war.

Once the war was over, other themes and other treatments began to emerge in both the fact and the fiction films. The documentalists quickly turned to the urgent problems of reconstruction—housing, food and health. And industry joined with government to sponsor films that would orient and encourage a war-weary people. Particularly pressing were the problems of the returning veterans, the paraplegics, the mounting numbers of mental cases directly or indirectly attributable to the war. Documentary rose to this challenge in dozens of films like *Out of True* (1950) and *The Undefeated* (1950), meeting each subject with a new flexibility of techniques. In *The Undefeated*, for example, Paul Dickson used re-enactments to tell the story of an R.A.F. flier who had lost both legs at Arnhem but learned to walk again on artificial limbs. The flier himself acted out the painful stages of his rehabilitation in the same hospitals and rest homes where they had taken place. Filmed for the Ministry of Pensions, it held out the hope for a similar recovery to thousands of crippled veterans—and informed millions of Britons of one more aspect of their government's service. *Out of True*, on the other hand, like many of the mental health films, was studio-made and cast with professional actors in the main roles. The complexity of its problem virtually dictated the kind of con trol that, under the circumstances, could best be obtained with actors, sets and scenario. Indeed, dramatization either with actors or with non-professionals permeated great areas of the postwar British documentary. The techniques of fiction gave the documentary film makers new points of contact with the British people, as evidenced by films as varied as *Children on Trial* (1946), dealing with juvenile delinquency; *Highland Doctor* (1948), an account of medical services in the all but inaccessible Hebrides villages; and *David* (1951), a warm and gentle portrait of a Welsh school caretaker, his simplicity, his kindness and his love for the traditions of his country.

One important adjunct of these films of social welfare that attracted many documentalists after the war was the educational field, the production of pictures for classroom use sponsored both by government and by private industry. The Shell Oil films, made under the supervision of Sir Arthur Elton (one of the original Grierson group), attained a rare precision and lucidity in their exposition of the principles of physics, aerodynamics and the like. The Ministry of Health sponsored a notable series of pictures on child care—*Your Children's Eyes* (1945), *Your Children's Teeth* (1946), *Your Children's Sleep* (1947), and so on, that was both informative and witty; while instructionals like *Instruments of the Orchestra* (1947) and *Steps of the Ballet* (1949), produced by the Crown Film Unit, proved entertaining enough to win theatrical bookings both in England and in the United States. There was, in short, a pressing need for fact films on a wide variety of subjects in the years just after the war—and the documentary people came forward to fill this need with a versatility that produced hundreds of pictures combining a high level of artistry with maximum utility.

Now, more than a decade after the war, it seems safe to say that the high watermark of British documentary has passed. As early as 1951 John Grierson had warned, "I think the time has come to say plainly that documentary as an art, documentary as a power of persuasion, documentary as a valuable instrument of national projection, is being allowed to go by default and a generation of film-makers ruined and lost to the State by a fumbling regime of sponsors unworthy of their predecessors and their origins." He was referring specifically to Britain's Labour government which, having gained power, strangely ignored the documentary film despite its long record of progressive sentiments and orientation. In the interest of economy, the Crown Film Unit, the direct descendant of Grierson's original Empire Marketing Board group, was dissolved. Grierson himself has become increasingly identified with feature film production, and other leading documentalists have been absorbed into the studios, government posts and television. Today, in a concerted drive to build her tourist trade, the government is putting primary emphasis upon the production of travelogues, one- and two-reel visits to various points of interest in the British Isles. Handsomely photographed, often in Technicolor, they continue to reflect the high level of Britain's fact-film technicians. Similarly, *The Conquest of Everest* (1954) revealed that the British documentarians are still able to organize and record the complexities of an extended operation in dramatic and meaningful images. But such films are a far cry from the high social purposes and ideals that had sustained the documentary movement through two decades. British documentary continues, but without the vigor, the prestige or the direction that marked its greatest years.

Like the documentaries, the British feature films sustained a high level during the difficult period of postwar reconstruction. Still fired by the wartime spirit of "we're all in it together," British directors continued to explore with humor and affection the quirks and crannies of the British character already demonstrated in films like *The Life and Death of Colonel Blimp* (1943) and *Tawny Pipit* (1944), that amusing side glance at the Britisher's traditional devotion to bird watching. There was Roger Livesey's daft Scottish laird in the delightful *I Know Where I'm Going* (1945) and Rex Harrison's satiric portrait of a *Notorious Gentleman* (*The Rake's Progress*, 1945). There were the deftly-drawn vignettes from Somerset Maugham's *Quartet* (1948), *Trio* (1950) and *Encore* (1951), not to mention Alec Guinness's mild-mannered rogue in films like *The Lavender Hill Mob* (1950) and *The Promoter* (1952)—all delightful, and specifically British, eccentric types. Britain's cultural tradition was recalled in David Lean's exciting adaptations of *Great Expectations* (1946) and *Oliver Twist* (1947), and in Sir Laurence Olivier's memorable trilogy of Shakespearean plays.

The realist tradition that resulted from the wartime fusion of documentary and fiction techniques made possible what was perhaps the most notable group of postwar films. Dramas like *Brief*

Encounter (1945), Carol Reed's *Odd Man Out* (1947) and *The Third Man* (1949) or the Boulting brothers' *Seven Days to Noon* (1950) all found their point of departure in the contemporary scene. It was in this field that the tiny Ealing Studio particularly excelled. The documentary people that Michael Balcon—now Sir Michael—had added to his staff during the war years were responsible for such successes as *Dead of Night* (1946), *The Cruel Sea* (1952) and *The Divided Heart* (1954), as well as that dizzying series of comedy hits, *Passport to Pimlico* (1949), *Tight Little Island* (1949), *The Lavender Hill Mob* and *The Man in the White Suit* (1951). But even as the documentaries had briefly flourished and declined after the first serious crises of reconstruction had passed, so too has an unfortunate lethargy settled over the British entertainment film. Part of the reason, to be sure, may be found in the waning of the strong sense of unity and purpose generated by the war and its aftermath; more of it lies in the postwar structure of the British film industry.

It has always been Balcon's contention that films should be produced to appeal primarily to the British market, and budgeted to show a profit within that market. Ealing's signal success had been based upon this policy. Oddly enough, it seems to have carried little weight with the other British studios. During the war J. Arthur Rank, the owner of Britain's largest theater chains, emerged as the strongest single figure on the motion-picture scene. He had bought into some studios, created others, financed independent producers on the grand scale. It was his dream to gain prestige for the British film—and for England—and ultimately to win over the vast American market for British movies. Costly films like *King Henry V* (1944), *Stairway to Heaven* (1946), *Red Shoes* (1948), and *The Tales of Hoffmann* (1951) became his "loss leaders," big films that he felt sure would edge their way into American theaters and, by their sheer opulence, create a demand for more British pictures. Hopefully, he named his American distribution organization Prestige Pictures. Certainly, it did much to enhance the prestige of British films—but at a cost to Rank of some $8,000,000. Popular in the art houses of the big cities, they failed to penetrate to the American mass audience. The motion-picture trade press on both sides of the Atlantic is still debating whether this failure has been due to public indifference or to the calculated sabotage of American distributors.

One thing is certain, however. In their second attempt to conquer America with big, lavish, costly productions, the British seriously over-extended themselves. The government itself unwittingly fostered this extravagance. In 1948 it set up the National Film Finance Company to distribute £5,000,000 in an all-out effort to support and encourage domestic production. With this new source of capital, many of the smaller companies unhesitatingly followed Rank's lead. Less than six years later Sir Alexander Korda alone had lost about £2,000,000 of the £3,000,000 his British Lion Company had received. This seemed a bit excessive even for the movie business, and in June of 1954 the government abruptly withdrew what remained of its loan. The decision probably saved British taxpayers £1,000,000, but it threw the film industry into a panic from which it has not yet recovered. British Lion shut down, as did many smaller studios. And within a short time, the brightest luminaries in the British film world— men like Laurence Olivier, Alec Guinness, David Lean, Carol Reed —were either working in Hollywood or on co-productions financed jointly by English and American or Italian studios and intended for the international market. Early in 1956 even Balcon closed the Ealing Studio, selling it to television and finding an American affiliation for himself. At the present writing, the industry is still in a state of crisis. Production has reached a new low, and scripts and stars are being chosen with an ever greater concern for the presumed tastes of the American public. The result of all this has been a marked diminution of those unique essays on British character and manners that gave the films from Britain their special distinction and appeal. It is unfortunate that, having raised up an entire generation of skilled, creative artists, England is no longer able to give them employment.

THE COURSE OF ITALIAN NEOREALISM

There had been signs of a new vitality in the Italian studios at the very end of the silent era, evidence that the film makers were beginning to catch up with the technical mastery that existed else-

where. Under the leadership of Alessandro Blasetti, both as a director and as editor of the magazine *Cinematografo,* Italian films were
breaking out of their moribund tradition of old-fashioned spectacles and cliché *romanzas.* Blasetti's first film *Sole* (1929) was a
drama based on Mussolini's vast project of draining the Pontine
marshes. Its immediate success suggested the possibility of turning
to other positive aspects of the contemporary scene as sources for
filmic material. But the established producers were hesitant; and
as they waited, sound arrived to put an end for the moment to
Blasetti's dream. The studios turned promptly to the stage for both
themes and actors, and the sweet strains of Neapolitan love songs
effectively drowned out any plea for greater realism or more imaginative techniques. The early years of sound in Italy were dominated
by the musicals, and by romances and boudoir farces drawn from
stage plays—"white telephone films," the Italians called them because so much of the action seemed to center about the white
telephone in the heroine's bedchamber.

As noted earlier, the Fascist government at first took little interest in the motion-picture field. There was, of course, official encouragement for historical films celebrating the rise of the Fascist
party or re-creating the life and times of such popular heroes as
Garibaldi, Ettore Fieramosca and Salvator Rosa, but nothing more
tangible. Fascist interests were, at that time, satisfactorily served
by the flow of propaganda shorts and newsreels turned out by the
government-owned LUCE. When the talkies arrived in 1930 this
company promptly added three sound trucks to its equipment, with
the result that impassioned harangues by Mussolini became part of
all their newsreels. These, together with any other shorts turned out
by LUCE, were shown by government decree in every motion-
picture house throughout Italy. But aside from such minor incon-
veniences, Italian producers, distributors and exhibitors were left
pretty much to their own devices until 1935. Between 1935 and
1940, however, things began to change. Mussolini was launching
those wars and campaigns through which he hoped to extend the
Italian empire and increase his own stature. National feeling, national pride had to be whipped up to a fever pitch. It was during
this period that the government gradually gained control of the
motion-picture industry, achieving this not by outright ownership

but by a weird and complicated form of patronage that the State held out to the eighteen accredited producing studios. Producers now could easily borrow up to 60 per cent of the cost of a picture from the State-controlled banks; if they were able to show that their film was either popular, artistic, or propagandistically useful, they had only to repay a small portion of the loan. Under such conditions, it became virtually impossible for a studio to lose money no matter how unsuccessful its pictures might be. Before long the studios were offering top jobs to political favorites because of their ability to wangle even more profitable concessions from the venal officials directing the banks and the State credit agencies. When Mussolini's son Vittorio entered the industry as head of Europa Films, Italy's largest studio, the pattern of nepotism and patronage was complete.

The government further increased its influence over the industry when it decreed that all foreign films shown in Italy had to be dubbed, and that the dubbing had to be done by Italians. This not only created more film jobs, it also made it simple to eliminate from foreign imports any sentiments that were not fully in accord with Fascist ideology—a neat, unobtrusive form of censorship. At the same time, the State awarded the valuable licenses for dubbing and distributing these films to those studios that produced the most or the most expensive pictures each year—a form of patronage that proved completely demoralizing. Indeed, no system could have been more ideally designed to encourage wastefulness and to discourage creativity.

Considering the amount of control the government actually held over the film industry both economically and by the appointment of political favorites to key positions, it is surprising how few of the pictures were made as outright Fascist propaganda. The Italians were satisfied, it would seem, with a primarily negative propaganda. They were content if their film simply ignored all ideas of democracy, civil rights, civil liberties or similarly "decadent" notions. Ettore Margadonna, one of the leading historians of the Italian film, has estimated that "out of more than five hundred feature films [produced between 1930 and 1942], those which were one hundred per cent Fascist in content may be counted on the fingers of one hand." These exceptions would include *Black Shirt* (1933),

Blasetti's *Old Guard* (1935), *The Siege of the Alcázar* (1940), proudly revealing Italy's part in the Spanish Civil War, and Carmine Gallone's soporific extravaganza *Scipio Africanus* (1937). Rumored to have been written by Benito Mussolini himself, it presumed to see in the ancient Italian victory in Africa the heroic counterpart of Mussolini's own campaign in Ethiopia. Filmed in Africa and on the giant stages of the new, State-financed Cinecittà, it was one of the most costly, most opulent productions of all time—and also one of the most overblown. Critics delighted in pointing to the telephone poles that sprouted from the hilltops of Imperial Rome, the wrist watches on the Roman legionnaires, and to the stupefying emptiness of the vast spectacle. Nevertheless, because it was an official film, the government made special efforts to have it shown abroad. Its reception did little to enhance the reputation of the Italian film makers. A few of the Italian opera films were also exported, notably Gallone's *The Dream of Butterfly* (1939), featuring long passages from Puccini's opera beautifully performed by Maria Cebotari, and a tear-stained story of a diva who, like Butterfly herself, loved not wisely but well. Aside from these—nothing.

But if the corrupt and corrupting Italian studios were unable to produce a masterpiece, at least they enabled talented people to gain a mastery of their art. Clearly, the neorealist movement that burst forth with such vitality after the war could only have come from men whose artistic impulses had long been bottled up, from men who knew the techniques of film making but lacked the opportunity to use them significantly. Many had been trained at the government-operated Centro Sperimentale, the official film school in Rome. Many had worked under the dispiriting studio conditions that marked the final years of Fascism. Vittorio De Sica, for example, had alternated between stage and screen as a matinee idol throughout the thirties. He turned to directing in 1940, specializing in sentimental comedies which he handled with a good deal of superficial charm and, on occasion, sharp insights into the behavior of children. Roberto Rossellini worked on a number of documentaries before being assigned as assistant director on *The White Ship* (1941), a wartime propaganda film almost totally lacking in human feeling. Two more features, *The Return of the Pilot*

(1942) and *The Man of the Cross* (1943), seem to have been equally devoid of any hint of his postwar style. Of the old guard, only Alessandro Blasetti gave any suggestion of the new themes and new techniques that lay ahead. His *Four Steps in the Clouds* (1943) for a moment took the Italian film out of the world of "white telephones" and official attitudes. It was a touching, warm-hearted comedy in which a kindly man from the city finds himself pretending to be the husband of a country girl he has met by chance—and the father of her unborn child. Though far from political, its picture of peasant life, its Italian peasant types and natural settings strongly foreshadowed the neorealist films of the postwar era. Indeed, when *Four Steps* was first shown in New York, undated, critics assumed it had been made *after* the war, as part of the movement touched off by *Open City.*

For all its excellences, *Four Steps in the Clouds* remains a modest work, a harbinger. But late in 1942, when Mussolini's hold on his people was fast disintegrating, there appeared Luchino Visconti's *Ossessione,* a true masterpiece that contained all the seeds of the postwar neorealist movement—the concern for people, the use of natural settings and types, the overwhelming sense of looking at life as it really is. An adaptation (although uncredited) of James M. Cain's *The Postman Always Rings Twice,* its sordid theme was played against the background of a small *trattoria* on the marshes of the Po and a fair at Ancona. And though Visconti used such familiar Italian actors as Massimo Girotti, Clara Calamai and Elio Marcuzzo, under his direction they performed with a naturalism that blended with the sweaty peasants who crowded the bar at the shabby inn and thronged the amusement booths of the *festa.* The camera work was always arresting, using long traveling shots to keep the principals in screen center as they moved through the crowds, using concealed cameras for sequences in public parks and streets, mounting the camera on a crane to rise from a close-up of an actor to panoramas of an entire landscape within a single shot. Here were the faces of real Italians, the sights and sounds of everyday Italy mobilized upon the screen to tell a powerful and affecting story. It was a revelation, a film so far beyond anything produced in the twenty years of fascism that its impression upon other Italian film makers could only have been profound. Unfortunately, it is a revelation that few Americans seem destined to share. Not only was Visconti's film a fairly flagrant violation of copyright, but the film rights to Cain's novel already belonged to M-G-M, which produced its own version of the story in 1946. M-G-M has been adamant in refusing to permit prints of *Ossessione* to enter the United States.

As the war progressed, film making in Italy became increasingly chaotic (as did life itself). Loyalties were divided. Some favored the Allies—or thought the Axis a losing cause; some clung to their Fascist beliefs. After the fall of Mussolini, with war still ravaging the south and the Nazis occupying the remainder of the peninsula, film making came to a virtual standstill. In 1944 only sixteen pictures were produced in Italy, most of them coming from Scalera's studio in Venice, the last stronghold of the Fascist elements in the industry. Meanwhile, anti-fascists went into hiding, awaiting the liberation of the Allied forces, awaiting the withdrawal of the Nazi army of occupation. Late in 1944, even before the Germans had completed their evacuation of Rome, Roberto Rossellini was already at work on *Open City,* the key film in the entire neorealist Italian revival. In it he sought to re-create, as accurately as possible, the tensions, the trials and the heroic resistance of the common people of Rome during the years of the Nazi occupation. Aside from the principals, few in the cast were professional actors. Many, indeed, were simply citizens—or Nazi soldiers—photographed on the fly by cameras concealed on rooftops or hidden in cars. Little of the film was shot in a studio, partly for financial reasons, partly because Rossellini (and Cesare Zavattini, who wrote the script) sensed that the documentary value of actual streets, apartments and courtyards would heighten the authenticity of their story.

What emerged was a film strikingly unlike anything that had been seen before. Technically, it was far from flawless. Rossellini had been forced to use whatever scraps of film stock he could lay his hands on, while the lighting—particularly in those interiors not taken in a studio—was often too weak for dramatic effects or even adequate modeling. Indeed, shooting had to be abandoned entirely several times while the director set about raising the necessary funds to continue. But the very passion that had inspired the production of *Open City* seemed to create the centrifugal force that held it all together. Its roughness, its lack of finish became a virtue. And the cumulative power of Rossellini's feeling for his subject was translated into a visual intensity that made the picture sometimes almost unbearable to watch. Here was true realism—the raw life of a tragic era. "This is the way things are," said Rossellini in presenting his film. It became the credo of the entire neorealist movement.

Within the next five years there appeared in Italy a cycle of films in every way as remarkable and exciting as the great Russian pictures of the late twenties—and inspired, like them, by the sudden discovery of a national identity and the simultaneous liberation of creative talents. The complete breakdown of the Fascist régime removed all previous restraints. The years of repression under the Nazi occupation forces, the disenchantment under the Allies produced a social awareness that found its fullest expression in the neorealist movement. At the outset, the mere ability to treat dispassionately the daily life of the ordinary Italian was inspiration enough for directors like Rossellini and De Sica. Rossellini's *Paisan* (1946) was an epic study of the last months of war in Italy. De Sica, the former matinee idol, revealed again his concern for children in *Shoeshine* (1946), but with a depth and passion unsuspected from his earlier films. It is a poignant, muted tale of an appealing group of Roman street urchins caught up in the black market that swept through Italy during the war years. The boys are jailed, then friend is set against friend so that their captors may gain a little more information on the gangsters who have been using them. De Sica makes it amply clear that the authorities are neither brutal nor stupid, merely hard pressed. But because they take the easy, obvious course, friends become enemies and murder is the final outcome. All of this is offered without either bitterness or cynicism as a dramatization of actual conditions. And if his revelations disturbed his audience it was, after all, up to them as citizens to do something about it. In such films can be detected the emergence of a truly democratic spirit—the objective presentation of social fact, with social action left to the conscience and the intelligence of the viewer.

With Rossellini and De Sica as its leaders, the neorealist movement quickly gathered momentum and was confirmed in the work of a dozen or more directors in the period immediately after the war. Drawn irresistibly to social themes, they were united by a common philosophy that was perhaps most clearly expressed in Luigi Zampa's *To Live in Peace* (1946). Zampa selected an incident from the very end of the war to suggest that all men—even Nazis—could live together in friendship if they followed their instincts instead of their ideologies. An Italian farmer has given shelter to two American soldiers caught behind the German lines, one white and one colored. During the night the German sentry from the village comes to the farm. In order to cover up the noises of the Negro drinking in the cellar, the farmer gets the German drunk. Suddenly the American bursts out of his hiding place, and there is a suspenseful moment as Nazi and Negro face each other. But all hate, all conflicting ideology has been drowned in the wine. The two wrap their arms around each other and go roaring through the village, "The war is over—Der Krieg ist kaput." In *Angelina* (1947), Zampa reiterated the same theme, that man's better instincts are subverted by his blind obedience to orders. In the title role, Anna Magnani gave a wonderfully funny and sympathetic performance as a working-class housewife who becomes the leader of all the women in her neighborhood against the local politicians and landlords.

Other directors took actual incidents from the postwar scene to create images of shocking or pitiable truth. In the first half of *Tragic Chase* (1947), Giuseppe De Santis drew a remarkable picture of the chaos, the lawlessness that followed the end of hostilities in northern Italy, and although a taste for melodrama marred its second part, his scenes of peasants organizing and fighting for the right to return to their land were both moving and convincing. Also quite melodramatic (almost inevitably) was Alberto Lattuada's *Without Pity* (1947), centered on another serious postwar problem in Italy, the Negro G.I.'s who had deserted the Army and were living lawlessly in the Tombolo, north of Leghorn. There was sensitivity in this story of a Negro and his love for a white prostitute, but sensationalism as well. (The film was cut drastically for exhibition in the United States.) From Visconti, the director of *Ossessione*, came a ponderous but searching and indubitably sincere study of the lives of impoverished Sicilian fishermen, *The Earth Trembles* (1948), made documentary-fashion without actors or studio settings—and in a dialect so special that not even all Italians could follow it. Again it was a film that said, with sympathy: "This is the way things are. What are we going to do about it?"

Out of all these films—and many more—there emerged the image of the ordinary Italian. With a vividness and humanity unequaled by any other nation, the drama of commonplace joys and sorrows was projected from the screen. Curiously enough, such pictures were not at first too well received in Italy itself. Perhaps they reflected the ordinary too accurately. What the Italians wanted was the glitter, the glamour, the romance of the Hollywood movies after their years of misery and privation. In any case, it was the critical reception abroad of such pictures as *Open City, Shoeshine, Bicycle Thief* and *To Live in Peace* that opened the eyes of most Italians to what they really had. All of them proved far more successful on their subsequent runs in their native land than when first released.

As economic stability began to return to Italy, the Italian producers began to consolidate their gains. In Cinecittà, just outside Rome, they had not only the largest and best equipped studios in all Europe but also, at the film school there, a well-trained corps of artists and technicians to draw upon. Furthermore, the new government took a healthy interest in film production, recognizing its value as a source both of good-will and of revenue for the country. Outstanding pictures were rewarded with special tax rebates. As an additional aid to the home industry, acting on a plan put forward by the Italian producers themselves, the government permitted the American studios to take out of the country a portion of their war-frozen dollars provided that some of this money were allocated to the development of a market in the United States for Italian pictures. In 1950 the American producers agreed—and found themselves in the unprecedented position of actively encouraging the growth of a rival industry in their own country. Except for the British, no nation has ever before made such a concerted effort to break into the American market. To overcome the resistance of the average moviegoer to subtitled foreign films, they even set up their own dubbing studios in New York, matching the voices of Broadway actors to the lips of the Italian performers. Today,

Italian pictures travel far beyond the art-house circuit, with frequent bookings in the profitable drive-ins and neighborhood theaters.

Indeed, the Italians have become so terribly anxious for wide box-office approval that, within the past few years, the original tenets of neorealism have been increasingly distorted. *Bitter Rice* (1949), for example, begins as a tale of migratory rice workers in northern Italy, but soon degenerates into a sordid melodrama of rape and violence. Both *Rome, 11 o'Clock* (1952) and *Three Forbidden Stories* (1953) tastelessly exploit an actual tragedy that shocked all Italy. Over two hundred girls had turned up at on office in response to an ad for a single position, thronging the stairs to await their turn. When the stairs gave way, scores were killed or injured. In *Rome, 11 o'Clock,* this incident is recreated and then, flash-back fashion, the film goes into the lives of several of the victims—a girl who had left home to live with an artist, a prostitute who wants to go straight, a girl disillusioned about finding a glamour job in radio, a shy girl in search of her first position. In *Three Forbidden Stories* the treatment is even more frankly sensational. One of its heroines is a lesbian, another a dope addict.

Most of the recent "realistic" films from Italy have had their origin in similar incidents, in real-life stories gleaned from the newspapers. All too often, however, the stories built out from these backgrounds have been an exploitation rather than a revelation of their themes. True, reality has not been prettied up in these films, as is so often the case with our own American pictures. On the contrary, there seems to be a concentrated effort to make everything as grim as possible—"this is the way things are"—but with increasing emphasis on such marketable aspects of reality as sex and sadism. And in place of the earthy, hearty Anna Magnani, the Italian screen now abounds in cover girls like Gina Lollobrigida, Silvana Mangano, Silvana Pampanini, Sophia Loren and Eleanora Rossi-Drago—sleek, well-developed creatures, delightful to look at, but scarcely ideal as the heroines of neorealistic dramas. In fact, as so often happens, the word itself has become little more than a catch-phrase today. The Italian cinema may continue to advertise its neorealism, but what we have been seeing of late is largely a series of melodramatic shockers photographed against natural exteriors.

In the meantime, several neo-neorealisms have emerged that hold new promise for the Italian screen—if the producers have the courage to follow them up. All of them are based firmly in the everyday life of ordinary Italians and motivated by a sympathy and affection for the common man. But a new dimension has been added, a new element of comedy, fantasy, even poetry. We can see now that De Sica's strange, fanciful *Miracle in Milan* (1951), with its hoboes soaring on broomsticks high above Milan's cathedral, was in fact the point of departure for this whole new genre. Renato Castellani's *Two Cents' Worth of Hope* (1952) and Luigi Comencini's *Bread, Love and Dreams* (1953), for example, created a fine sense of the reality of small-town life in the Italian hills, then used this as the background for broad comedy that also veered off into fantasy. Federico Fellini's *La Strada* (1954), a somber, tragic study of an itinerant sideshow strong man and a simple-minded girl clown, explored a new blending of realism and poetry, a heightening of emotion through skillfully stylized performances juxtaposed against natural backgrounds. *Love in the City* (1954), a project conceived and organized by Cesare Zavattini and directed by half a dozen youthful enthusiasts, also seems to mark a new direction. Here the emphasis is returned again to documentary realism, with people re-enacting their own tragedies or speaking urgently of their lives and problems directly in front of the cameras and microphones. But by skillful use of the camera, by dubbing and editing, Zavattini has transformed simple documentation into genuinely artistic creation.

Here is fresh ore for the Italian film, new directions to be explored and developed with all the passion and enthusiasm that marked the renaissance of the Italian film industry ten years ago. It is evident that the directors still have abundant vitality to tackle new themes and to work in new styles. The question now seems to be, will the Italian producers, obsessed with dreams of conquering the international market, permit them to do so? Will they be allowed to follow the lines sketched in by De Sica, Fellini, Castellani, Comencini, Antonioni and Zavattini? Or must they dissipate their talents on sordid studies of passionate drug addicts and frustrated telephone girls? Such pictures, sold not on their artistry but on their sensationalism, can only result in the eventual suffocation of first the art, and then the industry itself. For it is the artists in film—the directors and the writers—who tap the new and occasionally profitable veins of cinematic ore. The odd thing about movies is that once the industrial side moves in and begins to commercialize the operation, the outcome is frequently disappointing to the audiences, to the artists, and ultimately to the producers themselves.

THE CLASSIC ART OF THE JAPANESE FILM

Until Akira Kurosawa's *Rashomon* won the Grand Prize at the Venice Film Festival in 1951, it was generally assumed that the industry in Japan—like the studios in India or Egypt—simply turned out great quantities of films of dubious merit and purely local interest. Although pictures had been made there since 1904, almost since the time that movies started, few had been seen by the Western World and none had roused any particular enthusiasm. In fact, not until the thirties, when Japan began her campaigns of conquest in the Orient, was there an industry of any size. As so often happens, the films followed the flag. Through wars and economic penetration, Japan had captured for herself a vast potential audience in China, Manchuria, Indochina and Korea, a market long dominated by the European and Hollywood studios. With their particular gift for cheap imitation, the Japanese were soon turning out between seven and eight hundred films a year—mostly pseudo-French romances or American-style crime and action pictures. Through this flood of films, they effectively ousted or undersold all competitors in the Far East, a market that Japan controls to this day.

At the same time, Japan's studios also began to produce specifically for home consumption films that were designed to inspire the maximum loyalty and enthusiasm of the Japanese people for the innumerable wars their country was waging. Incidents from the campaigns in China and Manchuria, the border clashes with the Soviet Union provided the basis for many of them. Also important for this purpose were the *jidai-geki,* the period dramas designed to give the Japanese a heightened awareness of their cultural and historical past, a pride in their strength and their traditions—all very useful in time of war. Less useful, apparently, were the *kindai-geki,* those realistic studies of modern Japanese life which had been an out-standing film form of the late twenties. During the turbulent thirties, the tight military censorship saw to it that very few of these ever reached the screen. One of the rare exceptions was *Kimiko* (1936), a delicate and charming glimpse of Japanese domestic relations that received limited distribution in this country.

Soon after Pearl Harbor, the Japanese industry was nationalized and turned even more directly to propaganda purposes. Documentaries and fiction films combined to stress the duties, the honor of service to the Emperor—the privilege of dying gloriously for one's country. Such a film was *Volunteers of Death* (1942), the Japanese version of the Pearl Harbor attack. Despite the fate of its hero in the obviously staged battle scenes, it was considered to have a happy ending. The boy had died for his Emperor! The film, incidentally, was shown in Germany and distributed by the Nazis in occupied France as a demonstration of the might of the Eastern end of the Axis. At the same time, costume dramas were also being produced in great numbers—and apparently in very much the same style that has since won such recognition for the Japanese film makers. Hence the real liberation for Japanese talents, once the war was over, lay not in the field of period pictures but in their new freedom to comment upon the social conditions within the contemporary scene. Like the Italian directors under Fascism, the Japanese had acquired the skills and techniques of film making while producing the pictures demanded of them by their government. Now, with the war over and the old order swept away, with the Allied occupation forces everywhere and the devastation of the two atomic explosions that had shattered their cities still in evidence, they turned their creative energies to the world around them. And apparently, from the accounts of those who have been privileged to see any considerable number of these films, the Japanese directors have dealt with modern subjects in experimental forms as bold as the best of the Italian postwar films. Kurosawa's *Drunken Angel* (1948) and *Living* (1952), Imai's *Stained Image* (1953), Naruse's *The Echo* (1954), Toyoda's *Wheat Whistle* (1955) are only a few of the outstanding films on contemporary themes that are still awaiting distribution in the United States.

In the meantime, most Americans have had to judge Japanese

film making largely on the basis of the half-dozen or so costume dramas that have been released here in the wake of *Rashomon*. It is, of course, a serious critical error to attempt to generalize from a handful of pictures. But when that handful includes such radically different yet authentic masterpieces as *Rashomon* (1951), *Ugetsu* (1953), *Gate of Hell* (1954), *The Magnificent Seven* (1954) and *The Golden Demon* (1955), one may safely conclude that they are the products of an already mature industry that has at its core film makers of extraordinary scope and creativity. Today it is clear that *Rashomon* was not the first masterpiece of Japanese film making but simply the first to gain world-wide recognition. Its physical beauty, the virtuosity of its cinematic techniques and above all the exoticism of its 8th century setting and story prepared Western audiences in some measure for what was to follow. While our Occidental films have leveled off at a plateau of technical perfection, these films from Japan explored psychological, physiological and aesthetic paths that were, in their implications, not merely different but revolutionary. They do not ask us to "identify" with the characters in them, nor is there any attempt to heighten psychological tensions through photographic trickery or editing techniques. Our emotions are involved obliquely, through the mind rather than the nerves, while our eyes and senses are flooded by the unexpected beauties of a filmic art that derives from ancestral tradition. The camera frames each scene with the classic formalism of a Japanese print or painting. The performances of the actors are almost ritualistic, with attitudes and gestures drawn from the ancient Kabuki or No drama. Color, design, gradations of black and gray, the contrapuntal use of Oriental music add to an emotional tone that fortifies the sense of timeless tradition in these films. To the formalism of the past, however, has been added a new humanism, an interest in people that gives warmth and personality to their age-old themes, an intellectual and philosophic base to their art.

In *Rashomon*, for example, the center of the film is essentially an inquiry into the nature of truth. Its four principals have been involved in a murder and rape. Each recites his own version of the sequence of events. Each story, with its own protective colorations, is shown by the camera. The characters speak as to a tribunal, squatting directly before the camera, staring into its lens. It is the audience that must decide the relative truth of each one's testimony—if truth there be at all. The whole conception of *Rashomon,* both thematic and cinematic, was markedly different from Western conventions. Although Japanese critics spoke of its "European style," its closest relative is clearly Dovzhenko's daring and intense *Frontier* with its stylization and fluid movement of the camera. More important than its style or source, however, is the fact that *Rashomon* posed squarely a question that must have occurred to every thoughtful Japanese citizen during the years since the war. Their "divine" Emperor had been defeated, his myth of infallibility destroyed—and with it the entire elaborate structure of duties and obligations, the *chu* on which Japanese society was based. In place of the "truth" of unquestioning obedience, the Japanese were being force-fed the new "truth" of democratization. Through this story of the 8th century, Kurosawa sought some reassessment of the problems of today.

Similarly, *Ugetsu,* a legend of 16th century Japan, moved from the reality of the peasant wars onto a plane of supernatural fantasy as its hero, lured by the riches to be made in the cities, abandons his wife and farm and lives with a ghostly noblewoman in a mysterious castle. When eventually he returns to his home, he finds his dead wife waiting to receive him, to comfort him and give him rest. "What is truth?" asked *Rashomon;* "What is reality?" is the question posed by *Ugetsu. Gate of Hell,* based on a true story from the 12th century, is far more direct in its suggestion that, no matter what the form of a society may be, its basic strength derives from the code of personal honor that preserves the order, the moral fiber of a people. Its unhappy hero is a warrior, intoxicated by the beauty of a noblewoman whose life he has saved. He vows to have her even though she be married to another. When his rash persistence leads to her death, the man begs the husband to kill him. The husband refuses, and in a sudden, agonized gesture that is at once the mark of his repentance and an acknowledgment of the force of tradition, he crops his warrior's lock. The final shot shows him hurrying through the massive red temple gates of Kyoto to spend his remaining years as a monk.

Gate of Hell was the first Japanese film to use color, a carefully controlled color that not only enriched each beautifully composed shot but added immeasurably to the emotional values as well. Fiery red-oranges dominate the opening scenes of chaos in the Imperial palace, an icy blue bathes the scene in which the warrior, bent on assassination, approaches the home of his beloved. Japanese technicians spent three years in Hollywood mastering the technology of color. To these mechanical skills they added the age-old tradition of its use in Japanese art, an awareness of the psychology of color that made our own Technicolor films seem flat and one-dimensional by comparison. Shot on Eastman stock, its delicacy and subtlety so impressed the people in Rochester that they immediately requested a print for their own archives and research. Unquestionably, Japanese films will become an important influence in refining the future use of color on the screen. Since the Japanese have no color process of their own, and paying for American raw stock in American dollars is prohibitively expensive, the studios are prudently confining its use to themes that will not merely be enhanced but psychologically intensified by color. Its development can already be seen in such recent films as *The Golden Demon* and *Yang Kwei Fei* (1955).

Japan as a film-producing nation is once more on the rise. From approximately 250 pictures a year after the war, production mounted in 1955 to 422 features—almost 200 more than Hollywood in that same year. With only 5,000 theaters in Japan itself, the industry's economic base continues to be the 50,000 houses throughout the Far East that it services primarily with cheaply-produced action thrillers. But the producers are turning their thoughts toward the West. Masaichi Nagata, head of the Daiei Studio which produced *Rashomon, Ugetsu* and *Gate of Hell,* has declared that these films were specifically made as "prestige pictures" in the hope that their exoticism and pictorial beauty would interest European and American art-house audiences. Now that this acceptance has been established, one can only hope that the work of the same directors in the field of the contemporary Japanese social drama will soon find distribution here. Perhaps it will take another European festival and another grand prizewinner to pave the way.

INTERNATIONAL GLIMPSES

It is not possible in a book of this size to touch on production in every country where films are made. Nor, in fact, is that the intention. In many lands production is far too limited or too specialized to be of interest to the outside world. In others, the industry is too derivative or inept to claim serious attention. India, for example, turns out hundreds of pictures every year—far more than Hollywood does today—yet these are rarely seen by international audiences. Their techniques are crude by Western standards; their construction, their pace, their overemphatic acting are all alien to our tastes. The same holds true of China, which also produces pictures in great numbers; while the few serious films from Egypt that have been shown in Europe or in the United States literally rocked their audiences with laughter. One can merely note that such industries do exist and await the day when, like the Japanese or the Italian, out of the quantities of pictures they produce there begins to emerge a quality, a strength that makes them of more than purely local interest.

The history of film confirms that no masterpiece has ever sprung suddenly from hitherto barren ground. It seems that there must always be a period of preparation, a period during which the strengths of native production are explored, tested and developed. When at last a work of true merit is produced, there are today the great European film festivals to help it win world-wide distribution. Such festivals as those at Cannes and Venice, Berlin and Edinburgh and São Paulo are often lightly dismissed as tourist attractions for resort cities which, of course, they are. But they have grown increasingly important in recent years as a kind of international merchandise mart where the films of the world are placed on display and prospective distributors from all nations gather to discover the latest and best. It was at the postwar festivals of Venice and Cannes that the rebirth of the Italian film received international recognition. There also the resurgence of a Scandinavian industry was discovered, and the sudden, dramatic emergence of the Japanese film. It is at these festivals that one first notes enthusiasm turning into mastery, or a trend crystallizing into a national style.

In Sweden the first evidence of such stirrings was to be found in the experimental shorts of Gösta Werner and Arne Sucksdorff. Werner's *Midwinterblot* (1945) was an eerie evocation of a pagan ritual culminating in a human sacrifice. Imaginative sound and shadowy, deep-focus photography created the sense of an entire world in darkness. Sucksdorff, whose fascinating studies of wild life first attracted attention at the Cannes festival, spends months patiently waiting for his close-ups of birds on the wing or beasts on the prowl, then months more at the cutting bench. In such films as *A Divided World* (1948) and *Shadows on the Snow* (1948), he demonstrated his uncanny ability to capture and shape these moments of primeval life with a dispassionate hand. The killer kills, the captive waits, and elemental forces are neither sentimentalized nor transformed into moral fables. In *Symphony of a City* (1949) and *Summer Idyll* (1950), he applied the same objectivity to the people of Stockholm as they went about their daily tasks or made love at a nearby beach. Both Werner's and Sucksdorff's work was financed by Svensk Filmindustri, Sweden's leading studio. Even though Sucksdorff's shorts cost as much to make as an average feature film, Svensk had the feeling that the vitality of Swedish films depended upon such serious young craftsmen. They were not mistaken. The re-emergence of the Swedish feature film was heralded at Venice in 1947 with the screening of Alf Sjöberg's *Torment* (*Hets*), a suspenseful psychological study of a sadistic teacher given unbounded authority in his classroom. Since that time, despite severe financial restrictions, the Swedish directors have managed to maintain a high level of originality and integrity. Gone now are the Lagerlöf epics, the spectacular costume dramas; but the love of nature that once characterized the "Golden Era" of the Swedish film is still evident in such films as Sjöberg's *Miss Julie* (1950), Ingmar Bergman's *One Summer of Happiness* (1952) or Sucksdorff's first feature, *The Great Adventure* (1953). While pictures like *She Only Danced One Summer* (1953) or *The Naked Night* (1955) suggest that Swedish characters, despite their modern dress, still feel the same guilt, the same need for expiation through suffering as their cinematic forebears of 25 years ago.

Denmark, too, is slowly edging back into the spotlight shared by film makers of the world. A leader before World War I, she gradually disappeared from view as her foremost artists left for other lands. Late in the thirties, however, her greatest director, Carl Dreyer, returned to Denmark to write and, occasionally, to make a short art or documentary film. (Because of limited finances, Danish production continues to be primarily in the documentary field.) But a kind of spiritual rebirth took place with the release of Dreyer's first feature in almost twelve years, *Day of Wrath* (1943). This extraordinary film created on the screen the living image of early 17th century Denmark. In that time of puritanical repression and superstition, the young wife of a kindly parson, suspected of being a witch, finally comes to believe the horrible accusation herself. Dreyer unfolded slowly and forcefully his theme of the power of evil to corrupt the good. While the film was immensely popular in Denmark, the critics complained of its tempo. But, as Archer Winsten of the *New York Post* wrote in his vehement defense of the film, "That any critic can suggest that its slow movement is a fault reveals a deep-rooted depreciation of taste. Far too many sensational films, the critics' daily poison, all action and no thought, create this sad hypnotism."

Soon after the war, the Danish film industry was further strengthened by the work of two young documentary film makers, Bjärne and Astrid Henning-Jensen. Their first feature, *Ditte, Child of Man,* based on a work by the outstanding Danish novelist Andersen Nexö, told the story of an unwanted, illegitimate child. Presented at the 1947 Venice Festival, its unaffected use of peasant types and natural exteriors, its simplicity and sincerity recalled the great days of the Scandinavian cinema. But while *Ditte* has everywhere ranked high in critical esteem, its theatrical distribution has been limited almost entirely to its own country. Like *Day of Wrath,* it was deemed too slow for popular tastes elsewhere. Today the Henning-Jensens rank second only to Dreyer among Scandinavian film makers. Their delightful short, *Palle Alone in the World* (1951), has been repeated several times by request on the *Omnibus* television program; while their feature-length color film, *Where Islands Float,* a humane account of the difficulties of bringing medical care to the people of a small village in Greenland, won the top honors for documentary at the 1955 Venice Festival.

It is not too surprising that Denmark also won the Grand Prize in the feature-film category at the same festival with Dreyer's *The Word* (*Ordet,* 1955). For the Danes, in sustaining their tradition of limited, quality production across the years, have ignored the commercial stereotypes of glamour, sex and violence so often exploited on the screens of the larger nations. Though they release but a handful of films annually, these are apparently made without concern for any market beyond their own four million inhabitants. Certainly, it was this individuality, this preoccupation with the Danish land and its people, that distinguished *The Word* at Venice. There were dozens of other pictures, many of them sensational, most of them swift-paced, polished and adroit. Yet it was Dreyer's slow-moving, gentle story, shrouded in an atmosphere of almost mystic dedication, that caused the only true sensation at the festival. It is perhaps Dreyer's most personal film, with its strange theme of a young farmer obsessed by the belief that he is Christ. Though pitied and ridiculed by his family, a little girl's faith finally enables him to work a miracle. Like all of Dreyer's pictures, *The Word* is unconventional, deeply felt and lovingly wrought. Each scene, each unhurried action creates an anticipation that reaches its summit in the moment of the miracle. The effect is impressive, even shocking; but its quiet, deliberate exposition—typical not only of Dreyer but of Danish film makers in general—made its commercial success outside Denmark debatable. A "smash hit" in its native land, it has yet to be distributed in the United States or in most European countries at the present writing.

The Word, like many another outstanding picture shown at the festivals, accentuates a problem for which there is no easy solution. Foreign films are generally purchased for distribution by people who believe that they can market them profitably in their own countries. Distributors coming to these festivals are aware of their public's taste and preferences, and they search for such qualities in the pictures exhibited there. For an obvious box-office attraction, like Clouzot's thriller *Les Diaboliques,* there were frantic bidding and high prices. But an uncompromising film like Luis Buñuel's *The Young and the Damned* (*Los Olvidados,* 1951) found few bidders, even though it had won festival honors. A harrowing study of Mexico's juvenile delinquents, this picture could not be considered "commercial" by any ordinary standards and only a true film enthusiast like Edward Kingsley would dare to buy it for American art houses. Few distributors, however, could afford to risk the thousands of dollars required to purchase the rights to a foreign film of such dubious box-office appeal.

Clearly, festival honors are not enough to ensure international success. A wide box-office acceptance of these products of varying cultures depends not so much on cinematic art as upon the sophistication and maturity of the audience—a situation over which the film maker exercises no control. But though the festivals may not appreciably affect public standards, they still provide an invaluable meeting place where film makers, film distributors and a fraction of the film audiences of many nations can gather together to exchange ideas and keep an eye on developments in other lands. Far more important than the big commercial movies and the occasional "smash hits" that turn up at these festivals is the opportunity to observe the artistic growth of films from every country around the world.

VI

CHANGING TRENDS IN
THE AMERICAN FILM

THOUGH AMERICAN PICTURES ARE OFTEN CASUALLY DISMISSED AS "escapist entertainment," the forms of that escape vary from era to era and have their own significance. Successive waves or cycles of films characteristic of any given period, charted against changes in the political and social climate of the country, reveal something of the temperament, the social attitudes of the people themselves. Thus the pictures of the early thirties reflected the national disaster. The drawing-room comedies, the sophisticated plays, even the "canned" musicals—the staples of the first years of sound—had begun to pall. As banks failed and lifelong savings were wiped out, as unemployment spread across the land, these artificial and outdated forms of entertainment became unacceptable. The public did not suddenly demand "realistic" pictures, but it could no longer be amused by high society exchanging bons mots at the cocktail hour nor stirred by the matinee idyls of pretty sopranos and impoverished young tenors. In the first unhappy years of the depression, audiences sought a more recognizable image of their own problems on the screen. Sound had made possible a new degree of realism in motion pictures and when, late in 1930, Warner Brothers' *Little Caesar* brought throngs to the box office once more, the course was clear. What the public obviously wanted was a hard-hitting, naturalistic form of drama that took its themes from the headlines of the day.

The studios quickly brought to the screen not only a staggering succession of gangster pictures (fifty in 1931 alone!), but equally sensational exposés of rackets, political corruption, prison brutality, bank failures and newspaper scandal sheets. If there was any element of escapism in these films, it lay in their tendency to blame isolated individuals for what were in fact national problems. Audiences seemed to find some reassurance in the thought that everything could be solved by the jailing—or shooting—of a brutal warden, a hoodlum gangster or a power-hungry politician. In *The Big House* (1930), *Little Caesar* (1930), *The Front Page* (1931), *The Public Enemy* (1931), *The Secret Six* (1931) and many more, the public was given strong, unadulterated dramatizations of the stories behind the daily headlines. Often such films were cynical and cheap, but occasionally they proved to be sincere and perceptive investigations of evils and abuses aggravated by the depression. Indeed, the facts revealed by *I Am a Fugitive from a Chain Gang* (1932), based on an actual case, were so shocking that an aroused public forced a reformation of the chain-gang system.

Not only did the many topical films of this era reflect their times, but even the depression romances had a metallic twist. Their heroines—Constance Bennett, Tallulah Bankhead, Joan Crawford, Marlene Dietrich, Greta Garbo, Barbara Stanwyck—were frequently ladies who took to the streets or became rich men's mistresses in order to provide food for their babies, an education for their sisters or medicine for their husbands. Despite these sentimentalities, however, such films as *Susan Lenox* (1931), *Blonde Venus* (1932) and *Letty Lynton* (1932) were quite explicit in establishing the milieu of poverty that drove their heroines into a life of shame. Nor was it sheer coincidence that these virtuous prostitutes invariably encountered public enemies or crooked politicians in their rise from gutter to penthouse. In their own way, they were merely confirming the gangster theme that the only escape from depression-bred despair was to live outside the law. And the general public, if box-office returns are any index, not only condoned but applauded these fallen creatures, just as they were fascinated by the exploits of the gangsters and racketeers. The heroines may have sobbed a bit over their lost virginity, the Little Caesars may have ended up perforated by bullets, but while they lived there was a glamour and fascination to their lives that was in glaring contrast to the drab realities of 1931 and 1932.

Obviously, in making heroes of gangsters and heroines of prostitutes, the movie companies departed far from both the letter and the spirit of the Production Code they had so virtuously agreed to in the halcyon year of 1927. The depression had produced a new world, a new morality—and the studios, in giving the public what it wanted, reflected the seamiest side of the picture with unprecedented accuracy. Far too accurately for some tastes. Letters of protest began to reach the studios and the Hays Office from all the more respectable elements in communities across the country. Church groups, women's clubs and patriotic associations passed resolutions condemning the industry. Editorials appeared in the newspapers and sermons were preached from pulpits denouncing the growing immorality of the movies, urging the film producers to assume a greater social responsibility for the pictures they were turning out, prodding local censorship boards to increased vigilance and more rigorous standards. *Scarface* (1932), for example, at once one of the best and most brutal of the gangster films, was held up for months until the producers inserted several placatory scenes showing an aroused citizenry demanding action against what the film's subtitle described as "the shame of a nation." Even with these additions, *Scarface* was severely censored in many communities, banned outright in others. As a result of such efforts the films became, if not more moral, at least more moralizing. Sermons on civic responsibility became the price one had to pay for pictures that dealt realistically with the more sensational aspects of the social scene. Under the sustained pressure of the protest groups, the wave of gangster films began to subside. During 1933 it gradually merged into another cycle, with the F.B.I. men and other law enforcers as the new heroes. Actually, the G-men were simply gangsters in disguise, acting with as little concern for "due process" as the gangsters they were hunting. But official morality was once more being served.

With the election of Franklin D. Roosevelt and the prompt introduction of N.R.A. relief measures and reforms early in 1933, a new note of optimism appeared both in the country and in its films. The musicals, which only a short time before had been singing *Brother, Can You Spare a Dime* and *Ten Cents a Dance,* were now shouting out that *Happy Days Are Here Again,* or *Stand Up and Cheer*—"good times are here!" Indeed, the musical comedies reflected this new optimism not only in their songs but in their themes as well. Typical of the era were the plots of *Footlight Parade* (1933) and *100 Men and a Girl* (1937), in which groups of starving musicians, singers and dancers were rounded up by Dick Powell or Deanna Durbin and prodded into putting on a show. Their success provided employment and happiness for all. In much the same way, King Vidor's *Our Daily Bread* (1934) showed a heterogeneous band of unemployed city people finding their salvation by working together on a farm cooperative. "Back to the soil" was reiterated as the solution to urban hard times in such films as *Stranger's Return* (1933), *State Fair* (1933) and *As the Earth Turns* (1934).

In keeping with the reformist trend of the N.R.A. period, the topical films, the exposés of rackets, corruption and abuses of power took a more positive stand. Prohibition and gangsterism, juvenile delinquency, strikebreaking and prison reform were problems that an enlightened citizenry could do something about, once the facts were brought to their attention. It was in this spirit that the studios— and especially Warner Brothers—put into production such frankly controversial pictures as *Wild Boys of the Road* (1933), *Massacre* (1933), *Black Fury* (1935) and *The Black Legion* (1936), such vigorously anti-lynch films as *Winterset* (1936), *Fury* (1936) and *They Won't Forget* (1937). While the predominantly affirmative and constructive outlook of these films was encouraged by the growing liberalism of the era, it is also true that a new sense of caution and constraint was forced upon the industry by the formation of the Legion of Decency during 1933, set up to implement a new Production Code. Drawn up by Catholic churchmen and lay members, the new Code was a thorough revision of the original strictures established by the Hays Office during the "flaming" twenties—but this time reinforced by the power of the Church to bring economic reprisals against any studio that violated its rulings. Sex and crime had become so prevalent on the screen that when at last the Legion of Decency made its official appearance, in April of 1934, many of the Protestant denominations were ready to support it in its announced campaign to clean up the movies. The Code, with but few minor revisions, has remained in force ever since.

With the rise of the Legion, many of the crude excesses of the tough, realistic school of film making were quickly eliminated; but at the same time much of the forthright honesty of the period also disappeared from the screen as well. Mae West was an early victim. Her good-humored vulgarity and frank sexuality in films like *She Done Him Wrong* (1933) made her irresistible to the reformers. The biggest box-office draw of 1933–1934, she became a prime target for the outraged forces of decency. To conform to the new Production Code, her scripts were so bowdlerized that by 1936 the Mae West character had lost its sex and her films their appeal. Her few subsequent screen appearances consisted of innocuous parodies of her former roles in pictures like *My Little Chickadee* (1940) with W. C. Fields. To avoid a similar fate, James Cagney, Clark Gable and Edward G. Robinson, the movies' favorite gangsters of the early thirties, found it expedient to diversify their roles and lead more virtuous screen lives. The industry itself quite consciously began laying greater emphasis on purely escapist themes— big Westerns, costume dramas, historical films and adaptations of the classics. While treatment of the social scene was suffused with what Richard Griffith has aptly termed "the fantasy of good will," the feeling that if everyone were kind and generous to his fellow man, the depression could soon be overcome. This idea found its fullest and most popular expression in Frank Capra's *Mr. Deeds Goes to Town* (1936). Gary Cooper, a youthful millionaire, decides to give away his inherited fortune to the unemployed after discovering that his business associates are all parasites and cheats. The fact that no real-life millionaire has ever distributed his fortune with such openhearted innocence in no way diminished the attractiveness of the idea.

Mr. Deeds was one in a long cycle of films appearing during the mid-thirties that came to be called "screwball" comedies, pictures that did anything and everything for a laugh. But while the action in these films was always wildly at odds with any conventional response to a similar situation, most of them had as their point of departure the terrible realities of that period—unemployment, hunger and fear. In *My Man Godfrey* (1936), for example, William Powell plays one of the *"nouveaux* poor," a man ruined by the crash and reduced to living in the city dumps. Some scatterbrained socialites find him on a scavenger hunt and make him their butler. Because of his own experience with poverty, Godfrey is able to enlighten his employers and transform them into useful, social-minded citizens. In *Easy Living* (1937), Jean Arthur, an unemployed secretary, suddenly finds herself in possession of a priceless mink coat flung out the window by a millionaire in a moment of pique; her scathing denunciation of his thoughtlessness while others are starving was the high point of the picture. And yet both of these were presented—and taken—as comedies. As Lewis Jacobs has written, "If 'screwball' comedies successfully turned the world on its ear, that was perhaps the way it already looked to a depression generation which felt cheated of its birthright and apprehensively faced further loss in the steady approach of war."

As the thirties wore on, these growing tensions produced a notable series of films that rode the mounting wave of liberalism without recourse to either the "fantasy of good will" or "screwball" subterfuge. Labor unrest, slum housing, unemployment and dislocation aggravated by the dust storms of the mid-thirties—all of these were put on the screen with a directness that stressed the social and economic sources of such hardships. There were sympathy for the common man and new hope for a better tomorrow. In place of the contrived and improbable "happy endings" of the depression musicals and "back to the soil" films, there was now a forthright expression of belief in the inherent strength of democracy to bring about national recovery and a solution to these problems. Characteristically, when John Steinbeck's bitter novel *The Grapes of Wrath* was filmed by John Ford in 1939, the picture faithfully transmitted the shocking and desperate plight of California's migratory workers, but material in the book was freely transposed so that the film might end on a strong declaration of faith in the ability of the American people to win through. By 1941, with war raging in Europe, Capra himself had deserted his "fantasy" of the best of all possible worlds. His *Meet John Doe,* a daring and angry exposé of American fascism, was directed specifically against those manipulators of public opinion who were using the slogans of democracy to sell their program of blind reaction to the masses.

A belief in the democratic way of life was also implicit in an impressive and highly popular series of biographies that appeared throughout the late thirties. Some of these films—such as John Ford's *Young Mr. Lincoln* (1939) or *Abe Lincoln in Illinois* (1940)—

turned to American heroes whose lives and principles exemplified the democratic tradition. Others depicted great artists, scientists and political leaders in their battle with the bigots and reactionaries of their day. The careers of such international figures as Louis Pasteur, Dr. Ehrlich, Madame Curie, Emile Zola and Benito Juárez were presented as thinly-veiled sermons on behalf of democracy and enlightenment. *The Life of Emile Zola* (1937), for example, reached its climax in Zola's classic *"J'accuse"* defense of Captain Dreyfus, a scathing denunciation of anti-Semitism and intolerance in all its forms. Underlying all these films was the awareness that our cultural and intellectual freedom was a precious heritage that the growing forces of fascism both at home and abroad were threatening to destroy.

As World War II drew nearer, Hollywood films began increasingly to depict the joys, even the glamour of the military life. Though the government did not actually commission such pictures, the studios soon discovered that the War Department was willing to cooperate to the full in their production. A bomber, a battleship, even Annapolis itself was available to the producer of any film that might serve as a recruiting poster or simply as publicity for the various branches of the service. These films generally dealt with training rather than actual combat, using the Army, the Navy, the Marines or the Air Corps as a romantic background for a love story or a musical. Military preparedness was as far as the American people were willing to go at this time. They still clung desperately to the pacifism and isolationism of the thirties, echoing President Roosevelt's fervent declaration, "I hate war." But by the end of the thirties, with all of Europe in flames, American pictures began to take on a more ominous tone. In 1940 Alfred Hitchcock's spy thriller, *Foreign Correspondent,* chilled audiences across the nation when its hero, Joel McCrea, radioed the United States from bomb-torn London: "The lights are going out in Europe! Ring yourself around with steel, America!"

During this uneasy period of "lend-lease" and "bundles for Britain," the screen began a kind of orientation course, introducing the American people to their future allies, exposing the nature of their future enemies. From Hollywood came such graphic expressions of sympathy and admiration for the beleaguered British as

A Yank in the R.A.F. (1941), *This Above All* (1942), *Mrs. Miniver* (1942) and *Journey for Margaret* (1942). The Nazis began to appear as villains—for the first time—in such melodramas as *The Mortal Storm* (1941) and *Man Hunt* (1941). The dangers of a Nazi "fifth column" within the United States were exposed in the "prematurely anti-fascist" *Confessions of a Nazi Spy* (1939), while Chaplin in *The Great Dictator* (1940) spoke movingly of the dangers of fascism to the human spirit everywhere. And Russia, then linked to Germany by the Nazi-Soviet pact, was lampooned in such films as *Ninotchka* (1939) and *Comrade X* (1940).

But until the fateful morning of Pearl Harbor, on December 7, 1941, the United States was technically a neutral nation. Whatever the sympathies of the American people, whatever the implications of the government's "lend-lease" policies, most of the studios walked a wary line between 1939 and 1942, conscious that any overt declaration of partiality in their pictures could lead to economic reprisals on the part of the offended nation and outright bans in those countries anxious to maintain their neutral status. Furthermore, America itself was far from united. The strongly isolationist Midwest was cold to any film that threatened to involve us in European affairs, while as late as 1940 Hollywood was being investigated by a House Un-American Affairs Committee for daring to incorporate anti-fascist sentiments into pictures like *Confessions of a Nazi Spy*.

Once the United States was committed to the war, however, all such restraints vanished. Germans and Japanese immediately became the stock villains in film after film, while Nazi and Nipponese brutality was exposed, denounced—and exploited—in pictures like *Hitler's Children* (1943), *The Seventh Cross* (1944), *Behind the Rising Sun* (1944) and *Blood on the Sun* (1945). At the same time, our newly acquired Russian allies, who had been equally stock villains before Pearl Harbor, were suddenly turned into brave, solid, somewhat picturesque characters and lauded in films like *North Star* (1943), *Mission to Moscow* (1943) and *Days of Glory* (1944). Sympathy for the people of the occupied countries was expressed in an earnest and well-intended group of pictures—*The Moon Is Down* (1943), *Hangmen Also Die* (1943), *This Land Is Mine* (1943)—that sought to put on the screen some semblance of life under a Quisling dictatorship. Unfortunately, it was generally the Nazis who dominated these films while the people themselves remained shadowy and ill defined. Even more shadowy—although equally well intended—were their appearances as members of the anti-Nazi underground in the numerous war adventure films, where they smuggled American or R.A.F. fliers to safety beneath the very noses of the Gestapo. Certainly, these pictures served a useful propaganda function in depicting the French, the Poles, the Czechs and the Dutch as our friends and potential allies. But they also gave the quaint impression that all these people spoke an amusing pidgin English and led marvelously melodramatic lives in the underground when they weren't being tortured in Nazi prison camps. Needless to say, a sense of reality was not the strongest feature of these films.

When it came to showing American troops in action, however, Hollywood's directors became increasingly adept at creating a persuasive image of the war. They could scarcely have done otherwise, for as source material they had not only the weekly newsreels of actual combat but also a steady stream of magnificent documentaries from every theater of operations. These films were shown in theaters, factories, schools, union halls, clubs—wherever people gathered together for work or recreation. To make their own pictures properly convincing, the Hollywood directors were forced to match the realism of these documentaries in their studio-made versions of the fighting. By the end of the war, their vivid dramatizations of combat in films like *The Story of G.I. Joe* (1945), *A Walk in the Sun* (1945) and *Pride of the Marines* (1945) seemed to match frame for frame the footage sent back by the Signal Corps. Rarely did these films seek to glorify war, or attempt to make it seem a great adventure. On the contrary, most of them stressed the average American's distaste for killing and for regimentation—as well as his ability to rise to deeds of heroism when his country needed him. As in Britain, such films created a kind of group hero out of a platoon, a bomber crew or a patrol on a hazardous mission. The composition of these teams, however, was quite consciously—even self-consciously —American, with each group invariably composed of one Negro, one Jew, a Southern boy and a sprinkling of second-generation Italians, Irish, Scandinavians and Poles. America the melting pot was never more clearly in evidence.

This concern for the values of democracy was projected into the years immediately following the war in a series of films notable not only for their liberal sentiments but for their intelligent and courageous appraisal of the problems of the postwar world. The question of economic security for the hundreds of thousands of newly discharged veterans was squarely faced in a half-dozen or more films, and none more searching or honest than Samuel Goldwyn's *The Best Years of Our Lives* (1946). The emotional adjustments of returning veterans, the tragic loss of sons or fathers, the housing shortage, war profiteering and the black market were among the new themes that received serious consideration on the screen. Anti-Semitism was openly and thoughtfully discussed in *Crossfire* (1947) and *Gentleman's Agreement* (1947). In Capra's *It's a Wonderful Life* (1946) and *State of the Union* (1948), in Elia Kazan's *Boomerang* (1947) corruption in political life was admitted, but tempered by the honesty and sense of fair play of individual politicians. The wartime optimism, the belief in the American way kept all of these films from falling back upon the strident exposé techniques of the thirties.

On the other hand, the war had also familiarized movie audiences to the sight of blood and violence on the screen. In fact, it often seemed as if the stronger anti-Nazi and anti-Japanese films of the war period had used their themes as a pretext for sensational, even sadistic shots of torture, degradation and death. This suspicion was amply confirmed in the crime melodramas that took their place as the public tired of war themes. *Cornered,* appearing late in 1945, seemed to mark the transition. In it Dick Powell played an R.C.A.F. pilot who hunts down and wreaks personal—and violent—vengeance on the Nazis who murdered his wife. For a short while the heroes of these films continued to be ex-servicemen righting wrongs committed by Nazi spies or Gestapo agents. Very soon, however, this pose was dropped and they became simply rather shabby "private eyes" in the Dashiell Hammett—Raymond Chandler tradition, men who doggedly followed through on their sordid assignments despite knifings, druggings, beatings with whips and bludgeons and fierce hand-to-hand encounters. There had been violence in the gangster films of the thirties, sensationalism in the numerous exposés. But this was qualitatively different, a psychopathic kind of violence that recalled nothing so much as the tortures in the concentration camps and the cellars of the Gestapo. In films like *The Dark Corner* (1946), *The Big Sleep* (1946) and *The Lady in the Lake* (1946), the sadisms of the earlier anti-Nazi films were visibly engrafted upon the time-honored strain of film melodrama—and there they have remained to this day.

Added to this physical violence was a new interest in the refinements of mental torture. During the war it had become fashionable to depict the omnipresent Nazis as psychological monsters, men who got a grim satisfaction out of the emotional anguish they inflicted on their victims. Even before the war was over this type of villain was appearing in a more everyday guise in such films as *The Brighton Strangler* (1945), *Hangover Square* (1945) or *The Strange Affair of Uncle Harry* (1945). In this new kind of thriller, the audience knew from the outset who the murderer was. The fascination lay in the revelation of his twisted mind and the torments he devised for his victims. This morbid interest in abnormal psychology quickly spread to other genres. Films that had all the outward appearance of tragic romance, like *Love Letters* (1945) and *Leave Her to Heaven* (1945), veered off into paths of insanity and paranoia. Never before had there been pictures with heroines as sinister as *Mildred Pierce* (1945) or as sodden as the hero of *The Lost Weekend* (1945). The killers in the crime films—like Richard Widmark's laughing hoodlum in *Kiss of Death* (1947)—were presented as psychopathic personalities. And the mad psychoanalyst took his place alongside the mad scientist and the mad artist in Hollywood's gallery of arch-criminals available for horror pictures. In the search for values and stability after World War II, psychology and psychoanalysis seemed to be the key. But whether for good or ill, few could say.

By 1947 the liberalism of the Roosevelt years was fast running out. Russia had emerged from the war as a strong, militant and increasingly hostile power. In the growing hysteria, radicalism was almost instinctively linked with all shades of liberal thought. Conformity became the new order of the day, and congressional committees began to institute investigations into "un-American" activities in every sphere of American life. No investigations were more persistent—nor more publicized—than those into the motion-picture industry. The hearings of the House Un-American Activities Committee, begun in Hollywood in October of 1947, sent a chill of fear through the studios. Pictures like *Mission to Moscow* and *Song of Russia,* made during the years when the Soviet Union was an American ally in the war against fascism, were suddenly brought forward as evidence that the screen was being used to win converts to Communism. A committeeman claimed that he had detected Communist ideology in *The Best Years of Our Lives* and in *Margie,* an innocuous comedy based on the postwar housing shortage. But while the committee's charge that Communists had penetrated the industry was never substantiated, the investigations effectively dampened Hollywood's enthusiasm for controversial subjects. Jack L. Warner, after an uncomfortable probe into the details surrounding his production of *Mission to Moscow,* flatly stated that, so far as he was concerned, his studio would make no more pictures dealing with "the little man." Other producers were perhaps less forthright but no less decided. As William Wyler observed early in 1948, "I wouldn't be allowed to make *The Best Years of Our Lives* in Hollywood today. That is directly the result of the activities of the Un-American Activities Committee."

The fear, the uncertainty created by these investigations still pervades the movie colony. And though the restrictions, the unwritten taboos that they inspired have been relaxed a bit over the years, caution remains the industry's watchword. After two independent producers, Stanley Kramer and Louis de Rochemont, released *Home of the Brave* (1949) and *Lost Boundaries* (1949), several of the major studios made other films that attacked the problem of anti-Negro prejudice. Lynch law was condemned in such films as *Intruder in the Dust* (1949) and *The Lawless* (1950). But these pictures stand out as "message" films from an industry that was almost ostentatiously avoiding messages. Typical is the case of *Storm Center* (1956), a film depicting the effects of a book banning upon an entire community. Daniel Taradash, its author and director, has stated that he sought to make the picture for five years before the front office reluctantly gave its consent. If social problems have returned to the screen in recent years, it is once more in the form of sensational exposés rather than serious attempts to probe causes. And more often they are presented in terms of individual maladjustments than any deep-rooted national malaise. Alcoholics, drug addicts, juvenile delinquents, sex murderers and psychotics of every hue now throng the screen in films that are starkly documentary in reporting their heroes' problems, but strikingly noncommittal about the causes of these deviations. It is symptomatic of the film today that comedy—and especially the topical comedy that ridicules or satirizes the world around us—has completely disappeared from the screen. Perhaps the movie makers take themselves too seriously. Perhaps between the analysts, the anthropologists and the sociologists everything has been "explained" too carefully to admit laughter. But the time is clearly ripe for a new Mack Sennett, Groucho Marx or Will Rogers to brighten the scene with an irreverent wisecrack or a well-aimed pie flung in the face of convention.

THE RISE OF DOCUMENTARY

Documentary in the United States was a depression baby, born of hard times and the urge to influence public opinion toward one panacea or another. The pre-documentary pioneers of the twenties, men like Robert Flaherty and Merian C. Cooper, had already withdrawn from the field. Flaherty's lyric explorations of patterns of life in the remoter corners of the world were now alien to the harsh temper of the times; the early thirties found him in England working with John Grierson's new documentary unit there. While Cooper, who had skillfully combined ethnology with adventure in *Grass* (1925) and *Chang* (1927), moved to Hollywood to become a successful producer of studio films. These two men had sought to bring reality to the screen within the framework of the story-telling form. The new documentarians, however, were concerned with fact alone—the bitter fact of strikes, evictions, hunger marches and unemployment. Their techniques—and often their ideology as well—were derived from the Russian films of the late twenties, creating Left-tinged propaganda reels out of the violence and despair of the era. Inevitably, the theaters were closed to them. Shown primarily to the already convinced, their audience was limited, their influence slight. The development of a broader audience for documentary in this country resulted from the work of individuals and organizations quite apart from the scattered handful of dedicated souls who first introduced the form.

Clearly, the most important single step in this direction was the introduction of *The March of Time* early in 1935. Rightly called "a new kind of screen journalism," it stood midway between the ordinary newsreel and the probing social analysis of the British documentary school. It dramatized the news, getting behind the headlines to offer pertinent background information and editorial opinion. Not surprisingly, both its slant and its style bore striking resemblance to that of its successful parent *Time* magazine. The voice of *Time,* Westbrook Van Voorhis, was the voice of authority—strident, implacable, decisive. There was no questioning his figures, his facts, his conclusions. Everything had been carefully researched, properly thought out and knowingly packaged. One could not say nay to "The March . . . of Time!"—although documentary people on both sides of the water tended to look down their noses at it. They claimed that it was superficial and that its editing was as slovenly and haphazard as the average newsreel. Actually, despite its aesthetic shortcomings, *The March of Time* had created a distinctive style that punched information across with a maximum of intensity and interest. The editing, functional if not artistic, was so closely tied to the commentary that transitions were often introduced simply by a "but" or a "however" on the sound track. Personalities, authorities on the topic under discussion spoke their views glibly into the camera in interviews especially arranged for the reel. Dramatic re-enactments became an increasingly important part of the technique. In their thirteen issues a year the editors managed to keep their material timely, lively and even, on occasion, controversial. Indeed, so successful was *The March of Time* during the late thirties that RKO-Radio Pictures was inspired to launch a rival reel, *This Is America.* For most Americans, these spelled documentary. They knew nothing else.

In the meantime, however, American film makers were beginning to see examples of European documentary styles that suggested the variety of ways in which fact could be handled creatively on the screen. Robert Flaherty's English-made *Man of Aran* (1934), a feature-length study of the primitive pattern of existence on a barren Irish island, emphasized the concept of a personal, dramatic shaping of reality. Continental documentary was represented by Joris Ivens, the distinguished Dutch director who in 1936 brought a group of his pictures to this country and remained to form an important independent documentary group, Contemporary Historians. His vivid, frankly partisan reporting of the wars in Spain and China, *Spanish Earth* (1937) and *The 400,000,000* (1938), were the first extended accounts of those tragic preludes to World War II to reach the American screen. Even more widespread and influential was the work of the Museum of Modern Art Film Library. Founded in 1935, it soon acquired a number of British documentary films and began circulating them to schools, universities and museums throughout the country. Under its sponsorship, Paul Rotha, the English documentary producer, director and historian, was brought to this country to tour with the films and introduce them to American film makers. The impact of all these films and personalities upon the Americans produced both a broadening and refinement of their own work. Documentary was no longer thought of as the crude presentation of fact through an assemblage of highly realistic shots. It was, they began to realize, a complex, artistic form with reality at its core and an infinite variety of techniques by which the documentarian could make his subject meaningful and affecting to his audience.

With the appearance of Pare Lorentz' *The Plow That Broke the Plains* (1936), American documentary may be said to have come of age, assimilating the best of the European tradition and adding to it a spacious lyricism that was peculiarly American. Produced for the United States Resettlement Administration, one of the New Deal agencies, it was a dramatic account of the tragic misuse of our Great Plains that led to the disastrous Dust Bowl of the mid-thirties. Like President Roosevelt's famous "fireside chats," this was a report to the nation on its government's efforts to meet the emergency—and the first to be made by film instead of by radio. It was followed by *The River* (1937), a broadly conceived history of the Mississippi basin and the changes being wrought by the T.V.A. soil-conservation and flood-control program. The style of these two films was poetic— Lorentz wrote his commentaries in free verse—the approach, humanitarian. Implicit in each was the concern for people, for families blown off their land by the dust storms or forced to wrest a living from soil worn out by erosion and unscientific cultivation. There was a tragic grandeur in their evocation of the march of history, a thrill of pride as they recounted the government's efforts to combat the effects of generations of neglect, indolence and waste. These two films, not only pioneers but classics in American documentary, served as the recruiting ground for many of our leading documentary film makers. No less important, they began to focus public attention upon the form itself. Gradually foundations, public-service groups and even industry came forward in a very tentative way to sponsor production.

The real turning point for documentary in America, however, came with the New York World's Fair of 1939. Never before had such a variety of fact films been brought together in one place—sales films, promotion films, art films, travelogue and interest films as well as true documentaries. Never before had the many uses of the film medium been so graphically demonstrated. And what was quickly apparent was the popularity of the documentary with general audiences above all other forms except the outright entertainment feature. Crowds gathered throughout the day and night at the British Pavilion, where examples of the British documentary were on continuous display. Equally successful were the American documentaries, shown at the Little Theatre in the New York City Building. Outstanding, of course, were *The Plow That Broke the Plains* and *The River*. But the real hit of the show was *The City* (1939), a film made specifically for exhibition at the Fair by Willard Van Dyke and Ralph Steiner. Sponsored by the American Institute of Planners, it was a documentary on the need for city planning executed with great technical virtuosity and—what is even rarer in documentaries—considerable humor. By contrasting the peaceful New England scene against industrial slums and hectic glimpses of modern city life, it built a strong case for decentralized "green belt" communities—although ironically it never succeeded in making them seem quite as appealing as the ridiculously crowded and eminently human scenes of New York at its worst. The unmistakable popularity of documentaries at the Fair generated a greater interest in the form on the part of both the sponsors and the general audience, resulting in a sudden spurt in production during the years just before the war.

With more pictures being made, the problems of documentary distribution became more urgent than ever. For years the development of the field had been hobbled by its inability to make contact with the public. For the most part, theaters were closed to such films. They did not conform to the standard concepts of entertainment, and the educational channels through which they were available were unfamiliar to the average theater owner. When he wanted to play an informational short, he generally chose a *March of Time,* or perhaps an interest reel like Walter Futter's *Curiosities* or Lyman Howe's *Hodge-Podge.* Beginning in 1939, however, the documentary people instituted a vigorous program of publicity and information. Through the Rockefeller-financed American Film Center and their own Association of Documentary Film Producers they sought a wider public for their kind of film making. And to a degree they found it in the museums, the libraries, the clubs and schools— but rarely in motion-picture theaters.

This inability to break through to the mass audience proved doubly unfortunate. As the war drew nearer, the government needed hundreds of films to explain to the nation the reasons for a peacetime draft and lend-lease, the story behind America's increased production of tanks and bombers, the need for more women in industry and the necessity for closer cooperation with the Latin American countries. But since the government wanted to reach the vast moviegoing public, it turned not to the documentarians but to Hollywood. Through 1940 and 1941 came short after short from Hollywood writers and directors. Some of these official films were made by the studios, more of them by studio people who offered their services to the emergency organizations set up in Washington. But however good their intentions, it was soon apparent that their capacity to deal persuasively with factual material was limited. Most of their reels were pseudo-*March of Time* style, theoretically glamorized with narrations by such stars as Ingrid Bergman, Katharine Hepburn, James Stewart or Orson Welles. One recruiting film produced by M-G-M actually sought to induce Navy enlistments by showing sailors strumming their guitars while native girls danced on the beach at Waikiki. It was released only a few weeks before Pearl Harbor!

These pseudo-documentaries, distributed by the industry's efficient War Activities Committee, were shown in theaters all over the country. The experienced documentary film makers, on the other hand, were pointedly ignored by the government at this time. Some indication of the official attitude may be deduced from the fate of the Pare Lorentz unit. Organized into the U.S. Film Service, it had continued to produce distinguished documentaries for various governmental agencies throughout the late thirties—including Joris Ivens's *Power and the Land* (1940), Robert Flaherty's *The Land* (1941) and Lorentz's own feature-length *Fight for Life* (1940). But to a Congress growing restive under the Roosevelt administration, these smacked too strongly of New Deal propaganda. Early in 1941, at a time when the need for skilled documentarians had never been stronger, the Service was summarily disbanded. Congressionals preferred the less controversial style of the Hollywood people.

Once the war had started, however, film makers of every description were sought for the various branches of the government's vast information and education program. Thousands of training films were needed on every conceivable subject from military courtesy to the assembly of the M-1 rifle, from fighting venereal disease to spotting enemy aircraft. When the Army Signal Corps and the Navy could not keep up with the demand, the production of such pictures was parceled out under contract to the various Hollywood studios. Of even greater importance to the development of documentary, however, was the work of men like Frank Capra, John Ford, John Huston and William Wyler, men who left the studios completely to enter on wartime service in the Army Signal Corps or the Navy or Air Force. For most of them it meant a wholly new orientation, a self-imposed course in acquiring the techniques of handling fact on the screen through much the same process that Grierson's group had trained itself in England a dozen years earlier. Two styles of films resulted. One was the edited documentary, perhaps best represented by Frank Capra's *Why We Fight* series (1943–1945). Capra and his skilled editors drew their clips from feature films, newsreel and combat footage to create a panoramic background of the events leading to World War II, and the issues at stake. Others, like Huston's *San Pietro* (1944), Wyler's *Memphis Belle* (1944) and John Ford's *Battle of Midway* (1944), were masterpieces of on-the-spot war reporting, a combination of powerful images and thoughtful commentary that reached through to every American in or out of uniform. These films spoke the language. They made facts significant, dramatic. And perhaps because they were created by civilian soldiers rather than by the military itself, they never suggested that war was a heroic, glamorous business. It was always a means—a nasty, sordid, murderous but necessary means to a vital end—the preservation of democracy. What was even more laudable, the democracy that they extolled was implicit in the films themselves, ingrained in the spirit of the men who made them.

All of these were widely shown, both at home and to the soldiers in their camps and bases in every theater of operations. But there was another notable series of documentaries that, originally, was never intended for American eyes. These were the films produced for the Overseas Branch of the Office of War Information, an organization set up to prepare pictures on life in the United States— our traditions, our customs, the way we live—against the day when our armies became victorious. The people of Europe had lived so long under Fascist and Nazi rule, had been fed so long on Fascist and Nazi propaganda, that our own counter-propaganda had to be ready. To O.W.I. Overseas flocked the men who had been the leaders in American documentary production before the war— Irving Lerner (who became its production chief), Willard Van Dyke, Henwar Rodakiewicz, Irving Jacoby, Alexander Hacken- schmied, Jules Bucher, Joseph Krumgold and Sidney Meyers. They evolved a special style that was eminently adapted to the problem presented them. Because their pictures would be shown in many languages, direct dialogue obviously could not be used. They de- pended instead on a strong, clear narration, visually striking, indis- putably authentic images and exceptionally skilled editing. A mu- sical score, often prepared by such leading modern composers as Aaron Copland, Alex North or Virgil Thomson, completed the pic- ture. For foreign distribution, the narration was simply translated into the appropriate language.

Quite apart from such stylistic considerations, the films of O.W.I. Overseas were differentiated from the productions of the War De- partment and O.W.I. Domestic in a far more basic way. The reels prepared for the troops and the home front were related to the progress of the war; their whole effectiveness lay in their timeliness.

It was not, however, the passing moment that the Overseas unit sought to record. Its purpose was to discover typical and enduring elements in our culture that had grown from our European heritage, as well as those that might contribute to the postwar development of the liberated nations. The result was a series that included films like *Tuesday in November* (1945), a lucid explanation of the American electoral system; *A Better Tomorrow* (1945), examining the role of free education in the New York public schools in molding future citizens; *The Cummington Story* (1945), a true and touching incident in which a group of European refugees were welcomed and integrated into the life of a New England town. In anticipation of the liberation of Italy, there was a filmed performance by Arturo Toscanini and the N.B.C. Symphony of Verdi's *Hymn of the Nations* (1944). There were films on the public health services, the T.V.A. dam projects, the Library of Congress, the historic San Francisco Conference where the United Nations was born. It was a priceless collection, and one that might have been lost to the nation entirely had not the documentary people themselves urged distribution of these films in this country. Released at print cost through the U.S. Office of Education, they have become the backbone of many of today's school and university film libraries.

After the war, both the Army and the State Department, through its Information Service, extended the policy of O.W.I. Overseas, commissioning films that continued to "bring alive" the American scene for the people of Europe and Japan. Again it was predominantly the documentary makers who created these pictures of our cultural, intellectual and regional life in films like *Journey into Medicine* (1947) or *Land of Enchantment* (1948), a portrait of New Mexico as seen through the eyes of the artist Georgia O'Keeffe. Meanwhile, the Hollywood people had returned to the studios, taking with them their new techniques for handling reality on the screen. Louis de Rochemont, creator of *The March of Time,* had already introduced the documentary approach into the entertainment field with his anti-Nazi spy film *The House on 92nd Street* (1945). A re-enactment of an authentic case out of the files of the F.B.I., it was photographed against the actual backgrounds of the original story. The success of this experiment, which for de Rochemont has since hardened into formula, led to an increased use of "location" shooting on what were essentially studio films. Directors of ordinary cops-and-robbers pictures like *Naked City* (1948) or *Union Station* (1950) found it definitely advantageous to take their cameras and crews to New York's lower East Side or the Los Angeles depot. The real backgrounds lent a note of authenticity to their melodramatic plots. Documentary—or at least semi-documentary—had entered into the ordinary parlance of Hollywood.

During the years immediately after the war, the outlook for documentary in this country was brighter than ever. The wartime use of films had removed any doubts as to the efficacy of the medium in influencing public opinion. In education, tests had proved that men could master a process at least one-third faster if they saw it demonstrated first through motion pictures. The estimated 400,000 16mm projectors used during the war to show training and morale films created an unprecedented market for non-theatrical pictures. The schools were setting up elaborate audio-visual programs, and even the libraries were investigating the possibilities of circulating films along with books. Government, private industry, textbook publishers, foundations all came forward as potential sponsors. John Grierson arrived in New York to prepare a documentary series, *The World Today,* for United Artists release. When Robert Flaherty's feature-length documentary *Louisiana Story* (1948) began playing the art-house circuits, it seemed to presage a whole new era. Financed by Standard Oil and produced with unprecedented freedom at a cost of a quarter of a million dollars, it was a model of institutional film making. Its sponsor neither asked for nor received credit or mention in the film—simply the good-will that might accrue from its unaffected account of the discovery of oil in a Louisiana bayou and its effect upon a Cajun family. The picture's warm reception and the sponsor's expressed satisfaction added to the general optimism of the documentarians. They felt that the value of their kind of film making, their approach to reality, was at last receiving public recognition and support. They looked forward to the day when such enlightened public-relations programs would be the rule, not the exception. They envisaged a future in which the documentary would become as effective in peace as it had been in war. Unfortunately their hopes have yet to be realized.

Just what went wrong is difficult to say. Certainly, the rise of television drained off vast sums of money that might otherwise have been spent to sponsor institutional documentaries. TV's adverse effect on the movie box office also reached the documentarians: the market for shorts fell off so sharply that not only was the Grierson project scrapped but even the well-endowed *March of Time* was forced off the screen. Also since the war, in the interest of economy, both the Army and the State Department drastically curtailed their film production programs. Meanwhile, of course, documentaries are still being made. A few of them are privately financed, like Sidney Meyers' *The Quiet One* (1949), a moving and sensitive study of a disturbed Negro boy and the help he received at the Wiltwyck School. Some have been created on foundation grants, like the challenging series produced by Alberta and Irving Jacoby for the Mental Health Film Board. Others have been made with public funds to serve a specific purpose, to meet an urgent need—films like George Stoney's *Feeling All Right* (1949), dramatically effective in the fight against syphilis in Mississippi, or his simple and touching *All My Babies* (1954), produced for the State of Georgia to help train Negro midwives.

At present, however, inspired production is both scattered and sporadic. Increasingly, the documentarians have had to support themselves by routine commercial assignments tailored to rigid sponsor specifications. In the sharp struggle for such contracts, they have lost sight of their original goal. At its best, during the depression and the war, the documentary movement was characterized by a dedication to social change and public enlightenment. With the return of peace and prosperity, that spirit seems gradually to have ebbed away. Though there is still much to be learned, much to be said about the world and its people, the documentarians are no longer taking the lead in saying it. Without direction, lacking both leadership and enlightened sponsorship, they have become increasingly identified with technically proficient, uncreative industrial films whose main purpose is to promote a product or present a corporation's point of view. As we have noted earlier, a similar decline in vitality and purpose occurred in Britain after the war. It almost seems as if it takes a time of stress or crisis to crystallize the inherent strength of the documentary—its ability to build understanding in an increasingly complex world by revealing the relationship of man to his society, to his institutions and to his fellow men. This was Grierson's ideal, his concept of the mission of documentary film makers at all times. For true documentaries are concerned less with facts than with *meaning*. Mrs. Flaherty has called them "Films of Life," and in the deepest sense this is precisely what they are—life made meaningful by the creative artist. Their present eclipse can only be temporary. Documentary is too important a form to disappear entirely from the screen.

ART FILMS AND THE NEW AVANT-GARDE

The willingness to experiment, to try out new forms, new techniques and ideas, is as vital to the arts as it is to science. Today, through an unfortunate limiting of the word, experiment in film has come to be associated almost exclusively with the efforts of small avant-garde coteries working quite apart from the main stream of motion-picture production. In the truest sense, however, Griffith was experimenting when he pushed his camera closer to the actors than the conventions of the day accepted, when he lit, photographed and edited his scenes in ways no other director had dreamed of. *The Cabinet of Dr. Caligari* was an experiment in a new form of storytelling as well as in scenic design. The moving camera of Murnau, the editing principles of Eisenstein and Pudovkin, the realism of von Stroheim's *Greed* and the lyricism of Flaherty's *Moana*—all were experiments on the then-existing borders of the medium. The additions of sound and, more recently, the wide screens are technological innovations that forced creative film makers to attempt still further experiments with film techniques.

It was during the twenties, when the avant-gardists were in full swing on the Continent, that the idea of experiment became identified exclusively with their peculiar kind of film making. If a picture were abstract, baffling or downright incomprehensible, it could always be described as "experimental." And since these films came from Europe they were also considered "artistic," an assumption based largely upon the naïve American tradition that anything European is necessarily more artistic than the native product. Thus experiment acquired a certain honorific connotation, a quality that has clung to it ever since. And because the men who were experimenting in the studios never claimed that they were doing anything but making pictures as best they could, a certain preciousness and "little cinema" aura gathered about the word as well. This was strengthened by the ardent espousal of avant-garde film making by the film aesthetes of the late twenties. A new phenomenon, these young men and women were members of the first generation that had grown up with the movies as their most familiar form of artistic expression. Toward the end of the silent era, they gathered in the few small art houses that had become the last-ditch stand of the silent film and watched with enthusiasm the European avant-garde works. They wrote about them in the little magazines of the period and met together to discuss them in their film forums and societies. Under the influence of the Europeans, they even began to try their own hand at making city symphonies, impressionist studies, film poems and abstractions.

Once made, however, where could such pictures be shown? The handful produced on theatrical 35mm stock—like James Sibley Watson's expressionist version of *The Fall of the House of Usher* (1928) or Ralph Steiner's semi-abstract $H_2 O$ (1929)—might be booked for an occasional showing in an art house. But more of them were being made with the relatively new, relatively inexpensive 16mm equipment—and 16mm at that time was considered entirely the province of the amateur. Outside of screenings for home movie clubs or possibly a local art group, the audience for such early experimentalists as Emlen Etting, Henwar Rodakiewicz or Herman G. Weinberg was limited indeed. The final sweeping victory of the talkies, followed almost immediately by the depression, brought this first American avant-garde period to an abrupt close. With sound now a necessity for theatrical distribution, a film like Robert Florey's *Life and Death of a Hollywood Extra* (1928) could no longer be made for a mere $97. As in Europe, a number of the experimentalists turned to documentary; others abandoned the field entirely.

When the form re-emerged, in the years immediately after the war, it found a new audience waiting for it in the suddenly important 16mm field. The troops had seen their training and orientation films on 16mm projectors by day, then 16mm prints of the latest Hollywood features on the same projectors by night. The magnificent wartime documentaries had been shown to millions of civilians on the 16mm "smokestack circuit." No longer could 16mm be thought of solely in terms of classroom films or pictures of baby in the garden. It had achieved a new stature, a new degree of professionalism. It had arrived. During the same period, the Museum of Modern Art Film Library was distributing 16mm versions of film classics to schools, universities and museums around the country. With its circulating programs of features, documentaries and early avant-garde works, it provided a basis for the development of undergraduate film societies and workshops, stimulated independent experimental film production and helped create a new awareness of the film as an art form.

It was to this audience, already exposed to avant-garde films, that the new avant-garde first turned for sympathy and support. The indefatigable Maya Deren pioneered the field in 1945, booking her three short film poems—*Meshes of the Afternoon* (1943), *At Land* (1944) and *Choreography for Camera* (1945)—at a number of leading universities. Everywhere she went, in everything she wrote, she proselytized for the new form, for film as a personal expression. And the warmth of the initial response was astounding, suggesting that at least in the cultural centers—the big cities and the college towns—there had emerged a new breed of moviegoer. Such was indeed the case, for the programs of the film societies, museums and community art centers had begun to attract a public that wanted something not available in the average movie. Its slogans were vague—it knew only that it wanted pictures that were "more mature," "more controversial," "more artistic." Eager to see the offbeat and the different, it made an ideal audience for the new avant-garde. Not surprisingly, many of the postwar experimentalists came out of this same audience. They were impressed by the early avant-garde works, by the films of Maya Deren and by the thought that the motion picture was the true art of the 20th century. Furthermore, they found that by using the relatively cheap, highly flexible 16mm camera they could turn out films for a few hundred dollars that were both individual and technically acceptable for public showing. Above all, they were stimulated by the realization that an audience for such pictures already existed.

Some estimate of the growth of this audience during the past ten years may be gathered from the history of Cinema 16, America's largest and most successful film society. Organized by Amos Vogel in the fall of 1947, it held its first sessions at the tiny Provincetown Playhouse. The programs consisted of "outstanding social documentaries, controversial adult screen fare, advanced experimental films, classics of the international cinema and medical-psychiatric studies." In a short time Vogel's screenings had attracted such a following that he had to find a larger auditorium. Today, to accommodate upward of 5,000 members, Cinema 16 must run each of its eight programs five or six times in halls seating anywhere from 500 to 1,600. On a smaller scale, and for smaller audiences, Cinema 16's program pattern is now being followed by some 450 film societies around the country, most of them affiliated with schools, universities, museums or similar cultural enterprises. Frequently such showings became the nucleus for still more experimental production. In 1946, for example, when the late Frank Stauffacher arranged his first Art in Cinema series for the San Francisco Museum of Art, his programs consisted in the main of Museum of Modern Art films—plus four by Maya Deren, Hans Richter's *Dreams That Money Can Buy* (1946) and a handful of new West Coast experimentals. Two years later, through the San Francisco Museum's active encouragement of experimental work—and Stauffacher's own monumental enthusiasm—the West Coast avant-garde movement had grown to such proportions that Art in Cinema was able to present ten programs built entirely from contemporary works.

And what are these experimental films? What do they look like? How do they differ from ordinary movies? Actually, no single word, no simple explanation can quite answer those questions. Despite a multiplicity of styles and intentions, however, experimental work falls into two main categories—the abstract film and what might best be called the subjective film. The abstract film, concerned with color, form, texture, movement and spatial relationships, continues the line of inquiry set up in the twenties by Hans Richter, Fernand Léger, Oskar Fischinger and others. In most of them the primary concern is with the discovery and development of animation techniques that will impart movement to abstract or non-objective forms and designs. Fischinger, for example, still active in Hollywood, patiently draws a separate picture for each of the thousands of frames in every film he makes—an extension of the principle of the primitive thumb-books that existed years before the camera was invented. Francis Lee, a painter and photographer, combines cutouts that he moves from frame to frame with pastel backgrounds that shift and change as new colors are added under the camera. Douglass Crockwell, whose folksy paintings for beer ads have adorned the pages of most national magazines, worked out a fascinating technique in which thick, manipulative paints or molded wax forms are made to change their shape from moment to moment. In Mary Ellen Bute's "visual symphonies," commonplace objects—pins, buttons, collars—are photographed through distort lenses and animated to the music of the *Danse Macabre* or a Bach Toccata and Fugue. While in Canada, the witty and inventive Norman McLaren paints abstract designs directly upon strips of clear 35mm motion-picture film. In his *Begone Dull Care* (1950), fine wire-like lines move across a velvety dark screen to the accompaniment of a dreamy blues played by Oscar Peterson. Spots of light dart about, holding on the screen until a note fades away, appearing again elsewhere with the next note. Then, as the music turns into a frantic boogie-woogie finale, the whole screen seems to burst into a riot of swift, explosive color forms.

In all of these—and there are many more—the camera is used simply as a recording machine, an instrument that reproduces whatever materials the artist has painstakingly prepared for it and in the course of that reproduction creates the illusion of motion. Others have devised ways to bring the camera itself more fully into the creative process. James Davis, for example, an artist who has gained a considerable reputation for his mobiles of plastic, used film at the outset merely to record his compositions, building colorful, rhythmic patterns from the shifting flashes of light reflected or refracted from them. More recently, in films like *Through the Looking Glass* (1955) and *Analogies* (1955), he has played with the distorted images mirrored on irregular gold and silver surfaces. His most ambitious work to date, *Becoming* (1956), is a study in evolution expressed entirely in abstract visuals. Jordan Belson, perhaps the most talented and inventive of the younger West Coast abstract film makers, has devised a form of in-camera animation, building jazzy rhythms through swift glimpses of objects that fly by before the eye can fully identify them. In *Dime Store* (1949) Dorsey Alexander created a *ballet mécanique* through stop-motion photography, moving colorful spools of thread, marbles and tooth-picks in sprightly designs to the music of Offenbach's *Gaîté Parisienne*. Leonard Tregillus and Ralph Luce also used stop-motion to animate modeling clay in their amusing, semi-abstract telling of Lewis Carroll's *Proem* (1950). And Frank Stauffacher composed his *Zigzag* (1950) from shots of the night patterns of neon signs cut rhythmically to Stravinsky's *Ebony Concerto*.

Few of these films are intended to convey a message or even a mood, although the free association of forms may suggest meanings and symbols of which their creators are quite unaware. Primarily, however, they are made to give a sensual pleasure. When they succeed—as James Davis and Norman McLaren have so many times—they create moments of delight impossible to describe, a gratification that springs from the unexpected congruencies of line, form, color and sound. When they fail—which is not infrequent—there still remains quite often the fascination of techniques, ma-terials and visual effects found in no other kind of movie.

If the abstract film is concerned with technique, the subjective film is the story form of the avant-garde—stories told through the dream symbols and Freudian trappings first introduced on the screen by the surrealists of the twenties. Here is a field where any-thing goes, where the imagination is boggled and the sensibilities often chafed by the persistently personal imagery and deliberately sensational themes pursued by their makers. Often their objective is quite frankly to shock or, at the very least, to disturb the spectator with visuals and connotations of an unpleasant or downright per-verse nature. Even when the film maker avoids sensationalism, his work will still seem strange to the uninitiated. The normal story—the mystery, the comedy, the romance—can be handled on the screen with ordinary, straightforward techniques. But dreams, the drives and hungers of the subconscious, the performance of an occult ritual or the visualization of a surrealist poem—these require new forms, a feeling for symbol, for overtone, for the special rhythms of the world of unreality. Because such themes are generally avoided in the commercial movie, they offer a special challenge to the experi-mental film maker. In a sense, the subjective film bears much the same relation to ordinary pictures as poetry does to prose. Its successful realization depends entirely upon the sensitivity of the artist, his ability to project affectingly his own private vision. Unfortunately, simply because such films are so very personal, the field is quite inviting to pretentious frauds and precocious charlatans. So rarely does one have the opportunity to mask exhibitionism under the guise of art.

To this caveat it is necessary to add that many of the film makers of the new avant-garde are serious, honest and genuinely talented. As in any art form, only through repeated exposure can one begin to separate the sincere from the phony, the talented from the merely pretentious. The films of Maya Deren, for example, not only have a strong visual impact through her bold and unconventional use of the camera, but they create and sustain moods of dreamlike revelation with startling consistency. James Broughton, a San Franciscan poet and playwright, is less concerned with camera trickery than effects within the frame—adults playing children's games, incongruous juxtapositions of symbol-laden objects, the invention of absurd yet nostalgic business for his players and an over-all textural richness that recalls the paintings of Ivan Albright. By contrast, Curtis Harrington is almost abstemious in the amount of detail he includes in his scenes. His characters play against broad, unbroken backgrounds where every object shown—a large knitting needle, a white dress blowing against a sandy dune—acquires an added significance. While Ian Hugo's *Bells of Atlantis* (1954) with its glimpses of a sub-aqueous world seen through layers of masking, lattice-like designs—and set to the cool, bell-like poetry of Anais Nin—delights through the complexity of its textures and shifting, elusive forms.

In each instance the film maker has presented a highly personal vision of the world and filled it with subjectively meaningful imagery. And while there is narrative content in all these pictures, they evade literal interpretation. Their meanings emerge through the sensations they create in their audience, through a continuity of mood and feeling rather than any formal story line. Frequently they are shocking—sometimes merely by their strangeness, more often in a deliberate attempt to jolt the audience. It is impossible to view these pictures passively. They demand that the spectator participate both emotionally and intellectually in their presentation. It is this extraordinary sense of involvement that has won a special audience for these films—and perhaps also alienated those who were either unwilling or unprepared to make the effort required to appreciate this unconventional, challenging film form.

A striking parallel to the rise of the film-society movement in the United States since the war has been the spread of the art theater during the same period. These houses, devoted primarily to the showing of European films, numbered a scant dozen in 1946— and half of them were concentrated in New York City. Today there are over 250 in operation, and hundreds more that will book an outstanding foreign success like *Diabolique* or *Gate of Hell*. What makes these figures doubly impressive is the fact that within the same years box-office attendance in general has fallen off from an estimated ninety million per week to a new low of thirty-four million reported in June of 1956. Television, of course, bears the major responsibility for this startling decline. But television is not the sole culprit. Many informed commentators have written of the "lost audience," the audience of mature adults that rarely go to see a Hollywood film any more, the audience that has lost interest in stars, glamour and stereotyped happy endings. Some of these, the extremists, have found their way into the film societies. But more of them became patrons of the art houses, putting their faith in the discrimination of the management to bring them the type of entertainment they prefer. The names of Alec Guinness, Anna Magnani, Vittorio De Sica and Carol Reed have become as magnetic to art-house patrons as Marilyn Monroe or Cecil B. De Mille to the general public. The theaters themselves, generally small and intimate in design, cater to their special audience with luxurious seats and graceful lounges where coffee is served. No less important, the managers discovered that they needed a new kind of short to accompany their European features. Against the sophistication of a Guinness comedy, a Terrytoon seemed worse than puerile; while the cliché-ridden travelogue or sports reel made a singularly inappropriate prologue to an Italian neorealist drama. They began to look farther afield for their short subjects—turning, in fact, to the distributors who had been serving the colleges, universities and film societies. And they soon found that their audiences welcomed an interesting documentary on life in distant lands, an exciting reel on art or science, even an occasional abstract experimental work.

A great many of the shorts that now appear regularly on art-house programs come from Europe, and much credit must be given to those individual distributors like Thomas Brandon, Leo Dratfield, Rosalind Kossoff and Herman Starr who pioneered in the importation of such pictures. For importing a European film is not as simple as bringing over a bolt of cloth or a bottle of perfume. It can not be placed on a shelf until a customer comes along. A foreign documentary must be adapted for American audiences before it can be shown. It may need a completely new narration, new titles, re-editing—at the very least a re-recording of the sound track in English. Each of these processes is expensive. For a small distributor to undertake such costs in the market for cultural shorts as it existed even as late as 1950 required both courage and vision. Fortunately, once an awareness of the existence of this kind of material began to reach a more general audience, support was prompt and enthusiastic.

An important source of support was the formation of the Film Advisory Center in 1950 by Perry Miller. While in Europe preparing a film report for the United Nations, Miss Miller had become familiar with the vast quantities of outstanding short material that existed on the Continent. The Center was formed to encourage the importation of these pictures, as well as the production of similar films in this country. With Robert Flaherty as chairman, it succeeded in mobilizing prominent art and film authorities, journalists, teachers and museum people into a group which—by word of mouth, through the press and by special screenings—helped to stimulate a wider interest and awareness of these films. It provided distributors with expert advisers to collaborate on the adaptation of such pictures for the American market. It showed them to the managers of art houses and television stations, helped arrange courses at schools and museums, assisted in the organization of special film festivals. One of the most rewarding of the Center's activities was its participation in the First American Art Film Festival, held at the artists' colony of Woodstock, New York, during the hot Labor Day week-end of 1951. The sponsors had permitted themselves to hope that perhaps 600 people might turn up, the capacity of the summer theater where the screenings were to be held. Instead, over twice that many came—including distributors, exhibitors, artists, teachers and art and film critics. The experiences of that single week-end stimulated the production, distribution and utilization of art films in this country for the next few years.

"One good film helps another," Robert Flaherty used to say; and nowhere has this been truer than in the field of art films. The success of one makes it easier for a second to find distribution. Two successes lead inevitably to the production of a third, and so on. Flaherty's own presentation of *The Titan* (1950), a film on the life of Michelangelo, is evidence of this. In the years since the war there had been a slow accumulation of European-made films on the arts in the American market, but their distribution was limited, their influence slight. One of these neglected films was *The Titan*, made in Italy by Curt Oertel in 1940. Ten years later, when Flaherty's English version of it was released, the critical acclaim which it received helped focus attention on art films in general.

What became immediately apparent was the variety that existed in this field, the numerous ways in which art could be handled on the screen. In Oertel's film, for example, Michelangelo's life was told dramatically through his works. There were no actors, only the camera moving through the palaces, courtyards and countryside that Michelangelo had once known and pausing for extended, handsomely composed studies of his greatest statues and frescoes. Another style, typified by shorts like *Van Gogh* (1949) and *Gauguin* (1950), created an exciting form of film biography by showing the paintings of the masters accompanied by commentaries drawn from their own notebooks and letters. In others like *1848* (1949), *Images Médiévales* (1950) and *Balzac* (1951), contemporary works of art became the raw material out of which the film maker fashioned his interpretation of a moment in history, the manners of an era or the life of a great writer. Some of the art films took the camera into the homes and studios of famous painters—*Maillol* (1944), *Matisse* (1946), *A Visit to Picasso* (1950) and Clouzot's recent feature length *Le Mystère Picasso* (1956). In these the director presents a portrait of the living artist, showing something of his style, his inspiration, his intentions and, perhaps above all, his personality. Others explored with astonishing virtuosity the work of masters long dead. Two young Italians, Luciano Emmer and Enrico Gras, developed this technique during the war, moving their camera over photographic enlargements of the details from paintings like Bosch's fantastic *Earthly Paradise* (c1942) in the Escurial Palace near Madrid, or Giotto's murals on *The Drama of the Son of Man* (c1942) at Padua. With a true sensitivity for the style and mood of the originals—and a minimum of commentary—they revealed the suspense of terror and salvation implicit in the narrative content of these works. In *The Demon in Art* (1950), the art historian Dr. Enrico Castelli used the same technique with paintings by Bosch, Brueghel, Grünewald and others to visualize the grotesque struggle between man and the Devil that dominated the art of the late Middle Ages. While in *Rubens* (1948) and *From Renoir to Picasso* (1950) the Belgian art critic Paul Haesaerts boldly exploited the trick possibilities of the camera—animation, split screen and masking—to analyze the technique of Rubens and the major movements in modern French painting. By magnifying essential details, placing canvases side by side for immediate reference, using animated lines to emphasize the structure or the dynamics of a composition, by his discreet yet informative commentary Haesaerts carried art criticism forward to a new plane, endowing it with an immediacy and excitement possible only in motion pictures.

New in form, new in spirit, such films were made specifically for a cultivated European audience. In America, they were welcomed and admired in the art theaters. And their success, as Flaherty had predicted, led to the production of more pictures—this time by American film makers. Again the films followed many forms. Some—like the popular *Grandma Moses* (1950) or James Wong Howe's affectionate study of the Chinese painter *Dong Kingman* (1954)—were simple and unpretentious visits with the artists. Others, like *Jackson Pollock* (1951) and *Works of Calder* (1951), were concerned more specifically with explaining and interpreting the artists' techniques and intentions. Pollock, for example, narrates his film by describing his thoughts as he straddles a canvas and solemnly dribbles paint over it in his unique and controversial style. At one point, admitting quite frankly that he has "lost contact" with his painting, he abandons it and begins another. In the Calder film, for one beautifully cinematic moment grasses, leaves and waves all go out of focus under a hot summer sun, then the scene comes into focus again on the shimmering mobiles in Calder's studio—a perfect, unspoken statement of the sources of the artist's inspiration. Jean Lenauer's films on *Degas* (1950) and *Bosch* (1951), as well as the series produced by the Detroit Museum of Art, are more like visits to an art gallery. Such films bring the museum to the art lover wherever he may be, with one important difference: In place of the immediacy of the original painting, there is the camera's ability to emphasize, to enlarge, to reveal details that might go unnoticed under a less searching scrutiny. Other films, like Lewis Jacobs and Paul Falkenburg's *Lincoln Speaks at Gettysburg* (1950) and *Mathew Brady* (1954), follow the pattern of the French-made *1848* and *Balzac,* using art to document history, to tell through film the events of an era or a life that preceded the invention of the motion-picture camera.

Like the experimentals, most of the American art films have been made independently, with limited capital, by individuals working *con amore* on subjects that were of special interest to them. All of them were made initially on 16mm, although several of them have since been "blown up" quite successfully to 35mm for art-house distribution. In 1952, impressed by the size and enthusiastic reception of the art-film movement, 20th Century-Fox produced a series of seven art shorts for general distribution. Planned on the grand scale—at a cost of half a million dollars—the series included films on Botticelli, Vermeer, Degas, Renoir and Raphael, all photographed in the great European galleries. To make the subjects more "popular," rather inept little framing stories were devised for each—a G.I. going back to the Louvre to see the Botticelli that had inspired him in combat, an old art dealer reminded of Degas by a young ballet girl about to be married. Such mawkish introductions quite destroyed the films for the art-house audiences, despite the fact that their color reproduction was far in advance of anything seen at the time. Paradoxically, they were also rejected by the mass market as "too highbrow."

And yet the significant fact here is not that the Fox people burned their corporate fingers on art films, but that they tried to make art films in the first place. For years Hollywood has been turning out ten-minute travelogues, sportscopes and band shorts one so much like the other that one wonders why they even bother to make new ones. Now, amidst this standardized fare, the studios are also releasing an occasional cultural short of unusual quality and interest. Some have been acquired from abroad, like Jacques-Yves Cousteau's superb underwater films that poetically record the luminous, dreamlike world of fish and sunken ships. Others, like M-G-M's eloquent reconstruction of *The Battle of Gettysburg* (1956) from the plaques, statues and monuments of that tragic ground, or Walt Disney's enormously popular *True Life Adventure* series, are helping to raise the standards of domestic short-film production. The same may be said of the work of U.P.A. in the field of cartoons. The creators of *Gerald McBoing-Boing* and the near-sighted *Mr. Magoo,* U.P.A. has built up a wide following on the revolutionary principle that audiences in a movie theater have some intelligence and imagination of their own.

Since 1950 there has been a positive upbeat in shorts, a greater variety, a noticeable improvement in quality. No small part of this improvement is due to the work of individual film makers who, independent of studios or distributors, have seized upon the opportunities for experiment inherent in the form and turned them to their advantage. Such, for example, is Valentine Sherry's prize-winning *Coney Island, U.S.A.* (1952), a kaleidoscopic dawn-to-closing glimpse of New York's shopworn Lido, underlined by an unspoken pity for the people who must find their pleasures at this nightmare carnival. In quite another mood is a short by Shirley Clarke that captures the infectious delight of French children playing under the chestnut trees *In Paris Parks* (1955). While pure fantasy is the basis of *The Peppermint Tree* (1954), a charming animated film written by Broadway lyricist John LaTouche and narrated (all eight voices!) by comedienne Carol Channing. Numerous works of this caliber keep turning up, all of them indicative of the new vigor in the short subject field, all of them providing a freshness and diversity that is at last giving meaning to that classic program listing, "and selected short subjects."

THE STAMP OF THE STUDIO

The kind of individualism that has recently been cropping up in the field of short films has also in the past few years begun to creep into feature production. And this is a change of no small

INTERNATIONAL TRENDS: JAPAN

Gradually the films of the nations are finding their way to the screens of the world. The Japanese **Gate of Hell** (1954), directed by Teinosuke Kinugasa, exemplifies their skilled handling of traditional subjects with stylized performances, exquisite design and subtle use of color.

THE ART OF FILM: PRODUCTION DESIGN

Pre-production sketches, known as production designs, are often drawn as an aid not only to the set designer but to the camera-man and director as well. These comparison stills from Stanley Kramer's **The Pride and the Passion** (1957) reveal how closely the shots follow the original drawings.

THE ART OF FILM: THE WIDE SCREEN

Cinerama, introduced in 1952, gave rise to a dozen or more different techniques for achieving the same effect—a screen that would impress by sheer size alone, a shape that would contrast dramatically with the small screen in the parlor.

Cinerama—three 35mm strips projected side by side on a curving screen (actual size). (Scene from **Cinerama Holiday, 1955**)

CinemaScope "squeezed" 35mm frame (actual size), and as projected at 2.5:1 aspect ratio. (James Stewart in **The Spirit of St. Louis,** 1957)

The 70mm Todd-AO frame (actual size). (David Niven and Cantinflas in **Around the World in 80 Days,** 1956)

significance. American films have long been criticized as being overly standardized and routine, lacking the style and personality of the better European pictures. Almost any movie fan, after a few moments of gazing at a Hollywood film, can make a fairly accurate guess as to which company produced it without seeing either titles or trade-marks. On the other hand, aside from the work of a few top directors, a distinctive, personal "touch" is rare. By and large, it is the studio that leaves the strongest imprint on its films. A few years ago, for example, 20th Century-Fox produced an all-star omnibus feature, *O. Henry's Full House* (1952), with five first-rank directors handling the five separate stories that comprised the film. Yet when the picture appeared it was impossible to detect any evidence of stylistic differences. It might have been the work of a single individual. And in a sense, it was—the corporate individual known as 20th Century-Fox. The quality of the film's photography and sound, its settings, the characteristically lively tempo of its editing all bore the unmistakable stamp of the Fox personality.

And each of the other major studios has a style of its own that manifests itself in its choice of stars and story, in the physical mounting of its films and the technical aspects of the production. These corporate personalities grew and solidified during the twenties, when the American motion picture first achieved the status of a major industry. In the earlier days, when production was still simple and highly individual, men like Griffith, Chaplin or De Mille were free to make pictures pretty much as they pleased, as long as their films showed a profit. Frequently, the director was his own producer, not only making the picture but going out to find the financing and, ultimately, arranging for its sale or distribution. In any case, the producer at that time was invariably a part of the group that planned and created the film. Often, like Sennett and Ince, the producer had himself only recently graduated from the directorial ranks and knew at first hand the problems of film making. Sennett from his bathtub, Ince at his kitchen cutting bench personally shaped the pictures that came from their studios.

But as movies grew longer, more elaborate and expensive to produce, the problems of administration became increasingly demanding. The studios were forced to enlarge their operations to stay in business, the producers forced to devote more of their attention to matters of distribution and exhibition and less to production itself. The distance between the studios and the "front office" began to expand. And early in the twenties, when the movies turned into a vast, multi-million-dollar industry almost overnight, the creative talent was suddenly widely separated from the men who guided the financial destinies of their studios. Soon the studios were being spoken of as "the factory" or "the plant," and pictures became "the product." The movies had become big business; and since the very essence of big business is standardization and control, methods of production were introduced that would permit a close calculation of costs and a reasonably exact estimate of profits. Directors quickly learned their position in the complex chain of command that extended from the studio floor up through the new echelons of assistant producers, associate producers, producers, vice presidents in charge of production and on back to the board rooms and executive suites of the company's top brass, generally situated in New York.

It was at these levels that, until quite recently, virtually all production was planned. The ultimate decisions—the choice of stars, final script approval, the allocation of production funds—all of these came from the "front office." They represented a combination of the business acumen, the tastes and prejudices of such elder statesmen of the industry as the Schencks, the Balabans and the Skourases, filtered through studio chiefs like Dore Schary, Darryl Zanuck or Frank Freeman. These men left their ideological imprint upon every picture that their studio released. The company style enters at another level, in the organization of camera departments, art departments, music departments, sound departments and processing laboratories at each studio. Headed by men like Cedric Gibbons, Alfred Newman, Douglas Shearer or John Arnold, they persist where directors and producers come and go. Across the years these departments have evolved their own methods, their own standard operating procedures. With perhaps minor adjustments and adaptations for each new film that goes into production, they determine the physical appearance of their studio's pictures—the M-G-M gloss, the Paramount sparkle, the brassy brightness of the 20th Century-Fox releases, the ponderous pacing of the typical Warner film. It was this smooth-functioning machinery, the combination of "front office" and efficient departmentalism, that gave rise to the stamp of the studio. And until the early fifties, few directors had either the power or the individuality to surmount it. For most of them, it was a matter of adjusting their temperaments to the corporate identity of the eight major studios—or withdrawing from films altogether.

Today, however, they have an alternative, one that is proving attractive to an ever-increasing number of Hollywood's creative personnel. It is the possibility of independent production, with each film individually made, financed and marketed. The rise of this kind of production may be attributed to the success of a single firm, United Artists. Purely a distributing organization, U.A. handles films of all kinds—big and small, English and American, good, bad and indifferent. Unlike the other companies, it has no studios of its own, merely the facilities to advertise, promote and sell those independently-made productions that it agrees to distribute. In a sense, it carries out precisely the functions for which it was created back in 1919. At that time, the leading film makers of the day—Griffith, Chaplin, Fairbanks and Mary Pickford—formed United Artists as an outlet for their own pictures. They wanted complete autonomy of production, the freedom to make what they wished as they wished. And they realized that they had to break with the established studios to do so. Their ideal was quality, the custom-made film. During the twenties they were joined by such leading independents as Samuel Goldwyn and Joseph M. Schenck, later by David O. Selznick, Alexander Korda and Stanley Kramer. But there was a hard lesson in economics to be learned. By concentrating exclusively on independent quality production, United Artists lacked sufficient product to sustain the expense of a costly distributing apparatus. By the late forties the company's position had become desperate.

When United Artists was reorganized in 1951 by two young lawyers, Arthur Krim and Robert Benjamin, they immediately substituted a new policy of taking virtually anything they could get, low budget or high budget, domestic or foreign, in order to build up the volume of their business. And they soon discovered that quality does not always correspond to budget, that an inexpensive picture can be a gold mine while a multi-million-dollar all-star attraction can lay a multi-million-dollar egg. By carefully nursing the better small ones that came their way, and boldly exploiting such big ones as *The African Queen* (1951) and *Moulin Rouge* (1952), Krim and Benjamin gradually wiped away the tarnish that had gathered on the U.A. escutcheon. Today, while United Artists has its share of mediocre productions, it strikes a high average of excellence and interest. New independent outfits are flocking to the U.A. banner to produce films as modest as *Marty* (1955) or as vast as *The Pride and the Passion* (1957), as romantic as *Summertime* (1955) or as grim as *Attack* (1956). In some instances, United Artists has advanced the money that ensured their completion. The result is something quite different from the stamp of the studio. Each U.A. film has a personality of its own, a style that comes from its production team rather than from the accumulated habits, techniques and formulas characteristic of the other major studios.

The success of the United Artists pattern is having a profound effect upon the industry today. It is an industry in the midst of change—not merely the physical change imposed by wide screens and stereophonic sound, but a basic change in film economics. The Government's protracted antitrust action, begun in 1945, has at last succeeded in divorcing production from exhibition, splitting the studios away from their affiliated theater chains. As a result, pictures no longer get automatic play dates: they must be sold now on their own merits. And television, with its vast quantities of free entertainment on tap in the home, is fast eliminating the market for "B" pictures, that once-profitable staple of assembly-line production methods. At the same time, high income taxes since the war have made it more profitable for top stars and directors to incorporate into independent production units rather than work for a salary, however large, under a studio contract. An even greater attraction for many is the unprecedented artistic freedom possible under this system. And to proven talents like Hitchcock, Huston and Kazan, or teams like Hecht-Lancaster and Seaton-Perlberg, both banks and studios are happy to advance production money with relatively few strings attached. Increasingly the major companies, following the lead established by United Artists, are wooing the independents not only with financing but with their production and distributing facilities as well (for a sizable percentage of the finished film, of course). Since 1955 every studio has included some independent productions among its releases. Perhaps the most significant sign of change, however, is the resignation of Darryl F. Zanuck as executive producer on the 20th Century-Fox lot. For over two decades he supervised the thirty to fifty pictures made annually by that studio. But in 1956 he formed his own autonomous unit at Fox, with the intention of making perhaps two or three pictures a year— each personally chosen, personally produced. Many years ago Samuel Goldwyn said, "I make my pictures to please myself." The oldest and most conspicuously successful of all the independents, he has lived to see his private tenet become the watchword of a new generation of film makers in Hollywood.

As a result of all this, American movies are slowly acquiring a "new look"—not the stamp of the studio but the signature of the men who make them. It is this system that has made possible Elia Kazan's *On the Waterfront* (1954) and *Baby Doll* (1956), the Hecht-Lancaster production of *Marty* (1955), John Huston's production of *Moby Dick* (1956). It has fostered the return of controversial material to the screen, as in *The Man With the Golden Arm* (1955), Otto Preminger's painful film on the "forbidden" subject of dope, or Robert Aldrich's anti-war picture, *Attack* (1956), or *Storm Center* (1956), Daniel Taradash's daring film on Communist witch-hunting. This is not to suggest that the millennium is at hand. In the front offices, far from the scene of production, still sit the men who decide which pictures their studios will make or distribute. Basing their judgment on the script and star commitments, they retain the power to halt a picture before a foot of film has been exposed. The top stars are also in a commanding position today. Perhaps two dozen actors and actresses—hardy perennials like Crosby, Gable and Cooper—are regarded as gilt-edged investments by the film financiers. Money will be forthcoming for any picture they agree to appear in. But to get them, the independent producer must not only offer a considerable percentage of his profits but, more important, also consent to script changes that preserve the star's long-cherished conception of his screen character. And finally, there is the still unsolved riddle of the wide screen. It is axiomatic that as pictures grow wider, they grow more expensive to make. Today, most independent production is shot for the normal screen, much of it in black-and-white. But if, within the next few years, the wide screen and color become the accepted standard, will the independents be able to raise the enormous sums required for such production? And will the wide screens impose their own kind of standardization—the big musical, the big Western, the super-spectacle—upon the independent film maker?

These are questions that can only be answered in the future. For the present, it is heartening to note that the Hollywood film is struggling through to the kind of personal expression so admired in European pictures. At long last American production seems to be returning to the individuality and independence that characterized it back in the days when the movies were young.

VII

THE CHALLENGE OF TELEVISION

In the late thirties a small dark cloud loomed on Hollywood's horizon—television. At that time NBC and CBS, the two largest radio networks, had just begun taking a fatherly interest in the new medium, sending out several hours of experimental telecasts daily to the few hundred receivers scattered across the country. But World War II, which sent movie receipts booming, brought television to a temporary standstill. When wartime restrictions halted the production of TV sets, the networks abandoned their programming. In the huge profits of the war years, the film companies easily forgot about the possibility of competition from free pictures in the home. However, it proved only a brief respite. No sooner did the government relax its restrictions than the manufacture of television sets was resumed on a vast scale. TV programs returned to the air in force, this time with sponsors and big budgets. New stations began to open all around the country. "Uncle Miltie" and dozens of other personalities held audiences glued to the tiny 7" screens. By 1948 the movie makers were forced to acknowledge television as a major threat to their very existence. The history of the industry since that time has been dominated by its efforts to fight TV, to compete with it, and finally to work out forms of peaceful co-existence with this potent rival for the public at large.

Because of the vast quantities of program material that television must turn out every day—from ten to sixteen hours for most stations—it is all too easy to dismiss any serious claims that TV might indeed be a new art. Because much of its programming is devoted to the reproduction of ball games, prize fights and old movies, many profess to think of it primarily as a means of transmission, a channel of communication scarcely more creative than the telephone. Furthermore, because television operates under incredible pressures of time, space and sponsor demands, it is often criticized as a wholly commercial operation that cannot afford to be artistic. And finally, because of its rapid growth and grueling daily routine, it has had little opportunity to develop a style of its own. To date there has been no D. W. Griffith of television, no one with the vision to recognize its potential powers and, by an act of creative imagination, transform it into a truly distinctive art form. Instead, just as the early movies borrowed from theater, vaudeville and the Wild West shows for a decade or more, so television continues to draw on the stage, film and radio for its personalities, techniques and materials. At this point, television is primarily an exceedingly prosperous hybrid dominated by two constricting patterns of thought. According to some, TV is simply "radio with pictures." The rest think of it as "movies by air."

Just a glance at American television today confirms the prevalence of the "radio with pictures" point of view. The strict time schedules of commercial broadcasting have been carried over intact, imparting to TV its arbitrary segments of quarter-, half- and full-hour programs—in marked contrast to the movies where the unfolding of the story alone dictates the length of the picture. In addition, television's programs may be arbitrarily disrupted at any moment by "breaks" for the sponsor's message without regard for taste, logic or dramatic continuity. Because so many of television's top executives entered the field directly from radio, the propriety of these rigid schedules and frequent interruptions has scarcely even been questioned. That is how radio time was sold, and both the buyers and sellers of TV programs seem satisfied to continue under the old arrangements, despite growing audience resentment.

Similarly, the standard television script, like those for radio, places the emphasis almost entirely on dialogue. Camera position, camera movement, the cutting from shot to shot is generally left to the discretion of the director. It is the director who, along with the producers and cameramen, must translate words into pictures, supplying the visual interest that will keep audiences looking at their sets. At this level, therefore, radio patterns generally give way to the "movies by air" approach. While rehearsing his cast—generally in a bare room, far from the cameras—the director develops his ideas of how they will move from shot to shot, which cameras will view the various segments of his scenes, what action will be taken in close-up or long-shot. He also works out in advance, as far as he can, his plans for cutting—when to switch from one camera to another, where he might use two or three cameras in combination to heighten the tempo of his scene, cutting from left to right to center on quick, continuous action. Indeed, some TV directors have become so adept at this fluid filmic technique that their work almost looks like a movie! Which is scarcely surprising, since that is precisely what they are trying so hard to achieve.

Even the most skilled director, however, is limited to what his cameras give back to him once his show is on the air. For after days of rehearsal, after the preliminary dry runs with camera and the closed-circuit dress rehearsal, he must retire from the stage at the most crucial moment, the moment that his show begins. During the remainder of the program, confined in the control booth, he is completely at the mercy of his machinery—his cameras, his switches, his lights, his sound. Through throat microphones he has contact with his floor director and can correct the more glaring errors. But more of the time he is concerned with what he sees on the four small monitor screens within the control room. Three of them show exactly what each of his cameras is picking up; the fourth contains the image that is actually being transmitted to the audience. From these he does his cutting, determining the psychological moment to switch from camera one to camera three to camera two, signaling the technicians at the monitor panel when to punch the buttons that put one picture or another on the air.

But despite all his frantic activity, there is always the lurking anxiety that something unpredictable will suddenly mar the scene and destroy his carefully planned effects. A microphone may dip down between a girl and boy in the midst of a love scene. An important reaction shot, rehearsed as a tight close-up, may be lost when the hatbrim of a minor player comes between the camera and the performer. A camera moving into position may become momentarily snarled in a cable, forcing the director to hold a shot on the air longer than anticipated. The actress who blows up in her lines, the workman in overalls glimpsed at the trial of Socrates, the failure of camera two in the middle of the program—these are only a few of the hazards that confront the television director each time he puts a program on the air. For there is no going back, no possibility of re-shooting, no editing around a mistake. The director may improvise nimbly. The cast may cover up a fellow performer's lapse of memory so skillfully that it goes unnoticed by the general public. But inevitably some violence has been done to the original conception. And even though the original may have been no work of art (as is often the case in TV), there is always the sobering possibility that it might have been. In short, the element of *control* so essential to every art is lacking in live television. It is a lack that is particularly destructive to the realization of any work of creative imagination.

It is not surprising, then, that film is being used increasingly in the presentation of important dramatic and comedy shows. Its flexibility affords the director the maximum of freedom and control. If something goes wrong, the shot can always be made again. If a comedian's joke falls flat, it can be edited out. Also gone are the restrictions of time and space, those vexing physical limitations that harass the writers for live TV. A character can advance from youth to old age within a single half-hour without worries about the problem of make-up. Settings need no longer be limited to what can be crowded onto the floor of a single TV studio. All the world's a stage, just as long as you can get a camera there. At least, up to a point. Spectacular long-shots embracing a cast of thousands, vast scenic panoramas in which the individual is dwarfed by the wonders of nature—these will always come out as meaningless blurs on the small screen. The intimacy of television must still be respected when preparing films for it.

Aesthetic considerations are only one reason—and probably the least important—for the use of film on television. It has actually become an economic necessity for a station's operation. Not that films are any cheaper to produce than a live dramatic show—quite the contrary. But they relieve the studios of their two greatest pressures, time and space. No station could possibly afford to maintain the studio and staff that would be required for a 100 per cent live operation. One has only to look about in the major centers of television production—New York, Chicago and Los Angeles—to realize what vast amounts of high-priced real estate are already tied up in the presentation of live programs. Old theaters, old warehouses, riding academies and arenas are now television studios, while Hollywood's mammoth Television Cities cover whole city blocks. In radio, a group of actors can rehearse their script for an hour or two in a quiet room, carry it into a broadcasting studio and be done with it. By contrast, an hour-long dramatic show in television requires about two weeks of steady rehearsal—held in halls, hotel ballrooms and lofts all over town. The studios themselves must be reserved for on-camera rehearsals and the actual presentation of the program. And because of the time needed to build and strike the settings, most of them can only handle two or three shows weekly. While a really big program, like the *Omnibus* show, may tie up a whole studio for an entire week. It is not surprising, therefore, that the TV channels are overloaded with quiz programs, give-away programs and panel shows that need little or no rehearsal, and no props except a placard bearing the sponsor's name in large letters and a few tables and chairs. This is also the reason the telecasters are so eager to fill the air with special events originating outside the studio like baseball and football games, fights or political conventions.

And isn't it also possible that these are more truly the proper sphere for "live" television than the dramatic play? After all, TV made its first tremendous impact on this country through a series of live shows that, for many, transformed the home receiver from an expensive toy into a virtual necessity. The Kefauver crime investigations, the 1948 and 1952 presidential nominating conventions, the Army-McCarthy hearings—these were more than entertainment. They were an unforgettable education in democracy. They brought vast sections of the populace for the first time face to face with their legislators, their representatives, permitting them to see in close-up the complicated machinery of government, the even more tangled processes of government investigation. Taxpayers were turned into informed citizens—and relished the experience. Similarly, the telecasts of the World Series and other major sports events and, to a lesser extent, operas and symphony concerts, have permitted millions to participate in what had hitherto been limited to the privileged few who could afford the price of admission at stadium or concert hall. The popularity of such shows as Ed Murrow's *Person to Person*, NBC's *Wide Wide World* and even, on a much lower level, the innumerable interview programs that turn up on both national hookups and local stations, all are based on television's special appeals of intimacy and immediacy. Sets and props, demanding costly studio space, are either minimal or non-existent. Production values rise out of the thinking and planning that goes into such a program, and the intrinsic interest of the people and places that the cameras reveal. When it is good, it is live television at its best—exciting, informative, revealing.

But even this best is not good enough for the sponsors, most of whom insist that the heart of their shows, their advertising messages, be presented on film. Here, obviously, the question is not one of quality but of control over the effectiveness of their sales pitch. It just wouldn't do for the announcer extolling the virtues of a filtered cigarette to burst into a paroxysm of coughing. And what if he should commit a spoonerism on the name of the product, like the fabled "Buppert's Rear" of an earlier era in radio! No, the commercial must be foolproof, and completely encompassed in an even twenty-, forty-, or sixty-second segment, with not a precious moment wasted. The answer, for over 75 per cent of all TV shows, is the film commercial—with emphasis increasingly on the animated cartoon, the form that offers not only the highest degree of control but also the maximum amount of "sell" per second.

Aside from the commercials, perhaps the most familiar of all the pictures produced specifically for TV are those series built around a fictional character like *Our Miss Brooks* or featuring such star personalities as Groucho Marx or Loretta Young. In many of these, the camera is little more than the medium for recording a program that is staged before a studio audience. On the Groucho Marx show, for example, the use of film permits Groucho to run his brusque and hectoring interviews longer than actual air time and then, on the basis of audience response, edit out the weaker passages. (Marx began using this technique in radio, recording on tape and then cutting to air time.) What the viewing audience gets is, in effect, pre-tested material, "the best of Groucho." The TV film dramas or situation comedies, on the other hand, are more likely to be shot in a movie studio or on location, utilizing all the techniques of ordinary low-budget movie making while bearing in mind the special requirements of the small television screen. Such pictures are invariably tricked out with "canned" music and often, for the comedy shows, "canned" laughter as well.

Most of the programs of this kind were developed by independent agencies which sold their shows to the networks or to individual stations on the basis of a clever title, a fresh "gimmick" or a star name. They packaged them into 13-week series on the lowest possible budgets and syndicated them widely at the highest possible prices. It was, at the outset, pretty much of a catchpenny operation, dominated by the "fast buck" psychology. On shows that happened to strike the public's fancy, like *Hopalong Cassidy* or *The Cisco Kid,* the profits were enormous. The prints could be televised time and time again, often on the same stations. Since the early years of television, however, the big sponsors have grown increasingly chary of linking their products to shoddy, cheap-Jack entertainments. When they buy a program now their chief concern is not its price but its audience appeal. They are therefore willing to pay royally for a show that will rank high on the Nielsen and Trendex ratings. As a result, the inferior films are now being hawked to the smaller stations around the country, far from the green fields of Madison Avenue.

Curiously, while the dramatic films without exception have come from outside packaging agencies of one kind or another, the production of documentaries has been carried on primarily by the networks themselves. Both NBC and CBS have established units for this purpose, with personnel drawn largely from the ranks of the non-theatrical documentarians. Their main function is the creation of special shows—frequently unsponsored—that are presented as prestige or public-service features. Perhaps the most notable production to date has been NBC's *Victory at Sea,* 26 half-hour films covering the role of the United States Navy in World War II. Supervised by historian Henry Salomon, Jr., and masterfully edited by Isaac Kleinerman from millions of feet of on-the-spot combat footage, the series has been run and re-run on stations all over the country. The same unit has also been responsible for such hour-long documentaries as *Three-Two-One-Zero*, an illuminating exploration of the atom and the atomic age; *Nightmare in Red*, a concise history of the rise of Soviet Communism; and *The Jazz Age*, a backward glance at America during the twenties. In each of these, already existent feature, newsreel and documentary footage was assembled with immense skill to form a swift, informative and visually exciting narrative. Another NBC unit has been responsible for the *Elder Wise Men* series in which the camera plays the role of passive observer to present extended, half-hour interviews with people like Bertrand Russell, Robert Frost, Pablo Casals and Frank Lloyd Wright. By motion-picture standards these films seem static and unimaginative; in the theater they would be impossible. But somehow, when seen on the small screen in the home they acquire another personality altogether. Something of television's unique intimacy and immediacy takes the place of camera tricks and angles, and the wonderful close-range insights that they provide into the mind, face and character of these artists and philosophers creates a new aesthetic that stands halfway between film and live TV.

The CBS documentary units, on the whole, seem to follow more closely the line set down by the classic documentarians, building original films on people in relation to their institutions. For programs like *The Search* and *Adventure* teams of writers, directors and cameramen have been sent out to record the work being done in university research centers, on the Indian reservations, at government projects and in hospitals throughout the country. In *Out of Darkness*, for example, which Al Wasserman directed for *The Search*, the camera documents the slow rehabilitation of a mental patient in a California hospital. To broaden the significance of this theme beyond the treatment of a single case, sequences were interjected in which Orson Welles read from the diary of a patient in an 18th century asylum and Karl Menninger discussed in direct interview the growing seriousness of the mental health problem in the nation today. Ed Murrow has effectively adopted this kind of filmic on-the-spot reporting on many of his CBS shows. For his *Argument in Indianapolis*, his camera crews recorded at length the opposing factions in that city when the American Legion was fighting the formation of a branch of the American Civil Liberties Union. He also used this technique for his memorable sequence on Senator McCarthy's un-American investigations. In both instances the footage was later edited, and pointed, by Murrow's staff in New York.

Of the major shows, the Ford Foundation's experimental *Omnibus* has taken the lead in commissioning both dramatic and documentary films specifically for TV. Perhaps more clearly than any others, its staff has drawn the distinction between those subjects best handled in the studio and those for which the motion picture is most appropriate. Plays, operas, music and ballet—works conceived within the frame of the theater—are generally performed live, using the full resources of the TV cameras and staging techniques. On the other hand, adaptations of short stories that depend heavily on natural backgrounds for their atmosphere and effect are often shot on film—as for example, three tales by John Steinbeck whose setting was the rough farm country around Salinas, California. Frequently, *Omnibus* has commissioned documentary shorts on unusual people and places—a trip with a lobster fisherman in Maine, the training of a 10-year old ballerina for the Royal Danish Ballet or a hidden-camera glimpse of an emergency ward in a large city hospital. In addition, *Omnibus* has pioneered with a new type of commercial, short documentaries that make no effort to sell a product. Instead, they take the viewer behind the scenes of the sponsor's business to see how a Greyhound bus is serviced between runs or how Nash-Kelvinator's researches are solving the problem of preserving food *without* refrigeration. Lightly referred to by the staff as "Omnibusiness films," they are in fact a long step forward toward a more imaginative public-relations policy among TV advertisers. In all its programs, the Ford TV Workshop has tried to choose films that will either heighten dramatic expression or widen the span of interest and information. By skillfully alternating the filmed subjects with live studio performances, *Omnibus* has notably increased its vitality and broadened the cultural scope of its unique 90-minute variety show.

There is still another way in which film is used creatively on TV. It is a technique known as "integration," blending filmed segments with the live elements of a show to produce an integral whole. This method is seen occasionally on dramatic programs, where brief snatches of film—night shots of Times Square, a train racing through the English countryside—establish the setting and atmosphere of a play. It has been particularly effective, however, in the presentation of factual material on programs like *Adventure, Odyssey* and *Omnibus*. An early Ford Workshop presentation titled *Life in a Drop of Water*, for example, opened with a studio discussion between Burgess Meredith and a visiting biologist. From time to time, to enliven and illuminate their talk, specially prepared film clips flashed in on cue—footage ranging from the microscopic examination of protoplasmic forms to a deadly fight between shark and octopus. Because the films were silent, Meredith and the scientist supplied the accompanying narration, the scene switching back to them in person as each clip faded from the screen. Though such programs require extremely careful cueing and coordination, the results are worth the effort because "integration" adds greatly to the flexibility of a live telecast. Combining the immediacy and informality of TV with the precision of filmic visualization, it is perhaps the most appropriate and intelligent technique for using film on the air.

Unfortunately, the majority of films that are televised reflect little credit on either the telecasters who use them or the movie people who made them. Drawn for the most part from the dregs of pictures originally intended for theatrical exhibition, the only possible excuses for showing them are their accessibility and their low cost. It is always easier and cheaper for a station to rent a movie than to stage a live program—although even the shabbiest show might be preferable to some of the pictures that are screened during the late afternoon or late evening hours. And yet films that were inferior when they were first released a decade or more ago are run and re-run year after year on TV. For not only do they eliminate the need for rehearsals and standing sets, but they can also be quickly edited to fit any available time slot. It is not unusual, therefore, to find a picture that originally ran over an hour and a half sandwiched into a scant sixty minutes (with additional time out for the commercials). Violence, of course, has been done to the story, with great chunks lifted bodily out of the picture—sometimes entire reels eliminated. One recalls, in contrast, King Vidor back in the silent days going through his *Big Parade* shot for shot, painstakingly eliminating a few frames on either side of the splice in order to reduce the total footage by 800 feet, as his studio had ordered. Hard-pressed TV editors today have no time for this kind of perfection. And the truth is that few of the pictures they work on deserve such conscientious cutting. But when, on occasion, a classic like *Major Barbara* or *Paisan* falls into their hands, the results are painful to see.

No less painful are the frequent insertions of filmed commercials during the running of a feature picture. Most stations seem to regard a movie as simply the thread on which to string as many profitable beads as possible, halting the progress of the narrative every seven or eight minutes to splice in another sponsor's message. As long as the only films available to television remained cheap independent productions, ancient British "quota quickies" and a handful of foreign-language pictures, few artistic crimes were committed. No one, at any rate, felt compelled to protest the elision of twenty minutes or so from a third-rate thriller, Western or comedy. More recently, however, with programs like *Million Dollar Movie,* the telecasters have got their hands on some fairly distinguished material. Because of this, many of the stations have extended the time slots allocated to film showings, often running the entire picture without cuts—although, of course, the continuity is still blurred by frequent breaks for the sponsors' messages.

And here is the dilemma of the American television people today. They are willing to spend fabulous sums for first-rate films, but in order to pay for them they must destroy their effectiveness by the repeated insertion of disruptive commercials. When, for example, NBC offered the world première of Alexander Korda's British comedy, *The Constant Husband* (1955), as a Sunday-night "color spectacular," *Variety*'s reviewer was moved to comment, "If the web had set out to invite viewer resentment it couldn't have done a more imaginative job. . . . When four bankrollers share a 90-minute show, and each insists on being seen and heard, it's murder on the audience." With the Hollywood studios releasing some of their finest pictures to the networks, it seems inevitable that sooner or later this kind of mutilation will be vigorously opposed by the general public.

In contrast to the full-length feature, one might imagine that shorts—documentaries, travelogues, educationals, interest films of every kind—would suffer less from haphazard cutting and sponsored intrusions. Unfortunately, however, most program directors are more interested in the running time than the subject matter of the shorts they use. So prevalent is this attitude that at least one enterprising distributor makes it a practice to send out crates of film on consignment for the stations to play as needed. The reels are unassorted, unclassified, but each is carefully timed. The programmer has simply to reach into the pile for a film of the right length. It may be mediocre and completely inappropriate, but it will fit. In general, most short films are looked upon as stopgap fillers, the television equivalent of the staff pianist or organist from radio days who held himself in perpetual readiness for an occasional emergency performance.

Unquestionably, there is room for improvement in television's use of the film medium. Unquestionably, there will be even more room when the number of stations swells from a present total of approximately 500 to an anticipated 2,000 or more. When that happens, the already acute shortage of studio space will be aggravated to the point where films must become not the stopgap, but the very center of television programming. And while the live show, the on-the-spot coverage, the "you are there" spontaneity of television will inevitably remain its greatest asset, the dramatic, comedy and educational features that make up the bulk of its programs can only gain from this coming shotgun marriage with the movies.

In the meantime, the movie companies, originally sworn to a fight to the finish with their rival medium, seem to be finishing the fight on TV's own terms. By selling their pre-1948 pictures to the networks, they have netted millions in windfall profits. And where formerly the producers were writing clauses into their actors' contracts forbidding them to appear on TV, now they not only permit their stars to participate in telecasts but actively seek television recognition for their latest productions, donating performers and even generous clips from the film itself in return for the nation-wide publicity accruing from an airing on a major network show. But the final capitulation lies in the fact that almost all the largest studios are now creating programs specifically for the television screen, programs using their top directors, writers and stars.

All of this is only part of the rapidly changing scene in Hollywood. As feature production continues to fall off, many of the smaller studios have switched their entire operation to making films for television. And, of course, there are the numerous small, independent telefilm studios that have sprung up throughout the entire Los Angeles area. Even live shows that once emanated from New York and Chicago are moving to the Coast to take advantage of the superb facilities in Hollywood's Television Cities and the concentration of talent to be found there. The result is not only new jobs for technicians and performers but a stronger economic base for the entire industry. And every day, despite their antipathy, movie people are learning new ways not merely to adjust to but to profit from the rival medium.

One aspect of television that especially interests the movie industry—and has engaged the active financial participation of at least one major company to date—is toll TV, television free of sponsors and commercials, with the shows paid for by the viewers themselves. Its proponents point out that top-quality programs, including films, would be economically feasible under such a set-up. With a potential audience of millions paying to tune in the program, the entire production cost could be earned back in a single night. Several variations of the plan have already been worked out—including a coin-box arrangement, a rate card system, a coded card system and a special wire from the telephone company—but the essential idea is always the same. The picture is sent out scrambled, impossible to view without some special decoding device attached to the receiver in the home. A few of these methods have already had trial runs in specific communities. To date, however, the Federal Communications Commission, which regulates all aspects of television broadcasting, has refused to give any general go-ahead signal. Meanwhile, the local theater men, those who stand to lose the most should toll TV be successful, are fighting every test, protesting every advance. "Toll television conflicts with free enterprise," they maintain. "The airwaves belong to everybody." And they threaten reprisals against any studio daring to make its current product available to the toll TV experimenters. While tests with the various systems have been far too inconclusive to justify the

:adoption of toll television at the present time, the conflict of interests is already abundantly clear. Both the theater men and the tollcasters need pictures—new, expensive, all-star productions. The film studios can not afford to alienate the theater owners who are booking and running their product today; but at the same time they very much want to have one foot in the door should home "toll-evision" become a reality tomorrow. It is a situation that leaves the film people in a particularly awkward position.

There is, on the other hand, another form of toll television that has already won for itself the open enthusiasm of both the film companies and the theater men. It is, of course, theater TV, with the show piped into each subscribing house by special wire. Such events as a Metropolitan Opera production of *Carmen*, an all-star *ANTA Album* featuring excerpts from great plays, as well as numerous championship fights, have already indicated the potentialities of this medium. The closed-circuit telecast of the Rocky Marciano-Archie Moore bout in September of 1955, for example, hooked together 129 theaters in 92 cities to produce an unprecedented gross of over $1,000,000. Obviously, receipts like these do not displease the theater owners. Meanwhile, Fox is readying its closed-circuit, large-screen, color-TV-Eidophor system for theatrical installations, and RCA has demonstrated a similar closed-circuit TV process with a projected image almost the size of the average theater screen. Although it is not yet technically possible to transmit films over either of these systems, film distributors are not unmindful of the thousands of dollars they will save in print costs and shipping charges if ever they can pipe a single picture simultaneously into hundreds of theaters all over the country.

Thus, the interests of film and television touch at many points, sometimes harmoniously, sometimes in sharp conflict. Hollywood today is willing to "cooperate" with the networks, willing to make its old pictures available, happy to reap the supplementary rewards of originating new programs for TV. But until television can supply the millions of dollars—whether in tolls or sponsor commitments—that are required to make feature films, the Hollywood studios must continue to think first of their theatrical audience, jealously regarding every advance of television as a threat to their very existence. They know that every TV spectacular means sharply reduced movie attendance for that night. They know that several evenings of the week are already checked off as slow nights at the box office because of top-rating shows on TV. They are watching warily the steady advance toward color TV, for color brings new life, new depth, new reality to the small screen's image. And they know that it is already technically possible to enlarge the television screen to a proportion in the parlor that would just about equal the size in the theater.

And yet, as both movie men and theater men nervously reassure each other, people do like to go out for their entertainment. They want to get away from their homes, their routines, from the cares and problems of day-to-day living. And at the movies they can find this kind of freedom for a few hours by becoming part of the anonymous crowd. This kind of release, this utter forgetfulness of self, is something that television has never been able to duplicate. The small screen with its doll-sized figures is only part of the reason; more important is the familiar parlor furniture, the confining family circle, the recurrent commercials— all constantly impinging upon the consciousness, destroying the illusion, preventing the submergence of one's own personality in the people and problems of the story. One turns on the TV set for distraction or, perhaps, for information. One goes to the movies for refreshment and discovers there, on occasion, that heady sense of personal involvement and spiritual replenishment that only true art can give.

Although in the final analysis both films and television are wrestling for the same audience, the success of one does not mean the extinction of the other. The theater and the concert hall, the ball park and the tennis court, the magazine and book publishers are all catering to the public, all hoping to capture some fraction of the total for themselves. None of them, however, requires so wide an audience simply to stay in business as the movie and the television industries—a need that is driving them ever closer together. The studios are already benefiting from the new playwrights, directors and performers developed by TV. They are adapting its plays and adopting its cheaper production techniques. They want the publicity that TV can give them to interest people in their newest pictures, the money that TV will pay them for their older ones. On the other hand, the television people know that they cannot continue to hold their huge audiences without prodigious amounts of new program material—for which they must look increasingly to the motion-picture industry. They want the glamour of Hollywood star names, the smoothness of movie technique—and, above all, the films themselves. Despite their present rivalry, their common needs and inter-related talents and techniques would seem to predict a mutually profitable co-existence for these two dominant forces in the field of mass entertainment.

VIII

THE SHAPE OF THINGS TO COME

THE MOVIES HAVE ALWAYS FASCINATED AUDIENCES BY THEIR MAGICAL, larger-than-life image of the world. At the very beginning, the crude reproduction of movement was in itself enough to draw the crowds. Before this could pall, the film makers were using their imagination and artistry to extend the medium far beyond the limits of photographic duplication. Directors explored all the resources of the camera in their efforts to heighten the drama of their pictures, and soon they were able to offer audiences films that reflected not only the physical but the psychological aspects of reality as well. At the same time, the inventors were also seeking to enhance the film's sense of realism—by purely mechanical means. They increased the precision of the camera with faster lenses and more sensitive film stocks. Eventually they even succeeded in adding the dimensions of sound and color to the black-and-white images.

But each time the inventors introduced another facet of reality, the film makers were forced to begin their work all over again. For although innovations are always interesting, audience enthusiasm can only be sustained when reality has been shaped and transformed by art. Every invention, every technological advance, therefore, challenged the ingenuity of the film makers and replenished the creative vitality of the entire medium. This extraordinary capacity for evolving new forms and absorbing them into the fabric of filmic art was dramatically revealed during the turbulent year of 1953 when an anxious industry acted swiftly to check the inroads that television was making on movie attendance. The studios met the

313

crisis head on, adopting new processes and creating effects that TV could never hope to duplicate.

It was the astounding success of Cinerama, unveiled on Broadway in the fall of 1952, that first alerted the industry to the possibilities of wide screens and depth perception. But though the producers were willing to risk almost anything on the chance of getting people away from their TV sets and into the theaters once again, they were still practical enough to realize that Cinerama was not the answer. The process was too costly, the re-tooling so complex that any new productions would have been delayed for at least a year. What the industry needed was a system that could turn out 3-D pictures quickly, cheaply and without time-consuming changeovers. Early in 1953 it looked as if the solution had been found when a simpler, less expensive, completely different form of "depthie" made its appearance. This process, called Natural Vision, was a revival of the old concept of stereoscopic photography brought up to date by Polaroid lenses. Although *Bwana Devil*, the first film in Natural Vision, was unmitigated hokum, although patrons had to wear uncomfortable glasses in order to see it, nevertheless its special effects created an immediate sensation wherever it was shown. Audiences were fascinated by the sight of people, animals, trees and mountains all "in the round," delighted when spears and lions seemed to fly directly at them from the screen. And as *Bwana Devil* swept across the country, piling up spectacular grosses wherever it played, the studio heads became convinced that this was the weapon to use in their fight against television. Hollywood began its defense in depth.

Like Cinerama, Natural Vision had been privately financed and developed outside the industry. Unlike Cinerama, however, it required no major conversion of existing equipment or production techniques. Standard sets, standard lighting, standard plots—all could still be used. The only significant addition was a special, twin-lensed Natural Vision camera to shoot the pictures. This camera registered on separate reels two slightly different views of the same scene, each approximating the angle from which the eye would see it. In the theater, a pair of interlocked projectors equipped with Polaroid lenses flashed the two pictures simultaneously on the screen. When viewed through polarized glasses, the two images fused to form a single three-dimensional whole. Since the spectators were usually charged an extra dime for these glasses, the total cost to the theater owner for such an installation came to less than $2,000.

Once launched on its new campaign, Hollywood immediately began to exploit all the sensations of stereoscopic photography. Soon the air was filled with flying forms. Cartoon figures danced off the screen toward the audience, space creatures clawed them, sea monsters sprang at them. But though the producers worked full time devising new tricks to throw at the public, they wasted little effort on the unbelievably banal stories and slipshod productions that surrounded these effects. Anxious to cash in on the bonanza, they showed no respect for the taste, intelligence or sensibilities of their patrons. Month after month they bombarded them with ping-pong balls, pistol shots, beer barrels and bats. In one possibly symbolic scene, a Western bad man spat straight in the customers' eyes. As the novelty of this sort of thing began to pall, one art-film distributor cannily advertised, "What do you want, a good picture or a lion in your lap?" The answer was obvious. In less than a year Polaroid pictures were box-office poison and stereo had become synonymous with trash. As a result, *Dial M for Murder, Kiss Me Kate* and a few other quality films originally shot in 3-D were released flat. Hollywood's defense in depth, however, was far from finished. Behind the scenes, inventors and technicians were intensively experimenting with other systems that would eliminate the uncomfortable glasses and other mechanical shortcomings that had helped discourage the public.

In the meantime, Cinerama's initial triumph on Broadway was confirmed with each successive engagement. Throughout 1953, while the "depthies" flourished and waned, Cinerama continued to enjoy capacity business as it opened its own theaters in one city after another. Its multi-lensed camera and huge curving screen were completely revolutionary. The uncanny realism of its imagery literally brought the world into the theater and made the spectators feel as if they were in the very center of the scene. This startling effect was accomplished not by tricking the eye, but by reproducing virtually all that we normally see in just about the way we see it. When we look at our world, it is as though we were standing in the middle of a circle; everything that appears before us is instantaneously recorded on a curving arc of vision approximately 165° wide and 60° high. The ordinary movie camera can capture only the central segment of this arc, from 30° to 45°. The Cinerama camera, on the other hand, is able to encompass the entire range from central to peripheral vision. Fred Waller, the inventor of Cinerama, had discovered years earlier that it was peripheral vision—the scores of objects glimpsed around the rim of our visual arc—that supplies our brain with the hints and clues from which it builds its psychological impression of depth and space and distance. To record this panoramic view completely and within a single frame, Waller built a camera that was really three cameras in one—three lenses each registering in perfect synchronization one-third of the entire scene. In the theater, three separate machines project the segments simultaneously upon a huge curving screen, spreading across it a picture six times the size of the conventional movie. Because Cinerama parallels our field of vision both in its curve and range, we are no longer on the outside looking in on a scene that has been artificially foreshortened and tricked to give the illusion of depth. Rather, we have passed beyond the boundaries of another realm and are on the inside looking around. It is almost like being projected into the fourth dimension!

To supplement Cinerama's spacious vision of reality, the audio expert Hazard Reeves developed an equally revolutionary system of stereophonic sound that set new standards of high fidelity in the theater and also introduced the concept of linking each sound to its source. When a scene was being shot, six omni-directional microphones were situated at various points to record the sound on as many separate channels. In the theater these multiple tracks were reproduced by a veritable battery of speakers—five spread behind the screen, two at either side of the house, one or more at the rear. For the first time voices and music, dialogue and sound effects issued from the screen at a point corresponding to their visual sources. This new, directional sound system heightened immeasurably the sensation of being part of the scene, creating a sense of personal involvement, of physical participation that is far more than the simple identification of ordinary movies. In the famous roller-coaster sequence, for instance, the moviegoers feel as though they are actually in the front seat of a scenic railway. This impression is accentuated by the realistic clatter of the car on the rails and the screams that seem to come from all around—screams invariably supplemented by the spontaneous cries of the audience as the car plunges them with sickening speed into each new abyss.

Unfortunately, this kind of sensationalism has all too often obscured the full expressive powers of the medium. To date, the films have been little more than grab-bag travelogues superficially exploiting every avenue of obvious appeal. Nor have all the mechanical problems of the process been completely solved. The three panels of the curving screen frequently jiggle and fail to join; the sound must be kept at ear-splitting levels to maintain its "hi-fi" effect; horizons have a tendency to curl upward in the extreme long-shots. Generally speaking, however, the techniques of Cinerama far surpass the films that have been contrived for it. In fact one might even say that rarely has an invention so filled with promise been used with such a lack of taste, imagination or courage. Consequently, the beauty and eloquence inherent in the medium can be glimpsed only rarely—as in the La Scala sequence from the first Cinerama presentation. Here, in scenes from Verdi's *Aïda,* imagination and technique are in perfect harmony. The audience sees opera as it has never before appeared, close up and living, full scale in both image and sound. At such moments, Cinerama captures and conveys the living essence of reality in a way that no movie has ever before achieved and which all subsequent wide-screen processes have merely approximated.

In spite of its fame, however, in spite of the fact that ever since its inception it has rated as the top-grossing filmic entertainment of all times, Cinerama has remained a highly specialized operation. There are only 14 permanent installations in the largest cities of the United States, less than 30 throughout the world. And all of these are controlled by the Cinerama people themselves. They produce their own films, rent the theaters in which they are shown and make their own installations. At the outset, during the long years of research and development, they sought the economic support of the motion-picture industry—with a total lack of success. The studios found the process interesting but impractical. Even after it had made its Broadway debut, the industry considered

Cinerama far too costly and complex for general movie making. Merely equipping a theater with the screen, sound and three projection booths necessary for its presentation came to around $75,000— and none of this could be used to show any other kind of film. But as Cinerama broke box-office records in city after city, the idea of "something just as good" began to haunt the industry. In less than a year, Cinerama catapulted the movies into an era of change as radical and pervasive as the introduction of sound in 1928.

The year of the great transition was 1953. Even while the theaters were still running the 3-D "depthies," exhibitors saw the shape of things to come. In frank imitation of Cinerama they began enlarging their screens and blowing up normal pictures to unprecedented dimensions at the expense of clarity and definition of the images. In Hollywood, too, there were signs of the changing trend. Although most of the studios continued using the various Polaroid processes, at least one of them dared to risk all its vast resources in the development of a true wide-screen system. Early in January, Spyros Skouras, the head of 20th Century-Fox, announced that his firm had acquired the rights to Anamorphoscope, a process invented almost a quarter of a century earlier by the French physicist Dr. Henri Chrétien. Its basis was an anamorphic, or distorting, lens that "squeezed" an ultra-wide picture into the ordinary 35mm frame; when shown in the theater a compensating lens on the projector restored the picture and expanded it to more than twice its normal width on a special elongated screen. Ironically, when Dr. Chrétien had first demonstrated his invention in France in 1928, it was ignored in the stampede toward sound. Now, in the mounting TV crisis, Skouras hailed it as the true savior of the motion picture. With suitable fanfare Anamorphoscope was rechristened CinemaScope. Wisely, Fox refrained from rushing into the market with a hastily produced trick film that would cheaply exploit the new effect. Instead, in the fall of 1953 CinemaScope was introduced to the world with one of the studio's biggest productions —a five million dollar adaptation of Lloyd C. Douglas's Biblical best seller *The Robe*.

At the outset, Fox publicity stressed the similarities between Cinerama and CinemaScope. Like Cinerama, it could be viewed without glasses, and it too boasted a large, curving screen. But despite all claims, it was soon apparent that CinemaScope's illusion of depth was largely illusory. Not even its widest lens could encompass a field as broad as Cinerama's; as a result, it gave only the weakest approximation of peripheral vision. Quite naturally, its three-track stereophonic sound was considerably less "hi-fi" than Cinerama's seven. And in sharpness and brilliance of image it also fell short of the standards established by that process. But no one seemed to mind. CinemaScope was definitely the "something just as good" that the industry had been looking for. The size and shape of its new screen were undeniably impressive, and it had numerous practical advantages over Cinerama as well. Because the Cinema-Scope lens could be clamped to the ordinary projector, expensive machinery did not have to be scrapped; and the entire installation was available at a price most theater men could afford—about $20,000 for the lenses, the big screen and stereophonic sound. Not only was this much less costly than Cinerama, it was also far more flexible, as CinemaScope equipment could easily be adapted to show any kind of film simply by removing the anamorphic lens from the projector and masking down the screen to the desired dimensions. Furthermore, to encourage the sale of these installations Fox announced its readiness to lease cameras and lenses to rival studios, thus assuring exhibitors of a continuous flow of quality product in the process. With all these inducements in mind—and sparked by the tremendous public enthusiasm for *The Robe*— orders soon came pouring in from large and small theaters alike. By the spring of 1957, it had become standard equipment in some 17,500 of the 20,000 theaters in the United States alone—and the number continues to grow.

As CinemaScope installations fanned out across the country, the other studios abandoned 3-D to leap aboard the wide-screen bandwagon. And before long they were experimenting with the many variations of the anamorphic process that came crowding into the field. The Tushinsky brothers, for example, offered Superscope, an adaptation of Dr. Chrétien's "squeeze" principle that made it possible for theater managers to show films of any size or shape at the turn of a dial. For Warner Brothers, Zeiss-Opton in Germany prepared still another anamorphic system called WarnerSuperScope. In Europe, Cinepanoramic, a French invention, had already been adopted by the French and Italian studios; while in England an identical process was being used under the name of CameraScope. CinemaScope and Superscope, Vistarama and Thrillarama, Technirama, Vidoscope, Vistascope, Delrama—the list grew longer and longer as movie men all over the world dreamed up new ways to counter the challenge of the diminutive TV screen. Most of the studios, however, no matter what other systems they might be using for their ordinary films, invariably chose CinemaScope for their more elaborate pageants and musicals.

The sole exception was Paramount, which refused to go along either with CinemaScope's wide, wide screen (2½ times as long as it is high) or its "squeeze" principle of photography. Paramount's technicians protested—with considerable justification—that cramming an extra-wide picture into an ordinary 35mm frame produced a blurred and excessively grainy image on the screen. To answer this specific problem, they developed their own wide-screen variant, VistaVision. It involved an entirely new concept in motion-picture photography. Rather than "squeeze" the image, the VistaVision cameras shoot a normal scene on double-width 70mm negative; each frame is then optically reduced in the laboratories to produce the standard 35 mm release print. The effect is like reducing a snapshot; the amount of picture detail is increased and the picture appears sharper. As a result, VistaVision prints can be blown up tremendously in the theater without losing their intensity of color or crispness of focus. Furthermore, while VistaVision can produce a huge image, even to the extent of filling the entire proscenium of the mammoth Radio City Music Hall, the *shape* of its screen—the relationship of height to width—is less drastic than the long, narrow, rather ribbon-like CinemaScope aspect ratio. To show these films, of course, theater managers were obliged to purchase an additional lens for their projectors; but the same screen, with appropriate masking, could be used interchangeably for both CinemaScope and VistaVision. Like Fox, Paramount announced its willingness to lease cameras to other studios—and found ready takers on all sides. By 1954 the entire industry had abandoned its defense in depth for an all-out attack on a wide front.

As the wide-screen campaign gathered momentum, exhibitors throughout the country installed screens that extended as far as the walls of their theaters would permit. In some of the biggest houses the screens measured 60 feet in width, as much as three or four times their original area. These vast expanses soon revealed the inadequacies of the anamorphic system, weaknesses that had first been pointed out by the VistaVision technicians. The 35mm image, about the size of a postage stamp, could hardly be expected to fill such huge spaces with a picture that was bright, sharp and clear. And the larger the screen, the less satisfactory the projection. Black-and-white scenes looked fuzzy and gray; color films seemed pale and washed out. The reason was obvious—there just was not enough picture "information" within each frame to meet the extremes of magnification that the new processes demanded. The only possible solution was to increase the width of the film base itself. But though the studios knew this, most of them continued to cling to the standard 35mm film, realizing that any alteration in the size of release prints would necessitate costly changes in projection equipment for the theaters. They suspected that exhibitors would balk at such added expense following so soon after their investments in CinemaScopic screens and VistaVision lenses. Their suspicions were well founded. When Paramount tried in 1955 to push the distribution of 70mm VistaVision prints, the theater owners resisted so strongly that the entire project was hastily scrapped. At about the same time, 20th Century-Fox announced its CinemaScope 55, an improved version of CinemaScope in which films were photographed on a 55mm negative. Fox had also hoped to release prints to the larger theaters in this oversized version. But again the exhibitors refused to cooperate, and *Carousel* (1956), the first film completed in the process, was therefore distributed exclusively in 35mm reduction prints. Even in this form, however, CinemaScope 55 displayed distinct gains in clarity and color values over the earlier system.

Despite the theater owners' negative attitude, the projection of an extra-wide film was successfully introduced in the fall of 1955 when the 65mm Todd-AO process was unveiled to the public in an adaptation of Rodgers and Hammerstein's *Oklahoma!* To achieve this, veteran showman Mike Todd side-stepped the reluctant exhibitors and, following the formula worked out by Cinerama, leased theaters all across the country, equipping them specifically to show his picture. As one of the original backers of Cinerama, Todd became convinced that there must be a simpler, easier way to achieve the same end; and he left that organization in order to develop a process that would duplicate its effects without requiring three separate projector set-ups. He put the problem in the hands of Dr. Brian O'Brien, of the American Optical Company, who worked out the system now known as Todd-AO. In its deep-curving screen and ultra-stereophonic sound, Todd-AO obviously imitates Cinerama, but by using the wide 65mm film and a single projector it manages to avoid the jiggling join lines. Beyond this, the resemblance is purely superficial, for it provides little of Cinerama's exciting impression of depth or startling illusion of being in the picture. Only by comparison to Cinerama, however, does it suffer. As a wide-screen process it demonstrates conclusively the advantage of using a larger film base for both shooting and projection. Todd-AO fills the widest of wide screens with a clean, sparkling picture that is far brighter and better defined than anything possible in the 35mm anamorphic systems. In this sense it is a milestone in the field.

Just how long it will be before exhibitors are willing to re-equip their theaters is still problematical. But if the industry has anything to say about it, it will not be too long. Even while Todd-AO was making its bow, M-G-M announced that it was preparing to produce 65mm films in its own Camera 65 process for "the most gigantic of all screens." Meanwhile experimentation with various film widths still goes on, for most studio technicians are convinced that it is only a matter of time until one—or more—of the new sizes replaces the standard 35mm film which has proved inadequate for big-screen production.

With half a dozen processes, and almost as many widths, still in the promotion stage, there is little point in asking where it all will end. Today, exhibitors are facing precisely the same dilemma they met during the early years of sound. Obviously they cannot afford to keep buying new machinery—and if they purchase the equipment for a process that is soon outmoded, their losses could be substantial. Not only must they guess which inventions are likely to last, but they must also try to anticipate in which process the most popular pictures will be made. For there no longer seems to be any doubt that the wide-screen systems are here to stay. The question is simply, which one?

While the movie screens have been growing larger and larger since the advent of TV, statistics show that movie audiences have been growing steadily smaller. By the summer of 1956 film attendance had dropped to an all-time low of less than 35 million per week. Needless to say, this is still a tremendous following—enough to maintain the industry in the upper brackets of big business. Nevertheless, it represents a considerable comedown as compared to those halcyon postwar pre-television days of 1946 and 1947 when nearly everybody went to the movies. At that time an optimistic estimate placed weekly attendance at 90 million, although 85 million would probably be a more accurate figure. In either case, it is clear that in less than a decade the movies have lost more than half their public. And while every theater has been affected by this exodus, it is the small local houses that have suffered most. For they have lost the "habituals," those patrons who regularly went to the neighborhood movies several times a week regardless of what was being shown. Now, however, they are quite content to stay at home and watch old movies—and other programs as well—on their own TV sets.

The original impetus behind the wide-screen development was, of course, the desire—even the necessity—of regaining the support of the "habituals" and the more discriminating film fans alike. With so much ordinary—and sometimes extraordinary—entertainment available on tap in the home, the studios realized that the only way to get people back into the theaters was by offering them something impressively different, something that television could never hope to equal. And when the wide screens were first introduced, they did in fact lure a considerable portion of the public out of their living rooms. But with fifty million moviegoers missing at the box office, it is obvious that something is still lacking. Despite varying tastes, both the ex-"habitual" and the exacting devotee seem to agree on at least one thing. Size alone is not enough to win them. Dramatic, narrative and artistic values are still important—perhaps more important than ever before.

Unfortunately, these are the very qualities that have been most affected by the introduction of the wide screen. For though the 'vistas, 'scopes and 'visions certainly kept the customers from total retreat, they also succeeded in disrupting the entire artistic structure of the film. Consequently, despite a remarkable potential for increased realism, the first productions were singularly artificial and theatrical. Throughout this initial period producers, mindful of the added expenses of huge settings and complicated lighting set-ups, tried to promote important economies in shooting. They argued that close-ups and mid-shots were no longer necessary because the extreme magnification of the new screens made it possible to register even the slightest gesture in long-shot. They also felt that the additional picture information now included within the wide frame was enough to sustain visual interest without changing camera set-ups or varying the angles from which the scene could be viewed. Inevitably, the resulting films were static in the extreme. As shots grew longer and close-ups rarer, it became increasingly difficult for directors to achieve the dislocation of time, the singling out of detail, the freedom of action once implicit in the medium. Deprived of the very heart of film technique, they were left with no alternative but to impose theatrical patterns on their work, confining both cast and camera to conventional, consecutive movements from stage left to right to center. And because they were forced to use the camera literally and unimaginatively to record everything that passed before its wide-spreading lenses, their films lost the impact, the insight, the subtle shifts of emphasis produced by swiftly altering points of view. Even the most creative editors found these clumsy, almost static long-shots difficult to handle. They lacked the variety, the plasticity that was necessary to add rhythm or suspense, to accelerate the tempo or alter the mood of a scene. All that was really possible was the most primitive sort of editing, the piecing together of the lengthy strips into slow and ponderous scenes. As a result, although the audience now saw a great deal more than ever before, the sense of personal involvement was less. For all their size, the larger-than-life images looming on the screen seemed curiously lifeless and remote.

But it was not only the manipulation of giants that plagued the directors. There was also the uncertainty of not knowing how their films would look when they were eventually shown. The studios, on the other hand, did not seem to share these misgivings. Acting as if all wide screens were of equal size, they planned every production as though it were going to play the Music Hall. In actual fact, however, there no longer existed either a standard size or shape. Screens were now as varied as the dimensions of the auditoriums in which they were installed. Directors, therefore, had good reason to worry, because they could never be sure of their results. In *The Man Who Knew Too Much* (1956), for example, Alfred Hitchcock made a carefully planned trick shot showing in huge close-up the lips of a dying man frantically whispering his last words into Jimmy Stewart's ear. The effect of this vast mouth and immense ear filling a mammoth screen was somewhat gruesome and—as Hitchcock had no doubt intended—just a bit funny. Yet as shown on the smaller big screens of most theaters, the shot looked like almost any other close-up and its grisly humor was completely lost. In this case at least, the director had wittingly used the tremendous magnification to convey a grotesque impression; but often on the wide screens close-ups of details look equally grotesque without meaning to. In *The King and I* (1956), for instance, there was a medium close shot of Deborah Kerr attired in mid-Victorian hoop skirts. As presented at the Roxy, one could scarcely see the star for the skirts that billowed out over the entire 60-foot expanse!

Small wonder that directors are finding it difficult if not impossible to plan scenes that will take into account all the vagaries and variations of the screens on which their work will be seen. From theater to theater their pictures change in shape, appearance and effect. In VistaVision's *Strategic Air Command* (1954), for example, magnificent aerial views of huge B-36's and B-47's alternated with shots of James Stewart and his wife kissing each other goodbye in their bedroom. On the giant screen of the New York Paramount, the bedroom close-ups seemed overblown and absurd, while the shots of the silver bombers streaming trails of haze across the heavens superbly fulfilled the potentialities of the process. On smaller screens, however, the same splendid views looked dwarfed and cramped and, conversely, the star close-ups became more poignant and credible.

But even if all the wide screens were of the same magnitude and there were none of the complications of varying proportions, directors would still be faced with the difficulties of composing shots for these ungainly areas. For though they might easily cope with cattle stampedes and scenic views of lower Manhattan, less sweeping panoramas—or what one CinemaScope representative described as "the intimacies"—would continue to prove disconcertingly awkward to handle. Hence it is not at all unusual to see films these days in which two actors carry on a casual drawing-room conversation from opposite corners of a screen that often spans an entire city block. Even more perplexing is the handling of these "intimacies" when they must alternate on the same screen and in the same dimensions with scenes of eye-filling spectacle. It is both jarring and unnatural to see an actor stretched out 60 feet in length on a screen that only a moment before had held an entire battleship! On the old "postage stamp" screen of bygone days such transitions were readily accepted because the proportions were not so exaggerated. But the giant screen, with its emphasis on sheer size, makes every change in scale distressingly apparent, posing problems that none of the previous forms of film making have been able to solve. Obviously, until these outmoded methods are revised or replaced by a new body of techniques, the average director will continue to be baffled and harassed by the limitations of so much space.

In the meantime, Hollywood's best directors are cautiously exploring this strange terrain. Though dismayed by its immensity, they are determined to use it for something more substantial than pageantry and parade. But for all their ingenuity, they are seldom able to disguise its dimensions. The screen is there before them waiting to be filled. Its very shape demands the exaggeration of a scene far beyond its power to move or involve an audience. In their efforts to bring into focus dramatic, narrative and emotional expression, therefore, many directors have become reconciled to the use of theatrical techniques. They have found that they are better able to control and highlight action spread out across an entire screen if they stage it like a play. By drawing the attention now to this area, now to that; by leading the eye from point to point through carefully planned movements, groupings and lighting, they have gradually reduced one of the greatest hazards of wide-screen production—the strain of following a story sprawled shapelessly across an enormous surface. There have even been some attempts to meet this problem with filmic solutions as well. When too much space threatened to dissipate the dramatic intensity of a moment, some directors have boldly plunged the sides of their frame into shadow, leaving a bright playing area that, curiously enough, closely corresponds to the shape of the old standard screen. And despite studio strictures to the contrary, directors like John Ford and Robert Wise, masters of the art of cutting on movement, have persisted in their ways to prove that editing can still add pace and tautness to VistaVision epics and CinemaScope spectaculars. Directors of musical films have likewise done a great deal toward restoring mobility to the camera, although less by the number of shots and angles than in tracking, dollying or panning from one portion of the scene to another—a technique that is favored by production heads because it eliminates the need for frequent and costly readjustments of lighting set-ups.

At best, however, such methods represent a compromise with the medium and give no suggestion of its true potential. For though the wide screen has undoubtedly provoked numerous cases of agoraphobia, its magnification and largesse have also engendered occasional moments of inspired film making. In the Todd-AO production *Around the World in 80 Days* (1956), such an interlude occurs when the "intrepid adventurer" Phileas Fogg and his "antic servant" Passepartout set out on the second lap of their journey in a charmingly rococo balloon named *La Coquette*. Their take-off is somewhat marred by a typically theatrical hullaballoo; but from the instant their balloon rises above this contrived gaiety one is launched on an enchanted journey. At first she drifts leisurely through Paris, hovering uncertainly above rooftops, gliding past the gargoyles of Notre Dame. Then, gathering momentum, she sails out across the French countryside, past castles and rivers, over meadows and mountains. Far below the land spreads smiling and serene, while high in the skies both human and aerial elements combine to gladden the eye and the spirit. The solemn chilling of champagne with snow scooped from a passing Alp, the ceremonial toast between master and valet are not only extremely funny but touching as well. The silent shining atmosphere that surrounds the pantomime somehow conveys the gallantry that lies behind all the elab-

orate rituals of the human comedy, making it possible for men—
and especially Englishmen—to face the unknown with aplomb.

In this brief episode it is possible to glimpse the new medium
working with, rather than against, the filmic freedoms. It is a scene
that could have been approximated on the old screen, but never so
well. For here space, instead of inhibiting, actually enhances the
erratic, mercurial powers of the camera. As a result, the narrative
and visual demands of this particular scene are realized with an
eloquent simplicity. But once the balloon descends, the picture
promptly relapses into the characteristic excesses of the medium.
Though the film itself is robust enough to withstand this, much of
it would have been quicker, lighter, more persuasive within the confines of the standard screen. Especially since many sequences had
obviously been inserted simply to exploit the more spectacular aspects of the Todd-AO process. Time and again the story comes to a
standstill while these crowd scenes and travelogues run their course.
The action is further impeded by those frequent arrays of towering
figures spread out across the proscenium like penguins on parade.
On the smaller screen, much of the scenic grandeur would have
looked too unpretentious to warrant extensive footage, while the
static tableaux would probably have been eliminated entirely. For
the narrow field of the standard frame virtually compelled tighter,
more natural groupings as well as frequent changes of camera position and vigorous editing to unify the various shots into a sustained
dramatic development of the theme. Within this limited framework,
the director was able to organize and influence every element of his
production. The new medium, on the other hand, by its negation of
the best filmic techniques, drastically limited the director's creative
freedom—and the pictures suffered accordingly. For in the movies,
as in all the arts, the ultimate effect depends upon the artist's power
to shape and discipline his material according to the command of
his inspiration.

Though the new screens are far from perfect, we tend to forget
that the old screen, despite its many virtues, also had its faults. Its
horizontal rectangular form was neither wide enough for the composition of broad panoramic scenes nor narrow enough for shots in
which the stress was on the verticals. The wonder is that directors

managed as well as they did with a shape that had been chosen without the slightest concern for artistic or compositional requirements. Perhaps the most positive aspect of this recent period of transition, then, is the fact that it has focused attention once more upon the question of an ideal screen. It is a problem that was engendered by the very nature of the medium, by its dependence on machinery for every phase of production and exhibition. As long as cameras and projectors varied from firm to firm, or from country to country, the market for each picture was necessarily limited. Consequently, once the first crude flickers had gained a local following, their producers sought to increase the potential audience by standardizing all the complex apparatus of film making. The film image was confined in a rectangular frame approximately $1\frac{1}{8}''$ wide by $\frac{3}{4}''$ high. The aperture plates of both cameras and projectors were cut accordingly, and the screen—the final reflection of this mechanical hierarchy—was arbitrarily cast in the same mold. Though its size might vary from theater to theater, its shape merely duplicated on a larger scale the frame's proportion of 4 to 3.

Needless to say, as long as the movies were still in their formative stage, the shape of the screen mattered very little. It could have been square, round or oval for all the first film makers cared. Their only technique was to set the camera up in a fixed position and shoot whatever passed before its lens. But this static use of the camera did not last long. Movie makers soon learned how to compensate for its narrow field of vision by pivoting it on its axis in a pan or a tilt. And when narrative films became popular, they added to the liveliness and interest of their scenes either by taking numerous short shots from many different points of view, or by mounting the camera on wheels and following an action through as it developed. As their mastery increased, directors were able not only to create a more persuasive picture of the physical world but to reveal the inner reality of human emotions as well. Once film making had been transformed from a literal recording of events into an interpretative art, however, directors grew more and more aware of the limitations of the screen itself. The wealth of visual imagery that they were able to project made its fixed and static dimensions seem quite inadequate. Eventually some of the more gifted directors, led by D. W. Griffith, began to improvise ways of relating the shape of their screen to the mood, the action, the atmosphere of a shot, a sequence or a scene.

At that time, of course, there were no mechanical means of altering the shape of the screen. The most effective method was a manual one which consisted of slipping masks of cutout cardboard, metal or other material over the aperture of the camera during the shooting of a scene. Although the rectangular shape of the screen remained the same, the masks changed its appearance by blacking out portions of it and focusing attention on the remaining bright area. Because these masks varied in both form and texture, and could be readily changed from one shot to the next, the director could regulate the shape of his screen according to the fluctuating requirements of his narrative. As a result, masking soon became a common and popular device all over the world, and remained so until the introduction of sound. It even crops up occasionally in present-day films, although in the more prosaic form of realistic cutouts suggesting a peep through telescope, binoculars or keyhole. During the silent era, however, such conventional effects were considered less important than the opportunity of using the mask to enhance the dramatic value of individual shots. In *Intolerance,* for example, Griffith composed in squares, circles, triangles—whatever shape seemed most appropriate at the moment— now blacking out the unwanted portions of the screen with a hard mask, now imperceptibly shading the lighted areas down into darkness with gauze or gelatine filters. To emphasize the intense emotion of the young wife as she hears her husband's death sentence, he inserted a huge close-up of her anguished hands enclosed within a circular frame. Later, with the hero awaiting death on the gallows and the governor rushing to the prison with a last-minute reprieve, Griffith heightened the suspense by showing in an oval frame the hands of the executioners, their knives poised nervously over the cords that will spring the death trap.

Because Griffith could not actually enlarge his screen, he reserved its full area for those shots where size was most impressive—as in the vast court of Babylon, the streets of Jerusalem or a spacious ballroom scene. Even in his biggest scenes, however, Griffith often found use for the mask. To accentuate the far-flung hordes of Syrian warriors riding toward Babylon, for instance, he blacked out the top and bottom of the frame, producing a narrow, elongated frieze effect—strikingly similar to today's CinemaScope screen. But a moment later, when he wanted to emphasize the height of the walls of Babylon, he masked off the sides of the frame and showed the body of a single soldier hurtling down from the top of the ramparts in a vertical shaft of light.

Thus, by frequently varying the shape of the mask, Griffith was able to add to the visual interest and dramatic impact of his shots. But though this variety of compositional forms was artistically valid, the intercutting of static frames of different proportions often proved distracting. The constant shifting of margins seemed to call attention to the black masking elements almost as much as to the lighted images themselves. And despite all their ingenuity, there was little that either Griffith or his contemporaries could do to smooth over these abrupt transitions from one shape to the next. They had gone as far as their limited technical resources would allow in simulating a changing screen. Any further efforts to break the limitations of the frame required an actual change in the dimensions of the screen itself.

Although there had been attempts to introduce various wide-screen systems almost since the birth of the film, not until the mid-twenties did it become either technically or economically feasible to regard them as anything more than fleeting novelties. Perhaps the first to draw attention to the dramatic potentialities of such devices was the vast triptych screen designed by Abel Gance for the presentation of his film *Napoleon*. Introduced by him in Paris in 1926, it consisted quite simply of three standard screens placed side by side. As in Cinerama, three projectors were needed; these did not run continuously, however, for most of the story was told on the middle screen. Only when Gance came to his big scenes were the two supplementary projectors snapped on to augment the central image, creating such triptych effects as a stern close-up of Napoleon flanked by shots of his men riding off to battle. But while Gance achieved moments of impressive magnitude in this way, the film has also been described by those who saw it as both ponderous and confusing. Indeed, it might be said that by using three standard screens instead of one, he merely emphasized the problems of the static frame. Because it was impossible at that time to synchronize either the cameras or projectors, what he had in effect was three separate films running at one time! Fortunately, the equipment was far too unwieldy and impractical for general use, and after a few European engagements of *Napoleon* the triptych screen was discarded. At best, it may be regarded as an artistic step in the right direction, but technically it added nothing to the plasticity of the screen.

The first truly mechanical method for increasing the flexibility of the screen was an American invention, the Magnascope, designed specifically to enhance the spectacular sequences of the more expensive films. With a Magnascope lens fitted on the standard 35mm projector, it became possible to blow up an image to four times its normal size during the showing of a picture. Theaters using the process, therefore, had to install larger screens framed by special motor-operated movable black masks. At the climactic moment of a big film, the projectionist simply switched to the machine with the Magnascope lens and simultaneously touched a button that set these masks in motion. The resulting expansion of both screen and screen image contributed greatly to the excitement of the naval encounters in *Old Ironsides* (1926), the aerial dog fights in *Wings* (1927) and the massed stampede of wild elephants in *Chang* (1927). For though the studios had counted primarily on the magnification of the screen image to achieve their effect, it was obvious that the opening and closing of the screen frame also added to the dramatic momentum of such scenes. In the first talking version of *Moby Dick* (1930), for example, as the longboats pulled away from the mother ship, the screen began slowly to expand, the masking moving majestically back and up to reveal an ever wider view of the limitless sea. The entire pursuit of the great whale takes place on this enlarged screen until finally the monster turns on his pursuers. Then, just as the massive jaws are closing down on Captain Ahab, the sides of the screen contract, cutting off all possibility of escape. At such moments, with the movement of the frame intensifying both the psychological and visual impact of the story, the screen did more than passively reflect the scene; it became at last an integral part of the action.

The success of Magnascope, which was used primarily in the larger downtown houses, promptly inspired a number of imitations.

Paramount's Magnifilm, M-G-M's Realife, the Fox Grandeur Screen all duplicated its effect, but by using a wider film base they were able to produce a clearer, brighter image. The exhibitors, however, were seriously disturbed by this sudden epidemic of wide-screen systems occurring simultaneously with the advent of sound. Because film widths varied from studio to studio—ranging anywhere from 56 to 70mm—theaters wishing to show such pictures would have had to install not only new screens but new projectors for each process. And as many exhibitors were still paying for their expensive sound installations, they felt they were in no position to purchase the even more costly equipment required for wide-screen projection. The stock-market crash in October, 1929, merely confirmed this, making it impossible for most of them to assume further financial obligations. The studios, on the other hand, were not so easily discouraged—especially when they saw that the overwhelming popularity of the new sound films was carrying them safely through the first year of the depression. Quite naturally they were anxious to do all they could to sustain the public's interest, and hoped that by increasing the size and realism of their pictures they would add substantially to their appeal. Throughout 1930, consequently, they continued to experiment with various wide-screen techniques.

It soon became apparent to everyone, however, that if wide films were to be a permanent adjunct of the talkies, it was economically imperative to standardize both the width of the film base and the shape of the screen. In September, 1930, therefore, the Technicians Branch of the Academy of Motion Picture Arts and Sciences, in conjunction with the Directors and Producers Branches, called a special meeting of all their members. Its purpose was to consider the artistic, technical and economic advantages of adopting the wide film and, if possible, to establish an ideal screen shape. The invitations to the meeting were illustrated by drawings of three horizontal rectangles, each a bit more elongated than the other. These were offered as the most likely candidates for the new frame shape. Had one of them been chosen, proportions as awkward as the CinemaScope or VistaVision screen would have been established at the very dawn of the sound era. It was at this meeting, however, that Sergei Eisenstein, then working for Paramount, demolished all arguments in favor of increasing the rectangularity of the screen. In a somewhat pompous and involved but nonetheless prophetic speech, he dismissed the proposed proportions of these "creeping rectangles" as typical products of the "creeping mental- ity" of tradition-bound screen reformers. He warned that if they permitted "the standardization of a new screen shape without the thorough weighing of all the pros and cons of the question" they risked subjugating themselves to a frame even more oppressive than the present one whose horizontal stress had for the past 30 years excluded from the cinema 50 per cent of all vigorous, vertical, upright composition. "A shudder takes me," he said, when he saw that "instead of using the opportunity afforded by the advent of wide film to break . . . that passive horizontalism, we are on the point of emphasizing [it] still more." He urged them, therefore, to consider his own ideal concept of the wide screen, one that would free them forever from the inflexible dominion of the horizontal frame. He offered them, in short, the Dynamic Square—"the only and unique form equally fit . . . to embrace all the vertical and horizontal tendencies of a picture." For by virtue of its *squareness* it could accommodate "the crocodile basking extendedly in the sun [or] the upright standing giraffe, . . . the nostalgia of infinite horizons" or the steel and concrete towers of modern industry. In addition he pointed out that masking on the square screen would be much more effective because its balanced proportions made it equally adaptable to "every geometrically conceivable form" from square to rectangle to upright oblong. Directors would therefore be free to alter their compositions according to the artistic demands of each shot, the changes to be accomplished by the dynamic mask- ing of the film frame. Montage, he said, would then become "the rhythmic assemblage of varied screen shapes." What Eisenstein failed to explain was just how this was to be accomplished. Some of this obscurity may be attributed to his faulty command of English. Basically, however, it was due to the fact that his concept of the ideal screen was purely artistic, without any consideration of the mechanics involved. The practical realization of his dream still required long years of technical research and development. Not for another quarter of a century was the industry to hear again of the "dynamism of changeable proportions."

While Eisenstein's complex and highly theoretical exposition of the virtues of the Dynamic Square must have puzzled most of his listeners, there was no mistaking the meaning of his harangue against the proposed adoption of the Grandeur Screen. But though his analysis of its artistic deficiencies dismayed many of the directors at the meeting, far more important to the producers was a point that Eisenstein made almost casually toward the end of his speech—a reference to an Academy expert's estimate that the actual reconstruction and re-equipment of existing theaters for wide film would cost approximately 40 million dollars. Even this figure might not have deterred the producers because their recent experience with sound, which had won them the reputation of being a "depression-proof" industry, would have justified almost any investment in additional novelties. In 1931, however, the nation's economic distress finally caught up with the studios. And it was this fact—not aesthetic theories—that brought the wide-screen experiments to a halt. By mutual agreement Adolph Zukor, speaking on behalf of the Motion Picture Producers Association, assured the exhibitors that there would be no further attempts to change the standard screen.

Nevertheless, far from the studios experimentation continued. In Paris in 1937 Henri Chrétien again demonstrated his anamorphic lens which was to become the basis for CinemaScope some 15 years later. And in the summer of 1938 Fred Waller began work on the process that was to develop into Cinerama. But not until the period of postwar prosperity, when television plunged the industry into its own private depression, were the wide screens revived. Then under the stress of economic necessity all arguments for a more flexible screen, all warnings against over-extending its horizontal proportions were disregarded. Almost overnight directors were confronted by the immutable expanse of the new wide screens. If they had felt themselves inhibited by the old screen, they found that they were almost paralyzed by the new. A less resilient breed of artists might well have been dismayed by the enormity of the change. To their eternal credit, they accepted the challenge and continued to struggle valiantly with the welter of film widths and aspect ratios that appeared in the wake of Cinerama after 1952. Inevitably, however, in their efforts to restore some mobility to their pictures they were often forced to resort to extreme measures.

The director of an early CinemaScope musical, for example, wanted to include the entire Eiffel Tower on his elongated screen. The only way he could manage this was by tipping his camera over on its side and shooting his picture lengthwise! In *It's Always Fair Weather* (1955), another CinemaScope musical, Stanley Donen found that he could condense a ten-year interlude in the lives of his three principals by dividing his wide screen into three panels and telling their stories simultaneously. The effect was reminiscent of the old Gance triptych. Elsewhere in the film he went to the opposite extreme, reviving a favorite Griffith device, the iris, to isolate a single character on the huge screen. And there were still other stunts—some ingenious or amusing, some simply repetitious of techniques that, though valid for the old screen, were merely awkward on the new.

Clearly the need for a reappraisal of screen sizes and shapes exists far more urgently now than at any time in the past. Never before have directors been so rigidly restricted by the shape of the frame, for never before have the frame shapes been so very ungainly. Once again, as at the beginning of film history, the dimensions of the screen have been arbitrarily established without any regard for the aesthetics of cinematic composition. Fortunately, today there is an important difference because now, for the first time, the economic pressures are all on the side of art. The wide screens, hailed only a few years ago as the sure salvation of the industry, are at present regarded with serious doubts and misgivings. There is just too much space to fill, too much weight to carry, with the result that even the best wide films remain somewhat ponderous, theatrical and dull. And it is precisely these failings that are bringing the producers and their backers into the same camp as the creative film makers. For with movies facing the stiffest competition in their entire history, the artist's control of his medium becomes a decisive factor in the battle for audiences. Size alone is not enough—especially when it robs directors of their spontaneity and films of their vitality. Consequently, there has been a growing conviction on the part of everyone concerned with the survival of the motion picture that until the screens can be made more flexible, it will be impossible to produce better films. Today producers, technicians and artists alike are searching for ways to modify and improve the various wide-screen systems. Fred Waller, for example, whose Cinerama inaugurated the era, was aware of how quickly moviegoers grow accustomed to the magnitude of the wide screen. He realized that the only way to preserve its effectiveness was by contrasting the size of the images, playing most of the film on relatively small areas and saving the full screen for a film's more spectacular sequences. Shortly before his death he declared that he had worked out a way of changing the shape of the screen electronically, regulating the movement of its black masking framework by a system of notches along the edge of the film strip. The effect would probably have resembled Magnascope, but with one important difference: In Magnascope it was the projectionist who controlled the operation—and he often did so with an appalling lack of taste. By contrast, the Waller method would have made the movement of the frame an artistic decision to be predetermined by the director during the shooting and editing of his film.

Since Waller's death there has been no practical development of his idea, no means of providing a mobile masking framework for the screen. The importance—even the necessity—of such a mask, however, has been demonstrated repeatedly. From Griffith's time to the present we have seen that when only a part of the screen is used, the unused portion is still intrusive. Ideally, of course, a frame should be virtually unnoticed, focusing the attention completely on the picture itself. But because the blacked-out area of the screen is on the same spatial plane as the lighted image, it distracts the eye and overbalances the composition. Its surface seems to require an extra-dimensional covering to make it invisible— and it is precisely this definitive masking that Waller described.

Its eventual realization would seem to be a logical and necessary adjunct to the Dynamic Frame, an experimental process sponsored by the British Film Institute and introduced early in 1956 by its young American inventor, Glenn Alvey, Jr. Judging from the experiments and experiences of the past, this process comes closest to fulfilling all the demands for a more flexible screen. With it the director is at last liberated from the rigidity of the frame. He can choose any size playing area he desires and change it at will from a small square to a huge rectangle, from a narrow slit of light to full screen. These varying forms are made possible by a system of movable mattes that control the height and width of the image. Though very similar to the masks of the silent film, they are far more versatile. Whereas the old masks of necessity remained fixed throughout a shot, the mattes of the Dynamic Frame are operated within the camera to permit the alteration of shape not only from shot to shot but within the shot itself. Transitions can also be handled with the utmost fluency, either gradually, even imperceptibly, as in a mood sequence, or instantaneously for dramatic revelation or shock effect. Moreover, the Dynamic Frame is compatible with all wide-screen systems, requiring no changes or additions to existing projection equipment.

For his demonstration film, an adaptation of H. G. Wells's short story *The Door in the Wall*, Alvey worked with the 55mm VistaVision process. Using as his base an area considerably less than the full VistaVision screen, he was thus free to compose either horizontally or vertically, to increase or decrease the size of his images at will. For his drawing-room and conversational scenes, for example, he generally chose a medium-sized rectangular frame, blacking out the remainder with his mattes. In the fantasy sequences, however, the shape of the frame is varied to emphasize every change in mood and action. When the boy first discovers the little green door, the screen is small and square—just large enough to encompass the child, the door and a portion of the wall. Then as he passes into the enchanted garden beyond, the camera follows after him and the screen slowly widens out to full size before his wondering gaze. But when he sits down to rest at the base of a tree, the main part of the screen is blacked out again and the image is contained in a small rectangle at the lower left-hand corner of the frame. He is scarcely seated, however, when he realizes that the tree trunk is actually the leg of a tremendous beast! As he leaps up in alarm, the frame parallels his movement by shooting upward to reveal the monster. At another point the boy, now several years older, is hurrying on his way to school. Suddenly he sees again the tiny door he had been seeking. Though he longs to enter, the school bells remind him of his duty and he dares not linger. Even as he races on through twisting alleys hedged by high brick walls, the sides of the screen close in on him, the narrowness of the frame intensifying the sensations of pressure and confinement. At such moments, the shape of the screen kinesthetically transmits to the audience the emotional content of the scene in ways completely new to the motion-picture medium.

Unfortunately, episodes like this are all too rare in Alvey's film. He made *The Door in the Wall* to demonstrate his process, and as is so often the case with demonstrations, the result is an inartistic exploitation of technical effects. Yet even in this first self-conscious effort may be glimpsed the special excitement that accompanied the opening and closing of the old Magnascope screen, the freedom from the frame that Griffith longed for, the flexibility of compositional forms that Eisenstein hoped to achieve with his own Dynamic Square. And though the film gives only a glimmer of the creative potentialities of the process, it is enough to indicate that the Dynamic Frame depends entirely upon the taste, the skill, the perception of the director for its successful utilization. Because the shape of the screen must be constantly related to the mood and action of each scene, it requires a maximum of pre-production planning not only for the director but for the writer and cameraman as well. Paradoxically, the new spatial freedom that it affords demands greater artistic control than ever before.

At this moment in film history it is impossible to predict whether the Dynamic Frame will in fact become the frame of the future—or even if it will be generally adopted by the industry within the next few years. Too much depends upon such intangibles as the artistic ingenuity with which it is used in subsequent productions, the public's approval and support of the process, and the ever present possibility of other, more exciting inventions that may still be in the laboratory stage. For it is these three elements— the inventor, the artist and the audience—that ultimately determine what course the film will take. Inter-acting one upon the other, they have propelled the medium past the boundaries of silence, through sound and color and space. Together they have made possible its development from a crude peep-show novelty to an art form capable of touching the heart and the imagination of people throughout the world. The incredible thing is that all of this has been accomplished in only sixty years!

Today the motion picture is again in an era of transition. Once more the inventors have provided the film makers with a new dimension of reality to work with, and audiences everywhere have indicated their interest and enthusiasm. And once more the artists are faced with the necessity of developing skills and techniques that will serve to increase the scope and vitality of the entire medium. It is a challenge that accompanies each new technological development, each change in the basic tools of film production. But it is a challenge that the directors have met resourcefully in the past—and will meet again, inevitably, in the long years that lie ahead. For the capacity to change, to grow is the very essence of every living art—and especially of the movies, the liveliest of all the arts.

100 BEST BOOKS ON FILM

Any listing of 100 "best books" is, by its very nature, both arbitrary and artificial. As used here, it is meant to suggest only those books in English that the reader of the present volume might find especially useful and stimulating as supplementary references—particularly in the fields that have been slighted, such as documentary, experimental and animated films. Biographies have been chosen for the light they shed either on film history or on film art rather than on the individual personality. Works of a specifically technical nature have been pointedly ignored, partially because they date so quickly, but more importantly because they lie outside the province of this book. Books of special interest and merit have been marked with an *.

INTRODUCTORY

Barry, Iris: *Let's Go to the Movies*. Payson & Clarke, 1926. 278 pp.

    A witty, discursive and shrewd analysis of the silent film as seen by an English critic who loved the movies in spite of themselves. Especially valuable for its fresh, first-hand account of pictures that have since become "classics."

Clair, René: *Reflections on the Cinema*. Kimber, 1953. 160 pp.

    This engaging, somewhat saddening little book is cast in the form of a conversation between the youthful Clair of the twenties and the famous director of 1950, when the book was written. Clair intersperses the bright enthusiasms of his youth with the sober observations of a director who now almost too thoroughly knows the score.

Cocteau, Jean: *Cocteau on the Film*. Roy, 1954. 140 pp.

    A series of conversations with the French Jack-of-all-arts recorded by André Fraigneau. Cocteau is given to generalizing from his own highly special experience on matters of filmic creation, but his views on the relationship between an artist and his audience are both perceptive and provocative.

Cooke, Alistair, ed.: *Garbo and the Night Watchmen*. Jonathan Cape, 1937. 352 pp.

A compendium of good movie criticism in the mid-thirties as practiced by Cecilia Ager, Cooke, Otis Ferguson, Robert Forsythe, Graham Greene, Don Herold, Robert Herring, Meyer Levin and John Marks. All nine converge on Chaplin's *Modern Times* for the finale.

* Lindgren, Ernest: *The Art of the Film*. Allen & Unwin, 1948. 242 pp.

After presenting a brief introduction to modern studio production methods, Lindgren—the Curator of Britain's National Film Library—proceeds to actual films to illustrate various aspects of the art. Written with great warmth and lucidity, this makes an excellent introduction to film aesthetics, appreciation and criticism. Handsomely illustrated.

Manvell, Roger: *Film*. Penguin Books, 1946. 240 pp.

Dr. Manvell has unquestionably done more than anyone else in the world to popularize the idea of film as an art form. This book, a revision of his first important work on the medium, analyzes the essentials of film art and social aspects of the film. Frequent, vivid descriptions of outstanding pictures point up his brief historical survey.

Schmidt, Georg, Werner Schmalenbach and Peter Bächlin: *The Film: Its Economic, Social, and Artistic Problems*. Falcon Press, 1948. 140 pp.

An ingenious, if somewhat didactic, visual presentation of the essentials of film art (as differentiated, primarily, from theater, painting and photography), with diagrammatic presentation of the economic and social problems. Based on a wall show arranged for the first Basle Film Week (1943).

Sherwood, Robert E., ed.: *The Best Moving Pictures of 1922-1923*. Small, Maynard, 1923. 346 pp.

The late, distinguished playwright was also one of the first—and best—movie critics in this country. This book, intended as an annual, includes critical analysis of 16 outstanding films, among them *Nanook of the North, Grandma's Boy, Robin Hood, The Pilgrim* and *The Covered Wagon*. An account of the growing movie censorship of that period is included.

Wollenberg, H. H.: *Anatomy of the Film*. Marsland, 1947. 104 pp.

A brief introduction to film appreciation, based on a course given by the author at Cambridge. Includes a highly condensed history, an examination of techniques and economic problems—all with the purpose of promoting an awareness of the artistic and social values of the motion picture.

AESTHETICS

Arnheim, Rudolf: *Film*. Faber, 1933. 296 pp.

The first extended attempt to organize an aesthetic theory of film technique, analyzing both the physical and the psychological characteristics of the medium—and generally with concrete examples to illustrate abstract points. Though written at the dawn of the sound era, much of Arnheim's theory still proves valid.

* Balázs, Béla: *Theory of the Film*. Roy, 1953. 291 pp.

This posthumous edition of the summary work of one of the greatest European critics (he was also a film maker) is a valuable addition to the literature on the art of the film. Balázs writes with a broad frame of reference in all the arts; the art he loves, however, is film, and he is especially good at explaining the mechanisms that make it so affecting to audiences everywhere. The Soviet silent films provide most of his examples.

* Eisenstein, Sergei M.: *Film Form*. Harcourt, Brace, 1949. 279 pp.

A collection of essays—biographical and theoretical—collected by Jay Leyda, this book provides a summing-up of Eisenstein's artistic credo (or credos) on a somewhat more popular level than *The Film Sense*. Includes the long, penetrating study, *Dickens, Griffith and the Film Today*, in itself a splendid introduction to the problems of film form. If any one single theme runs through the book, it is Eisenstein's efforts to discover the contributions of kindred arts to the art of the film.

Eisenstein, Sergei M.: *The Film Sense*. Harcourt, Brace, 1942. 288 pp.

Eisenstein's theoretical writings make difficult reading for the layman—filled with allusions, often elliptical, rarely clarified by concrete illustrations. The power and originality of his thought, however, and the breadth of reference make this a constantly stimulating work. Edited by Jay Leyda, who has appended a valuable bibliography as well as excerpts from several of Eisenstein's scenarios.

Lindsay, Vachel: *The Art of the Moving Picture*. Macmillan, 1915. 289 pp.

The distinguished poet was one of the first of the American intelligentsia to embrace film as a popular art, and this astonishing book is his testament of faith in its future. Contains vivid descriptions and analyses of dozens of films (including *Judith of Bethulia* and *The Italian*) made between 1912 and 1915. Revised and enlarged for a new edition in 1922.

* Münsterberg, Hugo: *The Photoplay, a Psychological Study*. Appleton, 1916. 233 pp.

An eminent psychologist analyzes the techniques of silent films to discover how they work upon an audience. This first investigation into an important field is surprisingly little known—particularly since Münsterberg's insights into the processes of identification and empathy are even more meaningful in this age of the all-encompassing wide screen.

Nicoll, Allardyce: *Film and Theatre*. Crowell, 1936. 255 pp.

One of America's leading authorities on the theater compares the two media—and not always to the disadvantage of the film. Includes a penetrating analysis of the problems of filming Shakespeare, and the nature of film's reality.

Spottiswoode, Raymond: *A Grammar of the Film*. University of California, 1950. 328 pp.

A reprint of a work that appeared first in 1935, Mr. Spottiswoode has correctly appraised both its scope and its limitations in the preface to this new edition. For he has attempted nothing less than a formal outline of all the techniques that contribute to film art—untempered by any contact with the stern realities surrounding actual production.

HISTORY

Balcon, Michael, et al.: *Twenty Years of British Film, 1925–1945*. Falcon Press, 1947. 116 pp.

Balcon supplies the industry background, Ernest Lindgren writes of early English features, Forsyth Hardy on British documentary, and Roger Manvell on the war years in this compact, informative, well-illustrated little volume. One of the National Cinema Series.

Bardèche, Maurice, and Robert Brasillach: *The History of Motion Pictures*. Trans. by Iris Barry. Norton, 1938. 412 pp.

The artistic development of the film as seen through two pairs of French eyes, with special emphasis inevitably on the films from France and the United States. The authors' critical judgments and errors of fact are often tartly taken to task by their translator and editor in the copious footnotes.

Crowther, Bosley: *The Lion's Share*. Dutton, 1957. 320 pp.

In writing the history of Metro-Goldwyn-Mayer, Bosley Crowther, the distinguished critic of the *New York Times,* has in effect traced the growth of the entire American film industry. For M-G-M followed a pattern that was, in its main outlines, identical with that of every other major studio. Its story is perhaps especially interesting because of the many great stars and directors who worked there at one time or another—Garbo, von Stroheim, the Marx Brothers, King Vidor et al.

Dickinson, Thorold, and Catherine De la Roche, eds.: *Soviet Cinema*. Falcon Press, 1948. 136 pp.

Dickinson writes of the silent era, De la Roche of the sound era through the war years in the condensed, factual style that characterizes the National Cinema Series. Dickinson, himself a director, is especially good on the developing technique in the Soviet silent films.

Green, Abel, and Joe Laurie, Jr.: *Show Biz*. Holt, 1951. 613 pp.

Variety's able editor joined forces with comedian Joe Laurie, Jr., to cull the high-lights of a half-century of show business. The result is an amusing, discursive book filled with facts and figures on the film industry that are available nowhere else—and made readily accessible by a thorough indexing job.

Hampton, Benjamin B.: *A History of the Movies*. Covici, Friede, 1931. 456 pp.

Essentially, a history of the American *industry*, with detailed accounts of the patents wars and the growth of the major studios. Hampton is especially good on the battle for theaters that dominated the industry during the twenties, and the studio production techniques of that era.

Hardy, Forsyth: *Scandinavian Film*. Falcon Press, 1952. 62 pp.

Another in the valuable National Cinema Series, this covers the Danish, Swedish and (briefly) the Norwegian film. Accent falls on the sound period, particularly during the thirties—a period when Scandinavian films were rarely seen by the rest of the world. The text, stressing the adult qualities of these pictures, suggests how much we have lost by ignoring them.

* Jacobs, Lewis: *The Rise of the American Film*. Harcourt, Brace, 1939. 585 pp.

A detailed, superbly documented history of the American motion-picture industry revealing the inter-action between the public, the businessman and the film artist—all set firmly against the economic and social history of the period. An invaluable reference work.

Jarratt, Vernon: *The Italian Cinema*. Falcon Press (London) and Macmillan (New York), 1951. 115 pp.

Carefully balanced historical and critical appraisal of the Italian film from its great days before World War I through its renaissance after World War II. Especially valuable for its first-hand account of the industry during the years of its eclipse under Fascism. One of the best in the National Cinema Series.

* Kracauer, Siegfried: *From Caligari to Hitler*. Princeton, 1947. 361 pp.

In this authoritative history of the German film, the author relates the films themselves to socio-psychological traits of the German people —even down to the development of specific film techniques. Virtually every important German film down to 1933 is discussed, all film cycles and trends are examined, and the corporate structure of the German industry is analyzed. An invaluable appendix examines the techniques of the Nazi propaganda reels.

Low, Rachel: *The History of the British Film* (1896–1906, 1906–1914, 1914–1918). Allen & Unwin, 1948, 1949, 1950.

Three volumes have appeared to date in what was to have been a thoroughly documented account of British film history from its origins to the present day. Undertaken by the British Film Institute and under the supervision of Roger Manvell, these volumes cover perhaps the least-known years of the British film, examining both industry economics and artistic development. Revealing descriptions of typical films in each volume.

Museum of Modern Art Film Library: *Film Notes*, Part I, *The Silent Film.* Museum of Modern Art, 1949. 68 pp.

Compiled from notes designed to accompany films in the Museum's collection—which means, of course, that there are important omissions —this little pamphlet compresses a vast amount of factual and critical data within its carefully researched pages.

Quigley, Martin, Jr.: *Magic Shadows.* Georgetown University, 1948. 191 pp.

Subtitled *The Story of the Origin of Motion Pictures,* this admirable book follows the slow accretion of scientific knowledge from ancient Greece to the late 19th century when early principles of movement and the reproduction of images fused to form the movies. An elaborate chronology traces the growth of pre-screen inventions.

* Ramsaye, Terry: *A Million and One Nights.* Simon & Schuster, 1926. 868 pp.

This two-volume labor of love is probably the first book that one turns to for an accurate, lively account of American silent film history. Vol. I is a carefully researched investigation of pre-screen inventions in which Thomas Edison emerges as hero; Vol. II, largely first-hand and anecdotal, is a parade of the personalities and intrigues behind the industrial development of the film in America. Its superb index makes all this readily available.

Rotha, Paul, and Richard Griffith: *The Film Till Now.* Funk & Wagnalls, 1949. 755 pp.

A critical survey of the world cinema based on Rotha's classic history, first published in 1930, and updated by Richard Griffith, Curator of the Museum of Modern Art Film Library. An informative, argumentative, stimulating book, lavishly illustrated with well reproduced stills.

Sadoul, Georges: *French Film*. Falcon Press, 1953. 131 pp.

A history of the film in France by one of the leading French critics who is also a scrupulously exact historian. In this brief account, Sadoul relates film to the political and economic forces that shaped it from the turn of the century through the Nazi Occupation. One of the best in the National Cinema Series.

Vardac, A. Nicholas: *Stage to Screen*. Harvard, 1949. 283 pp.

A scholarly study of the nineteenth century theater that prepared the way for the motion picture, and the curious inter-action between stage and screen during the early years of this century. An important contribution to a sadly neglected phase of film history.

Wollenberg, H. H.: *Fifty Years of German Film*. Falcon Press, 1947. 48 pp.

First in the National Cinema Series, this is a somewhat arid account of the German film written with emphasis on its social implications rather than on its artistic development. A useful supplement to Kracauer's book, primarily for its history of the Nazi years. Fine selection of stills.

Wood, Leslie: *The Miracle of the Movies*. Burke, 1947. 352 pp.

A personal, garrulous, disorganized history of the movies by a British critic and writer. Valuable primarily for its detailed account of the dog days of the British studios. Unfortunately, no index.

BIOGRAPHY

Bainbridge, John: *Garbo*. Doubleday, 1955. 256 pp.

Bainbridge, one of the *New Yorker's* adroit profilers, presents a patiently researched, thoroughly readable but superficial biography of the screen's greatest actress. All the facts are here except perhaps the most important one: What was the nature of Garbo's art that was so perfectly suited to the screen? Good accounts of European and Hollywood production during the twenties.

Barry, Iris: *D. W. Griffith, American Film Master*. Museum of Modern Art, 1940. 40 pp.

An incisive, informative monograph on the great pioneer director, scrupulously documented; with a note by Beaumont Newhall on the contributions of Billy Bitzer's camera work to the Griffith films.

Cooke, Alistair: *Douglas Fairbanks*. Museum of Modern Art, 1940. 36 pp.

More than a biography, this fine monograph outlines the special nature of screen personality as opposed to screen acting. It traces the development of Fairbanks from the breezy juvenile of his earliest films, through his World War I status as "popular philosopher," and on into the swashbuckling romantic of the twenties—and always with an awareness of the industrial, social and personal drives that shaped his screen character. Includes a chronology of all his films.

de Mille, William C.: *Hollywood Saga*. Dutton, 1939. 319 pp.

A mellow and amusing autobiography by a director who, while eminent in his own right, was better known as "the brother of Cecil B." He uses that vantage point to make penetrating comments on the De Mille bedroom farces and spectacles, but adds to it his own perceptions of the movies' struggle toward artistry between 1915 and 1937.

Griffith, Richard: *Samuel Goldwyn: The Producer and His Films*. Museum of Modern Art Film Library, 1956. 48 pp.

This brief monograph attempts to evaluate the part of the producer in a film's creation. With a minimum of biographical detail, Griffith concentrates on the films themselves, from *Carmen* (1915) to *The Best Years of Our Lives* (1946). Includes a complete listing, with credits, of all Goldwyn's independent productions.

Huff, Theodore: *Charlie Chaplin*. Schuman, 1951. 354 pp.

The definitive Chaplin, at least as far as the factual background of his stormy life is concerned. Scrupulously researched, filled with descriptions and casts of all Chaplin films through *Verdoux*, this book contains everything except the evaluation of the nature of his genius.

Mayer, Arthur: *Merely Colossal*. Simon & Schuster, 1953. 264 pp.

A genial but shrewd autobiographical account of a life devoted to the film industry. With an appropriate anecdote for every occasion, Mr. Mayer discusses the problems of production, distribution, exhibition, the importation of foreign films—and the fickle public.

Payne, Robert: *The Great God Pan*. Hermitage House, 1952. 301 pp.

A good companion to Theodore Huff's admirable biography, Payne's work concentrates less on Charles Chaplin the man than upon the screen character he created—its sources, its changes from decade to decade, its significance to audiences all over the world. Filled with keen insights, and beautifully written.

Sennett, Mack: *King of Comedy*. Doubleday, 1954. 284 pp.

Chatty, anecdotal, disorganized, but still a fascinating and funny account of the early years of picture making in general, and the catch-as-catch-can methods that prevailed on Sennett's Keystone lot in particular.

* Seton, Marie: *Sergei M. Eisenstein*. Wyn, 1952. 533 pp.

Although described as a "definitive biography," this intense work by a friend and admirer of the great Russian director is far more than that. It is also a keen analysis of his working methods, a clear presentation of his theories and a vivid, sympathetic account of the ways of genius. Richly documented and illustrated.

Sinclair, Upton: *Upton Sinclair Presents William Fox.* Sinclair, 1933. 377 pp.

An almost embarrassingly adulatory account of the rise and fall of one of the pioneer American producers, but invaluable for its insights into the way the banks and utilities took over the film industry during the early years of sound.

Smith, Albert E., and P. A. Koury: *Two Reels and a Crank.* Doubleday, 1952. 285 pp.

Smith, one of the founders of the pioneer Vitagraph Company, offers a garrulous, random history of the early days. The problems of film makers at the turn of the century are especially well presented, but because the subsequent narrative leaps nimbly from era to era, rarely bothering with dates, the book is less than satisfactory as history. No index.

Tynan, Kenneth: *Alec Guinness. Rockliff* (London) and Macmillan (New York), 1954. 108 pp.

This slim volume is far more than simple biography. The brilliant young English critic tries to penetrate the secret of Guinness's chameleon-like ability to change personality with each role he plays. The result throws more light on the nature of screen acting than many more conventional works dealing directly with that subject. Superb illustrations.

Vidor, King: *A Tree Is a Tree.* Harcourt, Brace, 1953. 315 pp.

Vidor's candid autobiography, a summing up of over 50 years in films, presents vividly the changing production methods during this period. His faith in the audience remains unshaken, but it is amply clear that he longs for the freedom of expression possible when budgets were lower and risks were less.

TECHNIQUE

Alton, John: *Painting with Light.* Macmillan, 1949. 191 pp.

One of the top photographers in Hollywood gives a popular, readable account of studio camera techniques, with particular emphasis on lighting. Includes interior and exterior shooting and trick work. Profusely illustrated—and well.

Anderson, Lindsay, ed.: *Making a Film.* Allen & Unwin, 1952. 223 pp.

Anderson follows, step by step, the production of *Secret People* in Britain's Ealing Studio. It is a unique document, a diary of each day's work, reproduction of the shooting script, even the cuts and changes after shooting. Unfortunately, the film that it describes was not successful enough to be widely seen in this country.

Carrick, Edward: *Art and Design in the British Film.* Dennis Dobson, 1948. 133 pp.

This handsome volume, modestly identified as "a pictorial directory of British Art Directors and their work," gives brief biographical material on some 40 designers, accompanied by reproductions of characteristic designs, occasional photos of the sets built from them, and several continuity sketches to guide the cameraman as well as the architect.

Carrick, Edward: *Designing for Moving Pictures.* Studio, 1947. 104 pp.

A clear, non-technical account of problems (and personal solutions) of designing sets and properties for feature and documentary films by one of the leading British practitioners.

Cocteau, Jean: *Diary of a Film.* Roy, 1950. 214 pp.

Notes from Cocteau's diary during the production of *La Belle et la Bête,* detailing the difficulties of film making in postwar France and revealing a creative artist at work. A highly personal account by a completely personal film maker. Poorly edited, however, with no attempt to clarify technical processes or define technical terms for the lay reader.

Davy, Charles, ed.: *Footnotes to the Film.* Oxford, 1937. 346 pp.

A well organized and surprisingly undated anthology on film production techniques, industry and audience by such authorities as Hitchcock, Grierson, Alexander Korda and Alistair Cooke. The pieces are short but, for the most part, both informative and thoughtful.

Eisler, Hans: *Composing for the Films.* Oxford University, 1947. 165 pp.

There have been few serious considerations of film music between covers, and those are generally a chapter or two out of a longer work. Eisler—decidedly advanced in his musical ideas when he worked in Hollywood during the early forties—here outlines a theoretical base for film music that has since become almost standard practice.

Frayne, John G., and Halley Wolfe: *Elements of Sound Recording.* Wiley, 1949. 686 pp.

A somewhat technical but readable survey of all current recording techniques, including both magnetic and stereophonic sound. The many illustrations are helpful.

Gassner, John, and Dudley Nichols, eds.: *Twenty Best Film Plays; Best Film Plays of 1943–44; Best Film Plays of 1945.* Crown, 1943, 1945, 1946.

These three fat volumes, each with an informative introduction by script writer Dudley Nichols, contain the screenplays of dozens of outstanding American pictures, including *Little Caesar, It Happened One Night, Grapes of Wrath, Ox-Bow Incident, Miracle of Morgan's Creek* and *Double Indemnity.*

Lawson, John Howard: *Theory and Technique of Playwriting and Screenwriting.* Putnam, 1949. 464 pp.

Lawson's brilliant exposition of the techniques of writing for the stage, a standard work since the mid-thirties, is here expanded to include the technical and the artistic problems of writing for the screen.

London, Kurt: *Film Music.* Faber & Faber, 1936. 280 pp.

Hopelessly outdated as far as the techniques of recording are concerned, this thoughtful work traces the history of film music, its special uses and stresses the concept of "microgenic" music—music written with the special requirements of the microphone in mind. Thus, while recording characteristics have changed in the past two decades, the theory here outlined remains valid.

Milne, Peter: *Motion Picture Directing.* Falk, 1922. 234 pp.

Designed as a supplementary text for a photography school, this book contains interviews with leading directors of the silent era— Griffith, De Mille, Ince, Lubitsch, *et al.*—and affords valuable insights into early working methods.

Naumburg, Nancy, ed.: *We Make the Movies.* Norton, 1937. 284 pp.

A sketchy but informative account of studio production in Hollywood during the mid-thirties. Contributors include Jesse Lasky, Sidney Howard, Bette Davis, Paul Muni, John Arnold, Walt Disney and Max Steiner.

*Nilssen, Vladimir: *The Cinema as a Graphic Art.* Newnes, 1936. 227 pp.

A brilliant exposition by one of Eisenstein's early collaborators of the creative uses of the camera and the dynamics of composition. Both theory and illustrations are drawn from Soviet films of the late silent era, but the ideas are still valid and stimulating today.

*Pudovkin, V. I.: *Film Technique and Film Acting.* Lear, 1954. 357 pp.

Actually a reprint of two classic works by the great Russian director, with a new introduction by Lewis Jacobs. Although composed of essays from the late silent and early sound period, Pudovkin's observations on the techniques of his craft are still the most stimulating and comprehensive introduction to film art.

Quigley, Martin, Jr., ed.: *New Screen Techniques.* Quigley, 1953. 208 pp.

26 articles, largely non-technical, explaining the mechanics, problems and industry solutions of 3-D and wide-screen techniques (excepting VistaVision and Todd-AO). Well chosen diagrams and illustrations help considerably.

* Reisz, Karel: *The Technique of Film Editing*. Farrar, Straus & Young, 1953. 288 pp.

Reisz, with the aid of British film makers, has prepared a marvelously lucid, vividly illustrated account of the *art* of film editing (title notwithstanding). Not the mechanics but the reasons for assembling strips of film in any given order are discussed—in other words, editing in relation to direction, script, sound, etc.

*Ross, Lillian: *Picture*. Rinehart, 1952. 258 pp.

When Miss Ross's devastating observations on the production of John Huston's *The Red Badge of Courage* began appearing in the pages of the *New Yorker,* they threw the industry for a loop. Never before had Hollywood's operations been viewed with such acid understanding or objective derision. And never before has the production of a major film—from inception to final unveiling—been recounted with such sure instinct for the illuminating detail.

Schary, Dore: *Case History of a Movie*. Random House, 1950. 242 pp.

The former Vice-President in Charge of Production at M-G-M invites the reader behind the scenes to follow the step-by-step production of *The Next Voice You Hear*. Clear and well organized, although lacking the extra dimension of personality clash and temperament that gives *Picture* the ring of authenticity.

Spencer, D. A., and H. D. Waley: *The Cinema To-Day*. Oxford, 1956. 202 pp.

A thorough revision and updating of a text on basic cinematic techniques that, when it appeared, was a model of lucidity in explaining to the layman what made the movies move. The new edition, with added material on color, 3-D, wide screens and TV, improves on the original in both comprehensiveness and comprehensibility.

* Spottiswoode, Raymond: *Film and Its Techniques*. University of California, 1951. 516 pp.

A clear, thorough, detailed presentation of the techniques of factual film production, with special reference to the problems of 16mm. Invaluable to anyone this side of a major studio, it includes camera techniques, editing-room procedures, the laboratory and film library, color and 3-D. Excellent drawings clarify technical descriptions, and an extensive glossary explains technical terminology.

SOCIAL ASPECTS

Cogley, John: *Report on Blacklisting:* I, *Movies*. Fund for the Republic, 1956. 312 pp.

An effort on the part of Mr. Cogley, Editor of the *Commonweal,* to assess the extent and the effects of blacklisting in the motion-picture industry. Based on interviews and impressive research into the documents dealing with Communist activity in Hollywood, he has produced a comprehensive account of behind-the-scenes politics and policies in the studios.

Handel, Leo A.: *Hollywood Looks at Its Audience*. University of Illinois, 1950. 240 pp.

Hollywood's attempts to anticipate audience wishes by pre-testing stories, titles and casts are generally unknown outside the industry. This book, while written to outline the statistical methods employed, has the additional merit of introducing the lay public to audience-research activities.

*Huettig, Mae D.: *Economic Control of the Motion Picture Industry*. University of Pennsylvania, 1944. 163 pp.

In the years since this unique, penetrating investigation appeared, theaters have been divorced from the studios and independent production is now being encouraged. But because Mrs. Huettig approaches her subject historically—beginning with the Film Trust of 1909—time has in no way invalidated her lively, well-documented work.

Inglis, Ruth A.: *Freedom of the Movies*. University of Chicago, 1947. 240 pp.

The most thorough and comprehensive account of contemporary American film censorship, its history and effect upon the movies themselves. Prepared for the American Commission on Freedom of the Press, it is factual, dispassionate—and disturbing.

Manvell, Roger: *The Film and the Public*. Penguin, 1955. 352 pp.

Dr. Manvell skims through film history, reviews at length 23 film classics, then examines such problems as censorship, pressure groups, children and film, and finally television. Far too sketchy to lead to any conclusions, this book suggests the range of interests affected by the motion-picture medium.

Powdermaker, Hortense: *Hollywood, the Dream Factory*. Little, Brown, 1950. 342 pp.

Dr. Powdermaker, a noted anthropologist, has applied to Hollywood the methods and yardsticks by which primitive societies are studied; her purpose, to uncover "the patterns and ideas which control or influence the activities of its members"—and hence influence the content of films. A revealing work, particularly in its account of the power structure in Hollywood, a set-up that seems specifically designed to encourage mediocrity.

Robson, E. W. and M. M.: *The Film Answers Back*. John Lane, 1939. 336 pp.

Subtitled *An Historical Appreciation of the Cinema*, this lively, opinionated work is especially concerned with the relationship between the film and its audience—not only what it reveals of audiences in America, England, France, Germany and Russia, but how the people themselves helped shape the pictures that they see.

Rosten, Leo C.: *Hollywood: The Movie Colony and the Movie Makers*. Harcourt, Brace, 1941. 436 pp.

A vigorous, perceptive book, product of a 3-year investigation by a team of trained researchers into the attitudes of Hollywood's creative talent, set against the financial and organizational structure of the industry. A bit dated now, but still illuminating.

Seldes, Gilbert: *The Great Audience*. Viking, 1950. 299 pp.

Writing of movies, radio and television, Mr. Seldes examines the nature of their audiences and draws valuable distinctions between what the public wants, what it gets, what it deserves—and how it can get better entertainment. As always, Seldes is both discerning and provocative.

Seldes, Gilbert: *The Public Arts*. Simon & Schuster, 1956. 303 pp.

Some thirty years ago Mr. Seldes coined the phrase "the lively arts" to cover all forms of popular entertainment. In this volume he examines the three liveliest—films, radio and television—with special reference to their effects upon the tastes, habits and ideas of the American public.

Thorp, Margaret F.: *America at the Movies*. Yale, 1939. 313 pp.

A provocative account of the film as a cultural influence in our society—not only how we are influenced by the films we see and how we in turn influence film content, but how the film makers themselves consciously attempt to mold public opinion. Examples are drawn largely from films of the thirties.

Wolfenstein, Martha, and Nathan Leites: *Movies, a Psychological Study*. Free Press, 1950. 316 pp.

Two psychologists use the techniques of the couch upon the silver screen. Their discoveries are often fresh and interesting—the "good-bad girl," the heroine as mother, the screen's substitution of violence for sex. The effect, however, is more clever than conclusive, especially since the realities of production are firmly ignored. But they do introduce an important field for more purposeful investigation: to what extent and in what ways the film reflects the psychology of its public.

Wright, Basil: *The Use of the Film*. John Lane, 1948. 72 pp.

The veteran British documentary director has packed a vast amount of solid thought into a tiny but useful orientation work. Demonstrating the social value of both entertainment and documentary films, he looks toward the day when all producers will accept the implications of this fact.

SPECIALIZED FILMS

Baechlin, Peter, and Maurice Muller-Strauss: *Newsreels Across the World*. UNESCO, 1952. 100 pp.

A comprehensive, factual study of the newsreels—their history, production techniques, distribution and problems. Hardly exhaustive, it offers data on this little-studied field but attempts no conclusions. Includes an interesting section on the influence of documentary on newsreel formats and a commentary on newsreels for TV.

Chapman, William McK., ed.: *Films on Art*. American Federation of Arts, 1952. 160 pp.

The upswing of interest in films on art produced this excellent, comprehensive, critical survey of 453 films on painting, sculpture, gravure and the film itself as an art medium. Introductory essays cover the history of art films and recommended uses in schools and museums. Sources for the pictures are included.

Feild, Robert D.: *The Art of Walt Disney*. Macmillan, 1942. 290 pp.

A handsomely produced, carefully researched book by a professor of art who was also an enthusiast of the Disney organization. Includes historical information on cartooning and biographical data on Disney; but the meat of the book is a clear and detailed account of how an animated cartoon is made. Lavishly illustrated.

Film Council of America: *Sixty Years of 16mm Film, 1923–1983*. Film Council of America, 1954. 220 pp.

A symposium of authoritative, compact essays on the wide variety of uses of 16mm films in America, with the attendant problems of producing, distributing and exhibiting them to best advantage. Valuable both as a handbook and as an introduction to the field itself.

Griffith, Richard: *The World of Robert Flaherty*. Duell, Sloan & Pearce, 1953. 165 pp.

This unique biography of the great documentary pioneer is drawn largely from excerpts of journals, diaries and, at one point, the vivid letters that Mrs. Flaherty wrote from India during the filming of *Elephant Boy*. Mr. Griffith's running commentary not only ties the whole together but highlights the significance of Flaherty's contributions to the medium.

*Hardy, Forsyth, ed.: *Grierson on Documentary*. Harcourt, Brace, 1947. 324 pp.

A collection of John Grierson's writings on film, this is at once a history of documentary and an insight into the mind and philosophy of the man who has done the most to shape and direct its destiny. Introductory notes by Richard Griffith and Mary Losey help to orient the general reader.

Manvell, Roger: *The Animated Film*. Sylvan Press, 1954. 64 pp.

A beautifully prepared description—non-technical—of the processes involved in the creation of a cartoon film. Charts, stills, sketches and story boards are liberally included, all from the Halas & Batchelor version of George Orwell's *Animal Farm*. Includes a brief history of animation and a suggestion of its role in the future of the film.

Manvell, Roger, ed.: *Experiment in the Film*. Grey Walls, 1949. 285 pp.

An uneven but still informative collection of articles on avant-gardism around the world—uneven because it is quickly apparent that "experimental" means something different to each of the writers. Contributors include Lewis Jacobs, Grigori Roshal, Hans Richter and Edgar Anstey.

*Rotha, Paul: *Documentary Film*. Faber & Faber, 1952. 412 pp.

This history of documentary, a standard work since its first appearance in 1939, has been greatly expanded by Sinclair Road and Richard Griffith, the latter contributing a particularly valuable first-hand account of the wartime achievements of American documentarians. Rotha's theory of documentary has special application to the British movement.

*Starr, Cecile, ed.: *Ideas on Film*. Funk & Wagnalls, 1951. 251 pp.

Articles and reviews on documentary and informational films in the U.S. 16mm market, culled from the pages of the *Saturday Review*. Miss Starr has organized a wealth of material into highly usable form and selected 200 of the most important films available on 16mm for extended review. Distributors and regional film libraries are listed. Well indexed.

Stauffacher, Frank, ed.: *Art in Cinema*. San Francisco Museum of Art, 1947. 104 pp.

This guide to experimental production, created to accompany a film series at the San Francisco Museum, is perhaps the liveliest, most factual and revealing work yet published on the avant-garde. Statements by many of the leading experimentalists, and carefully prepared notes on classic films in the field suggest the wide variety of styles and personalities it embraces.

REFERENCE WORKS

Educational Film Guide. H. W. Wilson.

Issued quarterly with cumulative annual volumes, this is an invaluable guide to films in the 16mm field. Literally thousands of titles are arranged under the Dewey Decimal (standard library) subject headings and briefly described. A splendid index and complete data on sources and costs make this an indispensable reference work for all film program planners.

Educators' Guide to Free Films. Educators Progress Service.

An annual listing of thousands of free films, where and how to obtain them. Most of them are on 16mm, many in color, and all are grouped for subject matter. Especially useful for schools—but since most of these are pictures produced to advertise one thing or another, it might be well to forget that old proverb about looking gift horses in the mouth.

Film Daily Year Book of Motion Pictures. Film Daily.

A fat (over 1,000 pages) annual crammed with vital statistics of the industry and featuring a cumulative index to over 25,000 films released since 1915, full credits on all pictures produced during the year covered, corporate personnel, etc. Brief, authoritative articles reviewing the year complete each volume.

International Motion Picture Almanac. Quigley Publications.

An indispensable industry annual, featuring a "who's who" of the movies (including their main picture credits), listings of all pictures released in the U.S. in the 10 years previous to the volume, key corporation personnel, statistical information of every kind, and brief, informative surveys of major trends in the industry during the year covered.

U.S. Library of Congress: *Motion Pictures.* Library of Congress, 1951, 1953,—.

A cumulative compendium of all film titles, American and foreign, registered with the U.S. Copyright Office, including date, length, producing company and—especially in later entries—picture credits. Volumes to date: 1894–1912, 1912–1939, 1940–1949. An invaluable reference work.

*U.S. Work Projects Administration: *The Film Index.* Vol. I, *The Film* *as Art.* **Museum of Modern Art Film Library and H. W. Wilson, 1941. 723 pp.**

This little-known work is an invaluable guide to the literature of the film, covering history, technique and aesthetics and articles on thousands of important films and film makers. Superb indexing makes it easy to use. Unfortunately, the two projected volumes that were to accompany it have never appeared.

16MM FILM SOURCES

Code letters which appear in boldface following some of the entries in the Index to Film Titles refer to the agencies listed below which rent those films for 16mm use. In some cases, most notably the Museum of Modern Art, rentals are made only to educational organizations; however, most 16mm rentals are available to any group or individual for showing. Many of these distributors maintain branch offices in other cities.

A   Athena Films
165 West 46th Street
New York 36, New York

AA   American Art & History Films
41 West 47th Street
New York 36, New York

B   Brandon Films
200 West 57th Street
New York 19, New York

BIS   British Information Services
% Contemporary Films
13 East 37th Street
New York 16, New York

C   Contemporary Films
13 East 37th Street
New York 16, New York

CG   Cinema Guild
10 Fiske Place
Mount Vernon, New York

CMC   Center for Mass Communication
Columbia University Press
1125 Amsterdam Avenue
New York 25, New York

Col*   Columbia Pictures
711 Fifth Avenue
New York 22, New York

C16   Cinema 16
175 Lexington Avenue
New York 16, New York

D*   Disney Productions
16mm Division
2400 West Alameda Ave.
Burbank, California

deR   de Rochemont 16mm Library
13 East 37th Street
New York 16, New York

EB   Encyclopaedia Britannica Films
1150 Wilmette Avenue
Wilmette, Illinois

F   Films, Inc.
1150 Wilmette Avenue
Wilmette, Illinois

FA   Franco-American Distribution Center
972 Fifth Avenue
New York 22, New York

FI   Film Images
1860 Broadway
New York 23, New York

I   Ideal Pictures
50 E. South Water Street
Chicago 1, Illinois

IFB   International Film Bureau
57 East Jackson Boulevard
Chicago 4, Illinois

Ind	Independent 16mm release (these films are available from a number of 16mm libraries, including many of those listed on this page).		487 Park Avenue New York 22, New York
		R	Rembrandt Films 13 East 37th Street New York 16, New York
M	Museum of Modern Art Film Library 11 West 53rd Street New York 19, New York	**TW**	Trans-World Films 53 West Jackson Boulevard Chicago 4, Illinois
		U	United World Films
McG*	McGraw-Hill Text-Films 330 West 42nd Street New York 36, New York		1445 Park Avenue New York 29, New York
		UW-G*	United World Films—Government Division
MD	Maya Deren 35 Morton Street New York 14, New York		1445 Park Avenue New York 29, New York
P	Pictura Films		

—CECILE STARR

NOTE: A complete list of 16mm libraries is published by the Superintendent of Documents, Government Printing Office, Washington, D.C.; cost is seventy cents.

* These organizations do not rent their films, but will forward requests to the nearest 16mm dealer.

INDEX TO FILM TITLES

GENERAL INDEX